Neural Networks in Computer Intelligence

McGRAW-HILL SERIES IN COMPUTER SCIENCE

SENIOR CONSULTING EDITOR
C. L. Liu, *University of Illinois at Urbana-Champaign*

CONSULTING EDITOR
Allen B. Tucker, *Bowdoin College*

Fundamentals of Computing and Programming

Computer Organization and Architecture

Systems and Languages

Theoretical Foundations

Software Engineering and Database

Artificial Intelligence

Networks, Parallel and Distributed Computing

Graphics and Visualization

The MIT Electrical Engineering and Computer Science Series

ARTIFICIAL INTELLIGENCE

Bowen: Prolog and Expert Systems Programming
Fu: Neural Networks in Computer Intelligence
Horn: Robot Vision*
Levine: Vision in Man and Machine
Rich and Knight: Artificial Intelligence
Sangal: Programming Paradigms in LISP
Schalkoff: Artificial Intelligence: An Engineering Approach

*: Co-published by The MIT Press and McGraw-Hill, Inc.

Neural Networks in Computer Intelligence

LiMin Fu

University of Florida, Gainesville

McGraw-Hill, Inc.

New York St. Louis San Francisco Auckland Bogotá Caracas
Lisbon London Madrid Mexico City Milan Montreal
New Delhi San Juan Singapore Sydney Tokyo Toronto

NEURAL NETWORKS IN COMPUTER INTELLIGENCE

This book is printed on recycled, acid-free paper containing
a minimum of 50% total recycled fiber with 10% postconsumer
de-inked fiber.

2 4 5 6 7 8 9 0 DOC DOC 9 0 9 8 7 6 5 4

P/N 022637-7
PART OF
ISBN 0-07-911817-8

This book was set in Palatino by the author.
The editors were Eric M. Munson and Larry Goldberg;
the production supervisor was Camille Mahadeo.
The cover was designed by Merrill Haber.
R. R. Donnelley & Sons Company was printer and binder.

Library of Congress Cataloging-in-Publication Data:
Fu, LiMin, (date).
  Neural networks in computer intelligence / LiMin Fu.
    p.   cm.
  Includes index.
  ISBN 0-07-911817-8 (set)
  1. Neural networks (Computer science)   2. Artificial intelligence.
I. Title.
QA76.87.F82   1994
006.3—dc20   93-45343

About the Author

LiMin Fu is a Professor of Computer Science and Electrical Engineering at the University of Florida at Gainesville. He received his Ph.D. in Electrical Engineering from Stanford University and his M.D. in Medicine with highest honors from National Taiwan University. He is the author of many articles in journals and proceedings and two monographs in the areas of the brain, artificial neural networks, artificial intelligence, machine learning, expert systems, and genes. Dr. Fu has actively participated in various grant and research studies supported by the National Science Foundation and other funding agencies. He organized and chaired the First International Symposium on Integrating Knowledge and Neural Heuristics, and has established a foundation in this direction.

To Lienfen

Contents

Preface

The information processing principles of biological neural networks have been applied to building a computer system for solving difficult problems whose solutions normally require human intelligence. The neural network approach has attracted wide attention and found a growing number of applications especially in the last decade. This book describes various neural network computational models in theory and practice with emphasis on intelligent applications. Furthermore, since there is an urgent need for a bridge between the symbolic and the neural network approach to artificial intelligence (AI), the book looks back into the past as well as probes into the future in this perspective.

It should be noted, however, that a neural network can be investigated from a number of distinct perspectives, such as computer science and engineering, artificial intelligence, cognitive science, psychology, and neurobiology. The book adopts the first two perspectives, focusing on the structure and function of neural network models for accomplishing particular tasks. It is concerned with the performance and application aspects of the models rather than cognitive, psychological, and biological plausibility. But it does not rule out the possibility of cognitive, psychological, and biological modeling in this approach.

The book attempts a comprehensive treatment of artificial neural networks. Basic computational models and recent advances are contained. The book investigates not only AI problems but also important scientific problems such as mathematical modeling and causal learning in an attempt to broaden the scope and bridge the gap between conventional and new technologies. Among other things, the integration of knowledge engineering and neural networks is underlined.

The book is written in a coherent and consistent manner. It provides a step-by-step introduction to artificial neural networks and relates them to symbolic techniques where appropriate. Every important procedure or algorithm is highlighted and organized in a predefined format. Every effort has been made to produce a book that can be easily understood. With little technical background, readers can be guided through the book and develop a sufficient grasp of the material. Since it is infeasible to incorporate everything, the book provides a careful balance between the depth and breadth of the material included. An important technical goal is to provide sufficient information so that readers can apprehend and possibly implement all or most of the algorithms simply by following the book. References are provided at the end of chapters in case there is a need for further exploration of relevant matters. Each chapter is as self-contained as possible. So, the book need not be read from cover to cover, but it is advised to read the first two chapters in the beginning.

Important mathematical derivations and formulae are included as appropriate in order to provide sufficient technical depth of the subject. Basic knowledge about vector and matrix operations (vector dot product, matrix addition and multiplication) is the assumed background to use this book. Backgrounds in calculus and probability will be helpful for understanding mathematical notations in some places. Readers with insufficient mathematical background may skip mathematical analysis and can still learn concepts and techniques expressed in English.

The book is written for students interested in these topics. It is developed for courses on neural networks and can be adopted as a textbook for such courses. The ideas contained may also lead to interesting theses. The book is written for professionals with little background but with a strong interest in neural networks, artificial intelligence, knowledge-based systems, pattern recognition, or machine learning. The techniques offered by the book can be put into practice for coping with real-world problems. The book is written for researchers conducting scientific discovery; many useful techniques in this regard can be found there. The text is also written for people who have been engaged in traditional artificial intelligence research for a long time and wish to learn the neural network technology.

The book is divided into three parts. Part I is devoted to theory, methods, and applications, and is designed for one-semester neural network courses. The first three chapters are especially important because they establish the basic understanding and skill of neurocomputing. Part II is devoted to the interdisciplinary topics between neural networks and expert systems. In conjunction with Chapters 1 to 4, the second part can be used as a text for courses on neural network expert systems. This part also provides excellent supplemental material for neural network courses. Part III contains three case studies, intended as reference material for graduate students and researchers.

Writing this book is the most difficult project I have ever undertaken. The book could not have been successfully accomplished without support and constructive feedback. My first thanks go to Dr. Walter J. Karplus for his enlightening suggestions concerning how to organize the book as a useful text, and also for his encouraging remarks during the writing of it. I greatly appreciate Dr. Jenq-Neng Hwang's technical comments and additional references. I also thank Dr. Kenneth Magel, Dr. Edgar Sánchez-Sinencio, and Dr. Jack Gelfand for their suggestions about how to enhance the book. Finally, I would like to thank Mr. Eric Munson of McGraw-Hill for his patience and encouragement; Mr. Larry Goldberg, Mr. Chet Gottfried, and Mr. Joseph Siegel, for copy-editing and proofreading.

LiMin Fu

Acknowledgments

Portion reprinted, with permission, from *IEEE Transactions on Systems, Man, and Cybernetics*; 23(1), Fu, L.M., Knowledge-based connectionism for revising domain theories, pp. 173-182; January/February. Copyright 1993 IEEE. (Appears in Chapter 4).

Portion reprinted, with permission, from *IEEE Transactions on Systems, Man, and Cybernetics*; 24(8), Fu, L.M., Rule generation from neural networks. Copyright 1994 IEEE. (Appears in Chapter 14).

Portion reprinted from *Pattern Recognition*, 26(2), Fu, L.M., Yang, M., Braylan, R.C., and Benson, N., Real time adaptive clustering of flow cytometric data, pp. 365-373, Copyright 1993, with kind permission from Pergamon Press Ltd. Headington Hill Hall, Oxford OX3 OBW, UK. (Appears in Chapter 18).

Portion reprinted, with permission, from *Journal of Applied Intelligence*; 2, Fu, L.M., A connectionist approach to rule refinement, pp. 93-103; Copyright 1992 Kluwer Academic Publishers, Boston. (Appears in Chapter 4).

Portion reprinted, with permission, from *Artificial Intelligence in Medicine*; Fu, L.M., Polygenic trait analysis by neural network learning. Copyright 1994 Elsevier. (Appears in Chapter 16).

Part I

Theory, Methods, Applications

Chapter 1

Introduction

1.1 Background

Where does intelligence emerge? There are two important ways to answer this question from the computational point of view. One is based on *symbolism*, and the other, based on *connectionism*. The former approach models intelligence using symbols, while the latter using connections and associated weights. Evolving by different routes, they both have achieved many successes in practical applications. We shall briefly review their historical backgrounds and discuss the impact of their interaction on the design of future intelligent systems.

Artificial intelligence (AI) is the study of intelligent behavior and is also concerned with the implementation of a computer program which exhibits intelligent behavior. Perhaps, the most important assumption made by traditional AI systems is the *physical symbol system hypothesis* proposed by Newell and Simon (1976). The hypothesis states:

> A physical symbol system has the necessary and sufficient means for general intelligent action.

They define a physical symbol system as follows:

> A physical symbol system consists of a set of entities, called symbols, which are physical patterns that can occur as components of another type of entity called an expression (or symbol structure). . . . A physical symbol system is a machine that produces through time an evolving collection of symbol structures.

This hypothesis explains why AI languages such as LISP and PROLOG are oriented toward symbol manipulation.

One of the earliest AI programs is *Logic Theorist* by Newell, Shaw, and Simon (1963). The program was able to prove theorems from the first chapter of

Whitehead and Russell's *Principia Mathematica* (1950). Yet, the theorem-proving approach turns out unsuccessful in building a general system which can solve difficult problems consistently.

In the 1970s, it began to be realized that intelligent behavior can be displayed by a computer program if the domain it deals with is sufficiently narrowed. This concept has much to do with a new transformation in the field of AI, namely, the transformation from the logic-oriented toward the knowledge-based approach. The success of DENDRAL and MYCIN (Buchanan and Shortliffe 1984) has close tie to this transformation. And what we learn from it is that the "knowledge" rather than the inference mechanism makes the system intelligent. However, much human knowledge can only be represented symbolically.

In contrast to the symbolic approach, the neural network approach adopts the *brain metaphor*, which suggests that intelligence emerges through a large number of processing elements connected together, each performing simple computation. The long-term knowledge of a neural network is encoded as a set of weights on connections between units. For this reason, the neural network architecture has also been dubbed the *connectionist* (Feldman and Ballard 1982).

1.1.1   History of Artificial Neural Networks

The progress of neurobiology has allowed researchers to build mathematical models of neurons to simulate neural behavior. This idea dates back to the early 1940s when one of the first abstract models of a neuron was introduced by McCulloch and Pitts (1943). Hebb (1949) proposed a learning law that explained how a network of neurons learned. Other researchers pursued this notion through the next two decades, such as Minsky (1954) and Rosenblatt (1958). Rosenblatt is credited with the perceptron learning algorithm. At about the same time, Widrow and Hoff developed an important variation of perceptron learning, known as the Widrow-Hoff rule.

Later, Minsky and Papert (1969) pointed out theoretical limitations of single-layer neural network models in their landmark book *Perceptrons*. Due to this pessimistic projection, research on artificial neural networks lapsed into an eclipse for nearly two decades. Despite the negative atmosphere, some researchers still continued their research and produced meaningful results. For example, Anderson (1977) and Grossberg (1980) did important work on psychological models. Kohonen (1977) developed associative memory models.

In the early 1980s, the neural network approach was resurrected. Hopfield (1982) introduced the idea of energy minimization in physics into neural networks. His influential paper endowed this technology with renewed momentum. Feldman and Ballard (1982) made the term "connectionist" popular. Sometimes, connectionism is also referred to as subsymbolic processes, which have become the study of cognitive and AI systems inspired by neural networks (Smolensky 1988). Unlike symbolic AI, connectionism emphasizes the capability of learning and discovering representations. Insidiously, connectionism has become a common ground between traditional AI and neural network research.

In the middle 1980s, the book *Parallel Distributed Processing* by Rumelhart and McClelland (1986) generated great impacts on computer, cognitive, and biological sciences. Notably, the backpropagation learning algorithm developed by Rumelhart, Hinton, and Williams (1986) offers a powerful solution to training a multilayer neural network and shattered the curse imposed on perceptrons. A spectacular success of this approach is demonstrated by the NETtalk system developed by Sejnowski and Rosenberg (1987), a system that converts English text into highly intelligible speech. It is interesting to note, however, that the idea of backpropagation had been developed by Werbos (1974) and Parker (1982) independently.

Although the neural network approach rejects the notion of separating knowledge from the inference mechanism, it does not reject the importance of knowledge in many tasks that require intelligence. It just uses a different way to store and manipulate knowledge.

The symbolic approach which has long dominated the field of AI was recently challenged by the neural network approach. There have been speculations about whether one approach should substitute for another or whether the two approaches should coexist and combine. More evidence favors the integration alternative in which the low-level pattern recognition capability offered by the neural network approach and the high-level cognitive reasoning ability provided by the symbolic approach complement each other (Kandel and Langholz 1992). The optimal architecture of future intelligent systems may well involve their integration in one way or another.

1.2   Knowledge-Based Information Processing

The definitions of knowledge-based systems abound in the literature, but all the definitions are similar. A knowledge-based system is a computer program that acquires, represents, and uses knowledge for a specific purpose. Its basic structure, as shown in Figure 1.1, consists of a knowledge base which stores knowledge and an inference engine which makes inference using the knowledge. However, as Feigenbaum (1977) indicated, the power of such a system derives from the knowledge it possesses rather than from the inference method it employs. Still, there is much to say about the distinctions between *knowledge-based programming* and conventional programming.

A conventional computer program is characterized by algorithmic processing of data. In this programming paradigm, the knowledge concerning how to do things is encoded as a bunch of procedures, which are executed step by step to deal with the data entered. In knowledge-based programming, on the other hand, we represent what we know in a declarative manner and the knowledge is invoked under a certain inference strategy or driven heuristically. Although this paradigm does not exclude procedural representation, the emphasis on declarative representation is its main feature.

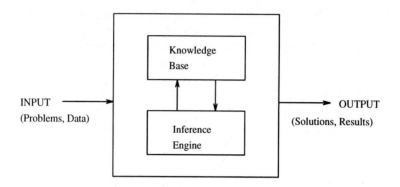

Figure 1.1: Knowledge-based information processing.

Another important distinction between the two programming paradigms is the feature of separating knowledge from control. In knowledge-based systems, knowledge is stored in the knowledge base while control strategies reside in the separate inference engine. This separation benefits the development and maintenance of the system because when knowledge is updated, the inference engine can be left alone, and when the inference process is changed, the knowledge base is not affected. Because of separation, a knowledge base can be run by different inference engines and an inference engine can drive different knowledge bases. This programming style revolutionizes the conventional procedurally oriented approach in which problem-solving knowledge and control knowledge are intermingled, and it is very difficult to manipulate one part without touching the other. As a consequence, a lot of time and effort can be saved using the knowledge-based approach. The comparison of knowledge-based and data-oriented information processing is provided in Table 1.1.

Domain knowledge means the knowledge specific to the domain in which the problem is defined. Researchers have recognized two important kinds of knowledge in building a knowledge-based system: deep knowledge and surface knowledge.

Surface knowledge is the heuristic, experiential knowledge learned after solving a large number of problems. It is the knowledge that human experts often rely on. It usually offers a quick, satisfactory solution, which is not necessarily the best though. The main problem with surface knowledge is its inadequacy in dealing with novel situations.

Deep knowledge refers to the basic laws of nature and the fundamental structural and behavioral principles of the domain. Invocation of deep knowl-

Table 1.1: Comparison of knowledge-based and data-oriented information processing.

Knowledge-Based Processing	Data-Oriented Processing
Declarative knowledge	Procedural knowledge
Separating control from knowledge	Integrating control and knowledge
Strategic and heuristic processing	Algorithmic processing
Symbolic processing (dominant)	Numerical processing (dominant)
Explanation capability	No explanation

edge for problem solving is sometimes called *reasoning from first principles*. In comparison with surface knowledge, deep knowledge has a stronger formal basis. It allows the derivation of a solution even for a novel situation, but the process may be time-consuming. One way to make it more efficient for use is to compile it. However, compiled deep knowledge may not correspond to surface knowledge since they come from different sources. In addition, there is no guarantee that every piece of surface knowledge can be proven based on deep knowledge. What is important in practice is how the two kinds of knowledge can be integrated so as to optimize the system performance.

In some knowledge-based systems, we make distinctions between *metalevel* and *object-level* knowledge. Object-level knowledge is the knowledge for solving the problem in the defined domain. Metalevel knowledge is the knowledge which controls the use of object-level knowledge. The employment of metalevel knowledge is intended to provide a better control of object-level knowledge. However, metalevel knowledge is not the same as the control knowledge housed in the inference engine. As a matter of fact, metalevel knowledge is also controlled by the inference engine. In a metalevel reasoning system, metalevel knowledge is invoked first, which then selects appropriate object-level knowledge to make inference.

The inference engine governs the use of the knowledge stored in the knowledge base. While the design of the inference engine is full of variety, we identify a general knowledge-based algorithm as follows.

The Knowledge-Based (Rule-Based) Algorithm (A general view)

Given a problem (initial conditions and the goal)

1. The inference engine selects a piece of knowledge from the knowledge base.

2. The inference engine executes the selected knowledge either to transform the goal or to generate a new fact.

3. If the goal (original or transformed) is solved (or deduced), then exit and succeed. If a certain stopping condition is met such as the case when the knowledge available is exhausted but the goal is not solved yet, then exit and fail. Otherwise go to step 1.

The description of knowledge-based systems in this section is by no means complete. We leave the details to Chapter 11 "Expert Systems."

1.3   Neural Information Processing

Biological neurons transmit electrochemical signals over neural pathways. Each neuron receives signals from other neurons through special junctions called *synapses*. Some inputs tend to excite the neuron; others tend to inhibit it. When the cumulative effect exceeds a threshold, the neuron fires and sends a signal down to other neurons. An artificial neuron models these simple biological characteristics. Each artificial neuron receives a set of inputs. Each input is multiplied by a *weight* analogous to a synaptic strength. The sum of all weighted inputs determines the degree of firing called the *activation level*.[1] Notationally, each input X_i is modulated by a weight W_i and the total input is expressed as

$$\sum_i X_i W_i$$

or in vector form, $\mathbf{X} \cdot \mathbf{W}$ where $\mathbf{X} = [X_1, X_2, ..., X_n]$ and $\mathbf{W} = [W_1, W_2, ..., W_n]$. The input signal is further processed by an *activation function* to produce the output signal which, if not zero, is transmitted along. The activation function can be a threshold function or a smooth function like a sigmoid or a hyperbolic tangent function.

A neural network is represented by a set of nodes and arrows, which is a fundamental concept in graph theory. A node corresponds to a neuron, and an arrow corresponds to a connection along with the direction of signal flow between neurons. As illustrated in Figure 1.2, some nodes are connected to the system input and others are connected to the system output for information processing.

The dynamic behavior of the neural network is described by either differential equations or difference equations. The former representation assumes continuous time and can be used to simulate the network on an analog computer, whereas the latter uses discrete time and is usually taken to simulate the network on a digital computer.

---

[1] In the neural network, connection weights and activations are sometimes referred to as LTM (long-term memory) and STM (short-term memory), respectively.

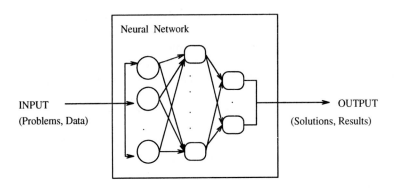

Figure 1.2: Neural information processing.

Neural networks solve problems by self-learning and self-organization. They derive their intelligence from the collective behavior of simple computational mechanisms at individual neurons. Computational advantages offered by neural networks include:

- Knowledge acquisition under noise and uncertainty: Neural networks can perform generalization, abstraction, and extraction of statistical properties from the data.

- Flexible knowledge representation: Neural networks can create their own representation by self-organization.

- Efficient knowledge processing: Neural nets can carry out computation in parallel. It is known as *parallel-distributed processing*, or PDP (Rumelhart and McClelland 1986). Special hardware devices have been manufactured which exploit this advantage. Thus, real-time operation is feasible. Notice that training a neural network may be time-consuming, but once it is trained, it can operate very fast.

- Fault tolerance: Through distributed knowledge representation and redundant information encoding, the system performance degrades gracefully in response to faults (errors).

Neural networks can recognize, classify, convert, and learn patterns. A *pattern* is a qualitative or quantitative description of an object or concept or event. A *pattern class* is a set of patterns sharing some common properties. *Pattern recognition* refers to the categorization of input data into identifiable classes by recognizing significant features or attributes of the data. In traditional pattern recognition theory, a pattern is an n-dimensional *feature vector* or a point in n-dimensional space. A feature vector is a vector of feature values arranged by a certain order. For example, suppose a person is described as a vector of [age, height, weight]. A pattern could be [30, 170, 160]. There is a great difference between patterns with numeric and nonnumeric (symbolic or linguistic) feature values. In the latter case, although we can encode values as discrete numbers (e.g., "no" as 0 and "yes" as 1), we cannot assign a metric to measure the distances between patterns. In the neural network approach, a pattern is represented by a set of nodes along with their activation levels.

1.4   Hybrid Intelligence

Integration of symbolic AI and neural networks results in a so-called hybrid intelligent system (Kandel and Langholz 1992). Under this approach, the fundamental assumptions on intelligence are as follows:

- Neither the physical symbol system nor the neural network is a necessary means for general intelligent action.

- The symbolic level and the connectionist level represent two different levels of abstraction for intelligent processes.

- Knowledge is power. Every intelligent being should have knowledge in one form or another.

Hybrid intelligence is a biologically plausible notion. Recall that humans store knowledge in certain complex molecules such as genes and proteins which determine what we are and how we behave, and at the same time, we have nerve systems to coordinate our behavior.[2]

Examples of research in this area include:

- *Knowledge-based neural networks*: Neural networks are built based on domain knowledge or theory. In this construct, neural networks model some aspects such as noise and uncertainty which knowledge is not dealing with.

- *Translation of neural network knowledge into symbolic knowledge*: This is important for interpreting neural networks, explaining neural network behavior, and learning knowledge under noise and uncertainty. The idea can also be applied to regularize the neural network and to prevent it from overfitting the data.

- *Learning by combining knowledge and adaptation*: It is concerned with how to build a better learning system than using knowledge or adaptation alone, how to build an incremental learning system, and how to build

---

[2]The term "knowledgetron" is introduced to represent a general concept of combining knowledge-based and neurally oriented computing concepts.

a useful discovery system. The central idea is to use knowledge as the initial crystal and then grow the crystal by adaptation.

- *Connectionist symbol processing*: It bears on how to represent symbolic information or knowledge in the framework of connectionists, how to process the information accordingly, and how to retrieve the information. The advantages of this approach include fault tolerance, space sharing, and special processing strategies offered by the distributed representation of connectionists.

- *Hybrid intelligent systems*: Such systems possess knowledge-based components and neural networks which are integrated in a certain manner so that each component performs the tasks for which it is best suited.

- *Expert networks*: They refer to neural networks that can perform as well as human experts. Explanation is an important issue for designing such systems.

1.5 The Outline of the Book

The book is divided into three parts. In Part I, we present the theory, the methods and computer algorithms, and the areas of applications.

- In Chapter 2, we describe general neural information processing algorithms and a number of important computational models based on the neural network. A general look at hardware implementation of the neural network is also provided.

- In Chapter 3, we state the differences between supervised and unsupervised learning and review important learning methods classified into four categories: statistical learning, AI learning, neural network learning, and genetic learning. Important learning algorithms are formulated. The purpose of this chapter is to provide readers with a good introduction to machine learning with the main focus on neural network learning.

- In Chapter 4, we treat the subject of knowledge-based neural networks. The main focus is the rule-based connectionist network, though other types of knowledge-based neural networks such as those based on decision trees will also be discussed. We show how to train the neural network in such a way that it can generalize over the sample space. And we describe how symbolic knowledge can be transferred to the neural network for revision and how revised knowledge can be translated back to symbolic form.

- In Chapter 5, we describe the fundamental principles of incremental learning and examine existing methods including both the symbolic and the neural network approaches. Then, we present knowledge-based neural networks with incremental-learning capability.

- In Chapter 6, we treat an important subject in science, namely mathematical modeling. While the subject has been investigated for a long time, many physical systems still lack good mathematical models. The neural network approach presents a promising solution to this problem because of its amazing mapping capability. We explore this approach and examine its mathematical basis. An important application is in the area of systems and control. Combining the idea of this chapter and that of Chapter 10 would be of great use for this application.

- In Chapter 7, we explore system architectures for complex neural networks. Our discussions are based on the classification of such architectures into hierarchical, differentiated, and parallel models. An important emphasis is placed on the design of control networks which involve some kind of temporal learning. The concept of complex networks is vital from the practical point of view because it shows how to decompose a real-world problem and exploit components with different capabilities in solving it. Through this concept, all simple ideas developed separately can be linked at once.

- In Chapter 8, we concern ourselves with the subject of machine discovery. We review symbolic methods including conceptual clustering, heuristic discovery, and search for laws. Then, we present neural network methods. Various neural network architectures for discovery are shown and related to their symbolic counterparts. The main idea is to combine knowledge and neural networks for purposes of discovery.

- In Chapter 9, we explore various connectionist representations and introduce a hybrid network approach for learning from structured data. The idea of this chapter serves to bridge the gap between knowledge representation and learning in the framework of neural networks.

- In Chapter 10, we explore various spatiotemporal neural networks (for learning spatiotemporal patterns), describe important learning procedures, and show how to apply knowledge to neural networks. The idea developed in this chapter is expected to lend itself to the areas of signal processing, communication, image understanding, linear and nonlinear systems, and temporal reasoning.

Part II is devoted to topics related to neural networks and expert systems.

- In Chapter 11, we examine major issues concerning expert systems (knowledge-based systems). Traditional issues include knowledge acquisition, knowledge representation, inference structures, and reasoning under uncertainty. We also explore the integration of neural networks and expert systems. This issue has attracted much attention recently and we present our view on it. An important emphasis is placed on fuzzy neural networks.

- In Chapter 12, we focus on causal modeling, which is an old yet important subject in many scientific disciplines. Since causal knowledge is often uncertain and since the neural network has the inherent ability to handle uncertainty, it follows that causal modeling can benefit from the neural network. Our goal is to explore the neural network approach for learning causal knowledge.

- In Chapter 13, we state the concepts fundamental to performance validation and describe general validation techniques. We examine this issue first in the context of learning systems and then in performance systems. We also explore approaches to verification. The aim of this chapter is to let readers know how to verify and validate an intelligent system.

- In Chapter 14, we formalize the relationship between rule-based systems and neural networks. In addition, we present a method for translating the knowledge of a neural network into a set of valid rules systematically yet heuristically. This method has a solid mathematical foundation and is also supported by empirical evaluations across a wide range of application domains. Various methods for rule extraction from neural networks are discussed.

- In Chapter 15, we investigate the problem of learning grammars (grammatical inference). This is a major problem in the areas of natural language understanding and syntactic pattern recognition. We show how grammars can be learned by neural networks and then extracted as symbolic rules. This process involves deriving a temporal order from recurrent weights.

In Part III, we present three case studies.

- In Chapter 16, we present the results of genetic pattern recognition. The program has successfully identified important gene patterns associated with insulin-dependent diabetes. Our purposes are to demonstrate the program's capability of searching through an enormous space as well as showing how to learn patterns associated with certain variables.

- In Chapter 17, we present the results of drug discovery. The importance of drug discovery is never overemphasized. The patterns learned in each drug-design cycle can help modify or discover a new drug in the next cycle.

- In Chapter 18, we present a computer program for the analysis of flow cytometric data and show how it can diagnose leukemia. This diagnostic task is difficult and may even elude a human expert. However, the neural network developed can easily recognize some subtle features that humans overlook.

The enclosed PC (personal computer) disk contains an object-oriented neural network software package. Read the file "README" in the disk before using it.

1.6 References

1. Anderson, J.A., Silverstein, J.W., Ritz, S.A., and Jones, R.S. 1977. Distinctive features, categorical perception, and probability learning: Some applications of a neural model. *Psychological Review*, 84, pp. 413–451.

2. Buchanan, B.G., and Shortliffe, E.H. (eds.). 1984. *Rule-Based Expert Systems*. Addison-Wesley, Reading, MA.

3. Feigenbaum, E.A. 1977. The art of artificial intelligence: Themes and case studies of knowledge engineering. In *Proceeding of IJCAI-77*, pp. 1014–1029.

4. Feldman, J.A., and Ballard, D.H. 1982. Connectionist models and their properties. *Cognitive Science*, 6(3), pp. 205–254.

5. Grossberg, S. 1980. How does a brain build a cognitive code? *Psychological Review*, 87, pp. 1–51.

6. Hebb, D.O. 1949. *The Organization of Behavior*. Wiley, New York.

7. Hopfield, J.J. 1982. Neural networks and physical systems with emergent collective computational abilities. In *Proceedings of the National Academy of Science*, 79, pp. 2554–2558.

8. Kandel, A., and Langholz, G. 1992. (eds.). *Hybrid Architectures for Intelligent Systems*. CRC Press, Boca Raton, FL.

9. Kohonen, T. 1977. *Associative Memory: A System-Theoretical Approach*. Springer-Verlag, New York.

10. McCulloch, W.S., and Pitts, W. 1943. A logical calculus of ideas imminent in nervous activity. *Bull. Math. Biophysics*, 5, pp. 115–133.

11. Minsky, M. 1954. Neural Nets and the Brain-Model Problem. Ph.D. thesis, Princeton University.

12. Minsky, M., and Papert, S. 1969. *Perceptrons*. MIT Press, Cambridge, MA.

13. Newell, A., Shaw, J.C., and Simon, H.A. 1963. Empirical exploration with the logic theory machine: A case study in heuristics. In *Computers and Thought*. McGraw-Hill, New York.

14. Newell, A., and Simon, H.A. 1976. Computer science as empirical inquiry: Symbols and search. *Communications of the ACM*, 19(3), pp. 113–126.

15. Parker, D.B. 1982. *Learning Logic,* Invention Report S81-64, File 1. Office of Technology Licensing, Stanford University.

16. Rosenblatt, F. 1958. The Perceptron: A probabilistic model for information storage and organization in the brain. *Psychological Review,* 65, pp. 386–407.

17. Rumelhart, D.E., Hinton, G.E., and Williams, R.J. 1986. Learning internal representation by error propagation. In *Parallel Distributed Processing: Explorations in the Microstructures of Cognition,* Vol. 1. MIT Press, Cambridge, MA.

18. Rumelhart, D.E., McClelland, J.L., and the PDP Research Group (eds.). 1986. *Parallel Distributed Processing: Explorations in the Microstructures of Cognition,* Vol. 1 and Vol. 2. MIT Press, Cambridge, MA.

19. Sejnowski, T.J., and Rosenberg, C.R. 1987. Parallel networks that learn to pronounce English text. *Complex Systems,* 1, pp. 145–168.

20. Smolensky, P. 1988. On the proper treatment of connectionism. *Behavioral and Brain Sciences,* 11, pp. 1–23.

21. Werbos, P.J. 1974. Beyond Regression: New Tools for Prediction and Analysis in the Behavioral Sciences. Ph.D. thesis, Harvard University.

22. Whitehead, A.N., and Russell, B. 1950. *Principia Mathematica,* 2d edition. Cambridge University Press, Cambridge, UK.

Chapter 2

Basic Neural Computational Models

2.1 Introduction

The neural network contains a large number of simple neuronlike processing elements and a large number of weighted connections between the elements. The weights on the connections encode the knowledge of a network. Though biologically inspired, many of the neural network models developed do not duplicate the operation of the human brain. Some computational principles in these models are not even explicable from biological viewpoints.

In many tasks such as recognizing human faces and understanding speech, current AI systems cannot do better than humans. It is conjectured that the structure of the brain is somehow suited to these tasks and not suited to tasks such as high-speed arithmetic calculation. Further, one may link the connectionist structure to the nonalgorithmic nature of perceptual or cognitive reasoning. Rather than by being programmed, an artificial neural network can solve problems simply by example mapping.

The intelligence of a neural network emerges from the collective behavior of neurons, each of which performs only very limited operation. Even though each individual neuron works slowly, they can still quickly find a solution by working in parallel. This fact can explain why humans can recognize a visual scene faster than a digital computer, while an individual brain cell responds much more slowly than a digital cell in a VLSI circuit.

Also, the "brain metaphor" suggests how to build an intelligent system which can tolerate faults (fault tolerance) by distributing information redundantly. It would be easier to build a large system in which most of the components work correctly than to build a smaller system in which all components are perfect.

Another feature exhibited by the brain is the associative type of memory.

17

The brain naturally associates one thing with another. It can access information based on contents rather than on sequential addresses as in the digital computer. The associative, or content-addressable, memory accounts for fast information retrieval and permits partial or approximate matching. The brain seems to be good at managing fuzzy information because of the way its knowledge is represented.

Thus, the brain-style computation points out a new direction for building an intelligent system, a direction which is fundamentally different from the symbolic approach. By now, more than a dozen well-known neural network models have been built, such as the Backpropagation net, ART, Hopfield net, Boltzmann machine, etc., each with distinct performance features. Applications are sought within disciplines as diverse as philosophy, psychology, engineering, economy, and medicine.

2.2   Basic Concepts of Neural Networks

A neural network has a parallel-distributed architecture with a large number of nodes and connections. Each connection points from one node to another and is associated with a weight. A simple view of the network structure and behavior is given in Figure 2.1. Construction of a neural network involves the following tasks:

- Determine the network properties: the network topology (connectivity), the types of connections, the order of connections, and the weight range.

- Determine the node properties: the activation range and the activation (transfer) function.

- Determine the system dynamics: the weight initialization scheme, the activation-calculating formula, and the learning rule.

2.2.1   Network Properties

The *topology* of a neural network refers to its framework as well as its interconnection scheme. The framework is often specified by the number of *layers* (or *slabs*)[1] and the number of nodes per layer. The types of layers include:

- *The input layer*: The nodes in it are called *input units*, which encode the instance presented to the network for processing. For example, each input unit may be designated by an attribute value possessed by the instance.

- *The hidden layer*: The nodes in it are called *hidden units*, which are not directly observable and hence hidden. They provide nonlinearities for the network.

---

[1] However, not all neural networks have a layered or slabbed structure.

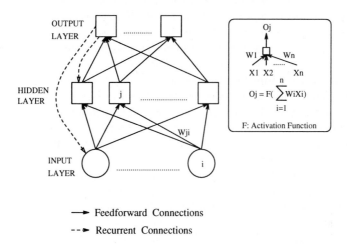

Figure 2.1: The neural network computational model. Recurrent connections distinguish feedforward from recurrent models.

- *The output layer*: The nodes in it are called *output units*, which encode possible concepts (or values) to be assigned to the instance under consideration. For example, each output unit represents a class of objects.

Input units do not process information; they simply distribute information to other units. Schematically, input units are drawn as circles as distinguished from processing elements like hidden units and output units which are drawn as squares in this book.

According to the interconnection scheme, a network can be either feedforward or recurrent and its connections either symmetrical or asymmetrical. Their definitions are given below:

- *Feedforward networks:* All connections point in one direction (from the input toward the output layer).

- *Recurrent networks:* There are feedback connections or loops.

- *Symmetrical connections:* If there is a connection pointing from node i to node j, then there is also a connection from node j to node i, and the weights associated with the two connections are equal, or notationally, $W_{ji} = W_{ij}$.

- *Asymmetrical connections:* If connections are not symmetrical as defined above, then they are asymmetrical.

A connection between nodes in different layers is called an *interlayer connection*. A connection between nodes within the same layer is called an *intralayer connection*. A connection pointing from a node to itself is called a *self-connection*. And a connection between nodes in distant (nonadjacent) layers is called a *supralayer connection* by some researchers. The term *connectivity* refers to how nodes are connected. For example, full connectivity often means that every node in one layer is connected to every node in its adjacent layer.

A *high-order connection* is a connection that combines inputs from more than one node, often by multiplication. The number of the inputs determines the order of the connection. The *order* of a neural network is the order of the highest-order connection. Neural networks are assumed to be of first order unless mentioned otherwise.

Connection weights can be real numbers or integers. They can be confined to a range. They are adjustable during network training, but some can be fixed deliberately. When training is completed, all of them should be fixed.

2.2.2   Node Properties

The activation levels of nodes can be discrete (e.g., 0 and 1) or continuous across a range (e.g., [0, 1]) or unrestricted. This depends on the activation (transfer) function chosen. If it is a hard-limiting function, then the activation levels are 0 (or -1) and 1. For a sigmoid function, the activation levels are limited to a continuous range of reals [0, 1]. Figure 2.2 shows the sigmoid function F:

$$F(x) = \frac{1}{1 + e^{-x}}$$

In the case of a linear activation function, the activation levels are open. The activation function is mentioned again when we discuss the system dynamics.

2.2.3   System Dynamics

The weight initialization scheme is specific to the particular neural network model chosen. However, in many cases, initial weights are just randomized to small real numbers.

The learning rule is one of the most important attributes to specify for a neural network. The learning rule determines how to adapt connection weights in order to optimize the network performance. It indicates how to calculate the weight adjustment during each training cycle. However, the rule is suspended after training is completed.

When the neural network is used to solve a problem, the solution lies in the activation levels of the output units. For example, suppose a neural network is implemented for classifying fruits into lemons, oranges, and apples. The network has three output units representing the three kinds, respectively. Given an unknown fruit, we want to classify it. So we present the characteristics of the fruit to the network. The information is received by the input layer

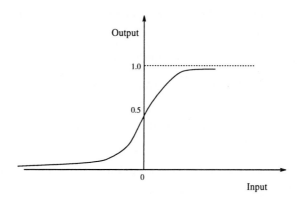

Figure 2.2: The sigmoid activation function.

and propagated forward. If the output unit corresponding to the class apple reaches the maximal activation, then the class assigned to the fruit is the apple. From this example, the inference behavior of a neural network involves how to compute the activation levels across the network. However, one should note that training a neural network also involves the same calculation, since we need to know the actual activation levels and the desired activation levels so as to calculate the errors, which are then used as the basis for weight adjustment.

The activation levels of input units need not be calculated since they are given. Those of hidden and output units are calculated according to the activation function used. Provided that it is a sigmoid function, the activation level (O_j) of unit j is calculated by

$$O_j = 1/[1 + e^{-(\sum_i W_{ji}X_i - \theta_j)}]$$

where X_i is the input from unit i, W_{ji} the weight on the connection from unit i to unit j, and θ_j the threshold on unit j. In the case of a hard-limiting activation function, the output of a neuron is given by

$$O_j = \left\{ \begin{array}{ll} 1, & \sum_i W_{ji}X_i > \theta_j \\ 0, & \text{else} \end{array} \right.$$

Occasionally, we *clamp* certain nodes so that they keep their present activation levels.

2.3 Inference and Learning

Building an AI system based on the neural network approach will generally involve the following steps:

1. Select a suitable neural network model based on the nature of the problem.

2. Construct a neural network according to the characteristics of the application domain.

3. Train the neural network with the learning procedure of the selected model.

4. Use the trained network for making inference or solving problems. If the performance is not satisfactory, then go to one of the previous steps.

Familiarity with existing applications will help determine the appropriate network architecture and select the best-suited computational model for learning and inference.

In the training (or learning) phase, a set of training instances is given. Each training instance is typically described by a feature vector (called an *input vector*). It may also be associated with a desired outcome (a concept, a class, etc.), which is encoded as another vector (called a desired *output vector*). In the above example, the three possible classes (the lemon, the orange, and the apple) can be represented by [1 0 0], [0 1 0], and [0 0 1], respectively. Starting with some arbitrary or random weight setting, the neural network is trained to adapt itself to the characteristics of the training instances by changing weights inside the network. In each training cycle, we present an instance to the network. It generates an output vector, which is compared with the desired output vector (if available). In this way, the error for each output unit is calculated and then used to update relevant weights. In a multilayer network, the errors of hidden units are not observed directly but can be estimated with some heuristic. Each weight change is hoped to reduce the error. When all instances are examined, the network will start over with the first instance and repeat. Iterations continue until the system performance (in terms of the error magnitude) has reached a satisfactory level. In practice, we choose an error criterion which will be minimized during training. Two criteria are commonly used for this purpose. One is the sum of squared errors,

$$\sum_p \sum_j (T_{j,p} - O_{j,p})^2$$

where $T_{j,p}$ and $O_{j,p}$ are, respectively, the desired and the actual activations of output unit j in instance p. The other criterion is the cross-entropy[2] (Hinton

---

[2] In this alternative, the activation of an output unit is construed as the probability of its designated concept. The cross-entropy criterion has more impact on the weight change than the squared-difference criterion when the actual activation is close to 0 and the target activation is 1

1989):

$$-\sum_{p}\sum_{j} P_{j,p} \log_2(Q_{j,p}) + (1 - P_{j,p}) \log_2(1 - Q_{j,p})$$

where $P_{j,p}$ and $Q_{j,p}$ are, respectively, the desired and the actual probabilities of output unit j in instance p.

In some network models, the error cannot be obtained at all since training instances are not provided with the desired results. Under this circumstance, a different learning procedure which updates weights by a different heuristic should be applied.

In the inference phase, the network propagates information from the input toward the output layer. When propagation stops, the output units carry the result of the inference. However, distinctions should be made between feedforward and recurrent networks. The lack of feedbacks in the former case allows one to define a clear endpoint of inference and ensures that the networks are *stable*.

Recurrent networks, on the other hand, are more complicated because they have feedback paths from their outputs back to their inputs. After applying an input, the output is calculated and then fed back to modify the input. The output is then recalculated, and the process repeats itself. For a stable network, successive iterations will produce smaller output changes and eventually a (near) constant output. That point defines the endpoint of inference. Networks in which the process never ends are said to be unstable. Cohen and Grossberg (1983) have devised a useful theorem which defines a subset of recurrent networks that are stable. The theorem sheds light on the design of such networks.

Despite some specific variations with different models, general learning and inference procedures can be extracted as follows.

The Neural Network Learning Algorithm (A general view)

Given n training instances,

1. Initialize the network weights. Set $i = 1$.

2. Present the ith instance to the network on the input layer.

3. Obtain the activation levels of the output units using the inference algorithm (described next). If the network performance meets the predefined standard (or the stopping criterion), then exit.

4. Update the weights by the learning rule of the network.

---

or vice versa. The cross-entropy criterion has been advocated by some researchers for domains in which output concepts are discrete in nature, such as classification tasks. Notice, however, when the error distribution is Gaussian, minimizing the error is equivalent to maximizing the likelihood.

5. If $i = n$, then reset $i = 1$. Otherwise, increment i by 1. Go to step 2.

The Neural Network Inference Algorithm (A general view)
Given a training instance,

1. Present the instance to the network on the input layer.

2. Calculate the activation levels of nodes across the network.

3. For a feedforward network, if the activation levels of all output units are calculated, then exit. For a recurrent network, if the activation levels of all output units become (near) constant, then exit; else go to step 2. However, if the network is found unstable, then exit and fail.

2.3.1   Data Representation

A discrete feature value (e.g., the feature *color* with values like *red, yellow, blue,* and so on) can be encoded by a single input unit. In this case, an activation of 1 corresponds to the notion of "yes," or "true," whereas an activation of 0 corresponds to "no," or "false." The activation may fall between 0 and 1, indicating the probability of the value.

Continuous feature values (e.g., the feature *age* with values ranging from 1 to 150) can be represented in several ways. In continuous representation, each feature is encoded by an input unit, and the feature value is mapped into the unit activation. In practice, the range of continuous values is often normalized to the interval between 0 and 1.

In discrete representation, the range of continuous values is divided into multiple intervals, each interval encoded by an input unit. Consider the range between a and b (a and b are reals, and $b > a$). Let us divide it into k intervals by introducing $k - 1$ points between a and b: $m_1, \ldots, m_{k-1}$. We may define $m_0 = a$ and $m_k = b$. In one approach, given the feature value x, if $m_i \leq x < m_{i+1}$, then the unit encoding that interval has an activation of 1 and the rest of the units have zero activations. In another approach, a unit has an activation of 1 if and only if the lower bound of the associated interval is less than or equal to x; that is, $m_i \leq x$. It is clear that in the second approach, one or more units will be activated at the same time for encoding a single value. Because of more distributive information encoding, the second approach is more resistant to noise than the first approach.

In the third scheme, a unit is activated to the extent determined by how close the associated interval is to the value. Again, this is a distributive encoding technique (see Chapter 4 "Knowledge-Based Neural Networks"). In the fourth scheme, a continuous-valued feature is encoded by fuzzy sets for fuzzy inference (see Chapter 11 "Expert Systems" for more details).

It is possible to represent a continuous value as a binary (rather than a decimal) number. For example, 8 is represented by four bits 1000; 7 is represented by 0111. This scheme does not make sense physically since two close values may have very different representations.

A relevant issue is how to enhance the information contained in the data by preprocessing. This step involves selection and transformation of data. Interested readers may refer to Stein (1993) and Chapter 17 "Drug Discovery."

It should not be overlooked that computational precision may affect the convergence property of the neural network. The precision of network weights or weight-updating calculations typically requires 13 bits including the sign for proper learning behavior (in fixed-point arithmetic); lower precision is possible with special scaling techniques (Hoehfeld and Fahlman 1992).

2.3.2 Functional Classification

Neural computational models can be categorized in terms of their applications:

- Classification: assignment of the input data to one of a finite number of categories.

- Association

  - Autoassociation: retrieval of an object (memory) based on part of the object (memory) itself.

  - Heteroassociation: retrieval of an object (memory) in one set using another object (memory) in a different set.

- Optimization: finding the best solution—often by minimizing a certain cost function.

- Self-organization: organizing received information using adaptive learning capabilities.

2.4 Classification Models

A neural network classifies a given object presented to it according to the output activation. For binary outputs, 1 corresponds to one class and 0 corresponds to the other. For continuous outputs between 0 and 1, 0.5 can be used as the threshold to make the decision. In the case of multiple outputs, the object is assigned to the class corresponding to the output node with the maximum activation. In this section, we examine classification models based on the neural network.

2.4.1   Single-Layer Perceptrons

A single-layer perceptron consists of an input and an output layer. The activation function employed is a hard-limiting function. An output unit will assume the value 1 if the sum of its weighted inputs is greater than its threshold. In terms of classification, an object will be classified by unit j into class A if

$$\sum W_{ji} X_i > \theta_j$$

where W_{ji} is the weight from unit i to unit j, X_i is the input from unit i, and θ_j is the threshold on unit j. Otherwise, the object will be classified as class B. Suppose there are n inputs. The equation

$$\sum_{i=1}^{n} W_{ji} X_i = \theta_j$$

forms a hyperplane in the n-dimensional space, dividing the space into two halves. When $n = 2$, it becomes a line. *Linear separability* refers to the case when a linear hyperplane exists to place the instances of one class on one side and those of the other class on the other side of the plane. Unfortunately, many classification problems are not linearly separable. The exclusive-or problem is a good example. A single-layer perceptron cannot simulate a simple exclusive-or function. This function accepts two inputs (0 or 1) and produces an output of one only if either input is one (but not both):

Inputs	Output
$(1, 1)$	0
$(1, 0)$	1
$(0, 1)$	1
$(0, 0)$	0

If we plot the above four points in the two-dimensional space as seen in Figure 2.3, it is impossible to draw a line so that $(1, 1)$ and $(0, 0)$ are on one side, and $(1, 0)$ and $(0, 1)$ on the other side.[3] To cope with a problem which is not linearly separable, a multilayer perceptron is required. The procedure given below summarizes the perceptron.

The Perceptron Algorithm

- **Weight Initialization**

  Set all weights and node thresholds to small random numbers. Note that the node threshold is the negative of the weight from the bias unit (whose activation level is fixed at 1).

---

[3] In contrast, the *or* function produces points which are linearly separable.

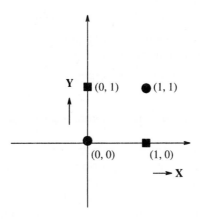

Figure 2.3: The exclusive-or function.

- **Calculation of Activation**

  1. The activation level of an input unit is determined by the instance presented to the network.
  2. The activation level O_j of an output unit is determined by

$$O_j = F_h\left(\sum W_{ji} X_i - \theta_j\right)$$

where W_{ji} is the weight from an input X_i, θ_j is the node threshold, and F_h is a hard-limiting function:

$$F_h(a) = \begin{cases} 1, & a > 0 \\ 0 \,(\text{or} - 1), & \text{else} \end{cases}$$

- **Weight Training**

  1. Adjust weights by

$$W_{ji}(t + 1) = W_{ji}(t) + \Delta W_{ji}$$

where $W_{ji}(t)$ is the weight from unit i to unit j at time t (or the tth iteration) and ΔW_{ji} is the weight adjustment.
  2. The weight change may be computed by the delta rule:

$$\Delta W_{ji} = \eta \delta_j X_i \tag{2.1}$$

where η is a trial-independent learning rate ($0 < \eta < 1$, e.g., 0.3) and δ_j is the error at unit j:

$$\delta_j = T_j - O_j$$

where T_j is the desired (target) output activation and O_j is the actual output activation at output unit j.

3. Repeat iterations until convergence.

The perceptron may use the delta rule to perform weight training. As seen in Eq. 2.1, the weight adjustment is proportional to the error. The adjusted weight will make the network output closer to the desired output. Furthermore, the weight adjustment also depends on the input (X_i). If the input is zero, there will be no adjustment. In this case, the weight does not contribute to the network output, so it should not be blamed. The learning rate η sets the step size. If η is too small, the convergence is unnecessarily slow, whereas if η is too large, the learning process may diverge.

The delta rule is a simple generalization of the perceptron learning rule.[4] According to the *perceptron convergence theorem*, if the data points are linearly separable, the perceptron learning rule will converge to some solution in a finite number of steps for any initial choice of the weights.

Example. In a single-layer perceptron, unit 1 receives inputs from units 2 and 3. Given that

$$W_{1,2} = -3, W_{1,3} = 2, X_2 = 1, X_3 = 1, \theta_1 = 1$$

calculate O_1.

$$O_1 = F_h(-3 \times 1 + 2 \times 1 - 1) = F_h(-2) = 0$$

Now, if the desired output $T_1 = 1$, how do we adjust weights? Assume that the learning rate $\eta = 0.3$.

$$\delta_1 = 1 - 0 = 1$$

$$\Delta W_{1,2} = \eta \delta_1 X_2 = 0.3 \times 1 \times 1 = 0.3$$

$$\Delta W_{1,3} = \eta \delta_1 X_3 = 0.3 \times 1 \times 1 = 0.3$$

$$W_{1,2} = -3 + 0.3 = -2.7$$

$$W_{1,3} = 2 + 0.3 = 2.3$$

---

[4] The perceptron learning rule is given by

$$W_{\text{new}} = W_{\text{old}} + \delta X$$

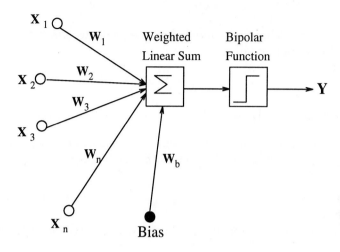

Figure 2.4: The adaline.

The threshold is the negative of the weight $W_{1,b}$ from the bias unit. That is, $W_{1,b} = -\theta_1 = -1$.

$$\Delta W_{1,b} = 0.3 \times 1 \times 1 = 0.3$$

$$W_{1,b} = -1 + 0.3 = -0.7$$

Thus, the threshold is changed to 0.7.

Adalines

The *adaline* (adaptive linear element) developed by Widrow is similar to the perceptron. The adaline has a single output (a single processing element) which receives multiple inputs. The processing element takes the weighted linear sum of the inputs and passes it to a bipolar function, which produces either $+1$ or -1, depending on the polarity of the sum. Its architecture is shown in Figure 2.4. A system with multiple outputs is implementable by using multiple adalines in parallel.

The *madaline* refers to multiple adalines which can be organized into multiple layers. The adaline and the madaline have found many useful applications in adaptive signal processing (Widrow and Winter 1988).

The problem dealt with by the adaline is to determine the weights in such a way that the output response is correct or the error is minimized. The training rule of the adaline is the LMS (least mean square) or the Widrow-Hoff rule:

$$\Delta W_{ji} = \eta \delta_j X_i$$

It differs from the delta rule employed by the perceptron in how the error is calculated for weight updating:

$$\delta_j = T_j - \sum W_{ji} X_i$$

The LMS Learning Rule

The adaline is trained on a set of instances. In instance k, the input vector is denoted by $\mathbf{X_k}$ and the desired, scalar output is denoted by Y_k. Let Y_k' be the network output given $\mathbf{X_k}$. That is,[5]

$$Y_k' = \mathbf{X_k} \mathbf{W}^T$$

where $\mathbf{W}$ is the weight vector. The LMS rule minimizes the mean squared error given by

$$\xi^2(\mathbf{W}) = E[(Y_k - Y_k')^2]$$

$$= E[(Y_k - \mathbf{X_k}\mathbf{W}^T)^2]$$

$$= E[(Y_k^2 - 2Y_k\mathbf{X_k}\mathbf{W}^T + \mathbf{W}\mathbf{X_k}^T\mathbf{X_k}\mathbf{W}^T]$$

$$= E[Y_k^2] - 2E[Y_k\mathbf{X_k}]\mathbf{W}^T + \mathbf{W}E[\mathbf{X_k}^T\mathbf{X_k}]\mathbf{W}^T$$

$$= a - 2\mathbf{b}\mathbf{W}^T + \mathbf{W}\mathbf{C}\mathbf{W}^T$$

where $E[\cdot]$ is the *expected value* operator, and the matrix $\mathbf{C}$ is the input correlation matrix. The best weight vector $\mathbf{W}^*$ is found by setting

$$\frac{\partial \xi^2(\mathbf{W})}{\partial \mathbf{W}} = 2\mathbf{W}^*\mathbf{C} - 2\mathbf{b} = 0$$

Thus, we obtain

$$\mathbf{W}^* = \mathbf{b}\mathbf{C}^{-1}$$

The LMS rule is actually a gradient descent rule. Consider the squared error for an individual instance:

$$\xi_k^2 = \frac{1}{2}(Y_k - \mathbf{X_k}\mathbf{W}^T)^2$$

The gradient descent technique minimizes the error by adjusting the weight vector as follows:

$$\Delta \mathbf{W} = -\eta \frac{\partial \xi_k^2}{\partial \mathbf{W}}$$

---

[5] We use horizontal vectors as the standard vector notation.

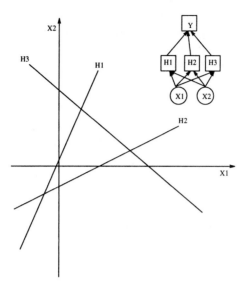

Figure 2.5: Decision regions created by a multilayer perceptron.

where η is the learning rate. This yields

$$\Delta \mathbf{W} = \eta(Y_k - \mathbf{X_k}\mathbf{W}^T)\mathbf{X_k}$$

which is the LMS rule.

2.4.2 Multilayer Perceptrons

A multilayer perceptron is a feedforward neural network with at least one hidden layer.[6] It can deal with nonlinear classification problems because it can form more complex decision regions (rather than just hyperplanes). Each node in the first layer (above the input layer) can create a hyperplane. Each node in the second layer can combine hyperplanes to create convex decision regions. Each node in the third layer can combine convex regions to form concave regions. The idea is illustrated in Figure 2.5. It is thus possible to form any arbitrary regions with sufficient layers and sufficient hidden units. Next, we briefly discuss the mechanism of combining information through layers.

---

[6] Conventionally, the input layer does not count. So, an n-layer perceptron has $n-1$ hidden layers, one input and one output layer.

Suppose an output node receives two inputs, its threshold is set to 1.5, and its input weights are both set to 1. It is clear that only when both input units are active (adopting the value 1), the output node will become active. In this case, the output node performs a logical AND operation. On the other hand, if the threshold is reduced to 0.5, then any active input can activate the node. In this case, the node performs a logical OR operation. Thus, by choosing a different set of weights and the threshold, a node can implement a different logical operation.

Example. Consider a two-layer perceptron. Let $\mathbf{W_{Hi}}$ and $\mathbf{W_{Oi}}$ denote the input weight vectors of hidden unit H_i and output unit O_i, respectively. Define the matrix $\mathbf{W_H} = [\mathbf{W_{H1}}^T, \mathbf{W_{H2}}^T, ...]$ and matrix $\mathbf{W_O} = [\mathbf{W_{O1}}^T, \mathbf{W_{O2}}^T, ...]$ where the superscript T means "transpose." Let $\theta_\mathbf{H} = [\theta_{H1}, \theta_{H2}, ...]$ and $\theta_\mathbf{O} = [\theta_{O1}, \theta_{O2}, ...]$ where θ_{Hi} and θ_{Oi} are the thresholds for the hidden unit and the output unit, respectively. Let $\mathbf{I}$, $\mathbf{H}$, and $\mathbf{O}$ be the input, the hidden, and the output vectors of activation levels. Then, we have

$$\mathbf{H} = F_h(\mathbf{IW_H} - \theta_\mathbf{H})$$

and

$$\mathbf{O} = F_h(\mathbf{HW_O} - \theta_\mathbf{O})$$

where F_h is a hard-limiting function. Given

$$\mathbf{W_H} = \begin{bmatrix} 2 & 1 & 0 \\ 1 & 2 & 2 \\ 0 & 3 & 1 \end{bmatrix}$$

and

$$\mathbf{W_O} = \begin{bmatrix} -1 \\ 1 \\ 2 \end{bmatrix}$$

and the input vector $\mathbf{I} = (3, 4, 0)$, calculate the output. Assume $\theta_\mathbf{H} = [0, 0, 1]$ and $\theta_\mathbf{O} = [1]$.

$\mathbf{H} = F_h(\mathbf{IW_H} - \theta_\mathbf{H})$

$\qquad = F_h([10, 11, 8] - [0, 0, 1])$

$\qquad = F_h([10, 11, 7])$

$\qquad = [1, 1, 1]$

$\mathbf{O} = F_h(\mathbf{HW_O} - \theta_\mathbf{O})$

$\qquad = F_h(2 - 1)$

$\qquad = 1$

So, the output is 1.

A major issue in designing a multilayer neural network is how many hidden units are optimal given a set of training patterns. Some analyses on this issue are available. For example, Mirchandani and Cao (1989) have developed a relationship as follows. In a d-dimensional space (d input units), the maximum number of regions $M(H, d)$ that are linearly separable using a single hidden layer of H hidden units is given by

$$M(H, d) = \sum_{k=0}^{d} \binom{H}{k}$$

where

$$\binom{H}{k} = 0, \quad H < k$$

For $H \leq d$, $H = \log_2 M$. Notice, however, that their analysis is limited to the case when the activation function is a hard-limiting function. More detailed discussion on network size is provided in Chapter 3 "Learning: Supervised and Unsupervised."

The number of hidden units can be determined empirically. Plot the test performance versus the number of hidden units, and then choose the number with the best performance. Since it is impractical to try all possibilities, pre-analysis may help select a good number to start with.

The delta rule does not apply to training a multilayer network since the error of a hidden unit is not known. The backpropagation rule (described in Chapter 3) overcomes this difficulty. The backpropagation network often uses a sigmoid function as the activation function. Its behavior is difficult to analyze because decision regions are bounded by smooth curves.

2.5 Association Models

In this section, we examine neural network models which exhibit associative-memory characteristics.

2.5.1 Hopfield Nets

Among all the autoassociative networks, the Hopfield network (Hopfield and Tank 1986) is the most widely known today. It is useful both for autoassociation and for optimization tasks. It applies the concept of energy surface minimization in physics to finding stable solutions in the neural network. Also, this network is relatively easy to implement in VLSI chips.

The main concept underlying the Hopfield network is that a single network of interconnected, binary-valued neurons can store multiple stable states. Suppose we create a network of binary-valued neurons, where each neuron is connected to the others but not back to itself. Assume all the connection weights

OUTPUT

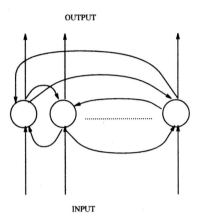

INPUT

Figure 2.6: The Hopfield network.

are symmetric. That is, $w_{ij} = w_{ji}$. This network can have a set of stable states. For each stable state, each binary neuron takes on a value (either -1 (0) or 1)[7] so that when it acts on its neighbors, the values of each neuron do not change. Given an input pattern, the network can converge to the stable state nearest to that pattern. This implies that we can use the network for autoassociation in which a noisy or partial pattern can stabilize at a nearby state corresponding to one of the originally stored patterns.

The architecture of the Hopfield net is shown in Figure 2.6. The number of the network units is the same as that of the bits or values contained in each stored pattern. Units update their states asynchronously by receiving inputs from other units. Once set, the weights in the Hopfield net are not trainable. The Hopfield net algorithm is displayed below.

The Hopfield Net Algorithm for Autoassociation

- **Weight Assignments**

  Suppose the network stores m patterns:

$$W_{ji} = \begin{cases} \sum_{p=1}^{m} P_{j,p} P_{i,p}, & i \neq j \\ 0, & i = j \end{cases}$$

---

[7]A neuron has a binary state: -1 (or 0) and 1. It is customary to use the bipolar version (-1 and 1).

where W_{ji} is the connection weight from unit i to unit j and $P_{i,p}$ is the ith component in the pattern vector p.

- **Calculation of Activation**

    1. At time $= 0$

    $$O_j(0) = P_j$$

    where $O_j(t)$ is the activation level of unit j at time t and P_j is the jth component of the input pattern.

    2. At time $= t$ $(t > 0)$

    $$O_j(t+1) = F_h(\sum_i W_{ji} O_i(t))$$

    where the function F_h is a hard-limiting function:

    $$F_h(a) = \begin{cases} 1, & a > 0 \\ -1\ (0), & a < 0 \\ O_j(t)\ (\text{i.e., unchanged}), & a = 0 \end{cases} \qquad (2.2)$$

    The hard-limiting function may be substituted by a smooth function. The Hopfield net is a nonlinear associator because of this nonlinearity.

    3. Repeat step 2 until equilibrium (i.e., the activation levels of nodes remain unchanged with further iterations). Then, the pattern of activations upon equilibrium represents the stored pattern that best matches the unknown input.

For problems other than autoassociation, the weight assignments depend on the network-energy function chosen, but the calculation of activation is similar to the above.

There are two major limitations with the Hopfield net. One is the tendency to local minima, which is good for association but disadvantageous for optimization. The other is the limited network capacity. For a network of N binary nodes, the capacity limit is of the order of N rather than 2^N. This issue is explored later.

Example. For the associative Hopfield net, let us use the outer products to construct the weight matrix as follows:

$$\mathbf{W} = \sum_i (\mathbf{X_i}^T \mathbf{X_i} - \mathbf{I}_n)$$

where $\mathbf{X_i}$ is the n-dimensional bipolar (-1 and 1) vector to be stored in the net and $\mathbf{I}_n$ is an $n \times n$ identity matrix. Given

$$\mathbf{X_1} = (1, -1, -1)$$
$$\mathbf{X_2} = (-1, 1, -1)$$
$$\mathbf{X_3} = (-1, -1, 1)$$

compute the weight matrix.

$$\mathbf{W} = (\mathbf{X_1}^T \mathbf{X_1} - I_3) + (\mathbf{X_2}^T \mathbf{X_2} - I_3) + (\mathbf{X_3}^T \mathbf{X_3} - I_3)$$

Thus,

$$\mathbf{W} = \begin{bmatrix} 0 & -1 & -1 \\ -1 & 0 & -1 \\ -1 & -1 & 0 \end{bmatrix}$$

Next, we use $\mathbf{X_1}$ as the probe vector:

$$F_h(\mathbf{X_1 W}) = F_h([2, 0, 0]) = [1, -1, -1]$$

which is exactly $\mathbf{X_1}$. In other cases, more than one iteration may be necessary for reaching an equilibrium. Whether all stored vectors can be retrieved correctly depends on the capacity of the net.

The brain-state-in-a-box (BSB) network (Anderson and Rosenfeld 1988) is similar to the Hopfield net. The difference is that the BSB network has self-connections while the Hopfield net does not.

Kanerva (1988) developed the sparse distributed memory (SDM) network in which a d-dimensional pattern is stored in a distributed manner within a certain metric distance of the pattern in d-dimensional space. Note that a pattern corresponds to a point (location) in the space but it is stored as multiple points within a critical radius of the pattern's location. This approach is well suited for storing very large, sparse pattern vectors.

Capacity of Hopfield Nets

The Hopfield net can be activated either synchronously or asynchronously. In the synchronous mode, the weights are updated simultaneously. In asynchronous operation, the network updates only one neuron at a time. The neuron is selected from n neurons with a probability of $1/n$.

To study the memory capacity of the Hopfield net, let us define what is a memory in the neural associative network. If a binary n-dimensional vector $\mathbf{X}$ is a memory, then for each component (neuron) $i = 1, ..., n$

$$X_i = F_h(\sum_{j=1}^{n} W_{ij} X_j) \qquad (2.3)$$

where F_h is the hard-limiting function in Eq. 2.2. Intuitively, this means that $\mathbf{X}$ is a memory if the network is stable at that point. The memory also tends to act as an attractor because it will pull states that are similar to map onto the memory. This has the effect of correcting some or all the errors in a probe vector. A probe vector refers to the vector we use to perform association.

Suppose we try to store m memory vectors X_i's of n dimensions. Each component in X_i is either $+1$ or -1. The m vectors are called fundamental memories. The outer product construction method is used to arrive at the appropriate weight matrix W as before. The weight matrix so constructed guarantees that the network will converge to a stable state. Additionally, if $m \ll n$, then the system will behave well.

Take an example given by McEliece et al. (1987). Suppose we wish to store three memories of five dimensions as follows:

$$X_1 = (+1, +1, +1, +1, +1)$$
$$X_2 = (+1, -1, -1, +1, -1)$$
$$X_3 = (-1, +1, -1, -1, -1)$$

Asynchronous operation is assumed. The weight matrix W is constructed by the outer products method:

$$W = \begin{bmatrix} 0 & -1 & 1 & 3 & 1 \\ -1 & 0 & 1 & -1 & 1 \\ 1 & 1 & 0 & 1 & 3 \\ 3 & -1 & 1 & 0 & 1 \\ 1 & 1 & 3 & 1 & 0 \end{bmatrix}$$

Assume that the probe vector is

$$X = (+1, -1, -1, +1, +1)$$

which is only a Hamming distance[8] of 1 from X_2. The product XW is computed and then hard-limited to $+1$, -1 to yield X':

$$X' = (+1, -1, +1, +1, -1)$$

Because of asynchronous operation, any element may be updated first. For this example, let the third element be chosen. The new probe will be

$$X' = (+1, -1, +1, +1, +1)$$

Now repeat the above step until a fundamental memory is reached. Eventually, the second element of X will be updated and give

$$X'' = (+1, +1, +1, +1, +1)$$

Note $X'' = X_1$. That is, the system does not converge to X_2 which is closest to the initial probe vector.

The above example reveals one of the problems with the Hopfield net. The probe may not settle onto one of the memories. If it is a memory, then it is not necessarily the closest memory.

---

[8] The Hamming distance calculates the number of bits which differ in two vectors.

It is desirable that fundamental memories are fixed points.[9] In the Hopfield net, a fixed point $\mathbf{X}$ satisfies

$$\mathbf{X} = F_h(\mathbf{XW})$$

Once the network settles in a fundamental memory, it will not leave. The fundamental memory should have the capability to attract states that are close to it. There are three possibilities for convergence.

The first possibility is direct convergence. In asynchronous operation, the probe vector lies within the basin of attraction and leads directly to the fundamental memory at the center. In the synchronous mode, this means convergence to the memory in one step.

In the second possibility, a random step will be in the correct direction with high probability. After several random steps, the probe vector will converge to the fundamental memory. This process can be thought of as a two-iteration convergence in synchronous operation.

In the third possibility, the probe vector moves back and forth but gets closer to the fundamental memory. After a finite number of iterations, the system will settle in a fixed point either on or close to the fundamental memory.

It has been conjectured that the maximum number of memories m that can be stored in a network of n neurons and recalled exactly is less than cn^2 where c is a positive constant greater than one (Wasserman 1989). In general, this bound is overly optimistic. Hopfield (1982) showed experimentally that the general capacity limit was about $0.15n$. If the m memories are chosen at random and if the input pattern is less than $n/2$ away in Hamming distance from a stored pattern, the maximum asymptotic value of m for which all the fundamental memories can be correctly recalled can be shown as (McEliece et al. 1987)

$$m \leq \frac{n}{4 \ln n}$$

The bound improves if we do not require the network to converge to the best memory.

2.5.2   Bidirectional Associative Memories

In autoassociation, a memory can be completed or corrected upon retrieval by self-association, given a partial or corrupted input. In contrast to this, the bidirectional associative memory (BAM) (Kosko 1987) can relate an input vector to another different vector and is capable of generalization over similar inputs. As seen in Figure 2.7, the BAM has a two-layer recurrent architecture in which the backward weight (from the output toward the input) matrix is the transpose of the forward weight (from the input toward the output) matrix. The sizes of the input and the output layers are determined by the dimensions of the pairs of associated vectors. An input vector $\mathbf{P}$ is applied to the weight matrix $\mathbf{W}$ and

---

[9]If $f(x) = x$, then x is called a fixed point of the function f.

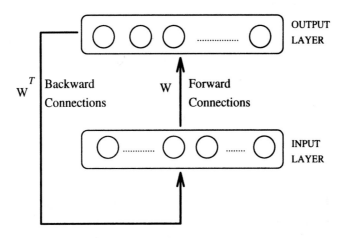

Figure 2.7: The bidirectional associative memory.

produces an output vector $\mathbf{Q}$, which is then applied to $\mathbf{W}^T$ to produce a new input vector. This process is repeated until the network reaches a stable point. The BAM uses the following procedure.

The BAM Algorithm

- **Weight Assignments**

  Suppose the network stores m pairs of patterns. Forward weights are given by

  $$W_{ji} = \sum_{p=1, q=1}^{m} P_{i,p} Q_{j,q}$$

  where W_{ji} is the connection weight from unit i to unit j, $P_{i,p}$ is the ith component in the pattern vector p, $Q_{j,q}$ is the jth component in the pattern vector q, and patterns p and q form an association pair. Then, set a backward weight W_{ij} = a forward weight W_{ji}.

- **Calculation of Activation**

  1. Initialize the input units at time 0 with

  $$O_i(0) = P_i$$

  where P_i is the ith component of the input pattern.

2. At time $= t$ $(t > 0)$

$$O_j(t+1) = F_h(\sum_i W_{ji}O_i(t))$$

where $O_j(t)$ is the activation level of unit j at time t and the function F_h is a hard-limiting function:

$$F_h(a) = \begin{cases} 1, & a > 0 \\ -1\ (0), & a < 0 \\ O_j(t)\ (\text{i.e., unchanged}), & a = 0 \end{cases}$$

Note that the hard-limiting function can be substituted by a sigmoid function.

3. Repeat step 2 until equilibrium (i.e., the activation levels of nodes remain unchanged with further iterations). Then, the pattern of activations upon equilibrium over the output units represents the stored pattern that is associated with the input pattern.

The results on the capacity of the Hopfield net can be extended to the BAM. It has been estimated that in general the maximum number of stored associations cannot exceed the number of nodes in the smaller layer. However, it has been suggested that the number of stable states can be increased by selecting the threshold for each node (Haines and Hecht-Nielsen 1988).

The Hebbian learning rule (described later) has been proposed to update the weights in the BAM (called the adaptive BAM). This capability enables the network to optimally extract the associated pattern even when the input pattern is noisy or incomplete.

Example. Use a BAM to store three pairs of vectors as follows:

Original vector	Associated vector
$A1 = [1, -1, -1]$	$B1 = [1, -1]$
$A2 = [-1, 1, -1]$	$B2 = [-1, 1]$
$A3 = [-1, -1, 1]$	$B3 = [1, -1]$

Use the outer products to construct the weight matrix:

$$\mathbf{W} = \sum_i \mathbf{A_i}^T \mathbf{B_i}$$

That is,

$$\mathbf{W} = \mathbf{A_1}^T\mathbf{B_1} + \mathbf{A_2}^T\mathbf{B_2} + \mathbf{A_3}^T\mathbf{B_3}$$

The result is

$$\mathbf{W} = \begin{bmatrix} 1 & -1 \\ -3 & 3 \\ 1 & -1 \end{bmatrix}$$

Suppose we use $\mathbf{A_1}$ as the probe vector.

$$F_h(\mathbf{A_1 W}) = F_h([3, -3]) = [1, -1]$$

which is $\mathbf{B_1}$. However, suppose we use $\mathbf{B_1}$ as the probe vector to perform reverse association.

$$F_h(\mathbf{B_1 W}^T) = F_h([2, -6, 2]) = [1, -1, 1]$$

It does not retrieve $\mathbf{A_1}$ correctly. More iterations may be needed. In this case, however, since $\mathbf{B_1} = \mathbf{B_3}$, there is always ambiguity.

2.6 Optimization Models

The optimization model offers solutions to various combinatorial optimization problems which often lack efficient solutions on a digital computer. In this section, we examine Hopfield nets and Boltzmann machines.

2.6.1 Hopfield Nets

In addition to serving as autoassociators, Hopfield networks can be applied to optimization and constraint satisfaction problems. The idea is to encode each hypothesis as a unit and to encode constraints between hypotheses by weights. Positive weights encode mutual supporting relationships, whereas negative weights encode incompatible relationships. As the Hopfield net settles into a stable state, the state reflects the assignment of truth and falsity to the various hypotheses under the constraints.

In a recurrent neural network like the Hopfield net, stability is a major issue. Cohen and Grossberg (1983) show that recurrent networks are stable if $W_{ij} = W_{ji}$ for $i \neq j$ and $W_{ii} = 0$ for all i. This can be proven using a Liapunov function as the energy function of the network:

$$E = -\frac{1}{2} \sum_i \sum_j W_{ji} O_i O_j - \sum_j I_j O_j + \sum_j \theta_j O_j \qquad (2.4)$$

where

E = network energy
W_{ji} = weight from unit i to unit j
O_j = activation level of unit j
I_j = external input to unit j
θ_j = threshold of unit j

In solving an optimization problem, this energy function is compared with another function built from problem constraints in order to determine the network weights.

Consider the well-known traveling salesman problem as an example. The problem is stated as follows: Given a group of cities and the distance between each city, find the shortest tour that visits each city only once and returns to the starting point. Given n cities, there are $n!$ possible solutions. To solve this problem, the Hopfield net involves n^2 units represented as an $n \times n$ array. O_{xi} indicates the activation level of the unit denoting that city x is the ith city in the tour, and d_{xy} denotes the distance between cities x and y. The energy function constructed from the problem constraints is

$$E = E_1 + E_2 + E_3 + E_4$$

where

$$E_1 = \frac{A}{2} \sum_x \sum_i \sum_{i \neq j} O_{xi} O_{xj}$$

$$E_2 = \frac{B}{2} \sum_i \sum_x \sum_{x \neq y} O_{xi} O_{yi}$$

$$E_3 = \frac{C}{2} [(\sum_x \sum_i O_{xi}) - n]^2$$

$$E_4 = \frac{D}{2} \sum_x \sum_{x \neq y} \sum_i d_{xy} O_{xi} (O_{y,i+1} + O_{y,i-1})$$

$A, B, C,$ and D are constants. Notice that E_1 reflects the constraint that each row contains no more than a single 1, E_2 reflects the constraint that each column contains no more than a single 1, E_3 reflects the constraint that there should be exactly n 1s in the array, and E_4 reflects the constraint that the shortest tour is favored (the term in the summation represents the length of any valid tour). By comparing this energy function with Eq. 2.4, the weight is given by

$$W_{xi,yj} = -A\delta_{xy}(1 - \delta_{ij}) - B\delta_{ij}(1 - \delta_{xy}) - C - Dd_{xy}(\delta_{j,i+1} + \delta_{j,i-1})$$

where $\delta_{ij} = 1$ if $i = j$ and otherwise is 0. Once the weights are determined and other system parameters chosen, the network uses the algorithm formulated below to solve the problem.

The Hopfield Net Algorithm for Optimization

- **Weight Assignments**

  1. Write an energy function based on problem constraints.

2. Compare the above energy function with the following energy function of the Hopfield net (a Liapunov function) to determine the weights:

$$E = -\frac{1}{2}\sum_i \sum_j W_{ji}O_iO_j - \sum_j I_jO_j + \sum_j \theta_jO_j$$

- **Calculation of Activation**

    1. At time = 0,
    $$O_j(0) = \text{a randomized small value}$$
    where $O_j(t)$ is the activation level of unit j at time t.

    2. At time = t ($t > 0$),
    $$O_j(t+1) = F_h(\sum_i W_{ji}O_i(t) + I_j)$$

    where the function F_h is a hard-limiting function:

    $$F_h(a) = \begin{cases} 1, & a > \theta_j \\ -1\ (0), & a < \theta_j \\ O_j(t)\ (\text{i.e., unchanged}), & a = \theta_j \end{cases}$$

    3. Repeat step 2 until equilibrium (i.e., the activation levels of nodes remain unchanged with further iterations). Then, the pattern of activations upon equilibrium represents the optimized solution.

The model formulated above is a discrete version. The continuous Hopfield model starts off with

$$C_j \frac{du_j}{dt} = -\frac{1}{R_j}u_j + \sum_i W_{ji}v_i + I_j \tag{2.5}$$

where u_j is the net input to unit j, v_j is its output (activation level), I_j is its external input, C_j is the capacitance, and R_j is the resistance. The input u_j lags behind the output v_j because of the capacitance, and they are related by

$$v_j = g_j(\lambda u_j) = \frac{1}{2}[1 + \tanh(\lambda u_j)]$$

where λ is a constant called the gain parameter. The continuous model uses the following energy function:

$$E = -\frac{1}{2}\sum_i \sum_j W_{ji}v_iv_j + \frac{1}{\lambda}\sum_j \frac{1}{R_j}\int_0^{v_j} g_j^{-1}(v)dv - \sum_j I_jv_j \tag{2.6}$$

In a continuous system, stable points move away from the vertices of the hypercube. Figure 2.8 shows an energy contour map with two stable points.

For example, in the 10-city traveling salesman problem, Hopfield and Tank (1985) used $A = B = D = 500$ and $C = 200$ and used the continuous activation function. Most of the trials converged to valid tours, and about half of them were optimal solutions. Results highly depend on the coefficients. Unfortunately, there is no systematic way to determine their values. For this particular problem, the Hopfield net is not superior to a specialized search algorithm, but it presents a general solution to optimization problems.

In addition, the Hopfield net can be used for parameter estimation in a system. For example, assume that

$$Y = \mathbf{X} \cdot \mathbf{p}$$

A set of instances of the form $(Y_k, \mathbf{X}_k)$, where $\mathbf{X}_k$ is a d-dimensional horizontal vector, is available to estimate the parameter vector $\mathbf{p}$ by minimizing the criterion of the sum of squared errors:

$$\sum_k (Y_k - \mathbf{X}_k \cdot \mathbf{p})^2$$

Translating this criterion into an energy function yields the weight matrix

$$\mathbf{W} = -2 \sum_k \mathbf{X}_k^T \mathbf{X}_k$$

The activation levels of network units at equilibrium are estimated parameter values. Alternatively, the problem can be solved by using the LMS rule.

Stability of Hopfield Nets

Here, we show how the selection of a Liapunov function as the energy function of a Hopfield net ensures stability.

Suppose neuron k changes its state from time t to time $t + 1$. From Eq. 2.4, the change to the energy level ΔE due to such a change is

$$\Delta E = E(t + 1) - E(t)$$
$$= -[(\tfrac{1}{2} \sum_i W_{ki} O_i) + I_k - \theta_k] \Delta O_k$$

where $\Delta O_k = O_k(t + 1) - O_k(t)$, and the sum of the first two terms is the total input to neuron k. Since a neuron assumes a state of either 0 or 1, there are three possible cases for ΔO_k:

- $\Delta O_k = 1$

- $\Delta O_k = -1$

- $\Delta O_k = 0$

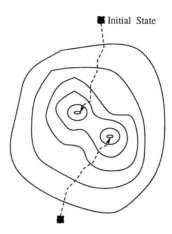

Figure 2.8: An energy contour map. The result of energy minimization depends on where it starts.

In the first case, neuron k changes its state from 0 to 1, and therefore, its total input must be greater than its threshold. It follows that $\Delta E < 0$. In the second case, neuron k changes its state from 1 to 0, so its total input must be less than its threshold. Again, $\Delta E < 0$. In the third case, $\Delta E = 0$. This shows that the energy level is always nonincreasing (decreasing or remaining constant) whenever a neuron changes its state. The network will eventually reach a minimum energy state and stop. The result follows.

2.6.2   Boltzmann Machines

The main problem with the Hopfield network is that it settles into local minima by constant energy minimization. This phenomenon is desirable for association but undesirable for optimization or constraint satisfaction. In the latter two cases, we seek the globally optimal state of the network. This state corresponds to a solution that satisfies the most constraints.

Simulated annealing, a technique which simulates the annealing process of metals,[10] is important in finding globally optimal solutions to combinatorial

---

[10] As early as 1953, Metropolis et al. proposed an algorithm for the efficient simulation of the evolution of a solid to thermal equilibrium. The basic idea behind annealing is that as a metal is gradually cooled, lower and lower energy states are formed and eventually the lowest-possible energy state is reached. Kirkpatrick, Gelatt, and Vecchi (1983) realized that there exists an analogy between minimizing the cost function of a combinatorial optimization problem and

problems. Hinton and Sejnowski (1986) combined Hopfield networks and simulated annealing to result in networks known as *Boltzmann machines*. In this technique, local minima are avoided by adding some randomness to the process of energy minimization, so that when the network moves toward a local minimum, it has a chance to escape. To implement this idea, the Boltzmann machine updates the binary states of individual neurons by a stochastic rather than deterministic rule. The probability that unit j will be active (in the state 1) is given by p_j:

$$p_j = \frac{1}{1 + e^{-\Delta E_j/T}}$$

where ΔE_j is the total input received by unit j and T is the "temperature" of the network. At thermal equilibrium, the probability of any global state is constant and obeys the Boltzmann distribution:

$$\frac{P_A}{P_B} = e^{-(E_A - E_B)/T}$$

where the probability ratio of any two states depends on their energy difference.

At high temperatures, the network exhibits random behavior, while at very low temperatures, it behaves like the Hopfield net. Annealing is the process of gradually reducing the temperature from high to low. Boltzmann machines run slow because of their stochastic nature.

To achieve a global minimum, Geman and Geman (1984) show that the temperature must be reduced in proportion to the inverse logarithm of time:

$$T(t) = \frac{T_0}{\log(1 + t)}$$

where $T(t)$ is the temperature at time t and T_0 is the initial temperature. In Cauchy machines where the Cauchy distribution replaces the Boltzmann distribution, run time is much reduced by following the schedule:

$$T(t) = \frac{T_0}{1 + t}$$

To train Boltzmann machines, we select one set of neurons to be input units and another set to be output units. Each weight is updated by

$$\Delta W_{ij} = \epsilon(P_{ij}^+ - P_{ij}^-)$$

where P_{ij}^+ is the expected probability (averaged over all cases) that units i and j are both active at thermal equilibrium through annealing when the input and the output vectors are both clamped, P_{ij}^- is the same probability when only the input vector is clamped and the network is free-running, ϵ is a constant. If ϵ is

---

the slow cooling of a metal.

sufficiently small, the weight-updating algorithm performs gradient descent in an information-theoretical measure G (Hinton 1989):

$$G = \sum_{x,y} P^+(I_x, O_y) \log \frac{P^+(O_y|I_x)}{P^-(O_y|I_x)} \tag{2.7}$$

where I_x is a state vector over the input units, O_y is a state vector over the output units, P^+ is a probability measured at thermal equilibrium when both the input and the output units are clamped, and P^- is a probability measured when only the input units are clamped. G is called the *asymmetric divergence*.

The Boltzmann Machine Algorithm

- **Weight Assignments**

  The same as the Hopfield net.

- **Calculation of Activation**

  1. Select an initial temperature.
  2. Until thermal equilibrium, repeatedly calculate the probability that unit j is active (adopting the state 1) by

$$p_j = \frac{1}{1 + e^{-\Delta E_j/T}}$$

  where ΔE_j is the total input received by unit j and T is the temperature. The activation level of unit j is set according to this probability.

  3. If the lowest temperature has been reached, then exit and the pattern of activations upon equilibrium represents the optimized solution. Otherwise, reduce the temperature by a certain annealing schedule and repeat step 2.

- **Weight Training**

  Each weight is trained by

$$\Delta W_{ij} = \epsilon(P_{ij}^+ - P_{ij}^-).$$

There exists a class of algorithms which also employ the notion of annealing to tackle difficult combinatorial optimization problems but with a deterministic approach. These algorithms are loosely called *deterministic annealing* or *mean field theory annealing* (Stolorz 1992). With mean field theory approximation, the stochastic process in the Boltzmann machine can be replaced by a set of deterministic equations (Peterson and Anderson 1987) which generally provide quicker solutions.

2.7   Self-Organization Models

The term *self-organization* refers to the ability to learn and organize information without being given correct answers for input patters. Thus, self-organizing networks perform unsupervised learning. This computational model may serve to explain some neurobiological phenomena such as how a baby learns since it does not know what is correct.

The self-organization model is effective for dealing with problems whose algorithms are too complicated to define, for example, modeling of irregular surfaces. In robotics, self-organization compensates for inaccuracies and noise in sensor readings and offers a method for dealing with unexpected and changing situations which lack mathematical descriptions.

In this section, we describe several models which exhibit this characteristic, including the Kohonen network, Hebbian learning, and competitive learning. The ART (adaptive resonance theory) network is self-organizing but it is treated in Chapter 3.

2.7.1   Kohonen Networks

The Kohonen network (Kohonen 1988) consists of a single layer of nodes (plus an input layer). Each node receives inputs from the environment and from the other nodes within the layer. When we build a Kohonen network, it is important to properly initialize the weight vectors of the nodes. Let us assume that both weight vectors and input vectors are normalized to a constant (typically unit length).[11] Each node computes by taking the dot product of its weight vector and the input vector. The result reflects their similarity (or distance). Symbolically,

$$N_j = \mathbf{X} \cdot \mathbf{W_j} \tag{2.8}$$

where N_j is the input activation of unit j, $\mathbf{X}$ is the input vector, and $\mathbf{W_j}$ is the weight vector of unit j. Suppose we place all weight vectors in a matrix called a matrix $\mathbf{W}$, and let the vector $\mathbf{N}$ represent the input activations of all nodes. Then we obtain

$$\mathbf{N} = \mathbf{XW} \tag{2.9}$$

Only the node with the maximum activation will produce an output (1). Next, we examine the functionality of the Kohonen network.

Clustering

Clustering is concerned with the grouping of objects (input patterns) according to their similarity. We will see how the Kohonen network can perform clustering through a competitive learning mechanism called "winner take all."

---

[11] If vectors are not normalized to a fixed length, the algorithm is modified. See Chapter 7 "Complex Domains" for the algorithm of self-organizing feature maps.

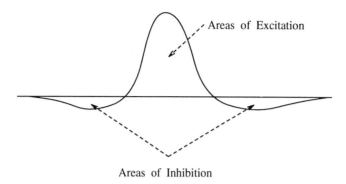

Figure 2.9: Lateral inhibition.

In essence, the node with the largest activation level is declared the winner in the competition. This node is the only node that will generate an output signal, and all other nodes are suppressed to the zero activation level. Furthermore, this node and its neighbors are the only nodes permitted to learn for the current input pattern.

The Kohonen network uses intralayer connections to moderate this competition. The output of each node acts as an inhibitory input to the other nodes but is actually excitatory in its neighborhood. Thus, even though there is only one winner node, more than one node are allowed to change their weights. This complex scheme for moderating competition within a layer is known as *lateral inhibition*. The inhibitory effect of a node can also decrease with the distance from it and assume the appearance of a Mexican sombrero (see Figure 2.9). The exact size of the neighborhood varies as learning goes on. It starts large and is slowly reduced, making the range of change sharper and sharper. To simulate lateral inhibition, we simply take the winner. This avoids the complexity of truly implementing this mechanism. However, the concept of lateral inhibition is vital in neurobiology.

After training, the weight vector of each node encodes the information of a group of similar input patterns. Given an input vector, it is assigned to the node with the maximum activation. Since the number of nodes is fixed, the net algorithm is similar to the k-means clustering algorithm (see Duda and Hart 1973). This kind of algorithm is more noise tolerant than algorithms which do not specify the number of clusters in advance, such as the ART network. Results, however, may depend on the presentation order of input data for a small amount of training data. The clustering function can be exploited in many ways. For example, the network can be used as a vector quantizer in a speech recognition system.

Learning

The winning node and its neighbors will learn by adjusting their weight vectors according to the following rule:

$$\mathbf{W}_{new} = \mathbf{W}_{old} + \eta(\mathbf{X} - \mathbf{W}_{old}) \qquad (2.10)$$

where $\mathbf{X}$ is the input vector and η is the learning rate.

Since the winner's weight vector generates the largest dot product with the input vector, it means that the winning weight vector is closest to the input vector. Kohonen learning is to make the winning weight vector even more similar to the input vector. As learning proceeds, the size of the neighborhood is gradually decreased. Fewer and fewer nodes learn in each iteration, and finally, only the winning node learns.

Example. The input weight vectors of the hidden units in a Kohonen network are given by

$$\mathbf{W}_{H1} = [0.530, 0.270, 0.801]$$
$$\mathbf{W}_{H2} = [0.424, 0.566, 0.707]$$
$$\mathbf{W}_{H3} = [0.440, 0.871, 0.220]$$

Suppose the input vector

$$\mathbf{X} = [0.208, 0.590, 0.780]$$

We calculate the dot products as follows:

$$\mathbf{X} \cdot \mathbf{W}_{H1} = 0.894$$
$$\mathbf{X} \cdot \mathbf{W}_{H2} = 0.974$$
$$\mathbf{X} \cdot \mathbf{W}_{H3} = 0.777$$

So, unit H_2 is the winner, and its weight vector is updated by (assuming that the learning rate $\eta = 0.3$ and that the radius of neighborhood is 0)

$$\begin{aligned} \Delta \mathbf{W}_{H2} &= \eta(\mathbf{X} - \mathbf{W}_{H2}) \\ &= [-0.065, 0.007, 0.022] \\ \text{new } \mathbf{W}_{H2} &= [0.359, 0.573, 0.729] \end{aligned}$$

Unlike the perceptron, the Kohonen network uses single-pass learning rather than multipass feedback and is potentially fast. This fact suggests its suitability for real-time applications.

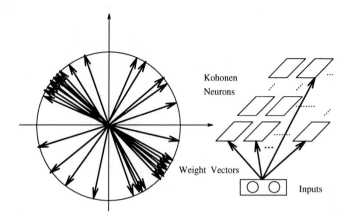

Figure 2.10: Statistical modeling.

Statistical Modeling

The Kohonen network has the ability to extract the statistical properties of the input data set. More specifically, it can estimate the probability density function of the input data. This property is very useful since we can apply the Kohonen network to statistical modeling. Kohonen has shown that in a fully trained network, if an input vector is randomly selected according to the probability density function of the input data set, then the probability of the vector being closest to any given weight vector is $1/k$ where k is the number of Kohonen neurons. This is the optimal distribution of weight vectors on the hypersphere if they are normalized to a constant length.

Figure 2.10 shows that normalized weight vectors align themselves in a unit circle so that their distribution reflects the probability density function of input patterns. The region where the weight vectors are more crowded is also the region where the input patterns fall more densely. The Kohonen network is able to model any statistical distribution which may lack a closed-form analytical expression.

The Kohonen network should be trained on data that is statistically representative or meaningful to the total input. In case the data statistics are not well understood, a large data set is often required for good modeling. On the other hand, the modeling capability is affected by the network size. In general, the smaller the network, the less accurate the statistical model.

Under the winner-take-all strategy, only one neuron gets activated for each input pattern. This is called the *accretive mode*. Another mode called the

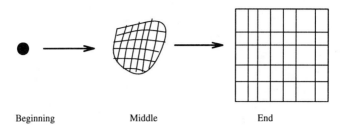

Beginning   Middle   End

Figure 2.11: The formation of a topology-preserving map (Lippmann 1987).

interpolative mode permits a group of neurons having the highest activations to be winners at one time. This allows the output of the network to be an interpolation of more than one best answer and is thus capable of representing more complex patterns and producing more accurate results.

Furthermore, if the statistical distribution of the input data changes over time (nonstationary statistics), the Kohonen network can be adapted to this change and continue to model the current distribution of the input data.

Topology Preservation

Consider a two-dimensional (2D) input space. The Kohonen network consists of nodes arranged in a 2D array (a matrix). We design a 2D plot in which each dot represents each node's weight vector and a line will be drawn linking the dots of nodes that are immediate neighbors in the matrix. If all the weights are zero, then we will have a plot containing a dot at the origin. If we randomize the weights, then the plot will just be a meaningless graph since there is no correlation between the position and the weight vector of the nodes.

The meaning of topology preservation becomes clear if we compare the plots before and after the network is trained. In a simulation run, the weights are initialized so that they occupy the same spot and continue to evolve as learning proceeds. Figure 2.11 shows the expansion of the weight vectors. After training is completed, the plot represents the topology map of input distribution. If we train the network on musical notes, then the network will develop sensitivity to frequencies and form a *feature map* just as the auditory pathway forms a topology (anatomical) map in relation to frequency response. In animal studies, geotopic maps have been found in the brain of the mouse that has learned a maze so that a specific neuron fires when the mouse is in a certain location of the maze. The capability of forming topology-preserving maps has also been utilized to model irregular surfaces in robotic applications. The detailed algorithm of Kohonen's self-organizing feature maps is given in Chapter 7.

Weight Initialization

In the Kohonen network, if we initialize weights randomly, most likely, they will not match the input distribution. During training, some weight vectors will be so far away from any input vector that they will never be trained and are hence wasted. A straightforward solution is to distribute the weight vectors according to the density of input vectors. Although we may not know the density before learning starts, several techniques produce good results.

The convex combination method sets all initial weights to $1/\sqrt{d}$ where d is the number of input units and is also the number of components in each weight vector. Thus, each weight vector has unit length. Each component X_i of the input vector is given the value of $\alpha X_i + (1 - \alpha)(1/\sqrt{d})$. α is gradually increased from a small value to a limit of 1. This allows the input vectors to separate and finally assume their true values. Another method gives each Kohonen neuron a "conscience." If a neuron has won more than $1/k$ (where k is the number of Kohonen neurons) of the time, its chance of winning is reduced by raising a threshold. This is an example of frequency-sensitive learning. See Wasserman (1989) for more discussions on this issue.

2.7.2   Competitive Learning

Despite some variations, competitive learning can generally be viewed as a procedure that learns to group input patterns in clusters in a way inherent to the input data. In this sense, competitive learning is closely related to clustering. In the previous section, we have seen how the Kohonen network performs competitive learning.

The heart of competitive learning lies in the winner-take-all strategy. Variations in competitive learning are often due to the differences in implementing this strategy. When vectors (weight and input vectors) are normalized, the winner is determined by the largest activation level (i.e., the dot product). This approach will fail if unnormalized vectors are used. In this case, we use the Euclidean distance as the measure, so that the weight vector at the least distance from the input vector is the winner. In fact, it can easily be shown that the Euclidean distance measure is consistent with the dot product measure in the case of normalized vectors. Thus, we can assume the Euclidean distance measure as a general measure to determine the winner in competitive learning networks. In psychology, however, different choices of distance functions have been explored in an attempt to arrive at more meaningful clusterings.

Once the winning neuron w is determined, its weight vector $\mathbf{W_w}$ is modified by

$$\Delta \mathbf{W_w} = \eta(\mathbf{X} - \mathbf{W_w}) \qquad (2.11)$$

where $\Delta \mathbf{W_w}$ is the weight adjustment and η is the learning rate. For any neuron j, its weight adjustment is given by

$$\Delta \mathbf{W_j} = \eta O_j (\mathbf{X} - \mathbf{W_j}) \tag{2.12}$$

where O_j is the activation of the neuron. When neuron j is not winning, $O_j = 0$ and hence no weight change is made. If neuron j is the winner, $O_j = 1$, and this equation is reduced to Eq. 2.11.

In the Kohonen network, the weights associated with the neighbor neurons of the winner are also adjusted. If we also allow a small weight change for every nonwinning weight vector, it is called *leaky learning*. The learning rate for these weight vectors is set to be much smaller than the rate for the winning neuron. If a neuron wins often, the chance of its winning is decreased. This is called frequency-sensitive competitive learning.

The quality of a clustering is often measured by the squared error criterion given by

$$E = \sum_p ||\mathbf{W_w} - \mathbf{X_p}||^2 \tag{2.13}$$

where $|| \cdot ||$ is the Euclidean distance operator, w is the winning neuron when input pattern $\mathbf{X_p}$ is presented, and $\mathbf{W_w}$ represents the center of the winning cluster corresponding to neuron w. We will show that the competitive learning algorithm actually seeks a local minimum for this squared error by performing gradient descent.

For each pattern $\mathbf{X_p}$, the criterion function is

$$E_p = \frac{1}{2} \sum_i (W_{wi} - X_{p,i})^2 \tag{2.14}$$

where the subscript i means the ith component. Gradient descent yields

$$\Delta W_{ji} = -\eta \frac{\partial E_p}{\partial W_{ji}}$$

where W_{ji} is the weight from unit i to unit j. If unit j is the winning neuron w, then the above partial derivative is reduced to

$$\frac{\partial E_p}{\partial W_{ji}} = W_{wi} - X_{p,i}$$

Otherwise, the derivative is simply 0. Then

$$\Delta W_{wi} = \eta (X_{p,i} - W_{wi})$$

which is equivalent to Eq. 2.11.

Vector Quantization

An important application of competitive learning is vector quantization, which is concerned with how to divide the input space into disjoint subspaces so that each input vector can be represented by the label of the subspace it belongs to. For example, input vector $\mathbf{X}$ is represented by w if it is the winning neuron when $\mathbf{X}$ is presented to the network. As in statistical modeling, vector quantization follows the probability density function of input patterns. In general, a more coarse quantization is obtained in those areas where inputs are more sparse.

In functional approximation, the network which performs vector quantization is combined with another type of network which performs mapping. What this architecture implements is essentially a lookup table. Suppose the combined network approximates the function F. To find the functional value of input $\mathbf{X}$, it is assigned to the winning neuron (the table entry), whose associated functional value is taken as an approximation of $F(\mathbf{X})$. We can train the vector quantization network first and then train the mapping network, or we train them as if they were a single network. In the latter case, a well-known example is the counterpropagation network, which is described in Chapter 7.

The multilayer backpropagation network gives a better approximation for most functions than the architecture integrating vector quantization and mapping. However, if the input space is of high dimension and the function to be approximated is discontinuous at numerous places, then the combined architecture is probably more efficient.

The *learning vector quantization* (LVQ) method also uses competitive learning rules in an attempt to define decision boundaries in the input space. Networks which perform LVQ are trained with supervision (because these networks are given a set of input patterns along with correct class labels) and perform discriminant analysis. The basic algorithm has the following descriptions:

1. Output unit j is associated with a class label O_j.

2. A learning instance consists of input vector $\mathbf{X}$ along with its correct class label T.

3. Determine the first (the best) and the second (the next-best) winning neurons w_1 and w_2.

4. Compare the class labels O_{w1} and O_{w2} associated with the two winning neurons and the label T. The learning rule (Eq. 2.11) is invoked when the labels (O_w and T) match. If the labels do not match, we penalize the weight vector by (Kohonen 1977)

$$\Delta \mathbf{W_w} = -\eta(\mathbf{X} - \mathbf{W_w})$$

2.7.3   Hebbian Learning

In 1949, Donald Hebb introduced an influential idea of learning by trying to explain how the brain learns at the cellular level. In the brain, a neuron receives many inputs from a large number of other neurons through synaptic connections. Hebb's law states that if a neuron A is repeatedly activated by another neuron B, then neuron A will become more sensitive to stimuli from neuron B and the synaptic connection from B to A will be more efficient. Thus, a synapse connecting two neurons is strengthened whenever both of them fire simultaneously. In essence, this idea can be conceived as strengthening a synapse according to the correlation between the activation levels of the neurons it connects. Hence, Hebbian learning is also referred to as *correlation learning*. The basic form of the learning rule is expressed as

$$\Delta W_{ji} = O_j O_i \tag{2.15}$$

where ΔW_{ji} is the weight adjustment for the weight from unit i to unit j and O_i and O_j are their respective activation levels. Hebbian learning explains how learning occurs without a teacher. In this learning system, learning is a local phenomenon without global feedback from the environment.

Hebbian learning suffers some limitations. First, it does not deal with inhibitory connections and cannot explain brain behavior in this aspect. Second, it does not show how a synapse can be weakened. If synapses can only be strengthened, a major concern is the stability of the system. In addition, from the computational point of view, some patterns cannot be learned in this way.

Linear Association

The linear associator network will associate one or more pairs of vectors $(\mathbf{X_i}, \mathbf{Y_i})$ so that given $\mathbf{X_i}$ as the input, the network will produce $\mathbf{Y_i}$. Furthermore, when a vector close to $\mathbf{X_i}$ is presented, the network will produce a vector close to $\mathbf{Y_i}$. Symbolically,

$$\mathbf{Y_i} = \mathbf{X_i W} \tag{2.16}$$

where $\mathbf{W}$ is the weight matrix of the network.

The Hebbian learning rule can be used to learn a new association pair $(\mathbf{X_i}, \mathbf{Y_i})$:

$$\Delta \mathbf{W} = \mathbf{X_i}^T \mathbf{Y_i} \tag{2.17}$$

Suppose the network has learned to associate m pairs of vectors. That is,

$$\mathbf{W} = \sum_{i=1}^{m} \mathbf{X_i}^T \mathbf{Y_i}$$

Further, assume that the vectors $\mathbf{X_1}, \mathbf{X_2}, \ldots, \mathbf{X_m}$ are orthogonal and of unit length (i.e., they are orthonormal): If $j = i$, $\mathbf{X_j X_i}^T = 1$; else it is 0. Then $\mathbf{X_j}$ can always be transformed into $\mathbf{Y_j}$ by the network without error because

$$\mathbf{X_j W} = \sum_{i=1}^{m} (\mathbf{X_j X_i}^T) \mathbf{Y_i} = \mathbf{Y_j}$$

In a d-dimensional input space, the maximum possible number of orthogonal vectors is d. Thus, the number of vector pairs that we can associate exactly is limited to d. If $\mathbf{X_i}$'s are not orthogonal, then we get an error when attempting to retrieve $\mathbf{Y_j}$ using $\mathbf{X_j}$. This error ϵ can be estimated by

$$\epsilon = \sum_{i \neq j}(\mathbf{X_j X_i}^T)\mathbf{Y_i}$$

In some cases, the weight matrix $\mathbf{W}$ can be chosen so that the error ϵ is small.

2.8 General Issues

Each computational model is often associated with some undesired problems. As neural network research continues to advance, it is possible to ameliorate and even to eliminate these problems. Here, we examine some of these problems which have long been investigated and explore their solutions based on current research.

The entrapment in a local minimum is a problem which often occurs with a gradient descent algorithm like backpropagation or with an energy minimization algorithm of the Hopfield net. Statistical methods such as simulated annealing have been employed to deal with this problem. In addition, genetic algorithms employ such genetic mechanisms as recombination, mutation, and selection in order to avoid local minima. However, these solutions tend to provide slow training and may have limited use in practical domains.

As the Bayes decision rule yields optimal decisions, the probabilistic approach offers a theoretical advantage to classification models. Practically, this approach relies on the availability of adequate samples for probability estimation. The neural network models developed under this approach are presented in Chapter 5 "Incremental Learning."

The knowledge-based approach to neural network design presents a direct and effective solution to the problem of local minima. With an optimal network configuration and initial weight setting, the likelihood of finding a global optimum is greatly increased. This approach is described in Chapter 4.

Slow learning is a notorious problem associated with iterative supervised learning algorithms such as backpropagation. Probabilistic neural networks and polynomial adalines (described in Chapter 5) offer efficient, one-pass learning. Radial basis function (RBF) networks provide fast learning by employing locally tuned processing elements which respond selectively to inputs over a small field of the entire input space much like biological neurons (Moody and Darken 1989). While not all neural models developed are biologically plausible, biological principles still remain a vital source of new concepts.

Generalization is an important issue which has drawn much attention. The generalization capability of a neural network can be improved by reducing the chance of overfitting the data. When a neural network is overtrained, it tends to fit the training data so closely as to lose its generalization over unseen data.

This issue is dealt with by properly designing the architecture and the training algorithm of the neural network. A detailed discussion is given in Chapter 3.

2.9   Hardware Implementation

Artificial neural networks have been built into chips for fully taking advantage of the parallel-distributed nature of information processing inherent in biological neural networks (Ramacher and Rückert 1991; Sánchez-Sinencio and Lau 1992). A neural chip can be used as a coprocessor inside a conventional computer and devoted to neurocomputing tasks.

In hardware, neural networks can be implemented in various ways. A neural network can be implemented as an analog or digital electrical circuit. Analog chips hold the potential to be faster and more economical than digital counterparts, whereas digital chips offer higher precision and ease of manufacture.

In analog implementation, connection weights can be coded as conductance, resistance, or capacitance. Node activation levels (signal strengths) can be represented by currents or voltages. The silicon retina (Mead 1989), for example, is an analog neural chip which emulates a biological retina.

Current digital technology can be applied to build neural chips. The issues behind digital neural chip design have been addressed by Hammerstrom and Means (1990). In one implementation, pulse-trains are used to represent weights and signal strengths (Caudill 1991). Pulse-trains reflect the frequency or probability that a neuron fires, simulating frequency modulation observed in biological neural networks. Multiplication of two pulse-trains is equivalent to taking their logic-AND, and summation is equivalent to the logic-OR operation.

In the aspect of learning, there are several design options. The weights in a neural chip can be fixed as a ROM (read-only memory), one-time programmable as a PROM (programmable ROM), many-times programmable as an EPROM (erasable PROM) or an EEPROM (electrically erasable PROM), or adaptive in the RAM (random access memory).

Optical technology provides an alternative way to implement neural networks. Optical neural networks promise a very large scale implementation. Unlike electrical beams, two light rays can pass through each other without interaction. By connecting neurons with light beams, signals are transmitted at the speed of light, and even more, significant orders of magnitude in the increase of interconnection density can be achieved. However, optical systems tend to be fragile, and the size of lasers and lenses is still a problem. Interested readers may consult McAulay (1991).

2.10   Summary

The learning rules described in this section are summarized as follows.

- **Delta Rule**

$$\Delta W_{ji} = \eta(T_j - O_j)O_i$$

where W_{ji} is the weight from unit i to unit j, η is the learning rate, O_i and O_j are the activation levels of units i and j, and T_j is the desired activation level of unit j. The backpropagation learning rule (described in Chapter 3) is a generalization of this rule.

- **Hebbian Learning Rule**

$$\Delta W_{ji} = O_i O_j$$

or in a differential form,

$$\Delta W_{ji}(t) = [O_i(t) - O_i(t-1)][O_j(t) - O_j(t-1)]$$

The rule stems from the idea of reinforcing a synapse according to the correlation between the activation levels of the neurons it connects.

- **Competitive Learning Rule**

$$\Delta W_{ji} = \eta O_j(O_i - W_{ji})$$

Under the winner-take-all strategy, this rule only updates the weights of the winning neuron. All other neurons are suppressed to the zero activation level. There are other variations of the competitive learning rule.

2.11   References

1. Anderson, J.A., and Rosenfeld, E. (eds.). 1988. *Neurocomputing*. MIT Press, Cambridge, MA.

2. Cohen, M.A., and Grossberg, S.G. 1983. Absolute stability of global pattern formation and parallel memory storage by competitive neural networks. *IEEE Transactions on Systems, Man, and Cybernetics*, 13, pp. 815–826.

3. Caudill, M. 1991. Embedded neural networks. *AI Expert*, April, pp. 40–45.

4. Duda, R.O., and Hart, P.E. 1973. *Pattern Classification and Scene Analysis*. John Wiley & Sons, New York.

5. Geman, S., and Geman, D. 1984. Stochastic relaxation, Gibbs distributions and Bayesian restoration of images. *IEEE Transactions on Pattern Analysis and Machine Intelligence*, 6, pp. 721–741.

6. Haines, K., and Hecht-Nielsen, R. 1988. A BAM with increased information storage capacity. In *Proceedings of the IEEE International Conference on Neural Networks* (San Diego), pp. I-181–190.

7. Hammerstrom, D., and Means, E. 1990. System design for a second-generation neurocomputer. In *Proceedings of IJCNN*, pp. 80–83.

8. Hinton, G.E. 1989. Connectionist learning procedures. *Artificial Intelligence*, 40, pp. 185–234.

9. Hinton, G.E., and Sejnowski, T.J. 1986. Learning and relearning in Boltzmann machines. In *Parallel Distributed Processing: Explorations in the Microstructures of Cognition*, Vol. 1. MIT Press, Cambridge, MA.

10. Hoehfeld, M., and Fahlman, S.E. 1992. Learning with limited numerical precision using the cascade-correlation algorithm. *IEEE Transactions on Neural Networks*, 3(4), pp. 602–611.

11. Hopfield, J.J. 1982. Neural networks and physical systems with emergent collective computational abilities. In *Proceedings of the National Academy of Science*, 79, pp. 2554–2558.

12. Hopfield, J.J., and Tank, D.W. 1985. "Neural" computation of decisions in optimization problems. *Biological Cybernetics*, 52, pp. 141–152.

13. Hopfield, J.J., and Tank, D.W. 1986. Computing with neural circuits: A model. *Science*, 233(4764), pp. 625–633.

14. Kanerva, P. 1988. *Sparse Distributed Memory*. MIT Press, Cambridge, MA.

15. Kirkpatrick, S., Gelatt Jr., C.D., and Vecchi, M.P. 1983. Optimization by simulated annealing. *Science*, 220, pp. 671–680.

16. Kohonen, T. 1977. *Associative Memory: A System-Theoretical Approach.* Springer-Verlag, New York.

17. Kohonen, T. 1988. *Self-Organization and Associative Memory.* Springer-Verlag, New York.

18. Kosko, B. 1987. Bi-directional associative memories. *IEEE Transactions on Systems, Man, and Cybernetics*, 18(1), pp. 49–60.

19. Lippmann, R.P. 1987. An introduction to computing with neural nets. *IEEE ASSP Magazine*, 4(2), pp. 4–22.

20. McAulay, A.D. 1991. *Optical Computer Architectures*. John Wiley & Sons, New York.

21. McEliece, R.J., Posner, E.C., Rodemich, E.R., and Venkatesh, S.S. 1987. The capacity of the Hopfield associative memory. *IEEE Transactions on Information Theory*, 33(4), pp. 461–482.

22. Mead, C. 1989. *Analog VLSI and Neural Systems*. Addison-Wesley, Reading, MA.

23. Metropolis, N., Rosenbluth, A., Rosenbluth, M., Teller, A., and Teller, E. 1953. Equation of state calculations by fast computing machines. *J. of Chem. Physics*, 21, pp. 1087–1092.

24. Mirchandani, G., and Cao, W. 1989. On hidden nodes for neural nets. *IEEE Transactions on Circuits and Systems*, 36(5), pp. 661–664.

25. Moody, J., and Darken, C.J. 1989. Fast learning in networks of locally-tuned processing elements. *Neural Computation*, 1(2), pp. 281–294.

26. Peterson, C., and Anderson, J.R. 1987. A mean field theory learning algorithm for neural networks. *Complex Systems*, 1, pp. 995–1019.

27. Ramacher, U., and Rückert, U. (eds.). 1991. *VLSI Design of Neural Networks*. Kluwer, Norwell, MA.

28. Sánchez-Sinencio, E., and Lau, C. (eds.). 1992. *Artificial Neural Networks: Paradigms, Applications and Hardware Implementations*. IEEE Press, New York.

29. Stein, R. 1993. Selecting data for neural networks. *AI Expert*, February, pp. 42–47.

30. Stolorz, P. 1992. Merging constrained optimization with deterministic annealing to solve combinatorially hard problems. In *Advances in Neural Information Processing Systems*, pp. 1025–1032. Morgan Kaufmann, San Mateo, CA.

31. Wasserman, P.D. 1989. *Neural Computing*. Van Nostrand Reinhold, New York.

32. Widrow, B., and Winter, R. 1988. Neural nets for adaptive filtering and adaptive pattern recognition. *Computer*, March, pp. 25–39.

2.12 Problems

1. Consider a two-layer perceptron (an input, a hidden, and an output layer). There are two input units, three hidden units, and one output unit. Name them I_1, I_2, H_1, H_2, H_3, and O_1, respectively. Let $\mathbf{W_{Hi}}$ and $\mathbf{W_{O1}}$ denote the input weight vectors of H_i and O_1, respectively. Define the matrix $\mathbf{W_H} = [\mathbf{W_{H1}}^T \ \mathbf{W_{H2}}^T \ \mathbf{W_{H3}}^T]$ and the matrix $\mathbf{W_O} = \mathbf{W_{O1}}^T$ where the superscript T means "transpose." Let $\theta_{\mathbf{H}} = [\theta_{H1}, \theta_{H2}, \theta_{H3}]$ and $\theta_{\mathbf{O}} = [\theta_{O1}]$ where θ_{Hi} and θ_{Oi} are the thresholds for the hidden unit and the output unit, respectively. Let $\mathbf{I}$, $\mathbf{H}$, and $\mathbf{O}$ be the input, the hidden, and the output vectors of activation levels. Then, we have

$$\mathbf{H} = F_h(\mathbf{IW_H} - \theta_{\mathbf{H}})$$

and
$$\mathbf{O} = F_h(\mathbf{HW_O} - \theta_O)$$

where F_h is a hard-limiting function. Assume the thresholds of all the hidden and the output units are zero. Also assume

$$W_{H1} = [-2, 2] \quad W_{H2} = [2, 2] \quad W_{H1} = [1, 3] \quad W_O = [1, 2, 1]$$

You are given two classes of patterns as follows:

$(7, 5), (6, 3), (2, 4) \in$ Class A
$(6, 0), (-1, -2), (3, -3) \in$ Class B

(a) Will this machine separate these patterns? (Hint: Calculate the output for each pattern, and then see whether one class of patterns output 1 and the other class 0.)

(b) Discuss the linear separability of these patterns.

2. Suppose the number of input units is four, the number of hidden units is four, and the number of output units is two. How many feedforward and fully connected network configurations are possible?

3. If the activation function of all hidden units is linear, show that a multilayer perceptron is equivalent to a single-layer perceptron.

4. What are the advantages of a sigmoid function as the activation function over a hard-limiting function?

5. Suppose an analog signal value is a nonnegative value ranging from 0 to 31 and we wish to convert the signal to a digital signal of 5 bits. Design this analog-to-digital converter using the Hopfield net.

(a) Specify the network structure.

(b) Specify the energy function. (Hint: Minimize the squared difference.)

(c) Specify the connection weights.

(d) Try several numbers in the range, and observe their digital representation produced by the neural network.

6. Use a Hopfield net to store four vectors as follows:

$$(+1, -1, -1, +1, +1, -1, -1)$$
$$(+1, +1, -1, +1, +1, +1, -1)$$
$$(+1, +1, +1, -1, +1, -1, -1)$$
$$(+1, -1, -1, -1, -1, -1, -1)$$

Use the outer product construction method to compute the weight matrix.

(a) Specify the network structure.

(b) Specify the connection weights.

(c) Examine whether the net can accurately retrieve the vector given the first 4 bits in each of the original vectors (the rest of the bits are set to zero).

7. Use a BAM to store three pairs of vectors as follows:

Original vector	Associated vector
$A1 = [1, -1, 1]$	$B1 = [-1, 1, 1, -1]$
$A2 = [-1, 1, 1]$	$B2 = [1, -1, 1, 1]$
$A3 = [1, 1, 1]$	$B3 = [-1, 1, 1, -1]$

(a) Specify the network structure.

(b) Specify the connection weights.

(c) Examine whether the BAM can accurately retrieve the associated vector given each of the original vectors.

8. The Boltzmann machine uses a stochastic rule to update the binary states of individual neurons. Given the probability that a given unit will be active, how do you determine its state in a simulation run? (Hint: Choose a random number between 0 and 1 with a uniform probability density function.)

9. In the traveling salesman problem, suppose there are four cities P, Q, R, and S. The distances between any two cities are given by

$$P-Q: 10 \quad P-R: 8 \quad P-S: 12$$
$$Q-R: 6 \quad Q-S: 11 \quad R-S: 7$$

(a) Design a Hopfield net to solve this problem.

(b) What is the solution?

10. Consider the same traveling salesman problem as defined in the last problem.

(a) Implement a Boltzmann machine to solve this problem. Assume that we set the initial temperature to 100 degrees and reduce the temperature by 10 degrees each time until 0 degree. At each temperature, we run the net until equilibrium and then move on to the next temperature. (Note that this annealing schedule is hypothetical.) How can you detect a thermal equilibrium? What is the solution?

(b) Is this solution different from the one found by the Hopfield net?

(c) Design a better annealing schedule as specified by

$$T(t) = \frac{T_0}{\log(1 + t)}$$

where $T(t)$ is the temperature at time t and T_0 is the initial temperature.

11. A sufficient (but not a necessary) condition for a stable recurrent neural network is that $W_{ij} = W_{ji}$ for $i \neq j$ and $W_{ii} = 0$ for all i. Can you find a class of networks which does not satisfy this condition but is stable? (Hint: All feedforward neural networks.)

12. A robotic arm moves in a three-dimensional (3D) Euclidean space with coordinates (x, y, z). The arm's movement is controlled by three joint angles with coordinates (θ, ϕ, ψ).

    (a) Design a neural network which can develop a topological map in the 3D space for the robotic arm.

    (b) Design a neural network which can generate proper joint angles in response to an activation in the 3D Euclidean space. (Hint: Use the counterpropagation network.)

Chapter 3

Learning: Supervised and Unsupervised

3.1 Introduction

The immediate benefit of machine learning would be to enable AI programs to improve their performance automatically over time. For example, a chess program can improve its game plan against its opponent through playing. A robot can recognize a particular kind of object more accurately though repeated presentation of the object image. At a more fundamental level, a machine with a clearly demonstrated ability to learn would answer the question of whether machines can exhibit true intelligence. Without this capability, a computer system cannot reason beyond the limit of its programmed intelligence. In fact, an entity can hardly be called intelligent unless it can learn.

The "knowledge bottleneck" was identified as the primary obstacle to implement expert or knowledge-based systems. Research is currently underway on transferring massive knowledge from an encyclopedia to a computer disk (using optic disk technology). However, the issue of knowledge acquisition requires far more than simple access to a collection of knowledge. This process also involves the representation, abstraction, organization, integration, and management of the knowledge in such a way that it can be used efficiently and properly. Yet, a great challenge is to expedite knowledge discovery by machines. There are still many unsolved real-world problems. The slowness of human learning may unnecessarily delay their solutions.

Somewhat surprisingly, many learning tasks at which humans are adept actually pose tremendous difficulties for machines, at least for sequential architecture ones. The massively parallel structure and processing mechanism of the brain give it an enormous computational advantage over such machines for tasks such as complex pattern recognition. Information processing in the brain provides an important clue to the design of an intelligent machine which can learn.

3.1.1 Definition of Learning

Inasmuch as a great variety of human experience can be described as learning, the term *machine learning* is sometimes obscure. A somewhat more focused definition suggested by Herbert Simon (1983) is based on the notion of *change*:

> Learning denotes changes in the system that are adaptive in the sense that they enable the system to do the same task or tasks drawn from the same population more efficiently and more effectively the next time.

Learning can refer to either acquiring new knowledge or enhancing or refining skills. Learning new knowledge includes acquisition of significant concepts, understanding of their meanings and relationships to each other and to the domain concerned. The new knowledge should be assimilated and put in a mentally usable form before it can be called "learned." Thus, knowledge acquisition is defined as learning new symbolic information combined with the ability to use that information effectively.

Skill enhancement applies to motor skills, such as learning to ride a bicycle, and applies to cognitive skills, such as learning to speak a foreign language. One aspect of skill enhancement which distinguishes it from knowledge acquisition is the role which repetition and practice plays. Skill enhancement can be interpreted in biological terms as reinforcing a pattern of neural connections for performing the desired function.

3.1.2 Historical Sketch

Research and development in machine learning have seen several major evolutionary changes. Over the years, different paradigms with different emphasis on objectives have been pursued. Four major periods can be distinguished, each centering around a different paradigm:

- Since 1940s and 1950s:

    - Paradigms: Neural network; decision-theoretical learning

    - Objectives: Neural modeling; pattern recognition

    - Examples: McCulloch and Pitts (1943); Rosenblatt (1958); Samuel (1959)

- Since 1960s:

    - Paradigm: Symbolic learning

    - Objectives: Concept acquisition; building knowledge-based or expert systems

- Examples: Winston (1975); Buchanan and Mitchell (1978)

• Since 1970s:

- Paradigm: Knowledge-intensive learning
- Objectives: Exploration of various learning strategies
- Examples: Mitchell, Keller, and Kedar-Cabelli (1986)

• Since 1980s:

- Paradigms: Neural network and connectionist learning; hybrid learning
- Objectives: Neural computers; robust learning; massive parallelism
- Examples: Rumelhart, McClelland, and PDP Group (1986); Goldberg (1989)

In the remaining sections of this chapter, we examine the differences between supervised and unsupervised learning and describe important learning methods in four categories: statistical learning, AI (artificial intelligence) learning, neural network learning, and genetic learning. The major focus is placed on neural network learning.

3.2 Supervised and Unsupervised Learning

The distinction between supervised and unsupervised learning depends on whether the learning algorithm uses pattern-class information. Supervised learning assumes the availability of a teacher or supervisor who classifies the training examples into classes, whereas unsupervised learning does not. Thus, unsupervised learning must identify the pattern-class information as a part of the learning process. In general, the task of unsupervised learning is more abstract and less defined. The learner must focus its attention, observe the regularity in the environment, and draw hypotheses.

Supervised learning algorithms utilize the information on the class membership of each training instance. This information allows supervised learning algorithms to detect pattern misclassifications as a feedback to themselves. Error information contributes to the learning process by rewarding accurate classifications and/or punishing misclassifications—a process known as *credit and blame assignment*. It also helps eliminate implausible hypotheses.

Unsupervised learning algorithms use unlabeled instances. They blindly or heuristically process them. Unsupervised learning algorithms often have less computational complexity and less accuracy than supervised learning algorithms. Unsupervised learning algorithms can be designed to learn rapidly. This makes unsupervised learning practical in many high-speed, real-time environments, where we may not have enough time and information to apply supervised techniques. Unsupervised learning has also been used for scientific discovery. In this application, the learner should focus its attention on interesting concepts, and the value of interestingness is determined in a heuristic manner.

One can similarly distinguish supervised and unsupervised learning in neural networks. Supervised learning usually refers to the search in the space of all possible weight combinations along error gradients. The supervisor uses class-membership information to define a numerical error signal or vector, which guides the gradient descent search. The performance of the neural network will deteriorate if overtrained.

Unsupervised learning refers to how neural networks modify their parameters in biologically plausible ways. In this learning mode, the neural network does not use the class membership of training instances. Instead, it uses information associated with a group of neurons to modify local parameters. Unsupervised learning systems adaptively cluster instances into clusters or decision classes by competitively selecting "winning" neurons and modifying associated weights. The fan-in weight vectors tend to estimate pattern-class statistics. Unsupervised learning involves more parameter tuning than supervised learning.

Some examples of supervised and unsupervised learning are given below:

- Supervised learning:

    - AI learning: Meta-DENDRAL (Buchanan and Mitchell 1978), version space (Mitchell 1978), ID3 (Quinlan 1983)

    - Neural network learning: Backpropagation (Rumelhart, Hinton, and Williams 1986)

- Unsupervised learning:

    - AI learning: AM (Lenat 1976), BACON (Langley, Bradshaw, and Simon 1983), conceptual clustering (Michalski and Stepp 1983)

    - Neural network learning: ART (Carpenter and Grossberg 1988), Kohonen (1988)

3.3   Statistical Learning

Statistical learning refers to learning based upon probability or statistical information of training instances. A representative example is Bayesian learning, which estimates probability density functions required by a Bayesian decision procedure. Related learning methods include learning linear discriminants for classification and learning transition probabilities in automata.

In pattern recognition and control systems, a decision concerns the assignment of an input to a predefined class. By defining a loss function that penalizes incorrect decisions, a Bayesian classifier can minimize the average loss and therefore can be used to model the unknown system. The problem of identifying the unknown system is then reformulated as one of estimating a set of parameters for certain probability density functions. These parameters, such as the mean vector and the covariance matrix, can be estimated from the training instances by applying Bayes' theorem. These methods rely on assuming a particular form (e.g., multivariate normal) for the probability distributions in the model. However, this assumption often does not hold in real-world problems. A description of this procedure is given by Duda and Hart (1973).

General Bayesian Learning

- The objective: Estimate the probability distribution function $p(\mathbf{x})$ for variable $\mathbf{x}$ from a set χ of n samples $\mathbf{x}_1, \mathbf{x}_2, \ldots, \mathbf{x}_n$ drawn independently according to $p(\mathbf{x})$.

- Basic assumptions:

    - The form of the function $p(\mathbf{x})$ is known (e.g., Gaussian), but the value of the parameter vector θ is not known exactly.

    - Our initial knowledge about θ is contained in a known prior probability $p(\theta)$.

    - The rest of our knowledge about θ is to be learned from sample χ.

- The learning equation is

$$p(\theta|\chi) = \frac{p(\chi|\theta)p(\theta)}{\int p(\chi|\theta)p(\theta)d\theta}$$

and by the independent assumption,

$$p(\chi|\theta) = \prod_{k=1}^{n} p(\mathbf{x}_k|\theta)$$

The probability of $p(\theta)$ is updated by the equation after observing sample χ. It can also be updated on a sample-by-sample basis incrementally.

3.4 AI Learning

This section gives the overview of learning in symbolic artificial intelligence. Important AI algorithms are formulated, but detailed discussions go beyond the scope of this book.

An important factor in the classification of learning strategies is the degree of inference required on the part of the learner. Michalski, Carbonell, and Mitchell (1983) provide the following classification scheme:

1. *Rote Learning*: It is equivalent to learning by memorization. This is the most primitive form of learning. There is no need to draw inferences from the facts memorized. In machine learning, it corresponds to representing knowledge directly in its original form. No further processing or transformation on the knowledge is required.

2. *Learning by Instruction*: This learning strategy is also known as learning by being told or learning by taking advice. Knowledge acquired from a teacher or textbook or a knowledge source is transformed by the learning system into an internal representation which facilitates the future use of the knowledge. The transformation process involves some inference. This learning mode closely parallels the formal educational model of how students learn from a teacher in the classroom.

3. *Learning by Analogy*: This mode of learning combines deductive and inductive learning. The first step is the inductive inference which finds the common structure between the problem domain and one of the domains stored in the knowledge base. The next step after generalization is to map the solution from the selected analogous domain to the problem domain. This analogical mapping is performed by deductive logic. In *transformational analogy*, the mapping involves only the final solution, while in *derivational analogy*, the mapping involves the detailed history of problem solving called a *derivation*.

4. *Learning by Induction*: This learning mode requires the greatest degree of inductive inference. In the literature, this learning mode includes learning from examples, learning by observation and learning by discovery. The first is a kind of supervised learning, but the latter two are kinds of unsupervised learning.

   Learning from examples involves the process of concept acquisition from a set of instances which are classified into positive examples (examples of the concept to be learned) and negative examples (counterexamples of the concept). The acquired concept should be general enough to explain all of the positive examples but exclude any counterexamples.

   Learning by observation and learning by discovery both take place without aid of a teacher. The learner infers general rules (theories) and regularities which explain the observations. This mode of learning may also involve clustering of objects based on similar and dissimilar relationships between them. The learner may passively observe the environment or actively perform experiments on it.

   Two basic operations in inductive learning are *generalization* and *specialization*. The former operation makes a description more general, whereas the latter makes it more specific. Description A is more general than description B if and only if an instance covered by (satisfying) B is also covered by A but not reversely. That is, A covers more instances than B.

"More specific" means the opposite of "more general." Generalization and specialization operators depend on how examples are represented. For instance, suppose a description consists of a set of attribute values. The description is made more general (specific) by removing (adding) one attribute value or replacing one value by a more general (specific) one. A generalization (specialization) operator will take multiple examples as the input and generate descriptions that are more general (specific) than these examples. An operator is called *selective* if it does not generate descriptors other than those present in the input examples. If it does produce new descriptors, then the operator is called *constructive*. We can thus distinguish induction into "constructive" and "selective," depending on whether constructive learning operators are involved.

5. *Learning by Explanation and Deduction*: The learner draws deductive inferences to explain an instance or a hypothesis from its knowledge base. The explanation can be further generalized to increase its utility. Since the learned result is implied by the original knowledge, what is learned is not new but something useful. Deductive learning also includes knowledge reformulation, compilation, and chunking which preserve the truth of the original knowledge.

3.4.1 Learning Theory

Learning using linear discriminant functions is examined first. Since the analysis on the two-category case can be extended to the multicategory case by special techniques such as Kesler's construction (Duda and Hart 1973), we primarily focus on two-category classification. Suppose there are n sample points in d dimensions. Each point is labeled either ω_1 or ω_2. A hyperplane separating the points labeled ω_1 from the points labeled ω_2 is called a *linear dichotomy*. The fraction $f(n, d)$ of linear dichotomies out of 2^n possible dichotomies of these n points is given by (Duda and Hart 1973)

$$f(n,d) = \begin{cases} 1 & n \leq d+1 \\ \frac{2}{2^n} \sum_{i=o}^{d} \binom{n-1}{i} & n > d+1 \end{cases} \qquad (3.1)$$

This means a hyperplane always exists to classify $d+1$ or fewer points correctly. However, to prevent a linear discriminant from being underdetermined, n should not be less than $d + 1$. A linear discriminant becomes more constrained as more samples are available. In principle it becomes overconstrained when n is greater than $d + 1$, but it is not effectively overdetermined until n is several times as large as d. At $n = 2(d + 1)$, which is called the *capacity* of a hyperplane, half of the possible dichotomies are still linear.

While the above analysis is limited to linear discriminant learning, the notion of capacity can be extended to AI learning algorithms. Consider an AI learning algorithm which learns one or more descriptions (rather than hyperplanes) to separate the instances labeled ω_1 from the instances labeled ω_2. Let the hypothesis space H be the space of possible descriptions. We next see how the capacity of H can be defined on the basis of the growth function of Vapnik and Chervonenkis (1971) and the Vapnik-Chervonenkis dimension.

Given a set of instances, a hypothesis h in H can partition the set into two groups: The instances in one group satisfy the hypothesis h and those in the other group do not. The partition is called the dichotomy induced by h. The maximum number of dichotomies induced by hypotheses in H on any set of m instances is defined as the *growth function* of H with respect to m. The Vapnik-Chervonenkis dimension (VCdim) of H is the largest m such that the corresponding growth function is equal to 2^m. That is, H can induce all possible dichotomies of m instances drawn from the instance space if and only if the Vapnik-Chervonenkis dimension of H is m. Thus, the Vapnik-Chervonenkis dimension of H measures the capacity of H. For example, the VCdim of a single perceptron with two input units is 3, since it is possible to find a set of 3 points that can be linearly dichotomized in all 2^3 ways but no set of four points can be dichotomized in all possible ways. It turns out that the VCdim of a single perceptron with an n-dimensional input is $n + 1$.

Valiant (1984) introduced the notion of "learnable." We say that a class of target concepts is learnable if the following condition is met: For every concept in the class and with any probability distribution on the instance space, there exists an algorithm which can produce a hypothesis such that its probability of error has a small upper bound. The probability of error is relative to the distribution of instances and is defined to be the probability of instances that are either in the hypothesis and not in the target concept or in the target concept and not in the hypothesis. When the error is small, the hypothesis is a good approximation to the target concept. This learning theory has been used as a basis for analyzing the properties of learning algorithms.

All learning algorithms employ some mechanism to restrict the hypothesis space or to rank hypotheses. This is referred to as *inductive bias*. Haussler (1988) describes a measure of bias based on the growth function and the Vapnik-Chervonenkis dimension in Valiant's framework. This measure quantifies inductive bias in a way that directly relates to learning performance. In his analysis, the least number of independently drawn examples for learning a concept within a given range of probability of error can be determined from the cardinality of the hypothesis space.

3.4.2   Version Spaces

Mitchell (1978) describes an approach to concept learning called *version spaces*. The learning task is to produce a description that is consistent with all positive examples (examples of the concept to be learned) but no negative examples (counterexamples of the concept) in the training set. This technique is designed to learn single conjunctive concepts.

The representational language in this learning system defines a partial

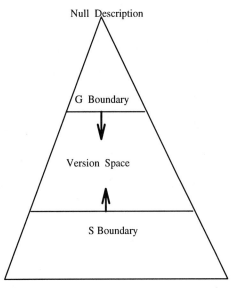

Figure 3.1: The version space.

ordering of descriptions in terms of generality. The ordering is partial because sometimes we cannot tell which description is more general than another. The entire partial-ordered descriptions in the language constitute the *concept space*. As we process training instances, we refine our notion of where the target concept might lie. Our current hypothesis can be represented as a subset of the concept space called the *version space*. The version space is the largest collection of descriptions that is consistent with all the training instances seen so far. As seen in Figure 3.1, the version space is often represented by the most general descriptions, which are called the G boundary, and the most specific descriptions, which are called the S boundary. Positive instances serve to make the S boundary more general, whereas negative instances make the G boundary more specific. When these two boundaries collide, the version space collapses into a single-concept description, which is the target description for the concept.

The Version Space Algorithm

1. Initialize G to contain one element: the null description.

2. Initialize S to contain one element: the first positive instance.

3. For a new instance,

- If it is a positive instance, then remove from G any descriptions that do not cover the instance and generalize the elements of S as little as possible so that they cover the instance.

- If it is a negative instance, then remove from S any descriptions that cover that instance and specialize the elements of G as little as possible so that they will not cover the instance.

4. Repeat step 3 until $G = S$.

The generalization and specialization in response to each new instance on arrival should be as minimal as possible to ensure that the traversal of the concept space is complete.

Example. Use the version space algorithm to learn a concept in the poker domain. Each instance and concept is represented as a feature vector "(rank, suit)," e.g., (4, heart). The initial version space has the G boundary = $\{(x, y)\}$ and the S boundary = nil, where x and y are variables. The first instance (3, diamond) is a negative instance. We may update the boundaries as

$$G = \{(\text{even}, y), (x, \text{heart}), (x, \text{black})\}$$
$$S = \text{nil}$$

The second instance (7, spade) is a positive instance.

$$G = \{(x, \text{black})\}$$
$$S = \{(7, \text{spade})\}$$

The third instance (4, club) is a positive instance.

$$G = \{(x, \text{black})\}$$
$$S = \{(x, \text{black})\}$$

Since $G = S$, we can stop, and the concept learned is (x, black). Note that this example is incomplete, because we did not supply rules of generalization and specialization. A complete example is given in the Problems section.

The version space will not eliminate any description unless there is sufficient information to indicate so. Thus, it is a *least-commitment* algorithm. Previous instance information is encoded in the version space, and there is no need to review old instances. This gives the system the ability of *incremental learning*. Because of the data-driven approach, the system is sensitive to data noise.

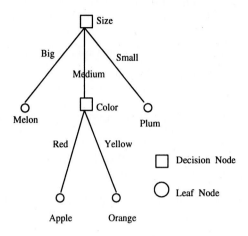

Figure 3.2: A decision tree for classifying fruits.

3.4.3 ID3

ID3 (Quinlan 1983) uses a tree representation for concepts. To classify a set of instances, we start at the top of the tree (see Figure 3.2) and answer the questions associated with the nodes in the tree until we reach a leaf node, where the classification or decision is stored.

ID3 begins by choosing a random subset of the training instances. This subset is called the *window*. The procedure builds a decision tree that correctly classifies all instances in the window. The tree is then tested on the training instances outside the window. If all the instances are classified correctly, then the procedure halts. Otherwise, it adds some of the instances incorrectly classified to the window and repeats the process. This iterative strategy is empirically more efficient than considering all instances at once. In building a decision tree, ID3 selects the feature which minimizes the entropy function and thus best discriminates among the training instances.

The ID3 Algorithm

1. Select a random subset W (called the "window") from the training set.

2. Build a decision tree for the current window.

   - Select the best feature which minimizes the entropy function H:

$$H = \sum_i -p_i \log p_i$$

where p_i is the probability associated with ith class. For a feature, the entropy is calculated for each value. The sum of the entropy weighted by the probability of each value is the entropy for that feature.

- Categorize training instances into subsets by this feature.
- Repeat this process recursively until each subset contains instances of one kind (class) or some statistical criterion is satisfied.

3. Scan the entire training set for exceptions to the decision tree.

4. If exceptions are found, insert some of them into W and repeat from step 2. The insertion may be done either by replacing some of the existing instances in the window or by augmenting it with the new exceptions.

In practice, a statistical criterion can be applied to stop the tree from growing as long as most of the instances are classified correctly.

Example. Use the ID3 algorithm to build a decision tree for classifying the following objects:

Class	Size	Color	Surface
A	Small	Yellow	Smooth
A	Medium	Red	Smooth
A	Medium	Red	Smooth
A	Big	Red	Rough
B	Medium	Yellow	Smooth
B	Medium	Yellow	Smooth

First, we calculate the entropy for each attribute:

$$\text{Size: } H = \tfrac{1}{6}(-\tfrac{1}{1}\log\tfrac{1}{1})$$

$$+\tfrac{4}{6}(-\tfrac{2}{4}\log\tfrac{2}{4} - \tfrac{2}{4}\log\tfrac{2}{4}) + \tfrac{1}{6}(-\tfrac{1}{1}\log\tfrac{1}{1})$$

$$= 0.462$$

$$\text{Color: } H = \tfrac{3}{6}(-\tfrac{2}{3}\log\tfrac{2}{3} - \tfrac{1}{3}\log\tfrac{1}{3})$$

$$+\tfrac{3}{6}(-\tfrac{3}{3}\log\tfrac{3}{3})$$

$$= 0.318$$

$$\text{Surface: } H = \tfrac{5}{6}(-\tfrac{3}{5}\log\tfrac{3}{5} - \tfrac{2}{5}\log\tfrac{2}{5})$$

$$+\tfrac{1}{6}(-\tfrac{1}{1}\log\tfrac{1}{1})$$

$$= 0.56$$

Thus, we select the attribute *Color* as the first decision node since it is associated with the minimum entropy. This node has two branches: Red and Yellow. Under the branch *Red*, only class A objects fall, and hence no further discrimination is needed. Under the branch *Yellow*, we need another attribute to make further distinctions. So, we calculate the entropy for the other two attributes under this branch:

$$\text{Size: } H = \tfrac{1}{3}(-\tfrac{1}{1}\log\tfrac{1}{1})$$

$$+\tfrac{2}{3}(-\tfrac{2}{2}\log\tfrac{2}{2})$$

$$= 0$$

$$\text{Surface: } H = \tfrac{3}{3}(-\tfrac{2}{3}\log\tfrac{2}{3} - \tfrac{1}{3}\log\tfrac{1}{3})$$

$$= 0.636$$

We use the attribute *Size* as the second decision node. The decision tree created is the following:

```
                Color
         Yellow/     \Red
              Size     A
         Small/  \Medium
              A     B
```

3.4.4 AM

AM (Lenat 1976) was able to *discover* many elementary mathematical concepts such as the concept of prime numbers from an initial set of set theory concepts. EURISKO is a descendent of AM in which heuristics themselves are considered concepts which can be discovered and evolved.

AM exploits a variety of AI techniques. It uses a frame-based system to represent mathematical concepts. One of the major activities of AM is to create new concepts and fill in their slots. AM also uses a heuristic search guided by 250 heuristic rules in order to discover "interesting" concepts. For example:

> If function f mapping from A to B is an interesting function, and subset C of B is interesting, then $f^{-1}(C)$ is interesting.

It employs the "generate-and-test" strategy to solve problems. Hypotheses are generated on the basis of a small number of examples and then tested against a larger set. An agenda is used to control the execution of the tasks proposed by those heuristics. In each operational cycle, AM chooses the most promising task from the agenda to perform. A general algorithm (Barr, Feigenbaum, and

Cohen 1981) is given below.

The AM Algorithm

1. Select a concept to evaluate and generate examples of it.

2. Check these examples by examining regularities. Based on the regularities,

   - Update the interestingness score of the concept.
   - Create new concepts.
   - Create new conjectures.

3. Propagate the new knowledge learned to other concepts in the system.

3.4.5   Meta-DENDRAL

Meta-DENDRAL (Buchanan and Mitchell 1978) is a program that discovers cleavage rules to explain the operation of a mass spectrometer. A cleavage rule states that "if the molecular structure matches a certain bond environment, then one or more bonds in that environment will break." A mass spectrometer is a device that bombards chemical samples with accelerated electrons to generate many charged fragments. The masses of these fragments can then be measured to produce a mass spectrum.

Meta-DENDRAL applies *heuristic search* to its learning task. The search starts with the most general hypothesis about molecular cleavage and continues to specialize a hypothesis in all possible ways until some optimality criterion is satisfied. The success of this system depends on how the heuristics employed can effectively prune the search space. Since the hypotheses are generated by a model and then tested by the data, Meta-DENDRAL illustrates a model-driven (top-down) approach to machine learning. This feature makes the system tolerant to data noise. Another notable feature is the application of background knowledge (the so-called half-order theory) to the learning task. The Meta-DENDRAL algorithm includes the following steps:

- RULEGEN (Rule Generation)

  1. Initialize H to contain the most general description.

  2. Pick a hypothesis from H and specialize it in all possible ways allowed.

  3. Test the hypotheses against the training instances. If all specializations of the hypothesis are worse than the hypothesis itself according to a predefined criterion, then the hypothesis is output as a new rule; else put in H the specializations which are better than the hypothesis and prune it.

  4. Repeat steps 2 and 3 until H is empty.

- RULEMOD (Rule Modification or Refinement)

  1. Select a subset of important rules according to a predefined function for calculating the performance score of individual rules.
  2. Specialize rules to exclude negative evidence.
  3. Generalize rules to include positive evidence.
  4. Select the final subset of rules using the same scoring function as in step 1.

3.4.6 Explanation-Based Learning

Unlike inductive learning, explanation-based learning (EBL) is characterized by learning based on single instances and a knowledge-intensive and analytic approach. An EBL system attempts to learn from a single example by explaining why a single example is an example of the target concept. The explanation is then generalized and added to the system's knowledge base. The learned knowledge is a logical extension of existing knowledge. The idea is to learn knowledge with a high utility value, which can improve system performance. Explanation-based generalization (EBG) (Mitchell, Keller, and Kedar-Cabelli 1986) is a typical EBL algorithm.

The EBG Algorithm

  1. Explain: Construct an explanation in terms of the domain theory that shows how the training example satisfies the goal concept definition.
  2. Generalize: Determine a set of sufficient conditions under which the explanation holds and which satisfies the operationality criterion.

The elements include:

- A goal concept: A description of what is to be learned

- A training example: An example of the goal concept

- A domain theory: A set of rules and facts that describe relationships between objects and actions in the domain

- An operationality criterion: A description of which concepts are usable

3.4.7 BACON

BACON (Langley, Bradshaw, and Simon 1983) is a data-driven program for discovery. In contrast to AM which discovers concepts in theoretical settings, BACON discovers empirical laws from data. BACON has been used to rediscover a wide variety of scientific laws, such as Kepler's third law, Ohm's law, and Joule's law.

BACON begins with a set of variables for a problem. It employs a set of data-driven heuristics to detect regularities in numeric and nominal data. These heuristics note constancies and trends, leading BACON to formulate hypotheses, to define theoretical terms, and to postulate intrinsic properties. Other heuristics allow BACON to reason by analogy. For example, if BACON finds a regularity in one set of parameters, it will attempt to generate the same regularity in a similar set of parameters.

3.5   Neural Network Learning

The neural network has also been dubbed the "connectionist." It contains a large number of simple neuronlike processing elements and a large number of weighted connections between the elements. The weights on the connections encode the knowledge of a network. It uses a highly parallel, distributed control, and can learn to adjust itself automatically. In this section, we describe important neural network learning algorithms.

3.5.1   Backpropagation

The backpropagation network is probably the most well known and widely used among the current types of neural network systems available. In contrast to earlier work on perceptrons, the backpropagation network is a multilayer feedforward network with a different transfer function in the artificial neuron and a more powerful learning rule. The learning rule is known as *backprop-agation*, which is a kind of gradient descent technique with backward error (gradient) propagation, as depicted in Figure 3.3.[1] The training instance set for the network must be presented many times in order for the interconnection weights between the neurons to settle into a state for correct classification of input patterns. While the network can recognize patterns similar to those they have learned, they do not have the ability to recognize new patterns. This is true for all supervised learning networks. In order to recognize new patterns, the network needs to be retrained with these patterns along with previously known patterns. If only new patterns are provided for retraining, then old patterns may be forgotten. In this way, learning is *not* incremental over time. This is a major limitation for supervised learning networks. In Chapter 5 "Incremental Learning," we show how to overcome this limitation. Another limitation is

---

[1] A gradient descent procedure searches for the solution along the negative of the gradient (i.e., steepest descent). Suppose $\mathbf{v}$ is the solution vector that minimizes the criterion function $J(\mathbf{v})$. Starting with an arbitrarily chosen vector $\mathbf{v}_1$, the procedure finds the solution vector by iteratively applying the following algorithm until convergence:

$$\mathbf{v}_{k+1} = \mathbf{v}_k - \eta_k \nabla J(\mathbf{v}_k)$$

where η_k is a positive scale factor that sets the step size, the subscript k denotes the kth iteration, and ∇ is the gradient operator.

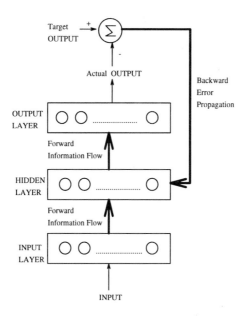

Figure 3.3: The backpropagation network.

that the backpropagation network is prone to local minima, just like any other gradient descent algorithm.

The backpropagation network in essence learns a mapping from a set of input patterns (e.g., extracted features) to a set of output patterns (e.g., class information). This network can be designed and trained to accomplish a wide variety of mappings. This ability comes from the nodes in the hidden layer or layers of the network which learn to respond to features found in the input patterns. The features recognized or extracted by the hidden units (nodes) correspond to the correlation of activity among different input units. As the network is trained with different examples, the network has the ability to generalize over similar features found in different patterns. The key issue is that the hidden units must be trained to extract a sufficient set of general features applicable to both seen and unseen instances. To achieve this goal, at first, the network must not be overtrained. Overtraining the network will make it memorize the individual input-output training pairs rather than settling in the mapping for all cases. To prevent this undesired effect, one way is to terminate training once a performance plateau has been reached. Another way is to prune the network, creating a bottleneck between the input and output layers. The bottleneck will force the network to learn in a more general manner. This issue is explored later.

The backpropagation network is capable of approximating arbitrary mappings given a set of examples. Furthermore, it can learn to estimate posterior probabilities $(P(\omega_i|\mathbf{x}))$ for classification. The sigmoid function guarantees that the outputs are bounded between 0 and 1. In the multiclass case, it is not difficult to train the network so that the outputs sum up to 1. With accurate estimation of posterior probabilities, the network can act as a Bayesian classifier.

The backpropagation network consists of one input layer, one output layer, and one or more hidden layers. If the input pattern is described by n bits or n values, then there should be n input units to accommodate it. The number of output units is likewise determined by how many bits or values are involved in the output pattern. Theoretical guidance exists for determining the numbers of hidden layers and hidden units (see later discussion). They can be recruited or pruned as indicated by the network performance. Typically, the network is fully connected between and only between adjacent layers. The backpropagation algorithm (Rumelhart, Hinton, and Williams 1986) is formulated below.

The Backpropagation Algorithm

- **Weight Initialization**

    Set all weights and node thresholds to small random numbers. Note that the node threshold is the negative of the weight from the bias unit (whose activation level is fixed at 1).

- **Calculation of Activation**

    1. The activation level of an input unit is determined by the instance presented to the network.

    2. The activation level O_j of a hidden and output unit is determined by

    $$O_j = F(\sum W_{ji}O_i - \theta_j)$$

    where W_{ji} is the weight from an input O_i, θ_j is the node threshold, and F is a sigmoid function:

    $$F(a) = \frac{1}{1 + e^{-a}}$$

- **Weight Training**

    1. Start at the output units and work backward to the hidden layers recursively. Adjust weights by

    $$W_{ji}(t + 1) = W_{ji}(t) + \Delta W_{ji}$$

    where $W_{ji}(t)$ is the weight from unit i to unit j at time t (or tth iteration) and ΔW_{ji} is the weight adjustment.

2. The weight change is computed by

$$\Delta W_{ji} = \eta \delta_j O_i$$

where η is a trial-independent learning rate ($0 < \eta < 1$, e.g., 0.3) and δ_j is the error gradient at unit j. Convergence is sometimes faster by adding a momentum term:

$$W_{ji}(t+1) = W_{ji}(t) + \eta \delta_j O_i + \alpha [W_{ji}(t) - W_{ji}(t-1)]$$

where $0 < \alpha < 1$.

3. The error gradient is given by:

   – For the output units:

$$\delta_j = O_j(1 - O_j)(T_j - O_j)$$

   where T_j is the desired (target) output activation and O_j is the actual output activation at output unit j.

   – For the hidden units:

$$\delta_j = O_j(1 - O_j) \sum_k \delta_k W_{kj} \qquad (3.2)$$

   where δ_k is the error gradient at unit k to which a connection points from hidden unit j.

4. Repeat iterations until convergence in terms of the selected error criterion. An iteration includes presenting an instance, calculating activations, and modifying weights.

The name "backpropagation" comes from the fact that the error (gradient) of hidden units are derived from propagating backward the errors associated with output units (as calculated by Eq. 3.2) since the target values for the hidden units are not given. In the backpropagation network, the activation function chosen is the sigmoid function, which compresses the output value into the range between 0 and 1. The sigmoid function is advantageous in that it can accommodate large signals without saturation while allowing the passing of small signals without excessive attenuation. Also, it is a smooth function so that gradients can be calculated, which are required for a gradient descent search.

Example. To solve the exclusive-or problem, we build a backpropagation network as shown in Figure 3.4. The network will be trained on the following instances:

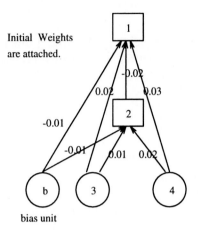

Figure 3.4: A backpropagation network for learning the exclusive-or function.

Inputs	Output
$(1, 1)$	0
$(1, 0)$	1
$(0, 1)$	1
$(0, 0)$	0

The weights are initialized randomly as follows:

$W_{13} = 0.02, W_{14} = 0.03, W_{12} = -0.02, W_{23} = 0.01,$
$W_{24} = 0.02, W_{1b} = -0.01, W_{2b} = -0.01$

Calculation of Activation: Consider a training instance with the input vector = $(1, 1)$ and the desired output vector = (0).

$O_3 = O_4 = 1$

$O_2 = 1/[1 + e^{-(1 \times 0.01 + 1 \times 0.02 - 1 \times 0.01)}] = 0.505$

$O_1 = 1/[1 + e^{-(0.505 \times -0.02 + 1 \times 0.02 + 1 \times 0.03 - 1 \times 0.01)}] = 0.508$

Weight Training: Assume that the learning rate $\eta = 0.3$.

$\delta_1 = 0.508(1 - 0.508)(0 - 0.508) = -0.127$

$\Delta W_{13} = 0.3 \times (-0.127) \times 1 = -0.038$

$$\delta_2 = 0.505(1 - 0.505)(-0.127 \times -0.02) = 0.0006$$

$$\Delta W_{23} = 0.3 \times 0.0006 \times 1 = 0.0002$$

The rest of the weight adjustments are omitted. Note that the threshold (which is the negative of the weight from the bias unit) is adjusted likewise. It takes many iterations like this before the learning (training) process stops. The following set of final weights gives the mean squared error of less than 0.01:

$W_{13} = 4.98, W_{14} = 4.98, W_{12} = -11.30, W_{23} = 5.62,$
$W_{24} = 5.62, W_{1b} = -2.16, W_{2b} = -8.83$

Backpropagation has been applied to classification tasks, speech synthesis from text (e.g., NETtalk), adaptive robotic control, scoring of bank loan applications, system modeling, data compression, and many others. In the classification problem, for example, the number of input units is determined by how many feature values are used, and the number of output units is determined by the number of classes under consideration. In functional approximation, the number of input units is determined by the number of arguments taken by the function and one output unit is needed.

A Derivation of Backpropagation Here, we show how to derive the backpropagation learning rule given by

$$\Delta W_{ji} = \eta \delta_j O_i \qquad (3.3)$$

If unit j is an output unit, then its δ_j is calculated by

$$\delta_j = (T_j - O_j)F'(\text{net}_j) \qquad (3.4)$$

where

$$\text{net}_j = \sum_i W_{ji}O_i$$

F is a sigmoid function, and

$$O_j = F(\text{net}_j) = F(\sum_i W_{ji}O_i)$$

If unit j is a hidden unit, then its δ_j is given by

$$\delta_j = F'_j(\text{net}_j)\sum_k \delta_k W_{kj} \qquad (3.5)$$

The backpropagation procedure minimizes the error criterion

$$E = \frac{1}{2}\sum_j (T_j - O_j)^2$$

Gradient descent yields

$$\Delta W_{ji} = -\eta(\partial E/\partial W_{ji})$$

By using the chain rule, we obtain

$$\partial E/\partial W_{ji} = (\partial E/\partial O_j)(\partial O_j/\partial W_{ji})$$

In the case when unit j is an output unit,

$$\partial E/\partial O_j = -(T_j - O_j)$$

and

$$\partial O_j/\partial W_{ji} = F_j'(\text{net}_j)O_i$$

Thus,

$$\begin{aligned}
\partial E/\partial W_{ji} &= (\partial E/\partial O_j)(\partial O_j/\partial W_{ji}) \\
&= -(T_j - O_j)F_j'(\text{net}_j)O_i \\
&= -\delta_j O_i
\end{aligned}$$

So, we obtain

$$\Delta W_{ji} = \eta \delta_j O_i$$

When unit j is a hidden unit, T_j is not given. Applying the chain rule gives

$$\partial E/\partial O_j = \sum_k (\partial E/\partial O_k)(\partial O_k/\partial O_j)$$

The output of unit k is given by

$$O_k = F(\sum_j W_{kj}O_j) \tag{3.6}$$

Thus, the term $\partial O_k/\partial O_j$ can be transformed by

$$\partial O_k/\partial O_j = F'(\text{net}_k)W_{kj}$$

As a result,

$$\begin{aligned}
\partial E/\partial O_j &= \sum_k (\partial E/\partial O_k)(\partial O_k/\partial O_j) \\
&= -\sum_k (T_k - O_k)F'(\text{net}_k)W_{kj} \\
&= -\sum_k \delta_k W_{kj}
\end{aligned}$$

Thus,

$$\begin{aligned}
\partial E/\partial W_{ji} &= (\partial E/\partial O_j)(\partial O_j/\partial W_{ji}) \\
&= -(\sum_k \delta_k W_{kj})F_j'(\text{net}_j)O_i \\
&= -\delta_j O_i
\end{aligned}$$

Then, we obtain

$$\Delta W_{ji} = \eta \delta_j O_i$$

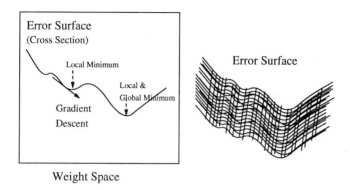

Figure 3.5: Search on the error surface along the gradient.

Step Size   A careful selection of the step size (the learning rate) is often necessary to ensure smooth convergence. It has been shown that a large step size may cause the network to become paralyzed. When network paralysis occurs, further training does little for convergence. On the other hand, if the size is too small, convergence can be very slow. Some have suggested to vary the step size adaptively during training. There appears to be more empirical guidance than theoretical understanding on this issue.

Local Minima   Figure 3.5 shows that backpropagation searches on the error surface along the gradient (steepest descent) in order to minimize the error criterion

$$E = \frac{1}{2} \sum_j (T_j - O_j)^2 \qquad (3.7)$$

It is likely to get stuck in a local minimum.

The problem of local minima has been tackled in a number of ways. Incorporating a random component into the weight adjustment is one way to escape the local minimum. As in simulated annealing, a parameter called the temperature is defined so that for a higher temperature, more randomness can be introduced into the training process. When the temperature goes down to zero, the process becomes completely deterministic. The genetic algorithm has also been applied to deal with this problem. It proceeds by starting with multiple initial weight settings and recombining trained weights during the process. The cost of either approach is the prolonged training time.

Learning Speed   Some techniques have been used to accelerate the convergence of a gradient descent technique like backpropagation. Newton's method uses the information of the second-order derivatives. Quasi-Newton methods approximate second-order information with first-order information. Conjugate gradient methods compute a linear combination of the current gradient vector and the previous search direction (momentum) for the current search direction. A detailed discussion on this issue is made by Shanno (1990).

The network training time can also be improved by some tricks, such as joggling the weights or using slightly noisy data (Caudill 1991; Stubbs 1990). It has been found that if the activation level is restricted to the range from $-1/2$ to $1/2$, convergence time may be reduced by half compared with the 0-to-1 range (Stornetta and Huberman 1987). This improvement proceeds from the fact that a weight coming from a neuron of zero activation will not be modified. This idea is implemented by changing the input range to $-1/2$ to $1/2$ and using the following activation function:

$$-1/2 + \frac{1}{1 + e^{-a}}$$

where a is the argument of the function. An alternative function is the hyperbolic tangent function (tanh), which lies in the range from -1 to 1.

Stopping Criteria   The process of adjusting the weights based on the gradients is repeated until a minimum is reached. In practice, one has to choose a stopping condition. There are several stopping criteria that can be considered:

- Based on the error to be minimized: In pattern recognition, one might consider stopping the procedure once the training data are correctly classified. When this is not the case, a fixed threshold is used so that the procedure is stopped if the error is below it.[2] However, this criterion does not guarantee generalization to new data.

- Based on the gradient: The algorithm is terminated when the gradient is sufficiently small. Note that the gradient will be zero at a minimum by definition.

- Based on cross-validation performance: This criterion can be used to monitor generalization performance during learning and to terminate the algorithm when there is no more improvement. See Chapter 13 "Validation and Verification" for cross-validation techniques.

The first two criteria are sensitive to the choice of parameters and may lead to poor results if the parameters are improperly chosen. The cross-validation criterion does not have this drawback. It can avoid overfitting the data and can actually improve the generalization performance of the network. However, cross-validation is much more computationally intensive and often demands more data.

---

[2]For example, the mean squared error per output unit is less than 0.01.

Network Size   The backpropagation network can approximate an arbitrary mapping only when the network is sufficiently large. In general, it is not known what size of the network will produce the best result for a given problem. If the network is too small, it cannot learn to fit the training data well. On the other hand, if the network is too big, the learning problem becomes underconstrained and the network is able to learn many solutions that are consistent with the training data but most of them are likely to be poor approximations of the actual model.

The network should have such a size as to capture the structure of the data and eventually to model the underlying problem. With some specific knowledge about the problem structure, one can sometimes form a good estimate of the proper network size.

With little prior knowledge, the size of the network must be determined by trial and error. One approach is to grow the network starting with the smallest-possible network until the performance begins to level off or decline. The network size is increased by adding more nodes in fixed layers or by adding new layers. The latter approach is illustrated by cascade correlation learning as described in Chapter 5.

Alternatively, we can proceed the other way around. That is, starting with a large network, we apply a pruning technique to remove those weights and nodes which have little relevance to the solution. In this approach, one needs to know how to select a "large" network to begin with.

In most cases, a two-layer network (with a single hidden layer) suffices to solve the problem. Numerous bounds on the number of hidden nodes in a two-layer network have been derived. However, most of them assume that the activation function is a hard-limiting function. Formal analysis will be more difficult in the case of a sigmoid function.

Complexity of Learning   It has been shown that the problem of finding a set of weights for a fixed-size network which performs the desired mapping exactly for given training data is *NP-complete*.[3] That is, we cannot find optimal weights in polynomial time. So, for a very large problem, it is unlikely that we can determine the optimal solution in a reasonable amount of time.

Learning algorithms like backpropagation are gradient descent techniques which seek only a local minimum. These algorithms usually do not take exponential time to run. Empirically, the learning time on a serial machine for backpropagation is about $O(N_w^3)$ where N_w is the number of weights in the network (Hinton 1989). The slowness of finding a local minimum is perhaps due to the characteristics of the error surface being searched. In the case of a single-layer perceptron, the error surface is a quadratic bowl with a single

---

[3]NP-complete problems refer to a class of problems which lacks a polynomial-time solution. The time taken by the best method we know for solving such problems grows exponentially with problem size. It has been proven that if a polynomial-time solution is found for one of the NP-complete problems, the solution can be generalized to the rest of the problems in this category. The question is, however, whether such faster methods exist.

minimum, and the search on it is relatively easy. By contrast, in the multilayer backpropagation network, the error surface is typically convoluted, which obviously prohibits an efficient search. Increasing the learning rate to speed up the learning process may cause instability when it reaches the steep part of the surface. Several alternative methods have been proposed, such as the momentum and the second-order methods mentioned earlier.

Generalization   Generalization is concerned with how well the network performs on the problem with respect to both seen and unseen data. It is usually tested on new data outside the training set. Generalization is dependent on the network architecture and size, the learning algorithm, the complexity of the underlying problem, and the quality and quantity of the training data. Research has been conducted to answer such questions as:

- How many training instances are required for good generalization?

- What size network gives the best generalization?

- What kind of architecture is best for modeling the underlying problem?

- What learning algorithm can achieve the best generalization?

It is often difficult to answer any of these questions without fixing some factors. But an important goal is to develop a general learning algorithm which improves generalization in most or all circumstances. This is addressed in the next section.

For simplicity, we focus our discussion on learning logic functions of d binary variables. In this problem, there are 2^d different patterns in the domain and there are 2^{2^d} possible functions. The network for identifying the true function should have d input units and one output unit. In general, the larger the network, the larger the set of functions it can form and the more likely the true function is in this set. We can think of the use of training data as a means of rejecting incorrect functions. Hopefully, at the end of training, there is only one function left which is the true function sought. If this is not the case, we wish the function learned to be the function that best approximates the true function. In this sense, the more training instances, the more likely the network can identify the true function. However, this is true only when the network is large enough (but not too large) to implement the true function.

Hush and Horne (1993) describe the approaches to study generalization and the methods to improve generalization. In one approach, the *average generalization* of the network is defined to be the average of the generalization values of all functions that are consistent with the set of training instances. The generalization value of a function is the fraction of the domain (of 2^d instances) for which the function produces the correct output.

In the second approach, the *generalization error* of the network is defined as the difference between the generalization on the training data (which forms an estimate of the true generalization) and the generalization on the actual problem. Since the network tends to fit the training data, the generalization with respect to it will be overly optimistic. However, in many cases, the generalization error can be bounded (a worst-case analysis), and this bound can be made arbitrarily small by increasing the number of training instances. Vapnik and Chervonenkis (1971) show that a useful bound can be established when the number of training instances exceeds the VCdim (defined earlier). The VCdim of a system can be infinite, and the bound on the generalization error in the worst case cannot be calculated. The VCdim of a one-hidden-layer perceptron with full connectivity between the layers is in the range (Baum and Haussler 1989, Hush and Horne 1993)

$$2[N_h/2]d \leq \text{VCdim} \leq 2N_w \log(eN_n) \tag{3.8}$$

where $[\cdot]$ is the *floor* operation that returns the largest integer less than its argument, N_h is the number of hidden units, N_w is the total number of weights in the network, N_n is the total number of nodes in the network, e is the base of the natural logarithm, and d is the number of input units. The upper bound holds no matter what the number of layers and the connectivity are. As a rule of thumb, the number of weights can give a rough estimate of the VCdim. The above results assume that the network uses the hard-limiting activation function. It is more difficult to determine the VCdim of the backpropagation network which uses the sigmoid as the activation function. In this case, Sontag (1989) suggests that it is at least twice as large.

Given the VCdim of the network, it is possible to determine the number of training instances required for good generalization. A useful heuristic in practice is that the number of training instances is about 10 times the VCdim, or 10 times the number of weights in the case of multilayer perceptrons. In many application domains, this heuristic means that we need a very large amount of training data and heavy computational efforts. It is, therefore, desirable to have a network as small as possible. The strategy of network pruning discussed in the next section meets this objective.

3.5.2 Generalization Methods

Cross-validation is the standard method for evaluating generalization performance. The data are divided into a training set and a test set. The network is trained on the training set, and its performance is evaluated on the test set. Statistically significant results are achieved by trying multiple independent data partitions and averaging the performance. The disadvantage of cross-validation is the lengthy time it takes.

Another technique for evaluating generalization performance is by measuring *predicted squared error* (PSE), which is defined by (Moody 1991)

$$\text{PSE} = \text{MSE} + \frac{2N_w}{P}\sigma^2 \tag{3.9}$$

where MSE is the mean squared error on the training set, N_w is the number of free weights (free parameters), P is the number of training instances, and σ^2 is the variance of noise. This measure applies to systems which are linear in their parameters. However, this measure may also provide an unbiased estimate of the predicted MSE for systems that are nonlinear in the parameters such as neural networks if their mappings are sufficiently smooth. As compared with cross-validation, this technique is much less time-consuming.

Methods which have been developed to improve generalization of neural network learning include:

- Network pruning

- Weight decay and elimination

- Weight sharing

In addition, it has been shown that combining the outputs from multiple neural networks can increase generalization capability. All these methods are not specifically tied to any specific learning algorithm and can be exercised as appropriate.

Network Pruning

In a fully connected network, there is a large amount of redundant information encoded in the weights. Thus, it is possible to remove some weights without hurting the network performance. This process is known as *pruning*. Reduction in the number of weights leads to better generalization and makes learning faster.

A straightforward approach is to eliminate small weights. However, this is not the best approach since the solution can be sensitive to some small weights and it may be difficult to determine what is "small." A much better solution is to delete the weights which have the least effect on the solution. The latter approach is illustrated by *optimal brain damage* (OBD) (Cun, Denker, and Solla 1990).

In OBD, the network is first trained using the backpropagation procedure. Then the weights with the smallest *saliency* are deleted. After this, the reduced-size network is retrained to obtain the final solution. The saliency for weight W_{ji} is given by

$$\text{saliency} = \delta E_{ji} W_{ji}^2 \tag{3.10}$$

where δE measures the sensitivity of the criterion function to small perturbations in W_{ji}. In OBD, the sensitivity measure is approximated by

$$\delta E_{ji} \approx \frac{\partial^2 E}{\partial W_{ji}^2}$$

The first-order derivative is not used since it is zero at a local minimum.

Similar to OBD, the method *skeletonization* (Mozer and Smolensky 1989) removes units with lower relevance. The *relevance* of a unit is defined as the difference in the value of the error function without the unit and with the unit in the network.

Weight Decay and Elimination

Generalization can be improved by favoring simple structures. In this approach, a term can be added to the criterion function to penalize complex structures. This type of criterion is sometimes referred to as a *minimum description length* (MDL) criterion. The total description length is the number of bits required to describe the model (model complexity) plus the number of bits required to encode the error. Thus, this model minimizes the cost function to provide a minimal description of the data.

In the *weight decay* approach (Hinton 1989), the effective number of weights is reduced by encouraging (near) zero weights in the learning process. This is accomplished by adding a term to the criterion function to penalize nonzero weights, as shown below:

$$E = \frac{1}{2} \sum_j (T_j - O_j)^2 + \frac{\zeta}{2} \sum_i W_i^2 \tag{3.11}$$

The ζ parameter is a small positive constant that is used to control the importance of model complexity relative to the squared error. With this additional term, the standard backpropagation algorithm is modified by subtracting a term in the form of ζW_{ji} from the weight adjustment. That is, the weight is decayed in an amount proportional to its magnitude. However, not all weights are decayed to small values. Only those weights which are not reinforced do so.

In the network, some weights have little influence or relevance to the solution. These weights may assume any arbitrary values or cause the network to overfit the data and result in poor generalization. Thus, generalization can be improved by encouraging these weights to take on small values. At the end of training, the magnitude of each weight is directly proportional to its influence on the error term, and we can safely delete weights of small values. A weakness of weight decay is that important weights are also biased toward slightly smaller values and moved away from the solution that minimizes the true error.

Another technique called *weight elimination* (Weigend, Rumelhart, and Huberman 1990) employs the cost function given by

$$E = \frac{1}{2} \sum_j (T_j - O_j)^2 + \zeta \sum_i \frac{W_i^2/W_o^2}{1 + (W_i^2/W_o^2)} \tag{3.12}$$

where W_o is a fixed weight normalization factor. When $W_i \gg W_o$, the term inside the summation is close to unity, and this criterion essentially counts the number of weights. When $W_i \ll W_o$, the term inside the summation is proportional to W_i^2, and this criterion behaves like the weight decay criterion. So, a small W_o encourages the network to settle with a few large weights, and a large W_o favors many small weights.

Yet, in another technique called *soft weight decay* (Nowlan and Hinton 1992), nonzero weights are encouraged to cluster into different groups so that weights in the same group have approximately the same magnitude. This technique is intended to combine the advantages of weight decay and weight sharing.

Weight Sharing

Through the use of local connections and weight sharing, the number of weights in the network can be reduced (Cun 1989). The network hidden units can be grouped so that each group covers the same region. In a single group, the adjacent receptive fields of individual hidden units overlap. For example, the first hidden unit connects to the first and second input units, the second hidden unit connects to the second and third input units, the third hidden unit connects to the third and fourth input units, and so on. With local connection, the number of weights per node is reduced, but the total number of nodes to solve the same problem may increase, and the total number of weights is not always reduced. However, when local connection is coupled with weight sharing, a significant reduction in weights can be obtained.

With weight sharing, nodes in the same group share the same weights, and thus the number of weights is reduced. In pattern recognition, nodes with identical weights are positioned at every possible registration point in the input pattern and extract certain local features.

3.5.3 Radial Basis Function Networks

A radial basis function (RBF) network (Moody and Darken 1989) is a two-layer network (see Figure 3.6) whose output units form a linear combination of the basis (kernel) functions computed by the hidden units. The basis functions in the hidden layer produce a localized response to the input. That is, each hidden unit has a localized receptive field. The basis function can be viewed as the activation function in the hidden layer.

The most common basis function chosen is a Gaussian function, in which case the activation level O_j of hidden unit j is calculated by

$$O_j = \exp[-(\mathbf{X} - \mathbf{W_j}) \cdot (\mathbf{X} - \mathbf{W_j})/2\sigma_j^2] \tag{3.13}$$

where $\mathbf{X}$ is the input vector, $\mathbf{W_j}$ is the weight vector associated with hidden unit j (i.e., the center of its Gaussian function), and σ^2 is the normalization factor. The outputs of the hidden unit lie between 0 and 1; the closer the input to the center of the Gaussian, the larger the response of the node. Because the node produces an identical output for inputs with equal distance from the center of the Gaussian, it is called a radial basis.

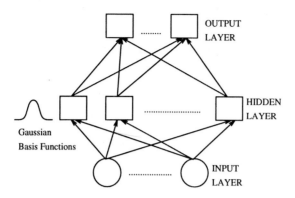

Figure 3.6: The radial basis function network.

The activation level O_j of an output unit is determined by

$$O_j = \sum W_{ji} O_i$$

where W_{ji} is the weight from hidden unit i to output unit j. Like a perceptron, a threshold component can be added. The output units form a linear combination of the nonlinear basis functions, and thus the overall network performs a nonlinear transformation of the input.

Learning in the RBF network can be divided into two stages: learning in the hidden layer followed by learning in the output layer. Typically, learning in the hidden layer is performed using unsupervised methods such as the k-means clustering algorithm,[4] while learning in the output layer uses supervised methods like the least mean square (LMS) algorithm. After the initial solution is found by this approach, a supervised learning algorithm (e.g., backpropagation) can be applied to both layers to fine-tune the parameters of the network, since the clustering algorithm does not guarantee an optimal set of parameters for the basis functions.

The normalization factor σ represents a measure of the spread of the data in the cluster associated with the hidden unit. It is commonly determined by the average distance between the cluster center and the training instances in that cluster. That is, for hidden unit j

$$\sigma_j^2 = \frac{1}{M} \sum (\mathbf{X} - \mathbf{W_j}) \cdot (\mathbf{X} - \mathbf{W_j}) \tag{3.14}$$

---

[4] Clustering is concerned with grouping objects according to their similarity. For k-means clustering, see Duda and Hart (1973).

where $\mathbf{X}$ is a training pattern in the cluster, $\mathbf{W_j}$ is the center of the cluster associated with hidden unit j, and M is the number of training instances in that cluster.

In the above approach, the number of hidden units is determined by the clustering algorithm. Some approaches use both a measure of fitness and model complexity to determine the number of hidden units. Some approaches adapt the width of the basis functions during learning in an attempt to minimize the overlap between clusters.

The RBF network can be used for both classification and functional approximation. For classification, the network can determine how close the given input is to the center of a Gaussian kernel by the response of the corresponding hidden unit. If only a single hidden unit is employed, the decision region is circular. From this perspective, the RBF is well suited for implementing an efficient classification model.

Using a set of nonlinear basis functions, the RBF network is capable of approximating any arbitrary mapping. The main difference between the RBF network and the backpropagation network is in their basis functions. The radial basis function in the former network covers only small regions, whereas the sigmoid function assumes nonzero values over an infinitely large region of the input space. For some problems, sigmoid basis functions provide better results, but for others, radial basis functions are more advantageous. For example, classification tasks are more amenable to the RBF network than the backpropagation network. This is especially true when the problem is extended to higher dimensions.

The Radial Basis Function Network

- **Weight Initialization**

  Weights in the hidden layer are determined by the clustering algorithm. Weights in the output layer are initialized to small random values.

- **Calculation of Activation**

  1. The activation level O_j of hidden unit j is calculated by

  $$O_j = \exp[-(\mathbf{X} - \mathbf{W_j}) \cdot (\mathbf{X} - \mathbf{W_j})/2\sigma_j^2]$$

  2. The activation level O_j of an output unit is determined by

  $$O_j = \sum W_{ji} O_i$$

- **Weight Learning**

  - In the hidden layer, use the k-means clustering algorithm.

– In the output layer:

1. Adjust weights by

$$W_{ji}(t+1) = W_{ji}(t) + \Delta W_{ji}$$

where $W_{ji}(t)$ is the weight from unit i to unit j at time t (or the tth iteration) and ΔW_{ji} is the weight adjustment.

2. The weight change is computed by

$$\Delta W_{ji} = \eta \delta_j O_i$$

where η is a trial-independent learning rate and δ_j is the error at unit j:

$$\delta_j = T_j - O_j$$

where T_j is the desired (target) output activation and O_j is the actual output activation at output unit j.

3. Repeat iterations until convergence.

Example. Hidden unit j is associated with the input weight vector:

$$\mathbf{W}_j = [0.9, 0.7, 0.3, 0]$$

Assume that the normalization factor $\sigma_j = 0.2$. Given the input vector

$$\mathbf{X} = [1, 1, 0, 0]$$

the activation of hidden unit j is calculated by

$$O_j = \exp[-(\mathbf{X} - \mathbf{W}_j) \cdot (\mathbf{X} - \mathbf{W}_j)/2\sigma^2]$$
$$= e^{-2.375} = 0.093$$

Complexity of Learning   In the aspect of learning, the RBF network is much faster than the backpropagation network. The primary reason for this is that the learning process in the RBF network has two stages and both stages can be made efficient by using appropriate learning algorithms. Although finding the optimal k clusters for a set of data is NP-complete, k-means is quite efficient and generally produces good results. Learning in the output layer is relatively easy because the network output is linear in the weights.

Generalization   We are interested in the number of training instances required for good generalization. Again, we use the VCdim as the main tool to get an estimate.

The results of Baum and Haussler (1989) can be applied to any feedforward network with binary outputs. The VCdim can be shown to be bounded by

$$\text{VCdim} \leq 2N_w \log(eN_n) \tag{3.15}$$

where N_w is the total number of weights in the network and N_n is the total number of nodes in the network. This bound is likely to be larger for nodes with continuous outputs, which is the case for the RBF network. We may analyze the lower bound on the VCdim by fixing the hidden layer. Then the VCdim for the output layer (viewed as a single-layer perceptron) is $N_h + 1$ where N_h is the number of hidden units.

3.5.4   Reinforcement Learning

Reinforcement learning refers to a class of algorithms for learning automata. The automaton takes one of a set of actions according to its corresponding probabilities. The environment or teacher responds to the automaton's action by showing "success" (+1) or "failure" (−1). We may call this feedback from the environment the global reinforcement signal. The automaton learns by altering the probabilities associated with the actions in response to the reinforcement signal. The learning process continues until the automaton behaves properly.

The extent to which a local decision or action is rewarded or penalized depends on how it correlates with the reinforcement signal. If enough samples are taken, the noise caused by the variations in the other variables is averaged out, and the effect due to a single variable becomes evident. Therefore, with a sufficiently long learning process, an optimal probability can be learned for each local variable.

In contrast to backpropagation learning, reinforcement learning does not have to compute derivatives. This feature makes it suitable in a complex system where derivatives are difficult to obtain. On the other hand, reinforcement learning is very inefficient in a large system. Additionally, it may get stuck in a local optimum.

An example of this class of algorithms is the linear reward-penalty (L_{R-P}) algorithm (Narendra and Thathachar 1974). In this algorithm, assume that there are r actions, $a_1, a_2, \ldots, a_r$, and the respective probabilities for these actions are $P_1, P_2, \ldots, P_r$. Let $P_i(k)$ denote the probability at iteration k. Suppose at iteration k, the action taken is a_i. When the reinforcement signal is +1 (i.e., positive feedback), the learning rule is

$$P_i(k+1) = P_i(k) + a[1 - P_i(k)]$$

$$P_j(k+1) = (1-a)P_j(k), \text{ for } j \neq i$$

If the reinforcement signal is −1 (i.e., negative feedback), the learning rule is

$$P_i(k + 1) = (1 - b)P_i(k)$$

$$P_j(k + 1) = \frac{b}{r-1} + (1 - b)P_j(k), \text{ for } j \neq i$$

In the above rules, a and b are learning rates. Thus, in the case of positive feedback, the probability of the current action is increased with relative decrease in the probabilities of the other actions. The adjustment is reversed in the case of negative feedback.

Barto and Anandan (1985) extended the above learning algorithm. In their algorithm called *associative reinforcement learning*, the environment provides not only the feedback signal but also the input vector. The network will learn to make right classification of the input vector. The teacher will determine how to reinforce or weaken the action taken, given the input vector. In other words, the teacher has knowledge stored in a two-dimensional array: one dimension is the input vector and the other dimension is the action.

Consider the case of two possible actions (classes) a_1 and a_2. Given the input vector $\mathbf{x}$, the Bayesian classifier will choose a_1 if $P(a_1|\mathbf{x}) > P(a_2|\mathbf{x})$, and choose a_2 otherwise. Suppose we use a vector θ such that

$$\theta \cdot \mathbf{x} \approx P(a_1|\mathbf{x}) - P(a_2|\mathbf{x})$$

Let z denote the correct class lable for $\mathbf{x}$ so that when $z = 1$, $\mathbf{x}$ is a_1 and when $z = 0$, $\mathbf{x}$ is a_2. It can be shown that when the expected value $E[(\theta \cdot \mathbf{x} - z)^2]$ is minimized, the error in classification is also minimized. Using the gradient descent procedure to minimize this criterion, we obtain the following learning rule (Robbins-Monro algorithm) to adjust θ:

$$\theta(k + 1) = \theta(k) + \eta[z - \theta(k) \cdot \mathbf{x}]\mathbf{x} \tag{3.16}$$

where η is the learning rate. It is not surprising that this learning rule is similar to the delta rule for perceptron learning. And the components of θ can be interpreted as weights on connections linking each component of the input to a single output unit.

If an element of randomness is added to this associative reinforcement algorithm, it becomes the associative reward-penalty (A_{R-P}) algorithm. The A_{R-P} algorithm reduces to other algorithms under certain conditions. For example, if the input vector is a constant and the random variable has a uniform distribution over the interval of -1 to 1, this algorithm reduces to the L_{R-P} algorithm. More discussions can be found in Zeidenberg (1990).

3.5.5 Temporal Difference Learning

A kind of problem is to predict future outcome by using past experience. This problem is quite common, for example, in game playing, weather forecast, and stock market prediction. Dealing with this problem, we are interested in on-line prediction. That is, we continue to make our predictions and adjust our belief and not wait until the last minute. The solution to this problem is especially important in the application domains where data continue to flow in and we have to make our decision or action in a real-time manner.

Sutton (1988) describes temporal difference methods which calculate parameter adjustment based on the difference between temporally successive predictions of the output, instead of the difference between the predicted and the desired outputs, and are thus different from backpropagation learning.

In game playing, for example, backpropagation cannot be used to update the weights after each move, since the outcome is not available until the end of the game. Even though it is possible to update the weights at the end, this approach requires the storage of all the information along the way. The temporal difference method, on the other hand, need not store all information. It saves weight update information at each move and performs on-line prediction. Besides storage efficiency, it is claimed that temporal difference methods are computationally more efficient than ordinary methods and converge faster to an optimum for multistep problems, the problems for which we make prediction several steps ahead of time. For example, predicting Sunday's weather based on Wednesday is a multistep problem. It can be argued that most prediction problems are of this type.

Suppose the neural network makes a sequence of predictions $O_1, O_2, \ldots, O_t$ up to time t. The weight vector is adjusted at time t by

$$\Delta \mathbf{W}(t) = \eta(O_{t+1} - O_t) \sum_{k=1}^{t} \nabla_{\mathbf{W}} O_k \qquad (3.17)$$

where $O_{t+1} = z$, the desired outcome in the end, η is the learning rate, and $\nabla_{\mathbf{W}} O_i$ is the gradient of O_i with respect to $\mathbf{W}$ yielding a vector of partial derivatives of O_i with respect to each component of $\mathbf{W}$. This learning rule looks similar to the backpropagation rule except that there is an accumulation of derivatives over time. As an extension, the family of learning procedures $TD(\lambda)$ is defined by

$$\Delta \mathbf{W}(t) = \eta(O_{t+1} - O_t) \sum_{k=1}^{t} \lambda^{t-k} \nabla_{\mathbf{W}} O_k \qquad (3.18)$$

where λ typically ranges between zero and one. In the $TD(\lambda)$ algorithm, the gradients into the past are weighted by decreasing factors of λ. This is analogous to the fact that our memory fades away with time. In the prediction task, it means that more recent experience is more important in making future decision. The adaptive heuristic critic (AHC) learning method is closely related to the $TD(\lambda)$ algorithm and is used to predict cumulative outcomes.

The last learning rule without λ involved is referred to as $TD(1)$, the first-order temporal difference procedure. It should be noted that the $TD(\lambda)$

algorithm actually minimizes the following criterion function:

$$E = \sum_{k=1}^{t} \lambda^{t-k}(T_t - O_k)^2 \tag{3.19}$$

where T_t is the desired prediction at time t.

Sutton used a simple problem to illustrate the advantage of the temporal difference method over ordinary supervised learning techniques. The problem involves a random walk through a linear sequence of states A to G. A and G are final states, and each of the other states (B to F) can move to either its right or left neighbor state, both with the probability 0.5. For example, the sequence $DCBCDEF$ is a walk. The problem is to learn the probability for each of the states B to F to end up in state A or G. The $TD(\lambda)$ algorithm was trained on 100 training sets of 10 walks each. The result showed that the error declined rapidly and was optimum when $\lambda = 0$.

The $TD(\lambda)$ algorithm has been successfully applied to game playing. A program based on this method has reached near-expert-level performance.

3.5.6 ART Networks

Adaptive resonance theory (ART) networks (Carpenter and Grossberg 1988) are most useful for pattern clustering, classification (e.g., signal classification), and recognition. They can also perform pattern association with some modifications. These networks can work on binary or analog-valued input. Their ability to generalize is limited because ART networks lack the hidden layer of neurons which perform feature recognition or pattern extraction in the backpropagation network. However, the ability of an ART network to create a new pattern class in its knowledge base on the arrival of a novel pattern makes it very suitable for applications such as automatic target recognition and spatiotemporal pattern recognition. Furthermore, when the network acquires new concepts, the old patterns are still kept in the memory. The network can learn incrementally without reviewing old instances. This nice feature is missing in supervised learning networks such as backpropagation.

The adaptive resonance theory suggests a solution to the stability-plasticity dilemma during the designing of learning systems. The dilemma asks: "How can a learning system be designed to remain adaptive in response to significant events and yet remain stable in response to irrelevant events?" It would be easy either to learn new patterns (learning plasticity) or to retain the knowledge of previously learned patterns (learning stability). However, designing a network that can achieve both objectives simultaneously is difficult. One of the key features in attaining learning plasticity and stability is the use of pattern resonance. The ART network, as shown in Figure 3.7, uses resonance of a pattern in the output layer, with a pattern in the input layer, to establish a good heteroassociative pattern match. A resonating network has two main layers. The first layer receives and holds the input pattern. The second layer responds with a pattern classification or association to the input pattern (the *recognition* phase) and verifies that by sending a return pattern to the first layer (the *comparison* phase). If this return pattern is correct (similar to the input pattern), then there is a match. If the return pattern is substantially different from the input pattern, then the two layers will resonate by communicating back and forth, seeking a match. If a novel input pattern fails to match stored patterns within the tolerance level (imposed by the so-called vigilance parameter), a new stored pattern will be formed.

In the recognition phase, the network finds the output neuron whose bottom-up weight vector ($\mathbf{B}$) is closest to the input vector ($\mathbf{X}$) in terms of their dot product:

$$\mathbf{B} \cdot \mathbf{X}$$

This is essentially the winner-take-all strategy.

In the comparison phase, the network performs the following vigilance test:

$$\left(\sum_i T_{ij} X_i\right) / \left(\sum_i X_i\right) > \sigma$$

where T_{ij} is the top-down weight from output unit j to input unit i, X_i is the activation level of input unit i, and σ is a vigilance parameter ($0 \leq \sigma \leq 1$). Assume binary values (0 and 1). The numerator is equal to the number of attributes possessed by both vectors (the top-down and the input vectors), while the denominator is the number of attributes present in the input vector. Therefore, this fraction reflects the similarity between the two vectors from the perspective of the input vector.

Both the lower layer (for comparison) and the upper layer (for recognition) are associated with gain control, called, respectively, Gain-1 and Gain-2. Both gain units output 1 if at least one component of the input vector is 1. Each neuron in the lower layer receives inputs from the input vector, Gain-1, and the feedback (top-down) signal from the upper layer. At least two of these three inputs must be 1 for a neuron to output 1. This is the *two-thirds rule*. In the comparison phase, if any component of the top-down vector is 1, Gain-1 is forced to 0. At this point, a neuron will fire only if its top-down signal matches its input signal (i.e., both are 1s) according to the two-thirds rule.

If the vigilance test is passed, then the input vector is assigned to the category designated by the output unit, and the weights associated with this output unit are updated. The top-down weights are updated by taking the dot product of the top-down weight vector and the input vector. This step prunes the components of the top-down vector (which characterizes the output unit) that do not match the input vector. The bottom-up weights have a similar update but with additional normalization. It should be noted that the ART network makes distinctions between slow learning (training) and fast learning. In the former case, weights are determined by the statistics of available instances, whereas in the later case, weights are determined by single instances on a one-by-one basis. What is formulated above is fast training.

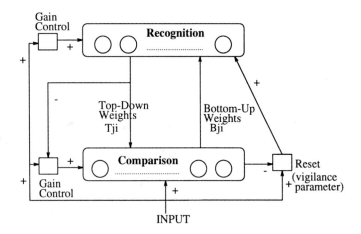

Figure 3.7: The ART network (Carpenter and Grossberg 1988).

If the vigilance test fails, the ART network will continue to search for another output neuron whose weight vectors best match the input vector. If all stored output neurons have been tried and all failed, then the network will allocate a new output neuron for the input vector. That is, a new category is formed. It is often the case that a lower vigilance value favors the formation of fewer clusters (stored patterns), while a higher value leads to more clusters.

These resonating networks are by no means simple. In fact, the underlying theoretical basis for their designs is more complex than that of the feedforward networks. However, they are interesting because of two useful properties: real-time learning and self-organization. In real-time learning, the system can identify a novel pattern and learn it fast, and every time the system recognizes a pattern, the system fine-tunes the weights for that pattern category. Due to the self-organizing capability, the system can be adaptive to new patterns and offer incremental learning capability. On the other hand, the system designer has little control over assigning particular patterns to a certain category, and the stored categories will evolve over time automatically. Thus, the system is more sensitive to data noise than clustering methods, such as the Kohonen network and the k-means clustering algorithm in which the number of classes is fixed.

In the ART network, the number of bits or values of the input pattern determines the number of input units, but the number of output units is dynamically adapted in the learning process. ART-1 processes binary inputs, and its later version, ART-2, accepts both binary and continuous inputs. ARTMAP (Carpenter, Grossberg, and Reynolds 1991) is a supervised version of ART, which can temporarily increase vigilance in order to rule out incorrect classification as supervised.

The ART (ART-1) Net Algorithm

- **Weight Initialization**

  The ART net consists of two layers: the input and the output layers. The connection weight $B_{ji}(t)$ (called a bottom-up weight) points from unit i in the input layer to unit j in the output layer at time t. The connection weight $T_{ij}(t)$ (called a top-down weight) points from unit j in the output layer to unit i in the input layer at time t. These weights define the stored pattern associated with output unit j:

$$T_{ij}(0) = 1$$

$$B_{ji}(0) < L/(L - 1 + m)$$

  where m is the number of input units, and $L > 1$ (L is a constant; typically $L = 2$).

- **Calculation of Activation**

  - The activation levels of the input units are determined by the input pattern.
  - The activation level of an output unit is calculated by the following procedure:
    1.

$$I_j = \sum_i B_{ji} X_i$$

    and

$$O_j = F_w(I_j)$$

    where O_j is the activation level of output unit j, X_i is the activation level of input unit i, and F_w is a winner-take-all function such that

$$F_w(I_j) = \begin{cases} 1 & I_j = \max_i\{I_i\} \\ 0 & \text{else} \end{cases}$$

    2. Vigilance test: Suppose output unit j is the winner neuron. If

$$\left(\sum_i T_{ij} X_i\right) / \left(\sum_i X_i\right) > \sigma$$

    where X_i is the activation level of input unit i, and σ is a vigilance parameter, $0 \le \sigma \le 1$, then update weights (see next); else set

$O_j = 0$, disable the output unit j, go to step 1, and repeat. If all committed output units (specifying stored patterns) are disabled, then a new output unit is allocated and its weights are initialized as stated.

- **Weight Training**

$$T_{ij}(t+1) = T_{ij}(t)X_i$$

$$B_{ji}(t+1) = \frac{LT_{ij}(t)X_i}{L-1+\sum_k T_{kj}(t)X_k}$$

Example. Suppose output unit j is the winning neuron. And suppose

$\mathbf{T}_j = [1,0,0,0,1,1]$
$\mathbf{X} = [1,0,0,1,0,1]$

and the vigilance parameter $\sigma = 0.6$ is used. Since

$(\mathbf{T} \cdot \mathbf{X})/(\sum_i X_i) = 2/3 > \sigma$

the top-down weight vector T_j is reset to $[1,0,0,0,0,1]$.

3.6   Genetic Algorithms

Genetic algorithms are algorithms for optimization and learning based on the mechanism of genetic evolution. The field of genetic algorithms was founded by John Holland (1975). Such algorithms have been applied to problems that are difficult and important, and are being applied to artificial intelligence systems. A good survey of applications is provided by Goldberg (1989).

A genetic algorithm consists of five components:

- A chromosomal representation of solutions[5]

- A way to initialize the population of chromosomes

- An evaluation function to rate solutions

- Genetic operators to alter the composition of chromosomes during reproduction, e.g., crossover

- Parameter settings for the algorithm, e.g., population size and probabilities of applying genetic operators

---

[5] Chromosomes carry genetic material inside a cell nucleus.

Over time, the population evolves to contain better individuals and finally converges to globally optimal (or near optimal) results. Let $m(H, t)$ denote the number of chromosomes of a particular configuration H at time t. Suppose during reproduction, a chromosome is copied according to its fitness, and the old population is replaced by the new population. Then, we may estimate the number at time $t + 1$ by (Goldberg 1989)

$$m(H, t + 1) = m(H, t)\frac{f(H)}{\bar{f}}$$

where $f(H)$ is the fitness of H and $\bar{f}$ is the average fitness of the entire population. Starting at $t = 0$ and assuming stationary fitness values, we obtain the equation

$$m(H, t + 1) = m(H, 0)(\frac{f(H)}{\bar{f}})^t$$

Thus, it is clear that the numbers of favorable (unfavorable) configurations will increase (decrease) exponentially. The genetic algorithm proceeds in the following steps:

1. Initialize the population of chromosomes.

2. If the termination criterion is met, exit; else repeat the following steps:

   - Select one or more parents (chromosomes) to reproduce children (chromosomes). Selection is stochastic, but parents with higher evaluations are favored. Children are produced by applying the genetic operators to the parents.

   - Children are evaluated, and promising ones are inserted into the population. The entire or a subset of population may be replaced.

Example. A chromosome is represented as a fixed-length string of 0 and 1. Two strings undergo crossover at a random position so that all bits are swapped from that position through the end. Suppose the initial population consists of four strings:

No.	String	Fitness
1	111000	90
2	010101	240
3	001011	150
4	101110	320

Now, suppose chromosomes 2 and 3 are selected for reproduction and crossover occurs at position 3 to yield two new strings:

No.	String	Fitness
5	011011	470
6	000101	80

Assume that the population size is fixed. At this point, chromosome 5 can replace chromosome 1 to give rise to a new population. Iterations like this continue until no further improvement for the population is seen.

A list of features has been identified which make a domain suitable for the application of genetic algorithms (Davis 1987): Domains should be multimodal; domains should not exhibit a high degree of epistasis (epistasis is the inhibition of one part of a solution by the action of another); domains should exhibit detectable and encodable regularities. The building block hypothesis has been suggested. Simple genetic algorithms depend on the recombination of building blocks to seek the best solutions. If the building blocks are misleading, the algorithms may still be clever enough to figure out (near) optimal solutions (by mutation, for example) but may take a longer time.

3.7 Summary

The intelligence of a computer-based system parallels the amount of knowledge it contains. Machine learning is an important topic not only because it would be an indispensable element in an intelligence system but also because it holds great promise in expediting scientific discovery. In this chapter, we have reviewed important approaches to machine learning and highlighted influential work. We have seen some fundamental differences between different learning paradigms, but we should keep in mind their potential cross fertilization. AI learning seems to place more emphasis on the representation and the use of symbolic knowledge. Connectionist learning, on the other hand, adopts the brain-style information processing. One may view the former learning as cognitive learning (at the conscious level) and the latter learning as perceptual learning (at the subconscious level). It is possible that they learn knowledge at different levels of abstraction on the same concept or process. As a matter of fact, their boundary is fuzzy. Connectionist models have now been applied to cognitive tasks such as medical diagnosis, while AI learning has been applied to speech recognition.

3.8 References

1. Barr, A., Feigenbaum, E.A., and Cohen, P.R. 1981. *The Handbook of Artificial Intelligence.* Kaufmann, Los Altos, CA.

2. Barto, A.G., and Anandan, P. 1985. Pattern recognizing stochastic learning automata. *IEEE Transactions on Systems, Man, and Cybernetics*, 15, pp. 360–375.

3. Baum, E.B., and Haussler, D. 1989. What size net gives valid generalization? *Neural Computation*, 1, pp. 151–160.

4. Buchanan, B.G., and Mitchell, T.M. 1978. Model-directed learning of production rules. In *Pattern-Directed Inference Systems*. Academic Press, New York.

5. Carpenter, G.A., and Grossberg, S. 1988. The ART of adaptive pattern recognition by a self-organizing neural network. *Computer*, March, pp. 77–88.

6. Carpenter, G.A., Grossberg, S., and Reynolds, J. 1991. ARTMAP: A self-organizing neural network architecture for fast supervised learning and pattern recognition. In *Proceedings of IJCNN* (Seattle), pp. I-863–868.

7. Caudill, M. 1991. Neural network training tips and techniques. *AI Expert*, January, pp. 56–61.

8. Cun, Y.Le. 1989. Generalization and network design strategies. In *Connectionism in Perspective*. North Holland, Amsterdam, Netherlands.

9. Cun, Y.Le, Denker, J.S., and Solla, S.A. 1990. Optimal brain damage. In *Advances in Neural Information Processing Systems II*, pp. 598–605. Morgan Kaufmann, San Mateo, CA.

10. Davis, L. (ed.) 1987. *Genetic Algorithms and Simulated Annealing*. Morgan Kaufmann, Palo Alto, CA.

11. Duda, R.O., and Hart, P.E. 1973. *Pattern Classification and Scene Analysis*. John Wiley & Sons, New York.

12. Goldberg, D.E. 1989. *Genetic Algorithms*. Addison-Wesley, Reading, MA.

13. Haussler, D. 1988. Quantifying inductive bias: AI learning algorithms and Valiant's learning framework. *Artificial Intelligence*, 36(2), pp. 177–221.

14. Hinton, G.E. 1989. Connectionist learning procedures. *Artificial Intelligence*, 40, pp. 185–234.

15. Holland, J.H. 1975. *Adaptation in Natural and Artificial Systems*. The University of Michigan Press, Ann Arbor.

16. Hush, D.R., and Horne, B.G. 1993. Progress in supervised neural networks. *IEEE Signal Processing Magazine*, January 1993, pp. 8–39.

17. Kohonen, T. 1988. *Self-Organization and Associative Memory*. Springer-Verlag, New York.

18. Langley, P., Bradshaw, G.L., and Simon, H.A. 1983. Rediscovering chemistry with the BACON system. In *Machine Learning*. Tioga Publishing Company, Palo Alto, CA.

19. Lenat, D.B. 1976. AM: An Artificial Intelligence Approach to Discovery in Mathematics as Heuristic Search. Ph.D. thesis, Stanford University.

20. McCulloch, W.S., and Pitts, W. 1943. A logical calculus of ideas imminent in nervous activity. *Bull. Math. Biophysics*, 5, pp. 115–133.

21. Michalski, R.S., Carbonell, J.G., and Mitchell, T.M. (eds.) 1983. *Machine Learning*. Tioga, Palo Alto, CA.

22. Michalski, R.S., and Stepp, R.E. 1983. Learning from observations: Conceptual clustering. In *Machine Learning*. Tioga, Palo Alto, CA.

23. Mitchell, T.M. 1978. Version Spaces: An Approach to Concept Learning. Ph.D. thesis, Stanford University.

24. Mitchell, T.M., Keller, R.M., and Kedar-Cabelli, S.T. 1986. Explanation-based generalization: A unifying view. *Machine Learning* 1(1), pp. 47–80.

25. Moody, J.E. 1991. Note on generalization, regularization, and architecture selection in nonlinear learning systems. In *Proceedings of the 1991 IEEE Workshop*, pp. 1–10.

26. Moody, J., and Darken, C.J. 1989. Fast learning in networks of locally-tuned processing elements. *Neural Computation*, 1(2), pp. 281–294.

27. Mozer, M.C., and Smolensky, P. 1989. Skeletonization: A technique for trimming the fat from a network via relevance assessment. In *Advances in Neural Information Processing Systems I*. Morgan Kaufmann, San Mateo, CA.

28. Narendra, K.S., and Thathachar, M.A.L. 1974. Learning automata—A Survey. *IEEE Transactions on Systems, Man, and Cybernetics*, 4, pp. 323–334.

29. Nowlan, S.J., and Hinton, G.E. 1992. Simplifying neural networks by soft weight sharing. *Neural Computation*, 4(4), pp. 473–493.

30. Quinlan, J.R. 1983. Learning efficient classification procedures and their application to chess end games. In *Machine Learning*, Tioga Publishing Company, Palo Alto, CA.

31. Rosenblatt, F. 1958. The Perceptron: A probabilistic model for information storage and organization in the brain. *Psychological Review*, 65, pp. 386–407.

32. Rumelhart, D.E., Hinton, G.E., and Williams, R.J. 1986. Learning internal representation by error propagation. In *Parallel Distributed Processing: Explorations in the Microstructures of Cognition*, Vol. 1. MIT Press, Cambridge, MA.

33. Rumelhart, D.E., McClelland, J.L., and the PDP Research Group. 1986. *Parallel Distributed Processing: Explorations in the Microstructures of Cognition*, Vol. 1 and Vol. 2. MIT Press, Cambridge, MA.

34. Samuel, A.L. 1959. Some studies in machine learning using the game of checkers. *IBM Journal of Research and Development*, 3, pp. 211–229.

35. Simon, H.A. 1983. Why should machines learn? In *Machine Learning*. Tioga Publishing Company, Palo Alto, CA.

36. Shanno, D.F. 1990. Recent advances in numerical techniques for large-scale optimization. In *Neural Networks for Control*. MIT Press, Cambridge, MA.

37. Sontag, E.D. 1989. Sigmoids distinguish more efficiently than heavisides. *Neural Computation*, 1, pp. 470–472.

38. Stornetta, W.S., and Huberman, B.A. 1987. An improved three-layer backpropagation algorithm. In *Proceedings of the IEEE First ICNN* (San Diego).

39. Stubbs, D.F. 1990. Six ways to improve back-propagation results. *Journal of Neural Network Computing*, spring, pp. 64–67.

40. Sutton, R.S. 1988. Learning to predict by the methods of temporal differences. *Machine Learning*, 3, pp. 9–44.

41. Valiant, L.G. 1984. A theory of the learnable. *Communications of the ACM*, 27(11), pp. 1134–1142.

42. Vapnik, V.N., and Chervonenkis, A. Ya. 1971. On the uniform convergence of relative frequencies of events to their probabilities. *Theor. Probab. Appl.*, 16(2), pp. 264–280.

43. Weigend, A.S., Rumelhart, D.E., and Huberman, B.A. 1990. Backpropagation, weight elimination, and time series prediction. In *Proceedings of the 1990 Connectionist Models Summer School*, pp. 65–80.

44. Winston, P.H. 1975. Learning structural descriptions from examples. In *The Psychology of Computer Vision*. McGraw-Hill, New York.

45. Zeidenberg, M. 1990. *Neural Networks in Artificial Intelligence*. Ellis Horwood, New York.

3.9   Problems

1. Use the version space algorithm to learn a concept in the poker domain. Each instance and concept is represented as a feature vector "(rank, suit)," e.g., (4, heart). The initial version space has the G boundary = $\{(x,y)\}$ and the S boundary = nil, where x and y are variables. The following instances are presented in sequence:

Classification (Label)	Pattern
positive	(6, spade)
positive	(8, spade)
negative	(J, diamond)
positive	(K, club)

Assume the generalization and specialization rules as follows:

Two specific even numbers are generalized into even numbers.
Two specific odd numbers are generalized into odd numbers.
Even ranks and odd ranks are generalized into all ranks.
Spades and clubs are generalized into blacks.
Hearts and diamonds are generalized into reds.
Blacks and reds are generalized into all suits.
All ranks are specialized into even ranks or odd ranks.
All suits are specialized into blacks or reds.
Blacks are specialized into spades or clubs.
Reds are specialized into hearts or diamonds.

(a) Update the version space incrementally.

(b) What is the concept learned?

2. Consider a collection of 10 objects. We use the attribute "size" (with two possible values: large and small) to group the objects into two subsets: five large objects and five small objects. Among the five large objects, three are class X and two are class Y. Among the five small objects, one is class X, one is class Y, and three are class Z. Calculate the entropy of the objects grouped under the attribute "size."

3. Use the ID3 algorithm to build a decision tree for classifying the following objects:

Class	Size	Color	Shape
A	small	yellow	round
A	big	yellow	round
A	big	red	round
A	small	red	round
B	small	black	round
B	big	black	cube
B	big	yellow	cube
B	big	black	round
B	small	yellow	cube

4. Implement a backpropagation network to simulate the exclusive-or function:

Input 1	Input 2	Output
1	1	0
1	0	1
0	1	1
0	0	0

(a) Try the architecture in which there is only a single hidden unit and all units are connected with each other (inputs units are also connected with the output unit). If the network uses a very steep sigmoid function, can you find a set of weights right away without running the learning algorithm? (Hint: In this case, the net behavior is similar to that of a multilayer perceptron.)

(b) Try the architecture in which there is a hidden layer with three hidden units and the network is fully connected (no supralayer connection).

5. The backpropagation network has been applied to medical diagnosis. A medical diagnosis problem is concerned with identifying the disease which is most likely to cause a given set of clinical findings. To solve this problem, we can use a backpropagation network in which the input units encode clinical findings and the output units encode possible diseases, and then train the network on a set of examples whose clinical findings and correct diagnoses are both known. Once the network is well trained, it can be used to diagnose the disease based on clinical findings. Suppose the domain concerned involves eight binary attributes to describe clinical findings, such as fever and jaundice, and three possible diseases. The available examples are listed below:

Input vector	Output vector
(1,1,1,0,0,0,0,0)	(1,0,0)
(0,1,0,0,1,0,0,0)	(0,1,0)
(1,0,0,0,0,1,0,1)	(0,0,1)
(1,0,1,1,0,0,0,0)	(1,0,0)
(0,1,0,1,1,0,1,0)	(0,1,0)
(0,0,0,0,0,1,1,1)	(0,0,1)
(0,0,0,1,0,1,1,1)	(1,0,0)
(0,1,0,0,1,1,1,0)	(0,1,0)
(0,0,1,0,0,0,1,1)	(0,0,1)
(0,1,1,0,0,0,0,1)	(1,0,0)
(0,0,0,0,1,1,0,0)	(0,1,0)
(1,0,0,1,0,1,0,1)	(0,0,1)

We will use a neural network with one hidden layer. The network is fully connected without supralayer connections. The number of hidden units is determined in the following way. We start with one hidden unit, then two, then three, and so on until we have the best performance. That is, the network cannot be further improved by adding more hidden units. To ensure good generalization, we use eight examples for training and the remaining four for testing. In practice, we should try multiple different partitions. In this problem, let us try three different partitions. We use the first four for testing in the first partition, use the second four for testing in the second partition, and use the last four for testing in the third partition. Upon convergence, the mean of the training error and the test error of the output units averaged over the sample is taken to measure the network performance. The best performance among these partitions determines the performance of an architecture being considered, and the associated trained weights are kept for future use.

(a) Design a backpropagation network for this domain.

(b) Train the neural network and show the trained weights.

(c) Call the three diseases encoded by the output vectors (1, 0, 0), (0, 1, 0), (0, 0, 1) as diseases A, B, and C, respectively. What are the diagnoses for the following two patients whose clinical findings are described by

   patient 1: (1,1,0,0,1,1,0,0)
   patient 2: (0,0,1,1,0,0,1,1)

6. The backpropagation network can be used for data compression. The idea is to map each pattern into itself, and the information encoded in the hidden layer represents the compressed data. In this application, we use a network with a hidden layer. Each pattern is presented on both the input and the output layers; they should be equal in size. The number of hidden units should be less than that of the input or output units in order to achieve compression. The original data is reconstructed from the compressed form using the weights between the hidden and the output layers. Suppose the following data vectors are to be transmitted:

$$(1, 0, 1, 1, 0, 0, 0, 0)$$
$$(1, 1, 0, 1, 1, 0, 0, 0)$$
$$(0, 0, 1, 1, 0, 1, 0, 0)$$
$$(1, 1, 1, 1, 0, 0, 1, 0)$$
$$(0, 0, 1, 1, 1, 1, 0, 0)$$
$$(1, 0, 0, 0, 0, 1, 0, 0)$$
$$(0, 0, 0, 1, 0, 0, 1, 1)$$
$$(0, 0, 1, 1, 1, 1, 0, 1)$$
$$(0, 0, 1, 1, 1, 0, 0, 0)$$
$$(0, 0, 0, 0, 0, 1, 0, 0)$$

(a) Design a neural network with a 2:1 data compression ratio.

(b) Write the equation for compressing a transmitted vector.

(c) Write the equation for decompressing a received vector.

7. Discuss how to use the backpropagation network as a noise filter in signal processing.

8. In the backpropagation network, the error is the target value *minus* the actual value produced by the network. Suppose the target value is a range (interval) rather than a point. Devise a simple scheme to calculate the error.

9. Derive the learning rule for the backpropagation network if the mechanism of weight decay is incorporated.

10. How can you approximate a Gaussian function by two sigmoid functions? In this view, how can you translate a radial basis function network into a backpropagation network?

11. Feed the following feature vectors into an ART network in the given order:

Order	Input vector
1	(1,1,0,0,0,0)
2	(0,1,1,0,1,0)
3	(1,0,0,1,0,1)
4	(1,1,0,1,1,0)
5	(1,1,0,1,1,1)
6	(0,0,0,1,0,0)
7	(1,0,1,0,1,0)
8	(1,0,0,0,0,1)
9	(1,0,1,1,1,0)
10	(0,0,0,0,1,0)
11	(0,0,1,1,1,1)
12	(1,0,0,1,1,0)

(a) Design an ART network and train it on the given data.

(b) Try several vigilance parameter values: 0.3, 0.6, and 0.9. For each vigilance level, how many clusters will be produced at the end? Discuss the results.

12. The ART-1 network is said to be stable for a finite number of training examples if the final clusters will not change with additional iterations on the same training set. Derive a bound on the number of iterations before the network reaches stability for N training examples, each with m inputs.

Chapter 4

Knowledge-Based Neural Networks

4.1   Introduction

In contrast to many symbolic machine learning programs, neural networks learn by encoding implicit generalized pattern information as connection weights which somehow reflect the statistical properties of the data. It has been indicated that the neural network approach could outperform symbolic learning programs, such as ID3 (Quinlan 1983), when data are noisy (Fisher and McKusick 1989; Mooney, Shavlik, Towell, and Gove 1989). This result leads to growing interest in exploring this approach for machine learning.

It has been found that a machine learning program can learn much more effectively if it can exploit existing domain theory (knowledge). Here, domain theory refers to a set of rules or facts to be used in explaining how a given example is an example of the goal concept. However, because theory-driven (or model-driven) learning such as explanation-based learning (Mitchell, Keller, and Kedar-Cabelli 1986) is not workable if the theory is weak and because data-driven (or empirical) learning, such as ID3, cannot learn well if data are inadequate, combining these two kinds of learning is a natural way to make the learning system more robust and useful. This consideration motivates the integration of domain theory (imperfect or approximate) into the neural network which then refines the theory empirically. This approach can also offer a more efficient and more reliable form of neural network learning.

A system combining connectionists and symbolic reasoning models is an example of a hybrid intelligent system. One major line of research on hybrid intelligent systems is knowledge-based neural networks, which are concerned with the use of domain knowledge to determine the initial structure of the neural network. Such constructions have been studied by Gallant (1988), Bradshaw, Fozzard, and Ceci (1989), Fu and Fu (1990), Fu (1992, 1993), Hall and Romaniuk

115

(1990), Yang and Bhargava (1990), and Lacher, Hruska, and Kuncicky (1992). The knowledge-based approach answers such questions as, "How many layers and how many hidden units are proper for a neural network?" Towell, Shavlik, and Noordewier (1990) demonstrated that a knowledge-based neural network could outperform a standard backpropagation network, as well as other related learning algorithms including symbolic and numerical ones. This impressive demonstration lays down a good foundation for this area of research.

This chapter explores knowledge-based neural networks with a main focus on rule-based neural networks. Decision tree–based and semantic-constraint-based neural networks are also discussed.

4.2 Rule-Based Neural Networks

A rule-based inference (or problem-solving) system can be mapped into a neural network architecture as follows. First, data attributes or variables are assigned input units (nodes), target concepts or final hypotheses are assigned output units, and intermediate concepts or hypotheses are assigned hidden units. Then, the initial domain rules determine how the attributes and concepts link and how the links are weighted.

Assume that the initial theory is in propositional Horn-clause format.[1] The syntax of rules is restricted to the form

If α_1 and $\alpha_2, \ldots,$ then β

where α_i is a condition and β is a conclusion or action. The conjunction of α_i's constitutes the rule's premise. The semantics of this rule is "if all α's are evaluated to be true, then β is true." However, in a knowledge-based (expert) system, the semantics of rules are determined by the inference engine which interprets them. Some inference engines allow the notion of "partially true." It would be appropriate to divide rules into two kinds: categorical (nonprobabilistic) and noncategorical (probabilistic). Categorical rules are not attached with any probabilistic or certainty factors, whereas noncategorical rules are. Accordingly, we may classify inference engines into categorical and noncategorical, which deal with categorical and noncategorical rules, respectively.

If rules are not in the above format, they can be rewritten into this form by applying the following equivalents:

- "If p then q and r" is replaced by "if p then q" and "if p then r."

- "If p or q then r" is replaced by "if p then r" and "if q then r."

- "If p and (q or r) then s" is replaced by "if p and q then s" and "if p and r then s."

---

[1] In logic, a Horn clause is a clause that has, at most, one positive literal. A clause is a disjunction of literals.

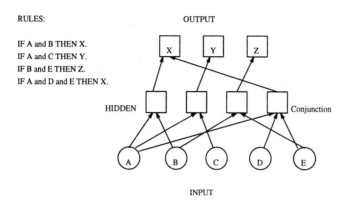

Figure 4.1: A rule-based connectionist network.

They can be recursively applied to handle cases involving nested "ands" and "ors."

As defined, each rule has an antecedent (premise) consisting of one or more conditions as well as a single consequent. In the network configuration, the premise is assigned a hidden unit, each condition corresponds to an assigned attribute or concept node, and the consequent corresponds to an assigned concept node. Each condition node is connected to the premise node which in turn is connected to the consequent node. Under such construction, the rule strength corresponds to the weight associated with the connection from the premise node to the consequent node. Notice that a hidden unit is introduced to explicitly represent the conjunction of one or more conditions in a rule's premise part.[2] Such a hidden unit is called a *conjunction unit*. An example network is given in Figure 4.1.

From the above description, mapping a rule, we need a three-level construct: The first level is the attributes of the if-part, the next level is the conjunction of these attributes to form the premise, and the third level is the consequent (in the then-part). A question is whether we can omit the conjunction level and link the attributes directly to the consequent. This approach would cause a problem when there are multiple rules because some combinations of the attributes involved in different rules may also activate the target concept. To avoid these possible unintended combinations, each rule's premise is assigned a conjunction unit which activates the target concept disjunctively. In an expert

---

[2]One variation is that if the premise contains only one condition, then the condition node can connect directly to the consequent node without introduction of a conjunction node.

or knowledge-based system, rules are often organized in a multilevel hierarchy, which can be mapped into a neural network of three or more layers.

We refer to this modeling technique as the *rule-based connectionist model* and call the neural network a *rule-based connectionist network* (RBCN). In this approach, the number of hidden units is determined by that of rules, and the number of hidden layers is determined by that of levels in the rule hierarchy.

We have just shown how to build a rule-based neural network. The rule strength can be adjusted by the backpropagation procedure (Rumelhart, Hinton, and Williams 1986). It would be adequate for refining rules if the fine tuning of rule strengths is all that is necessary. In general, we need a more flexible learning model which can carry out various forms of revision and learning.

The KBCNN (knowledge-based conceptual neural networks) model of Fu (1993) revises and learns knowledge on the basis of the network translated from the rule base which encodes the initial domain knowledge. When the network performance gets stuck during training, new hidden units are added to different layers in order to generate new concepts or rules. As a rule, we should not add more nodes than necessary. A newly introduced node is fully connected to adjacent layers by default.

Figure 4.2 shows an RBCN for the purpose of learning. In the figure, a filled circle is used for an attribute or a predefined concept (an intermediate or a final concept); a blank circle for an undefined hidden concept; a filled rectangle for a conjunction unit encoding the premise of an existing rule; and a blank rectangle for a conjunction unit corresponding to the premise of a possible (future) rule. The connection pattern for an existing rule is determined by the rule: The if-nodes (nodes denoting the attributes in the premise) connect to the then-node (the node denoting the consequent) through a conjunction unit (namely, the premise node). For a possible rule devoted to a certain concept (existing or nonexisting), the conjunction unit encoding its premise is fully (but could be partially if we have bias) connected to all nodes in the next layer closer to the net input. We may weakly connect (e.g., a typical weight value is 0.1) some nodes other than the if-nodes to the premise node of an existing rule in case the rule might incorporate those nodes for future specialization. We call those layers containing conjunction units *conjunction layers* and other layers except the input layer *disjunction layers*.

In the case of the CF-based activation function (described later), the weight value is bounded between -1 and 1. Suppose a rule's premise involves p positive attributes (attributes which must be present) and q negated attributes (attributes which must not be present). We set the initial threshold of the corresponding conjunction unit to about 0.2 (the threshold is the negative of the connection weight from the bias unit) and set the initial weight for each input connection from positive attributes to around $1/p$ and that from negated attributes to about $-1/q$ (to be different from randomized weights, both should be no less than a predefined magnitude, e.g., 0.3). The initial weights of tentative connections leading into a predefined conjunction unit are randomized to small values (e.g., between -0.1 and 0.1), as are those of connections pointing to an

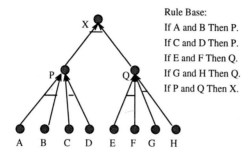

Rule Base:

If A and B Then P.

If C and D Then P.

If E and F Then Q.

If G and H Then Q.

If P and Q Then X.

(a) A rule base configured as a network

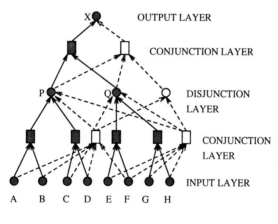

→ : Existing rules.   Filled nodes: Existing nodes

--➤ : Potential rules.   Blank nodes: Potential nodes

(b) A rule-based connectionist network for learning and revising knowledge

Figure 4.2: A rule-based connectionist network for learning and revising knowledge.

undefined hidden concept node. The initial weight corresponding to a rule strength is set strong (e.g., a typical weight value is 0.5) for existing rules, and weak (e.g., 0.1) for possible rules. Such a weight is associated with a connection pointing from a conjunction unit to a concept node (intermediate or final, existing or nonexisting). When an existing rule is attached with a belief value (for example in a MYCIN-like system), this value is indicative of the initial rule weight. The bias unit is not connected to any disjunction unit (a unit in a disjunction layer), which means its threshold is fixed at zero. The initial weights set in accordance with the above guidelines are further perturbed within a small range (e.g., ± 0.1) to avoid symmetry breaking problems (Rumelhart et al. 1986).

The KBANN system (Towell et al. 1990), in which the sigmoid function is used, sets weights from a positive attribute and from a negated one to ω (e.g., 3.0) and $-\omega$, respectively. The bias on the unit corresponding to the rule's consequent is set to $p * \omega - \phi$ where ϕ (e.g., 2.3) is the parameter chosen so that the consequent node has an activation ≥ 0.9 when the corresponding rule fires and an activation ≤ 0.1 otherwise.

KBANN requires a linear feature to be partitioned into multiple subranges, each encoded by a unit which uses the following activation function:

$$\Psi(\max\{0, [\text{Abs}(M - V) - \text{Range}/2]\}/\text{Range})$$

where M is the midpoint of a subrange, Range is the width of the subrange, V is the feature value, and Ψ is a function based on the normal distribution. Therefore, if the value is outside a subrange, the corresponding unit would still be active according to how close the value is to the subrange.

For hierarchical features, whenever a rule's premise refers to an element in a hierarchy, KBANN creates a high-weight link from the element to the rule's consequent and low-weight links from all ancestors and descendants of the element. This gives the network the capability to generalize or specialize the initial rule by the hierarchy. In the symbolic approach, the generalization hierarchy may be expressed in terms of the ISA relation. For example, Clyde "is a" bird and a bird "is an" animal. Thus, this technique also shows how to encode the ISA relation in the neural network. However, we should keep in mind that how to represent it will depend on how to use it.

4.2.1   The CF-Based Activation Function

The CF-based activation function adopts the following incremental updating formula of the CF (certainty factor) model (Buchanan and Shortliffe 1984) to combine activations:

$$f(X, Y) = X + Y - XY$$

This formula is applied to combine positive activations and negative activations separately. Then, the overall activation is the sum of combined positive activations and combined negative activations.[3] Nodal thresholds are dealt with here by sending activations from the bias unit. Application of this formula results in a nonlinear transfer function in replacement of the sigmoid function normally used in artificial neural networks. Note that this combining function maps $[-1, 1]$ (the interval of -1 and 1) into $[-1, 1]$. As a departure from the CF model, the KBCNN network handles conjunction and disjunction of activations by tuning weights and threshold values rather than using "min" and "max" functions in order to learn more smoothly. The system developed by Lacher et al. (1992) adopts a similar scheme but more rigorously follows the CF model.

Formally, we define the activation function F_{CF} based on the CF model as follows:

$$F_{\text{CF}}(x_1, x_2, ..., y_1, y_2, ...) = F_{\text{CF}}^+(x_1, x_2, ...) + F_{\text{CF}}^-(y_1, y_2, ...)$$

where

$$F_{\text{CF}}^+(x_1, x_2, ...) = 1 - \Pi_i(1 - x_i)$$

$$F_{\text{CF}}^-(y_1, y_2, ...) = -1 + \Pi_j(1 + y_j)$$

and x_i's are positive numbers and y_j's are negative numbers. Their partial derivatives are

$$\frac{\partial F_{\text{CF}}^+(x_1, x_2, ...)}{\partial x_i} = \Pi_{j \neq i}(1 - x_j)$$

$$\frac{\partial F_{\text{CF}}^-(y_1, y_2, ...)}{\partial y_j} = \Pi_{k \neq j}(1 + y_k)$$

Example. Calculate the following functional value:

$$F_{\text{CF}}(0.3, -0.5, -0.4, 0.7, -0.6)$$

$$= F_{\text{CF}}^+(0.3, 0.7) + F_{\text{CF}}^-(-0.5, -0.4, -0.6)$$

$$= [1 - (1 - 0.3)(1 - 0.7)] + [-1 + (1 - 0.5)(1 - 0.4)(1 - 0.6)]$$

$$= -0.09$$

Some criticisms against the CF model are due to the fact that this combining formula assumes independence between activations. However, if this is not the case, the connection weights can be adjusted properly through neural learning to offset their interactions.

In the CF model, the weights are confined to the interval $[-1, 1]$, as are the activations. An activation of 1 is interpreted as "true," -1 as "false," and 0 as "unknown." One caveat is that the activation of an output unit should be restricted to $[0, 1]$ when there is no disconfirming rule to inhibit the unit. In this case, for example, a vector of $[1, -1, 1]$ should be replaced by $[1, 0, 1]$. This consideration will affect how we encode a training instance.

---

[3]More complicated variants exist. However, they make more sense in a human model than a neural network one.

4.3   Network Training

In the designing of a neural network training procedure, an issue which has attracted much attention is "overtraining" (Drucker and Cun 1991; Sankar and Mammone 1991; Wada and Kawato 1991; Whitley and Karunanthi 1991). Overtraining is akin to the issue of overfitting data. The issue arises because the network matches the data so closely as to lose its generalization ability over unseen data (test data). Holding back part of training data has been found useful in our experiments. This fact suggests that we should try different data partitions for training and testing. It has also been suggested to use the information theoretical criterion rather than the least squared error criterion for training a neural network. Given a set of training instances, it can be shown that the likelihood of producing exactly the desired vectors is maximized when we minimize the cross-entropy (Hinton 1989). However, when the error vector distribution assumes a Gaussian distribution, maximization of likelihood is equivalent to minimization of squared error.

Another approach to the overfitting problem is to simplify and regularize the trained neural network. One useful way to improve the generalization of connectionist learning procedures is by building in an a priori bias in favor of simple models where there are not too many strong interactions between the variables (Hinton 1989). One method known as *weight decay* introduces an extra term into the error function so that the weight continually decays toward zero by an amount proportional to its magnitude (see Chapter 3 "Learning" for more details).

Full connectivity has been shown to hamper learning on some tasks (Rueckl, Cave, and Kosslyn 1988). Oversized networks are also undesirable. Generalization can be improved by pruning the trained neural network (Cun, Denker, and Solla 1989; Weigand, Rumelhart, and Huberman 1990; Sankar and Mammone 1991). Using existing knowledge to determine the connectivity presents a useful solution to this problem. The network structure can also be modified as a part of the learning process. More hidden units and connections can be added (e.g., Honavar and Uhr 1988) or removed (e.g., Kruschke 1988) during learning. Several algorithms for construction of neural networks are given by Gallant (1993).

The training scheme in the KBCNN model is based upon the backpropagation procedure developed by Rumelhart, Hinton, and Williams (1986) but modified under the above considerations. The training process involves two rounds of backpropagation. After the first round of backpropagation, the trained network then receives the following treatment in order to make each hidden unit carry different pattern information within a common layer. First, the input weights to each hidden unit are simplified by deleting small weights (e.g., the weights one or two orders of magnitude below the average). Then, the hidden units within the same layer are clustered on the basis of the similarity between their input weight vectors. The said similarity is based on $\cos \beta$ where β is the angle between two vectors. When this angle is zero, the two vectors point to the same direction in the vector space and are thus dependent. Using the Euclidean function as the distance measure is not justified. The clustering procedure is described below:

1. Start with no cluster. Incrementally scan the hidden units in a layer one by one.

2. Assign the first hidden unit to a new cluster.

3. For each of the remaining hidden units, find the most similar cluster, and then:

   - If the similarity between the unit's weight vector and the cluster's mean weight vector is greater than a threshold (e.g., 0.85), then update the latter vector with the former vector,

   - Else assign the hidden unit to a new cluster and initialize the cluster's mean weight vector with the unit's weight vector.

A new hidden unit with the average input weight vector and the average output weight vector will replace the hidden units in the same cluster within a layer. One exception is that predefined intermediate concepts shall not be removed. The clustering operation is followed by the second round of back-propagation, which completes the training process. The details of the KBCNN model for network training are given below.

The KBCNN Network Training Algorithm:

- **Weight Initialization**

  Weights are initialized according to the given domain knowledge formulated as rules.

- **Calculation of Activation**

  1. The activation level of an input unit is determined by the instance presented to the network.

  2. The activation level O_j of a hidden and output unit is determined by

  $$O_j = F_{\mathrm{CF}}(W_{j1}O_1, W_{j2}O_2, ..., -\theta_j)$$

  where W_{ji}'s and O_i's are input weights and inputs to unit j, respectively, θ_j is the threshold on the unit, and the function F_{CF} is the CF-based activation function. Another alternative is

  $$O_j = F(\sum W_{ji}O_i - \theta_j)$$

  where F is a sigmoid function.

- **The Learning Procedure**

  1. Backpropagation (adapted for the KBCNN model).
  2. Sparse transformation of the trained neural network by nullifying or deleting small weights.
  3. Clustering of hidden units.
  4. Backpropagation.

- **Weight Training in Backpropagation**

  1. Start at the output units and work backward to the hidden layers recursively. Adjust weights by

  $$W_{ji}(t+1) = W_{ji}(t) + \Delta W_{ji}$$

  where $W_{ji}(t)$ is the weight from unit i to unit j at iteration t and ΔW_{ji} is the weight adjustment.

  2. The weight change is computed by

  $$\Delta W_{ji} = \eta D_j \left(\frac{\partial O_j}{\partial W_{ji}} \right) - \zeta W_{ji}(t) \qquad (4.1)$$

  where η is a trial-independent learning rate, ζ is a weight-decay parameter ($\zeta = 0$ for knowledge-based connections), D_j is the discrepancy (error) between the actual and the desired output activation at unit j, and the term $\partial O_j / \partial W_{ji}$ is the partial derivative of O_j with respect to W_{ji}. Adding a momentum term is optional.

  3. The discrepancy is given by
     - For output units:
     $$D_j = T_j - O_j$$

     where T_j is the desired (target) output activation and O_j is the actual output activation at output unit j.
     - For hidden units:
     $$D_j = \sum_k \left(\frac{\partial O_k}{\partial O_j} \right) D_k$$

     where D_k is the discrepancy at unit k to which a connection points from hidden unit j. In the summation, each discrepancy D_k is weighted by the partial derivative of O_k with respect to O_j.

  4. Repeat iterations until stopping conditions are met.

  Recommended learning features:

  - Activation function: The CF-based function.
  - Weight range: Between -1 and 1.

- Activation range: Between -1 and 1. One exception is the case when an output unit receives no inhibitory connections, in which case the activation is confined to the interval [0, 1].

- Learning rate: Between 0.1 and 0.5 (tapered up to 0.005 if appropriate).

- Criterion function to be minimized: Sum of squared errors (or crossentropy).

- Stopping condition: The average mean squared error over the output units is less than 0.02 or converges to an asymptotic value with fluctuations less than 0.001.

The objective of the training algorithm is to make information more compactly encoded in hidden layers while preserving the network performance. In pruning the network, small weights are removed following the weight-decay procedure.[4] Therefore, the input weight vector of a hidden unit is determined by some instead of all attributes. This strategy is intended to make different hidden units encode noninteracting patterns. By favoring attributes with larger weights, the size of the attribute space in forming rules for each hidden concept is dramatically reduced.

Clustering of hidden units is the second strategy to prune the network. The combinatorial space of hidden units exponentially contracts as the number of hidden units decreases as a result of clustering. If there are too many initial hidden units, some will encode the same information. The clustering procedure reduces the likelihood of redundant encoding. On the other hand, clustering may cause nonconvergence because of an inadequate number of hidden units, especially in fine-grained mapping, but this would not be a problem if we allow more hidden units to be recruited if necessary.

4.4 Network Revision

A constantly raised question in neurocomputing is, "What are the semantics of connection weights induced by neural network learning procedures?" The semantics induced would depend on the kind of procedure applied. For backpropagation, two different views can be formulated. One view is the statistical regression model; the other is the rule-based (pattern-directed) learning model. Taking the latter view, we first define "semantically incorrect connections" and then describe how to refine rules on this basis in the following subsection.

---

[4] Weight decay is applied to hypothetical connections but not knowledge-based connections.

4.4.1   Semantically Incorrect Connections

The definition of semantically incorrect rules is given below:

Definition 1. Semantically incorrect rules are classified into three types. In the first type, a rule has a positive weight (strength), but its premise actually disconfirms its action. In the second type, a rule has a negative weight, but its premise actually confirms its action. In the third type, a rule has a positive or negative weight, but its premise neither confirms nor disconfirms its action.

In the RBCN model, a rule is mapped into a group of units and connections. A rule may be refined at the connection level rather than the rule level. For example, we wish to delete a condition from a rule rather than delete the whole rule. This consideration leads us to extend the above definition:

Definition 2. Semantically incorrect connections are classified into three types. In the first type, a connection has a positive weight, but its head node actually inhibits its tail node. In the second type, a connection has a negative weight, but its head node actually excites its tail node. In the third type, a connection has a positive or negative weight, but its head node neither excites nor inhibits its tail node.

The basic argument of the so-called consistent-shift algorithm is the following. A physical system at an equilibrium will tend to maintain that equilibrium when undergoing small perturbation. Likewise, when a neural network is moved away from an established optimum state, it will tend to restore (relax toward) that state. Suppose in a neural network that most of its connection weights are correct. Then, if we train the network with correct samples, the incorrect weights will be modified in the direction of minimizing their effect. As a result, the incorrect weights will move toward zero and even cross zero during training. Since this weight shift may be small quantitatively, it should be interpreted more qualitatively.

In the above, three types of semantically incorrect connections have been defined. Suppose we train the neural network with correct samples. We can expect the weight to shift toward zero and may cross zero in the first two types and to approach zero in the third type.

We are now in the position to introduce the notion of *consistent shift* for connection weights. If the absolute magnitude of a weight after training is greater than or equal to that of the weight before training and their signs are the same, then the weight shift is said to be semantically consistent with the weight before training; otherwise, the shift is inconsistent. The function *consistent-shift* is defined by

$$\text{Consistent-shift} = \begin{cases} w_a - w_b & \text{if } w_b > 0 \\ w_b - w_a & \text{if } w_b < 0 \\ |w_a - w_b| & \text{if } w_b = 0 \end{cases}$$

where w_a and w_b denote the weights after and before training, respectively. A shift of weight is said to be consistent if its consistent-shift value is greater than or equal to zero; else it is inconsistent.

Here is the definition based on the function of consistent-shift for semantically incorrect connections:

Definition 3. Let w_b, w_a, and w_{cs} stand for the weight before training, the weight after training, and the consistent-shift value of the weight, respectively. If $w_{cs} < 0$ and $|w_{cs}| \geq |w_b|$, then the weight before training is semantically incorrect.

The presence of inconsistent weight shifts does not necessarily imply that the weights concerned are semantically incorrect and vice versa. If the weight assigned to a semantically correct connection before training is overly high, an inconsistent weight shift may be observed after training. Thus, we define that a weight shift is inconsistent only if its consistent-shift value is less than a predetermined negative threshold. On the other hand, the weight shift of an incorrect connection may be less than expected. This is because the weights of correct connections will often be reinforced consistently in response to the effect of incorrect ones.

In an incremental learning scheme, the network is trained with sample instances one by one. The learning behavior of the network responding to a single instance is not so meaningful as responding to the sample instances as a whole. It is the knowledge gained through the process of generalization over the sample space that is significant. A correct weight may shift back and forth in the incremental process, resulting in a negligible overall shift. By contrast, an incorrect weight may shift largely in one direction, ending with a noticeable overall shift.

The above discussions lead to the following pragmatic rule for detecting semantically incorrect connections:

> If the consistent-shift value of a weight is less than a predefined negative threshold, then the weight shift is referred to as inconsistent, and it suggests that the pretraining weight is semantically incorrect.

A connection satisfying this rule and associated with an insignificant post-training weight is a good candidate for being deleted. However, empirical evaluation for each revision would be necessary.

Thus, revising the neural network includes the following steps:

1. Apply the backpropagation procedure until the system error converges on an asymptotic value.

2. Compute the consistent-shift value for each connection weight (excluding randomized weights).

3. Then:

- If the consistent-shift value is less than a selected negative threshold (e.g., -0.2), the absolute value of the posttraining weight is less than a selected positive threshold (e.g., 0.5), and deletion of the connection does not degrade the network performance by simulation, then delete it.

- Else, retain the connection.

Deletion of connections may bear different meanings. Deletion of a connection pointing from a conjunction unit to a disjunction unit means deletion of a rule (because the path between the rule's premise and the rule's consequent is cut), whereas deletion of a connection from a disjunction unit or an input unit to a conjunction unit corresponds to generalization of a rule (because removing an input connection from the conjunction unit makes the rule's premise more general). Likewise, addition of a connection pointing from a conjunction unit to a disjunction unit creates a rule, but addition of a connection from a disjunction unit or an input unit to a conjunction unit specializes a rule.

The complete algorithm for rule base refinement under the neural network approach is summarized as follows:

1. Map the rule base into a neural network.

2. Train the neural network by the backpropagation procedure on the training data.

3. Revise the trained neural network.

4. Translate the revised neural network into rules.

4.5 Issues

The level of the strength of the initial knowledge will affect our model design for revising the knowledge. If there is no knowledge at all, then we have to resort to a purely data-driven mode for learning. Namely, we build a multilayer neural network with full connectivity. If the initial knowledge is strong, then we can just map the knowledge into a neural network without adding extra hidden units and connections. In this case, computation is much easier, since no efforts are taken on searching for new rules and new concepts. If the knowledge is weak or incomplete, additional hidden units and connections should be added to the network as shown in Figure 4.2. In reality, however, we may not know how complete the initial knowledge is. If the initial knowledge fails to explain many instances, then we are inclined to think that the knowledge is weak. The level of completeness could be evaluated empirically. Yet, we need to know how many hidden units are deemed enough. Practically, this can be indicated by the error curve during training the network. Poor convergence reflects an inadequate number of hidden units.

When we map the given knowledge into a neural network, the initial topology and weight assignment accord with the knowledge. A target concept will be activated only under certain situations defined by the domain rules. Preserving intended initial semantics is crucial for keeping track of the revised knowledge. The semantics of a hidden unit is reflected by its input and output weight patterns (vectors). Even though the initial topology and weight assignment are based on the initial knowledge, the initial semantics may be lost or distorted due to information redistribution throughout the network during training. If a hidden unit mapped from a predefined concept totally changes its weight patterns after training, it would be necessary to rename the concept. It is also possible that a predefined concept shifts to another hidden unit or a concept splits or multiple concepts merge. Thus, it is desirable that a training scheme can conserve the intended semantics as much as possible. This issue has been found to be linked to the type of activation function employed by the neural network. In some knowledge-based neural networks, the sigmoid function is used, while in others, the activation function is derived from the model for combining belief values or certainty factors in expert systems. Empirically, we observed that the CF-based function tends to maintain more built-in semantics than the sigmoid function. In the latter case, when its slope gets steep, it becomes less predictable.

Another issue is the knowledge hierarchy. Intermediate-level abstraction can provide advantages in reasoning and explanation. However, improper introduction of intermediate concepts into the hierarchy may cause unnecessary increase of uncertainty and degradation of the system performance. It would be desirable to leave out those intermediate concepts and rules which undermine the system performance. The consistent-shift algorithm is suited for this purpose. On the basis of the vector change in weights after training, the algorithm hypothesizes which connections in the hierarchy can be deleted. A relevant question arises of how to test a new rule involving intermediate or hidden concepts against instances not described by such concepts. Again, we apply the consistent-shift algorithm to the rule to determine its acceptability.

4.6 Examples of Theory Revision

4.6.1 An Artificial Domain

Consider a domain with five binary-valued attributes, A1, A2, A3, A4, and A5, and three classes, C1, C2, and C3. We created eight mutually exclusive and exhaustive (covering all possible patterns) rules, which are shown in Table 4.1. We used this rule set to classify 32 possible input patterns into one of the three classes. Each input pattern along with its class formed a training instance. Since we had a complete set of instances, the amount of decision information they held was equivalent to that of the rule set. It was assumed that the rules were all correct and hence the instances generated. So, we had two equivalent

Table 4.1: The rule set used to generate the training samples.

Rule symbol	If-part	Then-part
R1	A1, A2, A3,	C1
R2	A1, A2, not A3	C2
R3	A1, not A2, A3	C2
R4	A1, not A2, not A3	C1
R5	not A1, A2, A3	C3
R6	not A1, A2, not A3	C1
R7	not A1, not A2, A3	C2
R8	not A1, not A2, not A3	C3

correct knowledge sources: One was rule-based, the other case-based. If we introduced errors into one knowledge source, the other knowledge source could be referenced in order to restore the integrity of that knowledge source. Using correct rules to revise the data is deductive, whereas using correct data to revise rules is inductive.

Next, we deliberately introduced various kinds of errors into the original rules and showed how the KBCNN model could revise them according to the training instances assumed correct. This arrangement was for experimental purpose and not for practical use since it has little meaning to perturb rules which are already correct.

It will be shown later that the rule set revised by the KBCNN model is in performance equivalent to the original rule set (i.e., able to accurately classify all the training instances) and also logically equivalent to the original rule set. In this experiment, we did not divide the samples into training and test sets because by so doing, the training data would not hold complete decision information for learning a complete set of decision rules. However, we will use the cross-validation strategy (training with a training data set and testing with a disjoint test data set) in the next example.

The correct domain knowledge was mapped into a two-layer RBCN with eight conjunction units. As shown in Table 4.2, the rule set was then perturbed in the following way:

- Addition of faulty rules, including R9 and R10

- Deletion of correct rules, including R4 and R8

- Qualitative change of correct rules, including R1 and R2: In rule R1, A3 was removed and A4, A5 were added; in rule R2, A2 was removed, A4, A5 were added, and the negation of A3 was reversed.

All these changes were mapped into the neural network by modifying weights.

Table 4.2: The perturbed rule set in the experiment.

Rule symbol	If-part	Then-part
R1	A1, A2, A4, A5	C1
R2	A1, A3, A4, A5	C2
R3	A1, not A2, A3	C2
R5	not A1, A2, A3	C3
R6	not A1, A2, not A3	C1
R7	not A1, not A2, A3	C2
R9	A1, A2, A4, A5	C3
R10	not A1, A2, A3	C1

Table 4.3: The training process. One iteration means one instance presentation to the neural network.

Iteration #	Error	Accuracy
0	0.383	50%
100	0.108	87.5%
200	0.037	100%
300	0.010	100%
400	0.0006	100%
500	0.0002	100%
600	0.00007	100%

For example, nullifying a weight is tantamount to deleting the corresponding connection, whereas increasing a weight above a certain threshold creates an effective connection.

The perturbed neural network was trained by the adapted backpropagation procedure (where the sigmoid logistic function was replaced with the CF-based activation function). As shown in Table 4.3, the training process converged rapidly. The end error was about zero.

The trained neural network was revised using the consistent-shift algorithm, resulting in a revised rule set. The consistent-shift value was computed for each connection weight, which is listed in Table 4.4 in increasing order of the value. We selected -0.2 as the tentative threshold for the consistent-shift value, so that if the value was less than -0.2, the pretraining weight was regarded as incorrect. Furthermore, we used 0.5 as the threshold for the posttraining weight, so that if the absolute weight was less than 0.5, the connection will not

Table 4.4: Consistent shift of the weights after training. "A←B" means a connection pointing from B to A.

Connection	Pretraining wts.	Posttraining wts.	Consistent shift
H2←A3	0.250	−1.000	−1.250
H7←A1	−1.000	−0.068	−0.932
C3←H1	0.500	0.003	−0.497
C1←H5	0.500	0.207	−0.293
H5←A1	−1.000	−0.733	−0.267
H2←A4	0.250	−0.003	−0.253
H2←A5	0.250	−0.002	−0.252
H1←A4	0.250	−0.002	−0.252
H1←A5	0.250	−0.002	−0.252
H8←A1	−1.000	−0.967	−0.033
H4←A3	−1.000	−0.985	−0.015
H6←A3	−1.000	−0.990	−0.010
H6←A1	−1.000	−0.994	−0.006
H4←A1	1.000	0.996	−0.004
H6←A2	1.000	0.998	−0.002
H4←A2	−1.000	−1.000	0.000
H7←A3	1.000	1.000	0.000
H3←A2	−1.000	−1.000	0.000
C2←H3	0.500	0.627	0.127
H1←A2	0.250	0.393	0.143
H2←A1	0.250	0.657	0.407
H3←A3	0.500	1.000	0.500
C1←H1	0.500	1.000	0.500
C2←H2	0.500	1.000	0.500
H5←A2	0.500	1.000	0.500
C2←H7	0.500	1.000	0.500
C3←H5	0.500	1.000	0.500
H3←A1	0.500	1.000	0.500
C1←H6	0.500	1.000	0.500
H5←A3	0.500	1.000	0.500
H1←A1	0.250	0.953	0.703
C1←H4	0.000	0.999	0.999
C3←H8	0.000	1.000	1.000
H1←A3	0.000	1.000	1.000
H2←A2	0.000	1.000	1.000

Table 4.5: The rule base revised by the KBCNN model.

Rule symbol	If-part	Then-part
R1	A1, A2, A3,	C1
R2	A1, A2, not A3	C2
R3	A1, not A2, A3	C2
R4	A1, not A2, not A3	C1
R5	not A1, A2, A3	C3
R6	not A1, A2, not A3	C1
R7	not A2, A3	C2
R8	not A1, not A2, not A3	C3

be translated in part or as a whole into a rule. The threshold of -0.2 appears to be a reasonable choice in the CF model. As shown in the table, there are nine incorrect pretraining weights, among which seven can be removed. In brief, the meanings of removing these connections are:

- Removing H7←A1: generalization of rule R7

- Removing C3←H1: deletion of rule R9

- Removing C1←H5: deletion of rule R10

- Removing H2←A4: generalization of rule R2

- Removing H2←A5: generalization of rule R2

- Removing H1←A4: generalization of rule R1

- Removing H1←A5: generalization of rule R1

Four new connections were recovered after training. They are the last four listed in the table. Their pretraining weights are 0 and posttraining weights are about 1. The meanings of these changes are:

- Adding C1←H4: addition of rule R4

- Adding C3←H8: addition of rule R8

- Adding H1←A3: specialization of rule R1

- Adding H2←A2: specialization of rule R2

Additionally, one connection weight changed its sign after training, i.e., H2←A3, which means that attribute A3 converts from a positive to a negative role in rule R2. The rule set revised by the KBCNN model is summarized in Table 4.5.

Table 4.6: A domain theory for promoters in terms of production rules (Towell, Shavlik, and Noordewier 1990).

R1	If contact, conformation	Then promoter
R2	If minus-35, minus-10	Then contact
R3	If @-37 "cttgac"	Then minus-35
R4	If @-36 "ttgxca"	Then minus-35
R5	If @-36 "ttgaca"	Then minus-35
R6	If @-36 "ttgac"	Then minus-35
R7	If @-14 "tataat"	Then minus-10
R8	If @-13 "taxaxt"	Then minus-10
R9	If @-13 "tataat"	Then minus-10
R10	If @-12 "taxxxt"	Then minus-10
R11	If @-45 "aaxxa"	Then conformation
R12	If @-45 "axxxa," @-4 "t" @-28 "txxxtxaaxxtx"	Then conformation
R13	If @-49 "axxxxt," @-1 "a" @-27 "txxxxaxxtxtg"	Then conformation
R14	If @-47 "caaxttxac," @-22 "gxxxtxc" @-8 "gcgccxcc"	Then conformation

The revised rule set can classify the training instances with 100 percent accuracy. Furthermore, the revised rule set is almost identical to the original rule set except that rule R7 is short of one attribute (i.e., A1) in the revised version. This is perfectly acceptable since revised R7 is simply a legitimate generalization of original R3 and R7. Thus, the revised rule set is logically equivalent to the original rule set.

4.6.2   A Real-World Problem

In this example, we demonstrate that the knowledge-based neural network KBCNN can effectively learn and revise the theory for recognizing promoters in DNA nucleotide strings. The data used were obtained from the public domain concerning machine learning. There are 106 instances in the data. Each instance consists of a DNA nucleotide string of four base types: A (adenine), G (guanine), C (cytosine), and T (thymine). The locations are specified relative to the site where transcription initiates. Fifty nucleotides before (minus) and six following (plus) this site describe an instance. Thus, each instance string is comprised of 57 sequential nucleotides. An instance is a positive instance if the promoter region is present in the string; else it is a negative instance. There are 53 positive instances and 53 negative instances.

Table 4.6 contains the initial domain theory for promoter recognition in the literature, as given by Towell, Shavlik, and Noordewier (1990). The theory is

Table 4.7: The promoter theory revised by KBCNN.

RR1	If minus-35, conformation	Then promoter
RR2	If minus-35, minus-10	Then promoter
RR3	If @-36 "tt"	Then minus-35
RR4	If @-36 "txga"	Then minus-35
RR5	If @-36 "txxxxa"	Then minus-35
RR6	If @-36 "txxac"	Then minus-35
RR7	If @-35 "tg"	Then minus-35
RR8	If @-34 "gxxa"	Then minus-35
RR9	If @-12 "a"	Then minus-10
RR10	If @-11 "a"	Then minus-10
RR11	If @-10 "a"	Then minus-10
RR12	If @-7 "t"	Then minus-10
RR13	If @-45 "aa"	Then conformation
RR14	If @-43 "t"	Then conformation

represented as a set of production rules (if-then rules). The first rule states that a promoter involves two regions called "contact" and "conformation." The second rule states that the contact region involves two regions: minus-35 and minus-10. The rest of the rules concern the string patterns for recognizing particular regions. In a string pattern, "x" denotes any nucleotide. In rule R4, for example, the string pattern specifies that the nucleotide at location -36, -35, -34, -33, -32, and -31 be $t\ t\ g\ x\ c\ a$, respectively.

Note that the initial theory fails to correctly classify any positive instance in the data base. This study was to demonstrate that (1) the KBCNN model can revise the initial theory in a way such that it can correctly classify all or most of the instances and (2) the model is able to generalize across different sets of samples (cross-validation).

The domain theory was mapped into a six-layer neural network (KBCNN) of 228 input units, 4 hidden units, 1 output unit, and 109 connections. The network was trained to classify the 106 instances with 100 percent accuracy, and then its knowledge was translated back into rules representing the revised theory shown in Table 4.7. The performance in terms of the error rate in classification of the given instances for the initial and the revised theories is 53/106 and 3/106, respectively. It is obvious that the revised theory improves considerably over the initial theory. However, there were three cases which cannot be explained by the revised theory without introducing new concepts into the hierarchy, accounting for the 3/106 error rate as shown. By adding new rules, the KBCNN model was actually able to revise the theory to achieve zero error rate (0/106).

How well the KBCNN approach revises the domain theory was further evaluated by cross-validation. An experimental methodology called "leave-one-out" was used. Leave-one-out (Fukunaga 1972) repeats n times given n instances (cases) each time, leaving one case out for testing and the rest for training. The average test error rate over n trials is the estimated error rate. Each instance was used as a test instance once. This procedure was repeated several times for different initial weight settings (though knowledge-based, they can be perturbed slightly).

For each leave-one-out experiment, we recorded the test performance of the trained neural network and the generated rule set. When we tested the performance of the rule set, there were two options. The first option was that we still ran the rule set using the neural network as the inference engine (a neural network noncategorical inference engine). The other option was that we used a categorical inference engine where rules were compared to the data base and were assumed with a certain ordering in terms of specificity and generality.

Among three initial weight settings tried, the best performance obtained in terms of the cross-validation error rate included: the neural network, $1/106$; the rules run by the neural network as the inference engine, $1/106$; the rules run by the categorical inference engine, $3/106$. The average performances were $2/106$, $2/106$, and $4/106$, respectively.

4.7   Decision Tree–Based Neural Networks

Brent (1991) indicated that a decision tree–based neural network is much faster than a fully connected backpropagation network. The topology of the network is determined by the decision tree, and therefore it is not necessary to specify the number of hidden units in advance.

As seen in Figure 4.3, the mapping strategy views each decision node in the tree as a hyperplane in the input space. Each leaf node corresponds to a decision region bounded by one or more hyperplanes. Thus, we can use the first layer of hidden units to implement these hyperplanes and use the second layer of hidden units to combine these hyperplanes to create decision regions. See the multilayer perceptron described in Chapter 2 "Basic Neural Computational Models."

Furthermore, since a hyperplane corresponds to the linear equation derived from the input weights and the threshold of a hidden unit, the knowledge about the hyperplanes (i.e., the decision nodes in the tree) can be applied to initialize the network weights. Gradient descent can be applied to train such a network if a smooth activation function is selected. The strategies of network training and revision described in previous sections would be as useful for a decision tree–based network as for a rule-based network.

In Chapter 14 "Rule Generation from Neural Networks," we will see that backpropagation neural networks can generate rules which outperform decision trees when the data are corrupted by noise. This result suggests that rule-based neural networks would be more advantageous than decision tree–based neural

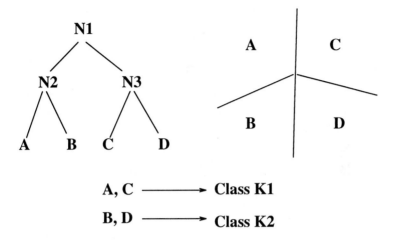

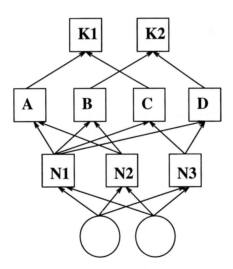

Figure 4.3: A neural network based on a decision tree.

networks if noise is present.

Decision Tree–Based Neural Networks

- Build a decision tree. For a discrete domain, each time select the best feature which minimizes the entropy criterion. For a continuous domain, each time select the best plane (hyperplane) which minimizes the entropy criterion.

- If the tree has m nonleaf nodes and n leaf nodes, then build a neural network with two hidden layers where the first hidden layer has m nodes and the second layer n nodes.

4.8 Constraint-Based Neural Networks

A neural network can also be constructed from semantic constraints. Each node designates a concept, and each connection encodes the relationship between two concepts. A positive weight signifies a supporting relationship, whereas a negative weight means an incompatible relationship.

In a constraint satisfaction network, three types of constraints can be identified as follows:

- Constraints between units: The absolute values of weights encoding these constraints reflect their magnitude.

- Direct constraints on individual units: These constraints are implemented as external, direct inputs to individual units. The external input serves to clamp the unit or modify its response.

- Constraints for prior information or probabilities: This type of constraint is implemented as a *bias* on each unit. In the absence of other evidence, a positive bias tends to turn a unit on, whereas a negative bias tends to shut it off.

Constraints that *must* be satisfied are referred to as *hard* constraints. For example, the external input clamping a unit is a hard constraint.

The constraint satisfaction problem is to seek a solution which satisfies as many given constraints as possible. Since, however, some constraints may be more important then others, constraints should be weighted appropriately. As suggested by McClelland and Rumelhart (1988), we can define the *goodness of fit (G)* value as the degree to which the desired constraints are satisfied by a solution:

$$G = \sum_j \sum_i W_{ji} O_i O_j + \sum_j I_j O_j + \sum_j B_j O_j \qquad (4.2)$$

where W_{ji} is the weight from unit i to unit j, O_j is the activation level of unit j, I_j is the external input to unit j, and B_j is the bias on unit j. In the above definition, the first term represents the degree to which the pairwise constraint between any two units is satisfied. If the weight is positive, presence of both hypotheses connecting by the weight will increase the G value, and presence of either hypothesis alone will decrease the value. The opposite is true if the weight is negative. The second term represents the degree of consistency between the external input and the actual activation of each unit. The G value is increased if the external input and the activation level are of the same sign; else it is decreased. The third term represents the influence of the bias on the unit. If the bias and the actual activation are consistent in their signs, the G value is increased; else it is reduced.

The constraint satisfaction problem is to find a solution which maximizes the G value as defined above. If we define the energy E of the system to be the negative of G, then we can apply the energy minimization procedure of the Hopfield net to find an optimal solution, as described in Chapter 2. The condition on the weight setting, $W_{ij} = W_{ji}$ and $W_{ii} = 0$, ensures that the network will reach a stable state. When this occurs, we say it has settled or relaxed to a solution. The energy minimization procedure seeks only a local optimum. Techniques like simulated annealing are needed for finding a global optimum solution.

If there is a large negative weight between two units and if these two units happen to be "on" initially, then this state will be discouraged when the network iterates seeking a solution. This causes a problem because the network may not leave either unit "on" and thus a desired solution may be missed. A solution to this problem is to update the states of units *asynchronously*. The asynchronous update rule will not allow more than one unit to update at a time. Thus, the two units will not inhibit each other simultaneously any more.

4.9 Summary

How to determine the neural network architecture (for example, the number of layers and the number of hidden units) is a major issue in neural computing. We have shown how to build a connectionist network based upon domain knowledge and extend it in a way such that it can learn new knowledge and revise old knowledge empirically. The initial domain theory determines the initial topology and connection weight assignments of such a network. The level of strength of the initial theory actually affects the model design. As the theory becomes weaker, more undefined hidden units and connections with randomized weights have to be added. How to preserve the initial intended semantics as much as possible is essential for keeping track of the revised theory. In this aspect, the choice of the network activation function is critical.

We have also shown how to decode the revised theory embedded in the neural network into the rule-based language. This capability is very important because without it we simply do not know what the revised theory looks like, despite the fact that the revised theory performs well in the network form.

4.10   References

1. Bradshaw, G., Fozzard, R., and Ceci, L. 1989. A connectionist expert system that really works. In *Advances in Neural Information Processing*, 2. Morgan Kaufmann, Palo Alto, CA.

2. Brent, R.P. 1991. Fast training algorithms for multilayer neural nets. *IEEE Transactions on Neural Networks*, 2(3), pp. 346–354.

3. Buchanan, B.G., and Shortliffe, E.H. 1984. *Rule-Based Expert Systems*. Addison-Wesley, Reading, MA.

4. Cun, Y.Le, Denker, J.S., and Solla, S.A. 1989. Optimal brain damage. In *Advances in Neural Information Processing Systems*, 2. Morgan Kaufmann, Palo Alto, CA.

5. Drucker, H., and Cun, Y.Le. 1991. Double backpropagation increasing generalization performance. In *Proceedings of IJCNN-91* (Seattle), pp. II-145-150.

6. Fisher, D.H., and McKusick, K.B. 1989. An empirical comparison of ID3 and back-propagation. In *Proceedings of IJCAI-89* (Detroit), pp. 788–793.

7. Fu, L.M., and Fu, L.C. 1990. Mapping rule-based systems into neural architecture. *Knowledge-Based Systems*, 3(1), pp. 48–56.

8. Fu, L.M. 1992. Knowledge base refinement by backpropagation. In *Data and Knowledge Engineering*, 7, pp. 35–46.

9. Fu, L.M. 1993. Knowledge-based connectionism for revising domain theories. *IEEE Transactions on Systems, Man, and Cybernetics*, 23(1), pp. 173–182.

10. Fukunaga, K. 1972. *Introduction to Statistical Pattern Recognition*. Academic Press, New York.

11. Gallant, S.I. 1988. Connectionist expert systems. *Communications of the ACM*, 31(2), pp. 152–169.

12. Gallant, S. 1993. *Neural Network Learning and Expert Systems*. MIT Press, Cambridge, MA.

13. Hall, L.O., and Romaniuk, S.G. 1990. A hybrid connectionist, symbolic learning system. In *Proceeding of AAAI-90* (Boston), pp. 783–788.

14. Hinton, G.E. 1989. Connectionist learning procedures. *Artificial Intelligence*, 40, pp. 185–234.

15. Honavar, V., and Uhr, L. 1988. A network of neuronlike units that learns to perceive by generation as well as reweighing of links. In *Proceedings of Connectionist Models Summer School*, pp. 472–484.

16. Kruschke, J. 1988. Creating local and distributed bottlenecks in hidden layers of back-propagation networks. In *Proceedings of Connectionist Models Summer School*, pp. 357–370.

17. Lacher, R.C., Hruska, S.I., and Kuncicky, D.C. 1992. Back-propagation learning in expert networks. *IEEE Transactions on Neural Networks*, 3(1), pp. 62–72.

18. McClelland, J.L., and Rumelhart, D.E. 1988. *Explorations in Parallel Distributed Processing*. MIT Press, Cambridge, MA.

19. Mitchell, T.M., Keller, R.M., and Kedar-Cabelli, S.T. 1986. Explanation-based generalization: A unifying view. *Machine Learning* 1(1), pp. 47–80.

20. Mooney, R., Shavlik, J., Towell, G., and Gove, A. 1989. An experimental comparison of symbolic and connectionist learning algorithms. In *Proceedings of IJCAI-89* (Detroit), pp. 775–780.

21. Quinlan, J.R. 1983. Learning efficient classification procedures and their application to chess end games. In *Machine Learning*. Tioga, Palo Alto, CA.

22. Rueckl, J., Cave, K., and Kosslyn, S. 1988. Why are "what" and "where" processed by separate cortical visual systems? *Journal of Cognitive Neuroscience*, 1(2).

23. Rumelhart, D.E., Hinton, G.E., and Williams, R.J. 1986. Learning internal representation by error propagation. In *Parallel Distributed Processing: Explorations in the Microstructures of Cognition*, Vol. 1. MIT Press, Cambridge, MA.

24. Sankar, A., and Mammone, R. 1991. Optimal pruning of neural tree networks for improved generalization. In *Proceedings of IJCNN-91* (Seattle), pp. II-219–224.

25. Towell, G.G., Shavlik, J.W., and Noordewier, M.O. 1990. Refinement of approximate domain theories by knowledge-based neural networks. In *Proceeding of AAAI-90* (Boston), pp. 861–866.

26. Wada, Y., and Kawato, M. 1991. Estimation of generalization capability by combination of new information criterion and cross-validation. In *Proceedings of IJCNN-91* (Seattle), pp. II-1–6.

27. Weigand, A.S., Rumelhart, D.E., and Huberman, B.A. 1990. Generalization by weight elimination with application to forecasting. In *Advances in Neural Information Processing Systems*, 3. Morgan Kaufmann, Palo Alto, CA.

28. Whitley, D., and Karunanthi, N. 1991. Generalization in feedforward neural networks. In *Proceedings of IJCNN-91* (Seattle), pp. II-77–82.

29. Yang, Q., and Bhargava, V.K. 1990. Building expert systems by a modified perceptron network with rule-transfer algorithms. In *Proceedings of IJCNN-90* (San Diego), pp. II-77–82.

4.11   Problems

1. A rule-based system has the following rules:

   If $A = 1$, $B = 1$, and $C = 1$, Then $M = 1$.
   If $A \neq 1$, $B = 0$, and $C = 1$, Then $M = 2$.
   If $D = 1$ and $E = 0$, Then $N = 1$.
   If $M = 1$ and $N = 1$, Then $X = 1$.
   If $M = 2$ and $N = 1$, Then $X = 1$.

   Variables A and M assume three possible values, 0, 1, 2, and all other variables are binary, 0 or 1.

   (a) Design a rule-based neural network based on the above rules.

   (b) Initialize the connection weights when the CF-based activation function is adopted. What if each rule is attached with a CF?

   (c) Initialize the connection weights when the sigmoid activation function is used.

2. A decision tree is given below:

   ```
                 A = 1
            yes/        \no
         B + 2C > 4      Class X
         yes/   \no
      Class X   Class Y
   ```

   (a) Build a neural network based on this decision tree.

    (b) Can the neural network handle arbitrary decision regions? Discuss the difference between a sigmoid and a hard-limiting function as the activation function.

3. Describe two ways in which the rule-based neural network performs generalization.

4. The rule-based neural network often handles continuous attributes by partitioning them into multiple ranges, each encoded by an input node.

    (a) Describe a method to determine which partition scheme is better. (Hint: Use the entropy criterion.)

    (b) Is there any other alternative to handle continuous attributes?

5. Among a set of variables, some are positively correlated and some are negatively correlated. Given the values of some variables, we wish to predict those of other variables. Design a neural network to solve this type of problem.

Chapter 5

Incremental Learning

5.1 Introduction

A learning system updates its hypotheses (or knowledge) when all available instances are seen or when an instance arrives. The latter strategy is referred to as *incremental learning*. Some machine learning systems process instances incrementally in one iteration and return to the first instance in the next iteration. In this case, learning is not really incremental. Therefore, a more specific definition of incremental learning is that the learning system updates its hypotheses as a new instance arrives without reviewing old instances. In other words, an incremental-learning system learns Y based on X, then learns Z based on Y, and so on.

It is a significant advantage for a learning system to acquire knowledge incrementally. An incremental-learning system is spatially economical and temporally efficient, since it need not store and reprocess old instances. Incremental learning is especially important for a learning system which continually receives input, since the system cannot wait for all instances to be available for learning. Moreover, one may argue that this learning mode is biologically plausible.

In symbolic learning systems, the version space approach (Mitchell 1978) is a good example of incremental learning. It encodes instance information in the version space and incrementally updates it. COBWEB (Fisher 1987) uses an incremental technique to build a classification hierarchy by conceptual clustering. On the other hand, ID3 (Quinlan 1983) based on the decision tree approach is not incremental. Although one can modify the tree incrementally by patchwork, the tree gradually loses its role of being the most efficient and representative in classification.

In the neural network approach, incremental learning again is a major issue for research. Not all neural network models are incremental. For example, despite its usefulness, the backpropagation network is not incremental. This network model will forget old instances if they do not join the training with new instances. The adaptive resonance theory (ART) of Carpenter and Grossberg (1988) suggests how to learn incrementally. In the ART approach, if a novel input pattern fails to match stored patterns within the tolerance imposed by the vigilance level (the vigilance parameter), a new cluster will be formed. The ART architecture proves quite capable of performing adaptive pattern recognition and clustering.

In the remaining sections, we first examine the fundamental principles of designing an incremental-learning system, review symbolic methods for incremental learning, discuss the neural network approach to this problem, and then describe rule-based connectionist networks with incremental-learning capability.

5.2   Fundamental Principles

How can a learning system discard old examples without forgetting them? An obvious answer is that the system must have a mechanism or device to store the information of old examples. Ideally, the stored information is equivalent to the actual information. In memory-based learning, the system simply stores every example encountered. This solution is expensive and does not actually abandon the examples. Moreover, memory-based learning does not address the issue of generalization, though it does provide some kind of inference, such as case-based reasoning, or nearest neighborhood. As such, it is not considered further.

In general, the information stored in a learning system is a generalization or abstraction of the actual information embedded in the examples. Thus, the stored information implies the actual information, but the reverse is not necessarily true. The stored information represents the current knowledge learned by the system. When learning is completed, it is hoped that the stored information (i.e., the learned knowledge) is equivalent to the true domain information. That is, the knowledge can apply to every example (seen and unseen) in the domain correctly.

In order to learn incrementally, the system should possess an information structure which can be updated incrementally (see Figure 5.1). This structure is referred to as an *incrementable information structure* (IIS). An IIS should conserve the information of examples as much as possible so that future updating can be constrained by this information. Therefore, it is important to store both first-order (information concerning individual variables or attributes) and high-order information (information concerning the interaction among variables or attributes).

Two general principles can be extracted from existing learning systems claimed to be incremental:

- The system uses an IIS to hold and update its knowledge, for instance, the version space, the concept hierarchy in COBWEB, the information

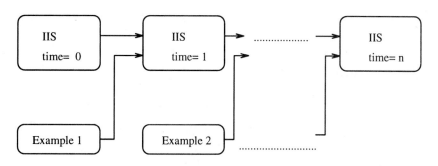

Figure 5.1: An incrementable information structure (IIS).

conservation scheme in LAIR (Elio and Watanabe 1991), and the rough set in FLORA (Kubat 1991).

- The system uses the principle of "minimal change" (i.e., change as minimal as possible) to revise its knowledge upon the arrival of a new example, for instance, the least-commitment strategy in the version space approach and the strategy of altering only the relevant nodes in the concept hierarchy in COBWEB.

A system may apply one or two of the above strategies for incremental learning. Initial knowledge can further constrain the incremental-learning process and will thus be important as well. Katsuno and Mendelzon (1991) examine the issue of minimal change in knowledge base revision in a theoretical framework.

In the design of an IIS, two observations on current systems can be made as follows:

- Probabilities are useful for storing information. Bayesian learning is a well-known method for incremental learning. In COBWEB, each node in the hierarchy is described by probabilistic information. Higgins and Goodman (1991) use probabilities as weights in their incremental-learning scheme.

- Clustering is a useful technique for incrementally acquiring new concepts, as demonstrated by the ART network. COBWEB learns new concepts through a technique known as *conceptual clustering* (see Chapter 8 "Discovery" for the definition).

5.3   Symbolic Methods

In this section, we examine several symbolic learning programs which address
the issue of incremental learning.

5.3.1   Version Spaces

The version space approach developed by Mitchell (1978) could be the first
work which adequately handles the issue of incremental learning. The version
space implements the so-called IIS, which performs generalization but at the
same time conserves the information of examples. Some earlier work may touch
this issue but involves no notion similar to the IIS. The version space algorithm
is described in Chapter 3 "Learning: Supervised and Unsupervised." Here, we
only focus on its ability of incremental learning.

The version space algorithm is designed to learn a single concept. The
version space contains all possible concept descriptions consistent with the
examples seen so far. The boundaries of the version space are modified
incrementally according to whether the new instance is a positive instance (an
example of the concept to be learned) or a negative instance (a counterexample).

Suppose the goal is to learn multiple concepts or disjunctive concepts. The
version space should be changed so that it can represent multiple concepts.
Equivalently, there should be multiple version spaces, each for a single concept.
In this situation, the learner should reason about which version space to
update for a given new instance. So, not only representation but also learning
gets much more complex than before. A similar approach can be taken
to handle an inconsistent set of examples. In this case, a version space is
created for each consistent subset of examples. Even though the version space
approach can be modified to learn incrementally (without backtracking) under
these circumstances, the algorithm may become intractable and the result be
nonoptimal.

5.3.2   COBWEB

COBWEB (Fisher 1978) is an algorithm for incremental concept formation.
In this algorithm, concepts are built as a hierarchy with more general nodes
higher in the hierarchy. Terminal nodes are always specific instances. Each
concept node in the hierarchy is described by the probabilities associated with
the concept and its attribute values. The probability of a concept is specified
relative to its parent (i.e., given that its parent concept is true). The probability
of an attribute value V for a concept C is the conditional probability $P(V|C)$.
The concept hierarchy is illustrated in Figure 5.2. As in many other learning
programs, each instance is represented as a set (conjunction) of attribute-value
pairs.

As formulated below, COBWEB interweaves classification with learning: If
it cannot classify, then it learns. The system initializes the hierarchy to a single

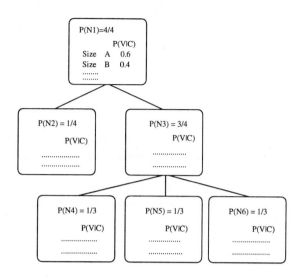

Figure 5.2: The concept hierarchy in the COBWEB system.

node on the basis of the first instance. Then, it sorts a new instance down
the concept hierarchy and alters the hierarchy in its passage. At a concept
node, COBWEB considers several alternatives in placing a new instance. These
alternatives include placing the instance in one of the child nodes of the
concept, creating a new node based on the instance, merging two child nodes,
and splitting a child node into two. The process is recursive in nature. It
proceeds until the new instance is settled in the hierarchy. While this is
reminiscent of divisive hierarchical clustering (top-down splitting), COBWEB
departs from this clustering scheme by allowing merging concepts (or clusters)
and processing instances one by one.

The COBWEB Algorithm

1. Initialize the concept hierarchy to a single node based on the first instance.

2. For every new instance, sort it down the concept hierarchy. At the
   current node, update its probabilistic information according to the current
   instance. If the node is a terminal node, then create two new terminal
   nodes under it, one based on the current instance and the other on the
   node before updating. Otherwise, calculate the score of:

- Placing the current instance in it for each of its child nodes
- Creating a new child node based on the instance
- Merging two child nodes with highest scores
- Splitting the child node with the highest score

Choose the alternative with the highest score from the above list.

3. Repeat step 2 until the current instance is settled in the hierarchy.

Merging two nodes: Creating a common parent node on top of them.
Splitting a node: Deleting the node and promoting its children one level up.

Suppose we call a set of clusters (concepts) with a common parent concept a *clustering*. COBWEB uses the following function to score (evaluate) the quality of a clustering for a parent concept:

$$\sum_k \sum_i \sum_j P(A_i = V_{ij})P(C_k|A_i = V_{ij})P(A_i = V_{ij}|C_k) \qquad (5.1)$$

where V_{ij} is the jth value for the attribute A_i and C_k is the kth cluster (concept). Via Bayes' rule, the above function can be transformed into

$$\sum_k P(C_k)\sum_i \sum_j P(A_i = V_{ij}|C_k)^2 \qquad (5.2)$$

This evaluation function reflects how well a concept can predict a certain attribute value and how well an attribute value can predict a concept. From this function, Gluck and Corter (1985) derives the following function which can compare clusterings with different numbers of categories (clusters):

$$\frac{\sum_{k=1}^K P(C_k)\sum_i \sum_j P(A_i = V_{ij}|C_k)^2 - \sum_i \sum_j P(A_i = V_{ij})^2}{K} \qquad (5.3)$$

where K is the number of clusters. This function uses the case of a single cluster as a baseline control and divides the gained merit by K. The program CLASSIT (Gennari, Langley, and Fisher 1989), which uses real-valued attributes in both instances and concepts, revises the above function into

$$\frac{\sum_{k=1}^K P(C_k)\sum_i^I 1/\sigma_{ik} - \sum_i^I 1/\sigma_{ip}}{K} \qquad (5.4)$$

where I is the number of attributes, σ_{ik} is the standard deviation for a given attribute in a given cluster, and σ_{ip} is the standard deviation for a given attribute in the parent node.

The ability of incremental learning in the COBWEB system can be ascribed to the use of a probabilistic structure which is incrementable. The concept hierarchy along with the contained probabilistic information constitutes an IIS.

5.3.3 Decision Tree Approaches

ID3 is the most representative work for the decision tree approach to machine learning. Its algorithm is described in Chapter 3. Because of ID3's nonincremental nature, research has been conducted to improve it in this respect. For example, ID4 (Schlimmer and Fisher 1986) maintains attribute-value and class counts at each node in the tree and uses this information to find the best attribute for splitting without reexamining the examples. ID5 (Utgoff 1988) saves examples and can reconfigure the tree structure by pulling up an attribute from below and recalculating attribute-value and class counts. By using the statistical information stored locally, some incremental change can be made at local sites. However, it appears unlikely to change the fundamental structure of the tree without reviewing old examples. Even change can be made incrementally; the tree may no longer be optimal. Adding a perceptron to the tree does not solve the problem, since the perceptron algorithm is not incremental.

5.4 Neural Network Approaches

Different neural network paradigms employ different learning rules to conduct generalization or extract statistical properties from a set of training examples. Quite often, a learning rule is advantageous in one aspect but disadvantageous in another. Backpropagation, for example, proves to be very useful for many problems, but it requires long computation time, is nonincremental in nature, and is prone to converge to local minima.

Recently, several neural network algorithms have emerged with emphasis on quick learning (or training). Two such examples are the probabilistic neural network (PNN) and the polynomial adaline developed by Specht (1990). Both methods involve one-pass learning algorithms (i.e., each instance needs to be presented to the neural network only once), in contrast to multipass backpropagation learning. Therefore, they can be orders of magnitude faster than backpropagation in training. Also, these two methods, based on the Bayes strategy, can avoid local optima. Although the polynomial adaline is derived from the PNN, the former can learn incrementally but the latter cannot. One should note that it is not the use of probabilities alone that "sufficiently" determines the capability of incremental learning. The incrementable information structure is all that is important.

A neural network which learns incrementally is well exemplified by the ART network. This network algorithm is described in Chapter 3 and hence omitted here.

In this section, we examine the PNN, the polynomial adaline, and the cascade correlation learning network and discuss what are essential network features for incremental learning.

5.4.1 Probabilistic Neural Networks

We start with the Bayes strategy for pattern classification. The Bayes decision rule is the rule that selects the category with minimum conditional risk. In the case of minimum-error-rate classification, the rule will select the category with the maximum posterior probability. Suppose there are c classes, $\omega_1, \omega_2, .., \omega_c$. Given a feature vector $\mathbf{x}$, the minimum-error-rate rule will assign it to ω_i if

$$P(\omega_i|\mathbf{x}) > P(\omega_j|\mathbf{x}) \text{ for all } i \neq j$$

Here, the posterior probability is used as the discriminant function. An alternative choice of the discriminant function to achieve the minimum-error rate is

$$P(\mathbf{x}|\omega_i)P(\omega_i)$$

Note that the risk factor can be incorporated into the function for consideration.

For every category c, let us define the probability density function (PDF) as follows:

$$f_c(\mathbf{x}) = P(\mathbf{x}|c)$$

We can use a set of training examples to estimate $f_c(\mathbf{x})$ for each category. Then, the Bayes (optimum) decision can be made based on these PDFs in conjunction with prior probabilities.

Parzen (1962) shows that a smooth and continuous density function can be approximated asymptotically by a class of PDF estimators. From this idea, Specht (1990) developed a particular estimator for the class PDF on the basis of training examples:

$$f_c(\mathbf{x}) = \frac{1}{(2\pi)^{d/2}\sigma^d} \frac{1}{m} \sum_{i=1}^{m} \exp[-(\mathbf{x} - \mathbf{X}_{ci}) \cdot (\mathbf{x} - \mathbf{X}_{ci})/2\sigma^2] \qquad (5.5)$$

where

$d = $ the dimension
$m = $ the total number of training patterns (examples)
$\sigma = $ a smoothing parameter
$\mathbf{X}_{ci} = $ the ith pattern from category c

Thus, $f_c(\mathbf{x})$ is the sum of Gaussian distributions centered at each training pattern. Note that the sum can approximate any smooth density function not limited to a Gaussian.

In the PNN, each training pattern $\mathbf{X}_{ci}$ is encoded as the input weight vector of unit i called a *pattern* unit. That is, $\mathbf{X}_{ci} = \mathbf{W}_i$. Thus, the net input to unit i is $z_i = \mathbf{x} \cdot \mathbf{W}_i$. Assume that both $\mathbf{x}$ and $\mathbf{W}_i$ are normalized to unit length. With some substitutions, Eq. 5.5 can be transformed into

$$f_c(\mathbf{x}) = \frac{1}{(2\pi)^{d/2}\sigma^d} \frac{1}{m} \sum_{i=1}^{m} \exp[(z_i - 1)/\sigma^2] \qquad (5.6)$$

This derivation suggests the design of the PNN (as shown in Figure 5.3) where the activation function of a pattern unit is defined to be

$$F(z) = \exp[(z - 1)/\sigma^2] \qquad (5.7)$$

It is clear that the PNN is not designed to be an incremental learner since old examples are represented explicitly in the network. Every new example demands the modification of the network architecture by the addition of another pattern unit and associated connections. The PNN (Specht 1990) is summarized below.

The Probabilistic Neural Network

- **Basic Structures**

    - Three layers: a layer of input units, a layer of pattern units, and a layer of output units.
    - There is one-to-one correspondence between pattern units and training examples. So, pattern units are equal to training examples in numbers.
    - Each output unit corresponds to a class (category).
    - A pattern unit connects to an output unit if and only if the corresponding example is labeled the corresponding class.

- **Weight Initialization**

    - The input weight vector of pattern unit i is initialized to the ith pattern (example) vector, which is normalized to unit length.
    - The input weight vector of every output unit is initialized to a vector of all 1s.

- **Calculation of Activation**

    1. The activations of input units are determined by the pattern (example) presented to the network. The input vector is normalized to unit length.
    2. The activation O_j of pattern unit j is given by

    $$O_j = \exp[(\sum_i W_{ji} X_i - 1)/\sigma^2]$$

    where W_{ji} is the connection weight from input unit i to pattern unit j, and X_i is the activation of input unit i.

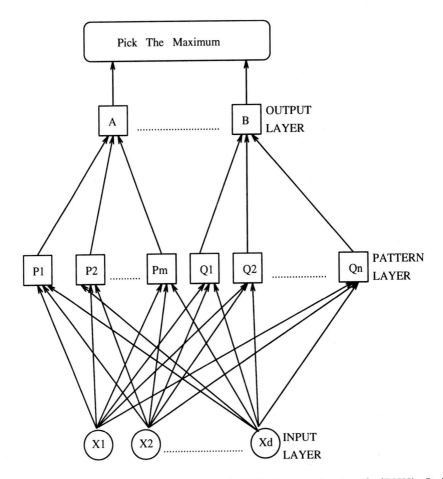

Figure 5.3: The architecture of the probabilistic neural network (PNN). It is constituted by three layers: the input, the pattern, and the output layers. Each pattern (example) is encoded by a pattern unit where a nonlinear activation function is used for smoothing out individual information. An output unit integrates information over pattern units encoding examples from the category designated by the output unit. As a whole, the network implements the Bayes decision surface.

3. The activation O_j of output unit j is given by

$$O_j = \frac{1}{m} P(\omega_j) \sum_i W_{ji} O_i$$

where W_{ji} is the connection weight from pattern unit i to output unit j, m is the number of training examples labeled class ω_j which corresponds to output unit j, and $P(\omega_j)$ is the prior probability of ω_j.

4. The decision of the network is the class corresponding to the output unit with the maximum activation.

- **Network Learning**

    - The weights are nonadjustable.
    - When a new example arrives, a new pattern unit is added and the associated weights are initialized as stated above

5.4.2   Polynomial Adalines

The polynomial adaline implements a general polynomial obtained through a Taylor's series expansion of the PNN decision boundary. The polynomial can asymptotically approach continuous Bayes-optimal decision surfaces. The coefficients of the polynomial can be calculated based on the training examples and can be incrementally updated on a one-pattern-at-a-time basis. These coefficients are directly mapped into connection weights in the neural network shown in Figure 5.4. The transformation of the PNN into the polynomial adaline is an example of the functional-link approach described in Chapter 6 "Mathematical Modeling."

Let

$$\mathbf{x} = [x_1, x_2, ..., x_d]$$

and

$$\mathbf{X_{ci}} = [x_{ci,1}, x_{ci,2}, ..., x_{ci,d}]$$

(Recall that X_{ci} is the ith pattern from category c.) Using the Taylor's series expansion, Eq. 5.5 can be written as

$$f_c(\mathbf{x}) = \frac{1}{(2\pi)^{d/2}\sigma^d} \exp(-\mathbf{x} \cdot \mathbf{x}/2\sigma^2) P_c(\mathbf{x}) \tag{5.8}$$

where

$$P_c(\mathbf{x}) = W_{c,0...0} + W_{c,10...0} x_1 + ... + W_{c,20...0} x_1^2 + ... + W_{c,k1k2...kd} x_1^{k1} x_2^{k2} ... x_d^{kd} + ...$$
$$\tag{5.9}$$

and

$$W_{c,k1k2...kd} = \frac{1}{k1!k2!...kd!\sigma^{2h}} \frac{1}{m} \sum_{i=1}^{m} X_{ci,1}^{k1} X_{ci,2}^{k2}...X_{ci,d}^{kd} \exp(B_{ci}/\sigma^2) \qquad (5.10)$$

where

$$h = \sum_{j=1}^{d} k_j, \quad B_{ci} = -1/2\mathbf{X}_{ci} \cdot \mathbf{X}_{ci}$$

When the ith example arrives, the coefficients (weights) of the polynomial are updated incrementally by

$$W_{c,k1k2...kd}(i) = [(i-1)/i]W_{c,k1k2...kd}(i-1) + \Delta W_{c,k1k2...kd}(i) \qquad (5.11)$$

where $W_{c,k1k2...kd}(i)$ is the coefficient (weight) after i examples are seen and

$$\Delta W_{c,k1k2...kd}(i) = \frac{1}{k1!k2!...kd!i\sigma^{2h}} X_{ci,1}^{k1} X_{ci,2}^{k2}...X_{ci,d}^{kd} \exp(B_{ci}/\sigma^2) \qquad (5.12)$$

The polynomial adaline can be adapted to follow nonstationary statistics. In a time-varying situation, the effect of a sample gradually decays over time. In this case, the coefficients of the polynomial are updated according to

$$W_{c,k1k2...kd}(i) = [(\tau-1)/\tau]W_{c,k1k2...kd}(i-1) + \Delta W_{c,k1k2...kd}(i) \qquad (5.13)$$

where τ is the time constant of the decay function measured in examples rather than in units of time and

$$\Delta W_{c,k1k2...kd}(i) = \frac{1}{k1!k2!...kd!\tau\sigma^{2h}} X_{ci,1}^{k1} X_{ci,2}^{k2}...X_{ci,d}^{kd} \exp(B_{ci}/\sigma^2) \qquad (5.14)$$

The polynomial adaline is an IIS because its connection weights can be updated incrementally without reexamining old examples. More specifically, instance information is encoded in the coefficients of the polynomial function, and the coefficients can be modified incrementally. The storage requirement increases only linearly with the number of coefficients used. In contrast, the PNN must store training examples. The polynomial adaline network (Specht 1990) is summarized below.

The Polynomial Adaline Network

- **Basic Structures**

  - Two layers: a layer of input units and a layer of output units.
  - Inputs are expanded by introducing high-order terms.

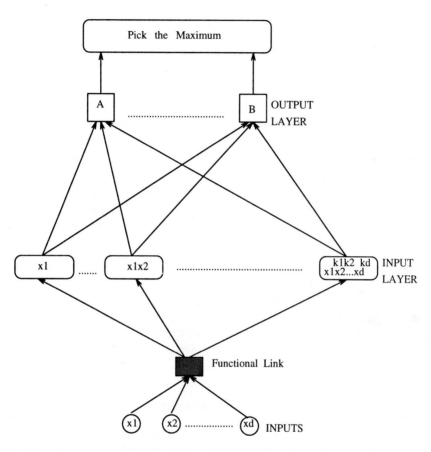

Figure 5.4: The architecture of the polynomial adaline. It has two layers: the enhanced input and the output layers. Original inputs are transformed based upon a polynomial function. Smoothing properties are built into the connection weights mapped directly from the polynomial coefficients. The polynomial adaline implements a polynomial decision boundary asymptotically, approximating the Bayes decision surface.

- **Weight Initialization**
  According to Eq. 5.10.

- **Calculation of Activation**

  1. The activations of input units are determined by the example presented to the network.

  2. The activation O_j of output unit j is given by

  $$O_j = P(\omega_j) \sum_i W_{ji} O_i$$

  where O_i is the activation of input unit i after expansion and $P(\omega_j)$ is the prior probability of class ω_j corresponding to output unit j.

  3. The decision is the class corresponding to the output unit with the maximum activation.

- **Weight Training**
  According to Eq. 5.11, or Eq. 5.13 in the case of nonstationary statistics.

Because individual instance information is smoothed out through the use of a smoothing parameter (σ in Eq. 5.10), the number of coefficients used in the polynomial can approach the number of training examples with little danger of overfitting the data. Note that the smoothing mechanism is also part of the PNN.

5.4.3 Cascade Correlation Learning

The cascade correlation algorithm of Fahlman and Lebiere (1990) is able to construct a multilayer, feedforward neural network incrementally and dynamically. It starts with a minimal network consisting only of an input and an output layer and then automatically adds and trains hidden units if the output error exceeds a predefined level. The term "cascade" is used because hidden units are added one at a time and do not change once added. Each hidden unit creates a new hidden layer placed just beneath the output layer. A new hidden unit receives trainable input connections from all the input units and from all preexisting hidden units, and is connected to the output units.

For each new hidden unit, the magnitude of the *correlation* between the new unit's activation level and the residual output error to be maximized is given by

$$\sum_j | \sum_p (H_p - \overline{H})(E_{j,p} - \overline{E_j})|$$

where $E_{j,p}$ and H_p are, respectively, the error at output unit j and the activation level of the hidden unit in instance p. The quantities $\overline{E_j}$ and $\overline{H}$ are the values averaged over all instances. The weight adjustment is derived as in the case of the backpropagation rule.

When a new hidden unit is added to the network, weight training proceeds as follows:

1. Train the input weights of the hidden unit while disconnecting it from the output units. The objective is to maximize the correlation defined above between the hidden unit's activation level and the residual output error.

2. Connect the hidden unit with the output units, freeze its input weights, and train the weights between the hidden unit and the output units.

Because the input weights of a hidden unit are frozen once it is incorporated into the network, learning only involves a single layer and requires no backpropagation of error signals and is hence fast.

It should be noted that incremental network construction does not imply incremental learning as defined in the beginning. Yet, an incremental-learning network may involve incremental network construction.

5.5   The Incremental RBCN

The success of ART motivates the idea of integrating adaptive resonance into the rule-based connectionist framework for incremental learning. The architecture so obtained is called an *incremental rule-based connectionist network* (IRBCN), which is depicted in Figure 5.5. The details of this model along with its design philosophy are described next.

The main idea behind this model is to add an additional layer for conducting resonance analysis.   Let us call this layer a *cluster layer* since its function is "cluster analysis" of the input patterns.   The winner-take-all strategy (a competitive learning strategy) is implemented so that the cluster node with strongest activation will shut down all the other cluster nodes. That node which solely remains active denotes the cluster assigned to the input instance. Since instances in the same cluster should bear similarities, the weights should be set in such a way that similar instances will activate the same cluster. This task is a kind of unsupervised learning since there is no cluster label for each training instance.

The IRBCN is an incremental version of the RBCN described in Chapter 4 "Knowledge-Based Neural Networks." The initial rule-based knowledge may be derived from a set of instances using a nonincremental-learning strategy. Once the incremental-learning mode is activated, the old instances are no longer used.

To make description easier, we assume that the original rule-based connectionist network has three layers, and thus its incremental version has four

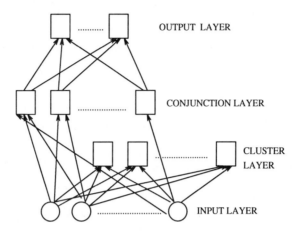

Figure 5.5: The incremental rule-based connectionist network (IRBCN).

layers. However, the network can have more layers, depending on the depth of the rule hierarchy. These four layers are the input, the conjunction, the cluster, and the output layers.

The initial architecture of an IRBCN is built out of an RBCN by introducing a new layer, the cluster layer, and connecting it with the input layer of the RBCN. Since each class of instances can have one or more clusters, initially we put the same number of nodes in the cluster layer as in the output layer. Each output node designates one class, and a cluster node is allocated for a distinct class at the outset. However, the size of the cluster layer is dynamically adjustable. A new cluster node will be allocated as needed. The number of cluster nodes can exceed that of the output nodes since different cluster nodes may be allocated for the same class (output) node. One should note the distinction between a class and a cluster in this context. The incremental-learning scheme of the IRBCN is described in the following respects.

Weight Initialization

- The initial weights between the input layer and the conjunction layer in the IRBCN are set as in the corresponding RBCN.

- The initial weights between the conjunction layer and the output layer in the IRBCN are set as in the corresponding RBCN.

- The initial weights between the input layer and the cluster layer are set according to the first relevant instance. For example, suppose an instance is labeled class X for which cluster A is allocated; the weight between cluster node A and an input node will be the activation level of the input node.

Calculation of Activation

1. The activation level of an input node is determined by the instance presented to the network.

2. The activation level of a conjunction node and an output node is the nonlinear transformation of the weighted inputs.

3. The activation level of a cluster node is $\cos \beta$ where β is the angle between the activation vector of the input layer (i.e., the vector formed by collecting the activation levels of the input nodes in sequence) and the input weight vector of the cluster node. The value of $\cos \beta$ reflects the similarity between the two vectors. When the desired activation level of an output node is zero, the activation levels of all cluster nodes assigned to it are set to zero. Under the winner-take-all strategy, only the cluster node with the strongest activation (the winner node) maintains the level of activation as calculated, and all other cluster nodes will be suppressed to the zero level. The activation level of a cluster node will not be calculated until its weights are initialized.

Allocation of New Nodes

When a new instance arrives, if the network cannot classify that instance correctly,[1] then the network is trained on that instance under the restriction that the weight change is bounded in a small range.[2] After training, if the network still cannot classify that instance, a new conjunction unit and a new cluster unit are added to the network if there is no inconsistency observed. The old weights are restored after this test regardless of the result. We determine an instance to be inconsistent with existing network knowledge if the network can clearly classify it[3] but the classification disagrees with the class label of that instance.

If the cluster layer has learned sufficient statistics of the domain, then the following heuristic is applicable. If the instance is labeled class X, the input weights of all cluster nodes assigned to class X have been initialized, and no cluster node has an activation level higher than a predefined threshold, then allocate a new node to the cluster layer and to the conjunction layer, respectively.

We allocate a new conjunction node in order to form a new rule for an instance which is dissimilar to previous instances in the same class. The

---

[1] Correct classification refers to the case in which the output unit of the largest activation matches the class label of the instance.

[2] The bound, determined empirically, is imposed in order to preserve previous network knowledge, perhaps, with emphasis on more recently acquired knowledge.

[3] The criterion is that the largest activation of output units is greater than the second largest activation by a predefined margin (say 0.2).

weights between the new cluster node and the input nodes are initialized as stated above. The weights between the new conjunction node and any other nodes connected below and above are initialized to small values consistent with the instance.

Weight Training

1. When no new nodes are allocated:

    (a) The weights between the input layer and the winner node in the cluster layer will be adjusted according to the Kohonen learning rule (Kohonen 1988). Other learning rules for cluster analysis are also possible.

    (b) The weights between the input layer and the conjunction layer and those between the conjunction layer and the output layer will be modified by the *minimal change backpropagation* learning rule (defined below).

2. When new nodes are allocated:

    (a) The weights between the new cluster node and the input nodes are initialized but not trained.

    (b) The weights between old conjunction nodes and any other nodes connected below and above are fixed.

    (c) The weights between the new conjunction node and any other nodes connected below and above will be set according to the new instance (which is treated like a specific rule but with a small rule strength).

The *minimal change* learning rule minimally changes weights encoding previous knowledge or instance information, when accommodating a new instance. To achieve this, an error margin and a weight-modification range are specified. Only when the error associated with a new instance is beyond the margin, the weights will be modified up to the point where the error is brought inside the margin or the magnitude of weight change exceeds the predefined range. Restriction of weight change to a range can reduce the disruptive effects of bad instances. The restriction is applied to single instances only. Accumulated weight change is not subject to this restriction so that bad knowledge can also be revised.

Since we start with initial knowledge, the learning rate should be smaller than it would be when there is no such knowledge. If we believe that this knowledge is strong, the rate can be set small so that the weights will be changed only little by little over time. We can set the rate larger so that new instances will have greater impact on the weights. Too small a rate will prohibit network weights from effective tuning, whereas too large a rate will deemphasize the initial knowledge. In the incremental scheme, at most one iteration of learning is performed for each new instance seen. Learning does not occur when the classification is correct and clear.

The IRBCN model is reminiscent of the counterpropagation network (Hecht-Nielsen 1987). Such a network model incorporates the Kohonen layer for competitive learning or cluster analysis. The size of the Kohonen layer is predefined, whereas the cluster layer of the IRBCN is dynamically adjustable. Another benefit with the IRBCN is that the conjunction layer between the input and the output layers provides nonlinearities and implements the rule-based knowledge.

In the above designed model, if a new instance is not similar to any of the previous instances, a new cluster will be formed and new rules will be learned without disturbing old knowledge; otherwise, the new instance will be absorbed into the current network by minimally changing the network weights. The cluster layer plays a monitoring role and does not affect the soundness of backpropagation. The purpose of cluster analysis in the IRBCN is to avoid *overgeneralization*. In symbolic learning programs, overgeneralization is detected when a generalization covers more than the allowed negative examples.

From the above discussions, the IRBCN model achieves incremental-learning capability by:

- Employing initial knowledge, which constrains future learning

- Creating an IIS through cluster analysis

- Using the minimal change learning rule

One concern is whether creating new rules would expand the network to an inefficient size for management. This issue will be resolved in two ways. First, the number of rules created for a particular instance is limited to a few. Second, the consistent-shift algorithm (described in Chapter 4) is applied to eliminate redundant rules.

Sensitivity analysis can be performed to determine the threshold for creating a new cluster. Too many clusters may jeopardize the capability of generalization. To achieve both generalization and incrementability is the desired goal.

Validating an incremental-learning system is just like doing any other learning system (see Chapter 13 "Validation and Verification"). One specific thing is, however, to supply training examples one at a time to the learning system. Figure 5.6 shows the learning curve for an IRBCN.

Higgins and Goodman (1991) reported a system which utilized an information theoretical measure for constructing a rule-based neural network. Consider a rule "If E Then H" where E is a conjunction of attribute values and H is a class. They developed the J-measure for evaluating a rule:

$$J(H, E) = P(E)\{P(H|E) \log[\frac{P(H|E)}{P(H)}] + P(\overline{H}|E) \log[\frac{P(\overline{H}|E)}{P(\overline{H})}]\}$$

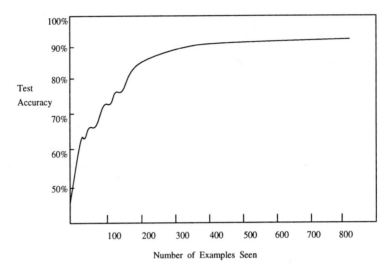

Figure 5.6: The learning curve of an incremental rule-based connectionist network.

In the neural network framework, the weight between the E node and the H node is set by (adapted)

$$W_{H,E} = \log P(E|H)$$

and the bias of the H node is set to $-\log[P(H)]$. Their neural network is just a three-layer RBCN (the input, conjunction, and output layers) where the activation of an output unit is the sum of its weighted inputs (minus the bias). The probability of the associated class is the exponential of the activation. They applied a symbolic method for incrementally constructing rules and mapped them into the network.

5.6   Summary

Incremental learning is a major issue in designing a machine learning system. The heart of systems equipped with such capability lies at an incrementable information structure (IIS) which not only performs generalization but also conserves the information of examples. The version space is a good example of IIS. The concept hierarchy in the COBWEB system is also incrementable. By contrast, the decision tree is not incrementable by its nature, though some techniques are available for overcoming this difficulty.

Two neural network paradigms related to this topic were examined. One is the probabilistic neural network (PNN) and the other the polynomial adaline. While the use of probabilities is important for achieving optimal results, it does not imply incremental learning automatically. The transformation of the PNN into the polynomial adaline illustrates how to acquire incremental-learning capability by creating an IIS. The coefficients of the polynomial approximating the PNN decision boundary are incrementable. In addition, this transformation reduces the computational and storage complexity. The smoothing properties inherent in both methods minimize the risk of overfitting data.

In the knowledge-based approach, we showed how to integrate incremental-learning capability into a rule-based connectionist network. Vital ideas include the use of initial knowledge to constrain learning, the creation of an IIS through cluster analysis, and the application of the minimal change learning rule.

5.7 References

1. Carpenter, G.A., and Grossberg, S. 1988. The ART of adaptive pattern recognition by a self-organizing neural network. *Computer*, March, pp. 77–88.

2. Elio, R., and Watanabe, L. 1991. An incremental deductive strategy for controlling constructive induction in learning from examples. *Machine Learning*, 7, pp. 7–44.

3. Fahlman, S.E., and Lebiere, C. 1990. The cascade-correlation learning architecture. Technical Report, Computer Science, Carnegie Mellon University, Pittsburgh, PA.

4. Fisher, D. 1987. Knowledge acquisition via incremental conceptual clustering. *Machine Learning*, 2, pp. 139–172.

5. Gennari, J.H., Langley, P., and Fisher, D. 1989. Models of incremental concept information. *Artificial Intelligence*, 40, pp. 11–61.

6. Gluck, M., and Corter, J. 1985. Information, uncertainty and the utility of categories. In *Proceedings of Seventh Annual Conference of the Cognitive Science Society* (Irvine, CA), pp. 283–287.

7. Hecht-Nielsen, R. 1987. Counter-propagation networks. *Applied Optics*, 26, pp. 4979–4984.

8. Higgins, C.M., and Goodman, R.M. 1991. Incremental learning with rule-based neural networks. In *Proceedings of IJCNN* (Seattle), pp. I–875–880.

9. Katsuno, H., and Mendelzon, A. O. 1991. Propositional knowledge base revision and minimal change. *Artificial Intelligence*, 52, pp. 263–294.

10. Kohonen, T. 1988. *Self-Organization and Associative Memory*. Springer-Verlag, New York.

11. Kubat, M. 1991. Conceptual inductive learning: The case of unreliable teachers. *Artificial Intelligence*, 52, pp. 169–182.

12. Mitchell, T.M. 1978. Version Spaces: An Approach to Concept Learning. Ph.D. thesis, Stanford University.

13. Parzen, E. 1962. On estimation of a probability density function and mode. *Ann. Math. Stat.*, 33, pp. 1065–1076.

14. Quinlan, J.R. 1983. Learning efficient classification procedures and their application to chess end games. In *Machine Learning*. Tioga Publishing Company, Palo Alto, CA.

15. Schlimmer, J.C., and Fisher, D. 1986. A case study of incremental concept induction. In *Proceedings of AAAI* (Philadelphia), pp. 496–501.

16. Specht, D.F. 1990. Probabilistic neural networks and the polynomial adaline as complementary techniques for classification. *IEEE Transactions on Neural Networks*, 1(1), pp. 111–121.

17. Utgoff, P.E. 1988. ID5: an incremental ID3. In *Proceedings of the Fifth International Conference on Machine Learning* (Ann Arbor), pp. 107–120.

5.8   Problems

1. Given nine objects as follows, we cluster them in two different ways:
   Clustering A:

Cluster	Size	Color	Shape
A	small	yellow	round
A	big	yellow	round
A	big	red	round
A	small	red	round
B	small	black	round
B	big	black	cube
B	big	yellow	cube
B	big	black	round
B	small	yellow	cube

Clustering B:

Cluster	Size	Color	Shape
A	small	yellow	round
C	big	yellow	round
C	big	red	round
A	small	red	round
B	small	black	round
B	big	black	cube
B	big	yellow	cube
B	big	black	round
B	small	yellow	cube

Use the function developed by Gluck and Corter (1985) to compare the two clustering schemes. Which scheme is better?

2. A clustering system maintains three parameters during learning: means, standard deviations, and covariances of clusters. Show how this system can perform incremental learning.

3. A probabilistic neural network is used to perform classification over six-dimensional data. The following training patterns are used:

Class	Pattern vector
A	$(1, 0, 0, 1, 0, 0)$
B	$(1, 1, 0, 0, 0, 0)$
C	$(0, 1, 0, 1, 1, 0)$
C	$(0, 0, 1, 1, 0, 0)$
A	$(1, 1, 0, 1, 0, 0)$
A	$(0, 0, 0, 1, 1, 0)$
B	$(1, 1, 0, 0, 0, 1)$
B	$(1, 0, 0, 0, 0, 1)$

(a) Specify the network structure.

(b) Specify the connection weights.

(c) Given an object with the pattern vector (1, 1, 1, 1, 0, 0) as the input, calculate the output vector of the network. How will the neural network classify this object?

4. Design a neural network based on Bayesian classification.

(a) Show how to set the connection weights and thresholds.

(b) Show how to update the connection weights incrementally.

Chapter 6

Mathematical Modeling

6.1 Introduction

A *system* is the connected units or parts that form a whole and operate together. The function of the system depends not only on the functions of constituents but also on how they connect to one another. A real or imaginary boundary separates a system from the rest of the real world, which is referred to as the *environment*. An *open system* is a system that is influenced by its environment, whereas a *closed system* is one isolated from its environment. The assumption of a closed system under certain restrictions is a means to simplify the analysis of system behavior.

System theory is the study of system behavior. The behavior refers to both external input/output characteristics and internal state change. The behavior can be described in terms of qualitative or quantitative relationships among variables defined for the system. A system can be imitated or simulated by something we call a *model*. A language is chosen depending on the aspect to be modeled. Mathematics is the natural language primarily for expressing quantitative theory and has been used in almost all scientific and engineering disciplines. This chapter focuses on how to build mathematical models of systems. Discussions on qualitative modeling can be found in Chapter 12 "Causal Learning and Modeling."

A system can be represented by a block diagram. In this representation, the system is treated as a "black box" whose internal behavior is opaque, and its behavior is described by external input/output relationships. The block diagram of a system may contain multiple blocks, each representing a subsystem. The connection pattern of blocks reflects the information flow in the system.

In block representation, static relations are given by

$$Y_j = F(X_1, X_2, ...)$$

where Y_j is an output variable, X_i an input variable, and the function F

describes the transformation of the system input into the system output. Dynamic relations are expressed by

$$Y_j(t) = F(X_1[t_0, t], X_2[t_0, t], ...)$$

where t is a time parameter such that $Y_j(t)$ is the value of Y_j at time t, t_0 is the starting time of the system, and

$$X_i[t_0, t] = \{X_i(s)|t_0 \le s \le t\}$$

This is a general representation since the current output can depend on the current and/or the past inputs. It should be noted that any system variable can be treated as an output variable if we are interested in its value and if it can be probed or measured. The variables put aside in the black box are either uninteresting or unobservable. For example, the output variable for an engine is the speed, and the input variables are gasoline flow and spark advance; the output variables for a chemical plant are yield and cost, and the input variables are material supply, time, and personnel; the output variable for drug clearance is the quantity of the drug excreted, and the input variables are circulation speed and metabolic rate.

In the rest of this chapter, we review traditional procedures for mathematical modeling, examine the neural network approach and its mathematical basis in this context, and then explore knowledge-based approaches to this problem.

6.2   Mathematical Modeling in General

In a scientific investigation, a model is constructed to explain a hypothesis or to simulate a practical system (see Figure 6.1). An experiment is performed to gather the relevant data for estimating model parameters or evaluating the model. A model needs to be refined or replaced if it does not provide sufficiently accurate results.

An important question here is how to construct a model. In this regard, we can divide modeling strategies into *theory-driven*, *data-driven*, and mixed. Treating modeling simply as a kind of curve fitting may be misleading since a polynomial can always be found to fit nicely to a finite amount of data. To avoid false models, a *bias* should be formed to favor certain models in the data-driven approach. The bias may be based on general or domain-specific heuristics. When domain knowledge and heuristics constrain the modeling process, it becomes theory-driven. Unless the theory is strong enough to specify or deduce the complete model, modeling cannot be purely theory-driven. A realistic approach is often a mixed strategy, namely, to construct a model based on theory and fill in its details according to the data.

As suggested by Eisen (1988), mathematical modeling generally consists of the following steps:

1. Define the problem for which a model is developed.

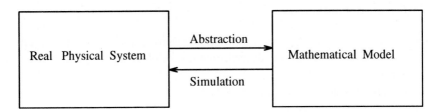

Figure 6.1: An overview of the problem of mathematical modeling.

2. Specify the purpose of the model.

3. Define the boundaries of the model.

4. Postulate the structure of the model, for example, in terms of the block diagram.

5. Define variables of interest.

6. Describe each element mathematically, based on physical laws.

7. Develop model equations and estimate model parameters from relevant data.

8. Test and analyze the model.

Modeling involves identification of:

- Variables which can be neglected

- Input variables (also called independent, or exogenous, variables) which affect the system but whose behavior is not modeled.

- Output variables (also called dependent, or endogenous, variables) whose behavior is modeled

Statistical analysis may aid in determining which factors can be neglected. It is important because model performance may be degraded if irrelevant variables are not removed.

Mathematical models can be classified in the following dimensions:

- Linear or nonlinear

- Static or dynamic

- Deterministic or stochastic

- Discrete or continuous

While most realistic systems are nonlinear, dynamic, and stochastic in nature, we may use linear, static, and deterministic models simply because they are easier to handle.

Traditional modeling techniques include:

- Classical and linear algebra

- Geometry

- Trigonometry

- Ordinary and partial differential equations

- Ordinary and partial difference equations

- Integral equations

- Functional equations

- Graphs

- Statistical models

- Simulation theory

- Linear and nonlinear programming

- Calculus of variations and dynamic programming

- Constrained and unconstrained optimization

- Information theory

The details of these techniques can be found in, for example, Kapur (1988).

Numerous mathematical models have been successfully developed and applied to fields as diverse as physics, chemistry, biology, medicine, engineering, economy, and sociology for various purposes, such as simulation, decision-making, prediction, and control. Despite this, there are yet more situations which are not modeled mathematically because they are too complex or because tractable models cannot be found. In these situations, other techniques may provide better solutions. For example, the rule-based technique is used to model human expertise, which lacks mathematical precision.

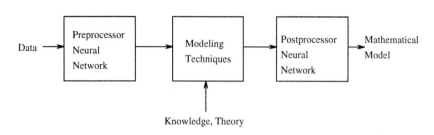

Figure 6.2: The integration of neural networks with other modeling techniques.

6.3 The Applications of Neural Networks

Given a physical system, a neural network can model it on the basis of a set of examples encoding the input/output behavior of the system. The neural network learns to map an input into a desired output by self-adaptation. This somewhat contradicts our previous emphasis on the need of domain theory to guide the design of the model. However, the modeling capability of the neural network can be ascribed to its ability to learn the mathematical function underlying the system operation, as discussed later. If the network is designed and trained properly, it can perform *generalization* rather than simple curve fitting. How to design and train is a kind of bias we impose on the network.

A neural network can be applied to mathematical modeling in several ways:

- As a preprocessor

- As a postprocessor

- As a mathematical model

- As a baseline control

Figure 6.2 shows how to integrate neural networks with other modeling techniques. Each application will be discussed next.

A difficult part of building a model is to determine which variables should be included in the model. Introducing irrelevant variables and missing relevant ones are both deleterious to the model. However, it may not be possible to define the boundary initially. A common practice is to select a tentative set of variables and refine the set successively. If the model is accurate, we are inclined to believe that the model possesses a correct set of variables. But if the desired form of model has yet to be determined, how can we evaluate the selected variables? On some occasions, a model can be evaluated only

Table 6.1: Correspondences between neural networks and mathematical models.

Mathematical Models	Neural Networks
• Linear models	Single-layer networks
• Nonlinear models	Multilayer networks
• Static models	Static networks
• Dynamic models	Temporal networks
• Deterministic models	Deterministic networks
	(e.g., the backpropagation network)
• Stochastic models	Stochastic networks
	(e.g., the Boltzmann machine)
• Discrete models	Discrete networks
	(with discrete values)
• Continuous models	Continuous networks
	(with continuous values)

after its variables are defined. Thus, we may face a dilemma. The neural network offers a possible solution to this dilemma by serving as a mapping machine. So, if the neural network cannot map input patterns into output patterns accurately, then some input variables are possibly missing. If an input variable can be removed without hurting the network performance, then the variable is possibly irrelevant. These two heuristics can be used to identify relevant variables for the model even if its form is still unknown. In this case, the neural network acts as a preprocessor for later modeling.

For a given problem, we seek the best model if possible. However, even the best model may not guarantee full accuracy because every model has its limit. Our ignorance and world fuzziness may further contribute to this fact. The neural network may help in this situation by being able to model unknown factors. Once we find the best model, we map it into a neural network architecture and then create additional units and connections in order to model what is still unknown to the model. The idea stems from the knowledge-based neural network (see Chapter 4 "Knowledge-Based Neural Networks"). In this case, the neural network acts as a postprocessor (i.e., a refiner) of the model.

The use of a neural network as a system model is increasingly common. This idea is based on the simple fact that a neural network can model a system by example mapping. If accuracy is the only concern for a model, then the neural network may well be a good one. However, it remains a philosophical question whether the neural network as a model is a cognitive model.

According to their nature, mathematical models can be related to neural networks in a way suggested by Table 6.1. A notable example is that a linear dynamic system can be implemented by a time-delay neural network. In the next section, we examine the issues of how and why we can use neural networks as mathematical models.

It is interesting to note that we can use the neural network as a baseline control while searching for the desired model. If a model cannot surpass a neural network which represents a system in an unknown manner, then the knowledge or theory embedded in the model cannot be good or can be improved. The assumption is that the neural network does not contain initial knowledge or theory of any sort and is simply a black box. In this way, the neural network provides a good performance standard for evaluating the model concerned.

6.4 Neural Networks as Mathematical Models

The basis of using neural networks as mathematical models is "mapping." Kolmogorov's theorem establishes a firm mathematical foundation for mapping networks. This section examines this subject, related issues, and applications.

6.4.1 Mapping Networks

Mapping networks in essence deal with the approximation of a mathematical function, as illustrated by Figure 6.3. More specifically, a mapping network implements a *bounded* mapping or function from a bounded set of n dimensions to another bounded set of m dimensions (where $n \neq m$ or $n = m$). Suppose we use a neural network to approximate a function f. Let F_{NN} denote the function directly encoding the network operation. The network is trained so that F_{NN} approximates f, i.e., $F_{NN} \approx f$. *Backpropagation* is the most common algorithm for training mapping networks.

For the purpose of training, a set of training examples are selected from the domain. Each example is represented by $(\mathbf{x}, \mathbf{y})$ where $\mathbf{y} = f(\mathbf{x})$. The ideal goal is that after training,

$$\mathbf{y} = f(\mathbf{x}) = F_{NN}(\mathbf{x})$$

for every $\mathbf{x}$ in the domain, not limited to the training set.

The main issue is *generalization*; that is, we want the neural network to generalize from the training examples to the entire domain. The design of the network architecture and the training algorithm is aimed at improving this capability. A related issue is *overtraining*, which refers to the deterioration of the network performance against test (instead of training) examples beyond a certain number of the training cycles. This issue is akin to *overfitting data*. When the network is overtrained, it tends to fit the training data so closely as to sacrifice its performance on the test data.

In the training process, we want to minimize the difference between F_{NN} and f. There are several criteria to define the difference. Among these, *mean squared error* is most commonly used. The squared error for a single training example is

$$E^2(\mathbf{x}) = |f(\mathbf{x}) - F_{NN}(\mathbf{x})|^2 \tag{6.1}$$

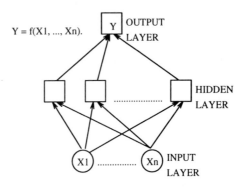

Figure 6.3: A mapping neural network.

The mean squared error over N training examples is given by

$$\overline{E^2} = \frac{1}{N} \sum E^2(\mathbf{x}) \qquad (6.2)$$

Alternatively, we can use the probability integral

$$\overline{E^2} = \int E^2(\mathbf{x})\rho(\mathbf{x})d\mathbf{x} \qquad (6.3)$$

where $\rho(\mathbf{x})$ is the probability density function. The least mean square (LMS) rule has traditionally been used in fields as diverse as control, pattern recognition, and statistics and gained a great deal of success.

The use of the LMS rule often leads one to wonder whether the neural network actually performs statistical regression analysis. However, the nonlinear nature of a multilayer network makes it transcend linear regression techniques. Experimental evidence has suggested that mapping networks are in general comparable to the best nonlinear statistical regression approaches and that mapping networks usually approximate a function more accurately than linear regression techniques. In fact, it is acceptable to regard the mapping neural network as a kind of nonlinear statistical technique. Yet, it is more powerful than traditional techniques by offering more functional forms and adaptive capabilities.

6.4.2   Kolmogorov's Theorem

An important theorem that illuminates the capability of multilayer neural networks was proven by Kolmogorov and is described in Lorentz (1976). This theorem states that any continuous function can be represented in terms of nonlinear and continuously increasing functions of *only* one variable.

Kolmogorov's mapping neural network existence theorem states that any continuous function from the n-dimensional cube $[0, 1]^n$ to the real numbers R can be implemented exactly by a three-layer feedforward neural network with n fanout elements in the input layer, $2n + 1$ processing elements in the hidden layer, and m processing elements in the output layer (from Hecht-Nielsen 1990). The processing elements of the hidden layer use the following activation (transfer) function:

$$h_k = \sum_{i=1}^{n} \lambda^k \psi(x_i + k\epsilon) + k$$

where the real constant λ and the real continuously increasing function ψ are independent of f (the function to be approximated), the constant ϵ is a positive rational number no greater than an arbitrarily chosen positive threshold, and x_i is the ith input. The processing elements of the output layer use the following activation function:

$$y_j = \sum_{k=1}^{2n+1} g_j(h_k)$$

where the real continuous function g_j depends on f and ϵ.

The proof of this theorem is not constructive. It does not indicate how to find the nonlinear activation functions ψ and g. This theorem only states that a three-layer mapping network must exist but fails to show us how to find it. Thus, it establishes the soundness of the neural network approach to functional approximation but may otherwise be of little use. It should be pointed out that the theorem can virtually be extended to apply to any compact (closed or bounded) set rather than just the unit cube.

Cybenko (1989) further showed that the finite sum of the form

$$y = \sum_i W_i \sigma(\mathbf{a}_i \cdot \mathbf{x} + b_i) \tag{6.4}$$

is dense in the space of continuous functions defined on $[0, 1]^n$, where the function σ is a continuous discriminatory function,[1] and b_i, $\mathbf{a}_i$, and W_i correspond to the bias, the input weight vector, and the output weight associated with hidden unit i, respectively.

6.4.3 Functional-Link Nets

The functional-link net has been developed by Pao (1989) for enhancing the computing power of the neural network. The idea of a functional link is the functional transform along a nonlinear link, as shown in Figure 6.4. By functional transformation, an input pattern (vector) is enhanced in its representation. The

---

[1] Refer to Cybenko (1989) for definition.

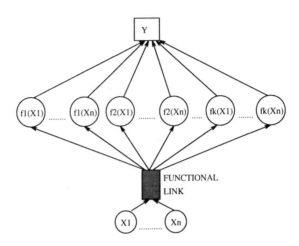

Figure 6.4: The functional-link approach to mathematical modeling.

neural network saves time to learn additional information obtained via such transformation since it is now given. Also, the network may not be able to learn this information given a specific training algorithm. These imply that the functional link can improve the network in both learning capacity and efficiency.

The theoretical background of the functional-link net starts with the observation that introduction of higher-order terms in the neural network can alleviate such difficulties as low learning rates, poor scaling, and low storage capacity. For example, sigma-pi units (Rumelhart, Hinton, and Williams 1986) have the net input in the form of

$$\sum_i W_{ji} \prod_k X_{i1} X_{i2}...X_{ik}$$

where the cross terms are higher-order terms. Lee et al. (1986) indicate that the storage capacity of the Hopfield net is improved significantly when higher-order connections are used. Sejnowski (1986) has similar findings on the Boltzmann machine.

Suppose each input node encodes a certain feature. Applying the function link to a feature causes it to multiply and generate more features. As a consequence, the expressive power of the network increases, as does its modeling capability. This is called the *functional expansion* model. Notice that the functional link should generate a set of linearly *independent* functions and evaluate these functions with the input pattern as the argument. It has been found that the use of functional links not only improves the network performance but also simplifies the network architecture and the training algorithm (backpropagation). Often, a flat net (a single-layer net) without hidden units suffices.

The benefit of the function link when applied to mathematical modeling is the increased accuracy of mapping through the expansion of the basis set. Suppose the function link contains the functions $f_1, f_2, \ldots, f_n$. An input x will be transformed into $f_1(x), f_2(x), \ldots, f_n(x)$, which are then fed into the network for further processing. The functions can be a subset of orthonormal basis functions. We may choose the functional link such as

- $x, x^2, x^3, \ldots$

- $x, \sin \pi x, \cos \pi x, \sin 2\pi x, \cos 2\pi x, \ldots$

- $x_i, x_i x_j \ (j \geq i), \ldots$

Note that the third example involves the cross products of different node values. It is called the *tensor model*.

The idea of the functional link is very close to that of series expansion. Let us look at two examples of well-known series. One is the Taylor series. A function f having derivatives of all orders in a neighborhood $x_o - h < x < x_o + h$ of x_o can be expanded into

$$f(x) = \sum_{n=0}^{\infty} \frac{f^{(n)}(x_o)}{n!}(x - x_o)^n \tag{6.5}$$

where $f^{(n)}$ is the nth derivative of f. If $x_o = 0$, the power series is reduced to

$$f(x) = \sum_{n=0}^{\infty} \frac{f^{(n)}(0)}{n!} x^n \tag{6.6}$$

which is often called an Maclaurin series of $f(x)$. Another example is the Fourier series. Any periodic function f can be expanded into the form

$$f(x) = a_o + \sum_{n=1}^{\infty}(a_n \cos n\omega x + b_n \sin n\omega x) \tag{6.7}$$

where ω is the frequency. From these examples, it is clear that the functional link can implement truncated series. As more terms are included, the function is better approximated. This discussion also gives a mathematical basis to the functional-link approach.

6.4.4   Wavelet Networks

In signal processing, an important issue is how to represent data. The wavelet transform, developed by Morlet (1983), offers a multiscale representation of waveforms. Applications of wavelet theory have been found in mathematics and signal processing (Chui 1992).

The wavelet transform of a signal $f(t)$ is to correlate it with a wavelet function ψ, with the resulting transform given by

$$F(b, a) = \frac{1}{\sqrt{a}} \int \psi(\frac{u - b}{a}) f(u) du \qquad (6.8)$$

where a is a dilation parameter, $a > 0$, and b is a translation parameter, $b \in R.$[2] The multiscale representation is obtained by selecting multiple values of a. The inverse transform for reconstruction is given by

$$f(t) = k \int \int \psi(\frac{t - b}{a}) F(b, a)\, da\, db \qquad (6.9)$$

where k is a constant scale factor for normalization.

The Fourier transform $\Psi(\omega)$ of a wavelet function should satisfy the condition

$$\int_0^{+\infty} \frac{|\Psi(\omega)|^2}{\omega} d\omega < \infty$$

A simple case is a Gaussian pulse

$$\psi(t) = \exp(-\frac{t^2}{a}) \exp(j\omega_o t) \qquad (6.10)$$

where ω_o is a frequency parameter.

Wavelet networks (Zhang and Benveniste 1992), based on the wavelet transform theory, can approximate any arbitrary nonlinear function. From Eq. 6.9, we design the *wavelet* network so that its output y is give by

$$y = \sum_i W_i \psi(\frac{\mathbf{x} - b_i}{a_i}) + \text{bias} \qquad (6.11)$$

where $\mathbf{x}$ is the input vector. To implement this network, we can let the wavelet function be the activation function in the hidden layer, or we use the wavelet function with various degrees of translation and dilation as the function link to transform the input. In the first approach, if the Gaussian wavelet function (Eq. 6.10) is adopted and $\omega_o = 0$, then the wavelet network is reduced to the radial basis function network (see Chapter 3 "Learning: Supervised and Unsupervised"). In the second approach, wavelet networks are just a kind of function link net in which wavelets are used as the basis functions.

---

[2] A pattern can dilate, translate, or rotate.

The wavelet network does not merely perform wavelet decomposition. More importantly, it can adapt the parameters (dilation and translation parameters, and weights) to a particular problem. A learning algorithm based on backpropagation and the heuristics for weight initialization has been developed by Zhang and Benveniste (1992).

6.4.5 General Regression Neural Networks

In this section, we describe the *general regression neural network* (GRNN) developed by Specht (1991). This network is akin to the probabilistic neural network (described in Chapter 5 "Incremental Learning"). However, unlike it, the GRNN provides estimates of continuous variables rather than discrete decisions. Statistical regression is briefly reviewed first.

One important mode of statistical reasoning is to predict the value of a variable from the known values of one or more other variables. Such predictions are important when some variable cannot be observed directly and must be estimated from other relevant variables. The variable to be predicted is called the *dependent variable,* and the variables used as the predictors are called the *predictor variables.* The method of *least squares,* which minimizes the squared difference between the predicted value and the actual value of the dependent variable, lies at the heart of regression. Statistical analysis based on least squares is known as *regression analysis.* When more than one predictor variable is involved, the process is known as *multiple regression.*

Let $f(\mathbf{x}, y)$ represent the known joint continuous probability density function of a vector random variable $\mathbf{x}$ and a scalar random variable y. And let $\mathbf{X}$ be a particular measured value of $\mathbf{x}$. The conditional mean of y given $\mathbf{X}$, called the regression of y on $\mathbf{X}$, is given by

$$E[y|\mathbf{X}] = \frac{\int_{-\infty}^{\infty} yf(\mathbf{X}, y)dy}{\int_{-\infty}^{\infty} f(\mathbf{X}, y)dy} \tag{6.12}$$

where $E[\cdot]$ is the expected value operator. When the density $f(\mathbf{X}, y)$ is unknown, we may take the Parzen (1962) window approach to estimate it from a sample of observations $\mathbf{X}_i$ and Y_i of $\mathbf{x}$ and y, as given by

$$\hat{f}(\mathbf{X}, Y) = \frac{1}{(2\pi)^{(d+1)/2}\sigma^{d+1}} \cdot \frac{1}{n} \sum_{i=1}^{n} \exp[-\frac{D_i^2}{2\sigma^2}] \cdot \exp[-\frac{(Y - Y_i)^2}{2\sigma^2}] \tag{6.13}$$

where n is the number of observations, d is the dimension of the vector variable $\mathbf{x}$, and

$$D_i^2 = (\mathbf{X} - \mathbf{X}_i) \cdot (\mathbf{X} - \mathbf{X}_i) \tag{6.14}$$

A sample probability of width σ is assigned to each sample (instance pair) $\mathbf{X}_i$ and Y_i, and the joint probability estimate $\hat{f}(\mathbf{X}, Y)$ is the sum of those sample probabilities.

Substituting Eq. 6.13 into Eq. 6.12 gives the desired (estimated) conditional mean, designated by $\hat{Y}(\mathbf{X})$. After some rearrangement and performing the indicated integrations, we obtain

$$\hat{Y}(\mathbf{X}) = \frac{\sum_{i=1}^{n} Y_i \exp(-\frac{D_i^2}{2\sigma^2})}{\sum_{i=1}^{n} \exp(-\frac{D_i^2}{2\sigma^2})} \tag{6.15}$$

The choice of the width σ (the smoothing parameter) is critical. If σ is too large, the estimate will be of little resolution; if σ is too small, the estimate will suffer from too much statistical variability. Parzen (1962) has shown that the density estimators of the form of Eq. 6.13 asymptotically converge to the underlying probability density function at all points (i.e., consistent estimators) where the density function is continuous, provided that $\sigma = \sigma(n)$ is a decreasing function with n such that

$$\lim_{n \to \infty} \sigma(n) = 0$$

and

$$\lim_{n \to \infty} n\sigma^d(n) = \infty$$

Inasmuch as the underlying distribution is not known, an optimum σ is obtained empirically. The value of σ producing the smallest cross-validation error should be used in the final network.[3] Also, it is usually necessary to scale all input variables so that they have about the same variances, for the underlying density function is estimated using the same width in each dimension.

The Gaussian kernel used in Eq. 6.13 could be replaced by any of the Parzen windows. For example, the following estimator

$$\hat{Y}(\mathbf{X}) = \frac{\sum_{i=1}^{n} Y_i \exp(-\frac{C_i}{\sigma})}{\sum_{i=1}^{n} \exp(-\frac{C_i}{\sigma})} \tag{6.16}$$

involves the use of the city block distance

$$C_i = \sum_{j=1}^{d} |X^j - X_i^j|$$

where the superscript j denotes the jth component of the vector.

When the number of observations is large, it is impractical to assign a separate node to each instance. Clustering techniques can be used to group instances so that a group is represented by only one node (the pattern unit). This process also endows the network with a higher degree of generalization over observations. See also the radial basis function network in Chapter 3 "Learning."

---

[3] Refer to Chapter 13 "Validation and Verification" for cross-validation.

Given m clusters, the estimator of Eq. 6.15 becomes

$$\hat{Y}(\mathbf{X}) = \frac{\sum_{i=1}^{m} A_i \exp(-\frac{D_i^2}{2\sigma^2})}{\sum_{i=1}^{m} B_i \exp(-\frac{D_i^2}{2\sigma^2})} \tag{6.17}$$

where A_i is the sum of the Y values, B_i is the number of instances assigned to cluster i, and D_i is the Euclidean distance of the input vector to the cluster center. So, $\mathbf{X}_i$ in Eq. 6.14 is now the center of cluster i. The parameters A_i and B_i are incremented each time a training observation Y_j for cluster i is seen:

$$A_i(k) = A_i(k-1) + Y_j$$

and

$$B_i(k) = B_i(k-1) + 1$$

where k denotes the parameter value after k observations.

To model a system with nonstationary (changing) statistics, a decaying (forgetting) factor can be incorporated in updating the parameters. If the new instance Y_j is assigned to cluster i,

$$A_i(k) = \frac{\tau - 1}{\tau} A_i(k-1) + \frac{1}{\tau} Y_j$$

and

$$B_i(k) = \frac{\tau - 1}{\tau} B_i(k-1) + \frac{1}{\tau}$$

Otherwise,

$$A_i(k) = \frac{\tau - 1}{\tau} A_i(k-1)$$

and

$$B_i(k) = \frac{\tau - 1}{\tau} B_i(k-1)$$

The constant τ corresponds to the time constant of an exponential decay function but is measured in update instances rather than in units of time.

Figure 6.5 shows the architecture of the GRNN. Each pattern unit is dedicated to one exemplar or one cluster center. The network algorithm is formulated below.

The General Regression Neural Network

- **Basic Structures**

  - Four layers: a layer of input units, a layer of pattern units, a layer of summation units, and a layer of output units. Each output unit corresponds to a continuous variable.

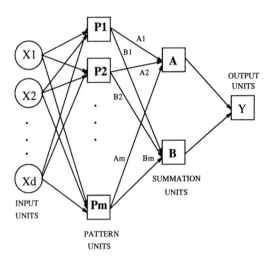

Figure 6.5: The general regression neural network for estimating continuous variables.

- There is one-to-one correspondence between pattern units and clusters.
- For convenience of description, assume that there is only a single output unit and two summation units.

- **Weight Initialization**

  - The input weight vector of pattern unit i is initialized to the ith cluster center.
  - The input weight vector of one summation unit is determined by A_i's (called unit A) and that of the other summation unit is determined by B_i's (called unit B).
  - The input weight vector of the output unit is unspecified.

- **Calculation of Activation**

  1. The activations of input units are determined by the example presented to the network.
  2. The activation O_i of pattern unit i is given by

$$O_i = \exp(-D_i^2/2\sigma^2)$$

where D_i is given by

$$D_i^2 = (\mathbf{X} - \mathbf{X}_i) \cdot (\mathbf{X} - \mathbf{X}_i)$$

and $\mathbf{X}_i$ is the center of cluster i.

3. The activation of each summation unit is a linear sum of weighted inputs from the pattern layer.

4. The activation of the output unit is the activation of unit A divided by that of unit B.

- **Network Learning**
  Perform adaptive clustering (e.g., the ART algorithm in Chapter 3 "Learning"), and update the cluster center and the associated parameters A_i and B_i as described earlier.

Like the PNN, the GRNN is memory-based (since it explicitly stores the information of each training instance in the network) and is a one-pass learning algorithm. The GRNN overcomes the disadvantage of slow training in the backpropagation network and lends itself well to real-time applications. Even with sparse data, the network provides smooth transitions from one observation to another. It converges to the underlying (linear or nonlinear) regression surface and can be applied to any regression problem without a specific assumption about the regressional form.

6.4.6 System Identification and Control

System identification is concerned with the construction of a model which describes an empirical relationship between the system input and the system output. In adaptive system identification, the true (desired) output and the model output are compared, and the error is fed back to a learning element which modifies the model in an attempt to reduce the error. This behavior is exactly the same as what the neural network does. However, the neural network combines both the model and the learning element in a single entity. The neural network learns to adjust itself. When learning concludes, the network identifies and simulates the system.

System identification is often necessary for a control problem. The control problem deals with the setting of the input so that the output follows a desired curve. A mathematical model which relates the input and the output can help us solve this problem because it allows us to calculate the desired input given a desired output. Suppose the model equation is

$$Y(t) = F(X(t))$$

where X and Y are the system input and output at time t, respectively, and F is the system function. If the function F is invertible, then the desired input can be calculated from the desired output by

$$X(t) = F^{-1}(Y(t))$$

Thus, the control problem is solved by inverting the system dynamics.

When the system function is not invertible either because it is not a one-to-one mapping or because it is too complex, the desired input cannot be calculated directly from the desired output using the system model. Under this circumstance, we may be forced to tune the input until the desired output emerges. The system model can be used in this way (i.e., the simulation approach), but it may be time-consuming especially when the input is multidimensional. A better solution is to construct a control model which can produce the desired input given the desired output. Now, the system input is taken as the controller's output, and the system output as the controller's input. However, if the system function is not a one-to-one mapping, then the control function cannot exist. Furthermore, in the event that the system has multiple inputs and outputs, only a few inputs can be manipulated, and a few outputs need to be controlled, the above alternative may fail to handle it. So, other solutions are sought.

For convenience, we call the input of the controller as the goal and its output as the action. The goal variables are some output variables of the system to be controlled, and the action variables are some of its input variables. The relationship between the system and the controller is shown in Figure 6.6. In the neural network approach, we implement two networks, one for the system and the other for the controller. Both networks are trained on examples properly set up. The system network is trained first and then fixed. Assume that the action variables are hidden. The error of the system network is backpropagated through the controller network during training of the latter. Once the controller network is well trained, it can be hooked up to the real system. The system model is no longer used. This approach has been applied to the control of real-time, dynamic, nonlinear systems by Beale and Demuth (1992). More examples of using neural networks for control can be found in Miller, Sutton, and Werbos (1991).

Cerebellatrons such as CMAC (cerebellum model articulation controller) of Albus (1981) are a class of neural networks designed for control of motor action of robotic arms. These networks act as command sequence memories, which store and replay command sequences, and are capable of combining multiple command sequences with different weights to interpolate motion smoothly.

See Chapter 7 "Complex Domains" for more details about *control neural networks*. See also Chapter 10 "Learning Spatiotemporal Patterns" for how to model a system whose behavioral description involves time.

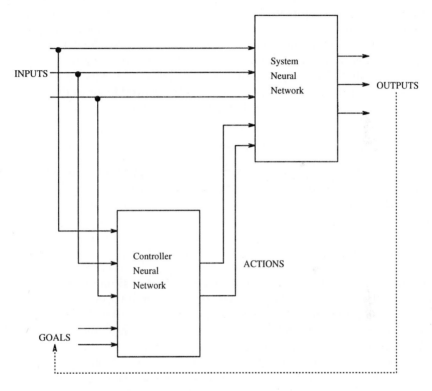

Figure 6.6: A neural network–controlled system. The system network maps inputs into desired outputs. The controller network decides its actions according to goal and input conditions. When action variables are unobservable directly, the error of the controller network can be estimated by the backpropagation technique. The training of the controller network follows that of the system network. The weights of the latter network are fixed during training of the former network. The overall objective is that, given desired goal (output) conditions, the controller network can generate proper actions in order to achieve the goal.

6.5   Knowledge-Based Approaches

The neural network approach seems to suggest that a mathematical model can be built from scratch. However, there are pros and cons for this view. The main argument in favor of this approach is that a mapping network can approximate a mathematical function, as discussed in the last section. Reversely, several arguments can be raised against this view: The neural network just provides an "approximation"; a bunch of nodes and weights cannot be called a mathematical model; complacency with the neural network may hinder one from discovering more scientifically meaningful models; and even for a small, elegant function, there is a good chance that the neural network approach results in a cumbersome network. The central focus of this section is placed on the application of knowledge to alleviate these concerns.

6.5.1   The Use of Knowledge

It is useful to know the modeling technique most appropriate for a particular situation. In the first place, we may need to examine the problem nature and decide between linear and nonlinear, static and dynamic, deterministic and stochastic models. After the technique is chosen, the model prototype is developed based on the laws of physics or chemistry or relevant disciplines. Thus, modeling demands two types of knowledge: the knowledge about modeling in general and the domain knowledge or theory. In a novel situation, we may apply to it the knowledge from an analogous situation; this is known as *learning or reasoning by analogy*. Reviewing old examples in the literature or a data base is a common exercise for finding a suitable model. But the bottleneck is often the process of model development, which generally requires ingenuity and expertise as well as time-consuming experiments.

The neural network approach seems to offer a shortcut solution to modeling because it bypasses the need of expensive expertise. However, even in such approach, we can find a better model if we know what activation functions should be used on the processing nodes and what functional forms or bases included in the network. Equally important is the knowledge as to the design of the network architecture and topology and the initialization of the interconnection weights.

6.5.2   Graph-Based Approaches

Mathematics can also deal with qualitative relationships. Some examples of qualitative relations are A causes B, A points to B, A is a member of B, and so on. Such relationships can be naturally represented by graphs. A graph consists of a set of vertices and edges. An edge connects two vertices in the graph. Figure 6.7 presents some types of graphs:

- A *directed graph*, or a *digraph*, in which every edge is directed with an arrow

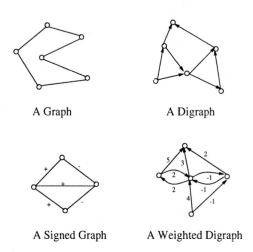

A Graph · A Digraph

A Signed Graph · A Weighted Digraph

Figure 6.7: Some types of graphs.

- A *signed graph*, in which every edge has either a plus or minus sign associated with it

- A *weighted graph*, in which every edge has a weight associated with it

A graph-based model is constructed based on domain knowledge that indicates (from the weakest to the strongest level):

- Which edges are joined

- How edges are directed

- How edges are signed

- How edges are weighted

The first three levels provide qualitative information, the last level quantitative information. A graph can make inference up to the level of the knowledge it contains.

A graph-based structure can be directly mapped into a neural network by mapping a vertex into a node and an edge into a connection. By so doing, the knowledge contained in the graph is also transferred to the network and hence a knowledge-based neural network. The edges in the graph determine how the nodes in the network should be linked; the arrows indicate how the information should flow. The signs suggest how to set the signs for initial weights, and

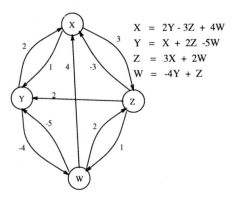

Figure 6.8: A neural network transformed from a system of equations.

the weights suggest how to initialize weights. A primary advantage of this practice is that we can apply the neural network learning algorithm to improve existing knowledge initially encoded in graphs. Another implication is that graph theory could be applied to neural network design.

6.5.3   Equation-Based Approaches

A system of algebraic equations can be represented as a weighted digraph, as seen in Figure 6.8. Since a graph can be mapped into a neural network, it follows that a set of equations can be implemented by a neural network with coefficients translating into weights. The network so constructed does not distinguish between input, hidden, and output nodes. The nodes encoding the variables with known values are input nodes, and the nodes whose values need to be known are output nodes. So, which are input and which are output nodes vary with cases. Depending on the equations, the network architecture can be feedforward or recurrent. "Recursion" on equations translates into "recurrency" on the network. This approach can handle equations involving complex functions by incorporating them into the activation functions on relevant nodes.

Equation-based neural networks can find several different applications, for example,

- When certain coefficients are missing, they can be found or estimated empirically by the neural network.

- When certain coefficients are uncertain, they can be refined empirically by the neural network.

- When the equation system is too complex to solve analytically, it can be dealt with numerically by the neural network.

- When certain variables are missing, some nodes can be recruited by the neural network.

The fundamental idea is to let neural networks improve the knowledge of and retrieve information from the equations.

Neural networks can also be used to implement dynamic differential or difference equations. This subject is treated in Chapter 10.

6.5.4 Rule-Based Approaches

The primary application of the rule-based approach has been qualitative modeling, such as modeling expert knowledge. Its application to quantitative modeling is seldom noticed. Here, we examine two such applications:

- Use rules to build a connectionist model, which is then converted to a mapping network.

- Identify patterns or rules associated with certain variables. Then, convert these patterns to functional forms.

Qualitative models are often viewed as the abstraction of quantitative models. For example, given that $y = f(x)$ where the function f is a monotonically increasing function, we know that as x increases, so does y. But if we only know that the increase of x is always accompanied by the increase of y, this information is too little for identifying the function f. Since quantitative models are more informative than qualitative ones, why do we want the latter? A common answer is that sufficient quantitative knowledge is not always available. In fact, humans appear to memorize qualitative knowledge more easily than quantitative knowledge.

Now, an important question can be raised here, namely, "How can we build a quantitative model based on qualitative knowledge?" One approach is the following:

1. Represent qualitative knowledge as rules.

2. Build a rule-based connectionist network (RBCN).

3. Convert the RBCN to a *quantitative mapping network* (QNMN). An additional hidden layer may be inserted under each conjunction layer to increase mapping accuracy, as seen in Figure 6.9.

4. Use quantitative data to train the QNMN.

A QNMN differs from an RBCN in the following aspects:

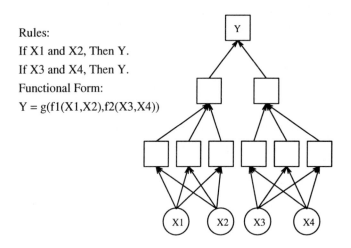

Rules:

If X1 and X2, Then Y.

If X3 and X4, Then Y.

Functional Form:

Y = g(f1(X1,X2),f2(X3,X4))

Figure 6.9: A mapping neural network for functional forms translated from rules.

- Input values are continuous (and often normalized to the range from 0 to 1) in a QNMN but discrete in an RBCN.

- Output nodes have no nonlinearities in QNMN.

In this approach, we use qualitative knowledge to determine the topology of the network and then use the neural network to learn quantitative knowledge from the data.

It is possible to write a rule as a functional form. For example, the rule "if X_1 and X_2, then Y" is written as "$Y = f(X_1, X_2)$," where the function f is yet to be found. This transformation has two advantages. First, it suggests which variables should be included in the model of a given variable. Secondly, it suggests how the functional form can be written. In this example, X_1 and X_2 should be included in the model of Y. What if there are multiple rules concluding the same variable? So, for example, another rule says, "If X_3 and X_4, then Y." Now, there are two possible functional alternatives:

- $Y = g(f_1(X_1, X_2), f_2(X_3, X_4))$

- $Y = f(X_1, X_2, X_3, X_4)$

In the first form, the function g in quantitative domains corresponds to the logical "or" function in qualitative domains.

The next task is to identify or approximate the functions involved in the functional form. Traditional techniques can certainly be tried. A mapping neural network offers another solution to this problem, as indicated by Figure 6.9. In this approach, we should be concerned about the choice of the activation functions.

6.6 Summary

Throughout the ages, scientists have been involved in finding mathematical models for particular problems. Despite a lot of successful examples, mathematical modeling remains a challenging field for us to investigate since many situations still lack good mathematical models. Traditional techniques often rely on a great deal of ingenuity and expertise. The neural network approach, on the other hand, appears attractive since it does not require expertise as much as traditional approaches. The neural network is able to find a good mathematical model for predicting the system behavior simply by example mapping. Kolmogorov's theorem provides a sound basis for mapping neural networks but tells little about how to find them. The functional-link approach simplifies the network architecture and the training algorithm. One caveat about the neural network approach is that one should not be satisfied with a neural network model so much as to cease seeking a more meaningful model.

A neural network can be integrated with traditional techniques by serving as a preprocessor or postprocessor. In addition, the neural network can provide a baseline control in quest of better models.

An important area of application for mathematical modeling is "control." Once a mathematical model is developed which simulates the system behavior, the system can be controlled according to the model. The neural network approach holds a great promise in this application since neural networks are capable of identifying a system whose behavior is hard to understand.

Knowledge plays a vital role in mathematical modeling. When knowledge is represented in graphs, they can be directly transferred to neural networks which then improve the knowledge by learning empirically. Moreover, graph theory may aid in the design of the neural network. When knowledge is represented as a system of equations, they can also be implemented by a neural network. Equations involving complex functions and even differential equations may be handled in this way. When knowledge is represented in rules, they can be used to build a mapping network for modeling. Rules associated with a certain variable can be written as a simple or nested functional form in which unknown functions can be identified through traditional techniques or can be approximated by a mapping network. Identification of correlated patterns can effectively narrow down the search space for possible mathematical models.

6.7 References

1. Albus, J.S. 1981. *Brains, Behavior, and Robotics*. BYTE, Peterborough, NH.

2. Beale, M., and Demuth, H. 1992. Preparing controllers for nonlinear systems. *AI Expert*, July, pp. 42–47.

3. Chui, C.K. 1992. *Wavelet Analysis and Its Applications*. Academic Press, San Diego, CA.

4. Cybenko, G. 1989. Approximation by superposition of a sigmoid function. *Mathematics of Control, Signals and Systems*, 2, pp. 303–314.

5. Eisen, M. 1988. *Mathematical Methods and Models in the Biological Sciences*. Prentice-Hall, Englewood Cliffs, NJ.

6. Hecht-Nielsen, R. 1990. *Neurocomputing*. Addison-Wesley, Reading, MA.

7. Kapur, J.N. 1988. *Mathematical Modelling*. John Wiley & Sons, New York.

8. Lee, Y.C., Doolen, G., Chen, H.H., Sun, G.Z., Maxwell, T., Lee, H.Y., and Giles, C.L. 1986. Machine learning using a higher order correlation network. *Physica 22D*, pp. 276–306.

9. Lorentz, G.G. 1976. The 13th problem of Hilbert. In *Mathematical Developments Arising from Hilbert Problems*. American Mathematical Society, Providence, RI.

10. Miller, III, W.T., Sutton, R.S., and Werbos, P.J. (eds.). 1991. *Neural Networks for Control*. MIT Press, Cambridge, MA.

11. Morlet, J. 1983. Sampling theory and wave propagation. In *Issues on Signal/Image Processing for Underwater Acoustics*. Springer-Verlag, New York.

12. Pao, Y.H. 1989. *Adaptive Pattern Recognition and Neural Networks*. Addison-Wesley, Reading, MA.

13. Parzen, E. 1962. On estimation of a probability density function and mode. *Ann. Math. Statis.*, 33, pp. 1065–1076.

14. Rumelhart, D.E., Hinton, G.E., and Williams, R.J. 1986. Learning internal representation by error propagation. In *Parallel Distributed Processing: Explorations in the Microstructures of Cognition*, Vol. 1. MIT Press, Cambridge, MA.

15. Sejnowski, T.J. 1986. Higher-order Boltzmann machines. In *Proceedings of American Institute of Physics Conference, No. 151: Neural Networks for Computing* (Snowbird, Utah), pp. 398–403.

16. Specht, D.F. 1991. A general regression neural network. *IEEE Transactions on Neural Networks*, 2(6), pp. 568–576.

17. Zhang, Q., and Benveniste, A. 1992. Wavelet networks. *IEEE Transactions on Neural Networks*, 3(6), pp. 889–898.

6.8 Problems

1. Consider a neural network with a single hidden layer. There are two input units, three hidden units, and two output units. The network is fully connected (no supralayer connection). Each weight is quantized to n bits. What is the information content stored for each weight setting in the network? (Hint: Let the probability of each weight setting be P_W. The information content is $-\log_2 P_W$.)

2. Suppose a continuous function f from a compact set to real numbers is expanded in terms of a set of orthonormal sine wave basis functions. Show that each sine wave function can be approximated by combining the output of some hidden-layer units with sigmoid nonlinearity. In this way, show that the backpropagation network can approximate the function f arbitrarily closely.

3. Kolmogorov's mapping neural network existence theorem indicates the requirement of $2n + 1$ processing elements in the hidden layer. Is there a possible justification for this requirement?

4. It is a common problem to learn a function. Suppose the function f maps from one scalar to another scalar domain:

$$f : x \longrightarrow y$$

where x is a real number ranging from 0 to 20. We have the following examples available for learning the function f:

$$
\begin{array}{lll}
f(0) = 0 & f(1) = 1 & f(2) = 4 \\
f(3) = 9 & f(4) = 16 & f(6) = 36 \\
f(8) = 64 & f(10) = 100 & f(12) = 144 \\
f(14) = 196 & f(16) = 256 & f(18) = 324
\end{array}
$$

(a) Design and train a backpropagation network on the above examples in order to model the function f. The network should have one input unit, one output unit, and a hidden layer. The number of hidden units should be properly chosen to ensure good generalization, as described in the problem section of Chapter 3 "Learning." In addition, since the input domain is continuous, we suggest it be normalized to the range from 0 to 1, for example, by

$$x' = \frac{x - \min}{\max - \min}$$

where min and max are the minimum and the maximum of the input domain and x and x' are the original and the normalized values, respectively.

(b) Use the trained network to estimate $f(11) =?$ and $f(15) =?$

(c) Solve the same problem using a functional net with the basis functions: 1, x, and x^2.

(d) Can you guess the analytical form of the function f?

5. Consider the function g which maps from a vector to a scalar domain:

$$f : (x, y) \longrightarrow z$$

where x and y are both real numbers ranging from 0 to 20. Available examples are given below:

$$
\begin{array}{lll}
g(0, 0) = 0 & g(1, 2) = 5 & g(2, 4) = 20 \\
g(3, 7) = 72 & g(4, 5) = 41 & g(6, 8) = 100 \\
g(8, 14) = 260 & g(10, 16) = 356 & g(12, 10) = 244 \\
g(14, 2) = 200 & g(16, 12) = 400 & g(18, 9) = 405
\end{array}
$$

(a) Design and train a backpropagation network on the above examples in order to model the function g. The network should have two input units, one output unit, and a hidden layer. Use the same considerations as in the last problem. Both the inputs x and y are normalized to the range from 0 to 1. That is, the input domain is normalized to a unit square.

(b) Use the trained network to estimate $f(11, 4) =?$ and $f(15, 10) =?$

(c) Solve the same problem using a general regression neural network. Assume that each instance forms a distinct cluster.

(d) Can you guess the analytical form of the function g?

6. In a neural network–controlled system, the training of the controller network follows that of the system network. When these two training processes cannot be separated in a dynamic situation, what constraint becomes necessary then?

Chapter 7

Complex Domains

7.1 Introduction

When a simple neural network is incapable of solving a complex problem, the combination of multiple networks presents a solution. A loosely coupled architecture contains two or more, similar or different, networks which interact in one way or another. These networks are arranged in a parallel or hierarchical fashion to allow different types of information processing on the same data set or different subsets, or to offer different levels of data abstraction. A tightly coupled architecture, on the other hand, is a hybrid of multiple existing network types.

Here, we distinguish between two major ways in which we can integrate multiple neural networks. One is to merge the features of two or more network types in a single hybrid network so that it exhibits some desirable properties which cannot be obtained by solely connecting the networks together. The limitations with this approach are that a hybrid network cannot possess many functions and neither can it handle more than one task at a time.

The alternative approach is to create a system of interacting networks, with each devoted to a specific task. This architecture should be considered when the problem requires multiple stages of processing or multiple levels of abstraction or multiple views of interpretation. Like structured and object-oriented programming, this modular approach facilitates the development and maintenance of network systems. However, without coupling their dynamics, it seems unlikely that new functionalities other than those defined by individual components can emerge in this approach.

There is no universal solution to the design of a system of neural networks. It depends on the nature of the problem. If we can decompose a complex problem into multiple subproblems, then we may assign each one to a functionally suitable network. Research in the field of artificial neural networks has matured to a point that permits us to create a system of neural networks for a particular problem in this way. In practical domains, however, it may not be easy

197

to find a clear-cut way to divide and conquer. In addition, there could be *uncertainty* and *opportunity* involved in the process of problem solving, and thus the information flow characteristics between networks may not be determined precisely in advance. These facts complicate the design problem.

When a problem is so complex that a brute-force approach is simply inadequate, some degree of abstraction or heuristic search is demanded. The research on knowledge-based systems has resulted in a rich body of heuristics to deal with complex domains, from which we can borrow here.

In a system of neural networks, the relationships between two components can be classified into three categories:

- *In parallel*: Two components act in parallel.

- *In sequence*: One component acts before the other.

- *In control*: One component controls the other.

We can divide and then map an arbitrarily complex problem topologically into a system of neural networks in which the relationship between any two is specified by one of the three relationships stated. Similar or different networks can be related in ways where appropriate. Basic types of system architectures grow from these basic relationships between component networks. For example, a hierarchical cascade of clustering networks can be designed for the task of building a taxonomy of objects; a vector quantization net can be used as a front end to a backpropagation network for classification.

In complex domains, the issue of control structures is especially important. Here, it does not refer but is related to the use of neural networks in solving the engineering control problem. Although neural networks are parallel-distributed processing models, a control mechanism is often indispensable for integration of multiple networks into a system. In one extreme, all networks behave independently and hence in parallel, and a control structure can be very trivial. In the other, the quality of the overall solution depends on the order of network invocations, and the control structure plays an important role, emulating the brain rather than simple neural networks.

In the following sections, we explore system architectures for complex neural networks. Our discussions are based on the classification of such architectures into *hierarchical*, *differentiation*, and *parallel* models. Hybrid models in general fall in the first group. An important emphasis is placed on the design of control networks.

7.2   Expert System Heuristics

Expert systems are intelligent computer programs capable of solving difficult problems which require experts' knowledge. Intensive research in this area has produced abundant knowledge concerning how to design an inference

Table 7.1: Application of knowledge-based principles to the design of neural network systems.

Knowledge-Based Principles	Neural Network Systems
• Abstraction with fixed sequences	A cascade of networks
• Abstraction without fixed sequences	A hierarchy of networks
• Divide and conquer	Parallel-distributed networks
• Multiple lines of reasoning	Parallel networks
• Multiple knowledge sources	Control networks
• Constraint-based reasoning	Recurrent networks

architecture for a complex problem. This knowledge is readily transferable to the design of complex neural network systems, as suggested below:

- *Abstraction with fixed sequences*: A problem is partitioned into multiple stages or steps. This heuristic can be implemented by a cascade of networks with each dedicated to a single stage.

- *Abstraction without fixed sequences*: A problem is organized at multiple levels of abstraction. It can be mapped into a hierarchical system of networks with each level bearing on some level of abstraction.

- *Divide and conquer*: This is a classical approach to complex problems. It can be realized by a system of networks working in a parallel-distributed yet cooperative manner.

- *Multiple lines of reasoning*: A problem is analyzed from multiple perspectives. It can be worked upon by multiple networks in parallel with each focusing on a different aspect of the same data. This is useful when a single line of reasoning is too weak or unreliable to reach a meaningful conclusion.

- *Multiple knowledge sources*: Sometimes, a problem cannot be solved without consulting multiple knowledge sources. The *blackboard* architecture (Hayes-Roth 1985) is well known for integration of multiple knowledge sources. The blackboard can be implemented by a control neural network. Its details are described later.

- *Constraint satisfaction and propagation*: When a problem consists of multiple interacting subproblems, constraint propagation is a vital technique to achieve a final solution. Problem constraints can be dealt with by recurrent neural networks, such as the Hopfield net.

These heuristics and their neural network implementations are further summarized in Table 7.1.

7.3   Hierarchical Models

In the hybrid (tightly coupled) approach, a hierarchical network is a multilayer network in which functionally similar or different subnetworks stack one on another. A similar definition applies to the system (loosely coupled) approach. A hierarchical network system is comprised of functionally similar or different networks concatenating one to another, as shown in Figure 7.1. In the former case, subnetworks learn conjunctively, whereas in the latter case, component networks learn separately but coherently. In both cases, the output of a network is taken as the input of the network on top of it and the information cascades. The main advantage of the hierarchical approach is the powerful capability of information abstraction.

7.3.1   Neocognitron

The neocognitron (Fukushima, Miyake, and Ito 1983) is a representative work of hierarchical neural networks. This work shows how to synthesize a neural network model in order to endow it with pattern recognition capability and with position and deformation-invariant responses.

In the neocognitron (see Figure 7.2), processing elements on each layer or subnetwork only receive connections from a localized subset of those on the previous layer or subnetwork. This implies that each processing element can only act on the partial information it perceives. Processing elements at deeper layers visualize a larger field (the pyramid effect), have the tendency to respond selectively to a more complicated feature of the stimulus pattern, and are more insensitive to the shift in position of the input pattern. Since each processing element needs only to process a limited amount of information obtained from the previous layer, it is less distracted to irrelevant signals, and the overall network behavior may thereby be regularized. The details of the neocognitron procedure are given below.

The Neocognitron (adapted)

- **Basic Structures**

    - A multilayer network with a hierarchical structure.
    - Each layer consists of two arrays of cell planes: an array of S (simple) planes and an array of C (complex) planes.
    - The layered structure is in the form of

        $$\text{Input} \longrightarrow [S \longrightarrow C] \longrightarrow [S \longrightarrow C] \ldots \longrightarrow [S \longrightarrow C]$$

    - A cell plane is an $n \times n$ array of cells (neurons).
    - A connection area is an $m \times m$ array of cells that have their synaptic connections leading to a single cell in a deeper layer.

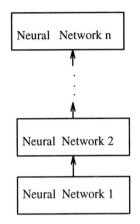

(a) A linear hierarchy

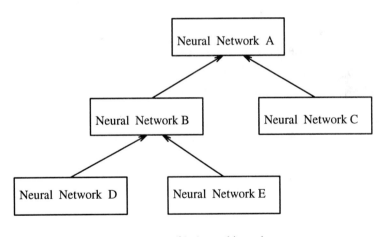

(b) A tree hierarchy

Figure 7.1: Hierarchical network models. (*a*) Information is processed in a linear sequence. (*b*) Information processing is structured as a tree where there are sequential relationships between levels but parallelism can be introduced on the same level.

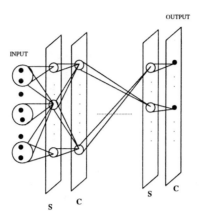

Figure 7.2: The neocognitron network architecture (Fukushima, Miyake, and Ito 1983).

- S cells acquire the ability to extract a specific stimulus feature or pattern, and their input weights are modifiable during learning. The synapses to an S cell are excitatory and inhibitory in nature.

- C cells respond to the same stimulus feature as the preceding S cells but are less sensitive to shift in position, and their input weights are determined in such a way that they will fire when at least one of their preceding S cells fires. The synapses to a C cell are only excitatory, and the associated weights are unmodifiable.

- All the inputs and outputs of cells are analog.

- **Weight Initialization**

  - The modifiable weights are set to zero.
  - The unmodifiable weights are set heuristically, as stated above.

- **Calculation of Activation**

  1. The output of an S cell is given by

  $$U_s = r \cdot \phi\{\frac{1 + E}{1 + \frac{r}{1+r} \cdot I} - 1\} \tag{7.1}$$

  where
  $\phi(x) = \max(x, 0)$

r = a parameter which controls the intensity of the inhibition

$$E = \sum_i a_i U_i$$

$$I = b \cdot V$$

where
E = the total excitatory input
I = the total inhibitory input
a_i = the weight of the ith excitatory synapse
b = the weight of the inhibitory synapse
U_i = the output of the ith (excitatory) C cell
V = the output of the inhibitory cell

$$V = \sqrt{\sum_i c_i U_i^2}$$

where
c_i = the synaptic strength (weight) of the connection from the ith C cell to the inhibitory cell

2. The output of a C cell is given by

$$U_c = \psi\{\sum_j d_j U_j\}$$

where
d_j = the weight from the jth S cell (all excitatory)
U_j = the output of the jth S cell

$$\psi(x) = \begin{cases} x/\alpha + x, & x \geq 0 \\ 0, x < 0 \end{cases}$$

where α is a positive constant which determines the degree of saturation of the output.

- **Weight Training**

  - Learning in the l layer is performed after completion of the learning in the $l - 1$ layer.

  - Learning of cell planes is done one at a time.

  - In order to train a cell plane, a cell is chosen as a representative cell. The desired input pattern is applied to the cell's input connection area, and the changes in the weights are calculated. All the other cells in that cell plane have their input weights modified in the same way as their representative.

– Only the weights through which nonzero signals are coming are
updated, and only the weights leading to S cells are modifiable:

  1.

$$\Delta a_i = q \cdot c_i \cdot U_i$$

where
q is a learning constant
c_i = the (unmodifiable) weight between the ith C cell and the
inhibitory cell
U_i = the output of the ith C cell

  2.

$$\Delta b = q \cdot V$$

where
V = the output of the inhibitory cell

– Learning is unsupervised in the original version, as seen above.
However, supervised learning (omitted here) has also been used
later.

The weights in the neocognitron can increase without bound. It seems that
the network would produce an arbitrarily large output. This is, however, not
the case because of the balance between excitatory and inhibitory inputs. In
contrast to many networks we have seen before like the perceptron, the output
of a neocognitron neuron (S cell) is determined by the ratio of the excitatory to
the inhibitory inputs, rather than their difference. If both types of input increase
at the same rate, the value of the output is limited. It can be shown that the
behavior of neocognitron neurons closely parallels the nonlinear input/output
characteristics of the sensory neurons in biological systems.

S cells play the cardinal role of learning a specific feature, and so their input
weights are modifiable. C cells respond to the same stimulus feature as their
preceding S cells. However, C cells further augment what S cells have learned
by being less sensitive to a shift in position. To achieve this effect, a C cell fires
when at least one of its preceding S cells, which register at different points in
the input pattern, fires.

Let us take a moment to make analysis of Eq. 7.1 in order to gain a better
understanding of the learning behavior of S cells. Let

$$S = \frac{E}{I}$$

If both E and I are sufficiently large, then

$$U_s = r \cdot \phi\{\frac{1+r}{r} \times S - 1\}$$

If $S > r/(r+1)$, then $U_s > 0$ and the cell responds; else the cell does not respond. The larger the value of r, the better the cell can discriminate patterns of different classes. However, the high selectivity of the cell's response decreases its ability to tolerate the deformation of patterns and is not always desirable. Thus, the proper value of r should be a compromise between these two considerations.

The total excitatory input E of the S cell is the dot product of the excitatory weight vector and the input vector (from preceding C cells). Since the excitatory weights are modified according to previous input vectors, it follows that the S cell responds if it judges there is sufficient similarity between the current input and previous inputs.

In one experiment, Fukushima et al. used a four-layer neocognitron to learn handwritten Arabic numerals from 0 through 9. The output layer (more specifically, the C plane of the final layer) consists of 10 units, each designating a numeral. Given an input (which is the image of a pattern), the neocognitron recognizes it as a certain numeral if the corresponding output unit has a high activation. The results showed that the neocognitron could learn to recognize deformed handwritten numerals considerably well. However, it missed some distorted numerals which a human can recognize.

7.3.2 Complex Networks

A neural network system can be created to handle complex tasks by hierarchically linking together a number of networks of the same or different types. In a hierarchical network system, the interface connections between two consecutive networks are determined by the relationship between the tasks assigned to them. So, the connections are knowledge-based. For example, in a hierarchical clustering system, the cluster node on one level connects into the input nodes encoding cluster features on the next level.

Carpenter and Grossberg (1990) show how ART-1 networks can be combined for complex, high-level pattern recognition through hierarchical search. When ART networks are combined into a system, top-down priming stimuli can descend across multiple layers to reevaluate the features presented as input. This contrasts to some hierarchical clustering systems driven entirely bottom-up.

Not only clustering networks but also classification networks can be hierarchically linked. For example, a hierarchical system of backpropagation networks can be devised for the task of speech recognition. This system can process information at different levels of abstraction, such as phonemes, letters, syllables, and words. One may wonder whether we can collapse this hierarchical set of networks into a single backpropagation network. The research on knowledge-based systems has indicated that the hierarchical approach can improve the accuracy and/or efficiency of inference. Moreover, such an approach does make the system more understandable and verifiable since intermediate results are also observable and usable. And we can evaluate the system performance at each level of processing.

A hierarchical system can also be configured as a tree (rather than a single line) where a network may receive inputs from more than one other network. Again, the topological structure reflects how the problem is decomposed. Suppose the task is to model a complex, unknown function f and we know that it involves two smaller unidentified functions f_1 and f_2. Symbolically,

$$f(x_1, x_2, ..., y_1, y_2, ...) = g(f_1(x_1, x_2, ...), f_2(y_1, y_2, ...))$$

where the functions f, f_1, f_2, and g are all unknown. Instead of building a single neural network to learn the function f, we can use three networks to learn f_1, f_2, and g, respectively, assuming that we can obtain training examples for each of them.

If a system involves different types of networks, it is called a heterogeneous system. For example, a vector-quantization network is used as the front end to a backpropagation network, an autoassociative network as the postprocessor of an heteroassociator. Kadaba et al. (1990) used two self-organizing backpropagation networks to encode and decode data sent to a main backpropagation network. The self-organizing backpropagation network uses the same pattern vector as both input and desired output and compresses the original vector into a smaller one stored in the hidden layer. The compressed data are then used as input to the main network.

Hirsch (1989) investigated convergence properties of cascades of networks. This issue is nontrivial since convergence on each level does not guarantee the overall convergence of the whole system. If a cascade of networks behaves like a multilayer network, then the issue could be examined accordingly. Since, however, in the cascade system, the learning dynamics of individual networks are not so closely coupled as in a single multilayer network, the output of one network must meet the convergence assumption of the next one it leads into.

7.3.3 Modular Neural Networks

The modular neural network developed by Jacobs, Jordan, Nowlan, and Hinton (1991) is composed of multiple different *expert* networks plus a *gating* network that decides which of the experts should be invoked for each training case (see Figure 7.3). To see why this idea is useful, consider the problem of functional approximation. If the data suggest a discontinuity in the function being approximated, then it would be more accurate to use a separate model on each side of the discontinuity than to fit a single model across the discontinuity. The role of the gating network is to divide the training data set into different subsets (or more generally, to divide the input space into different subspaces), each best dealt with by a distinct expert network.

Each expert network is a feedforward network (a perceptron or a radial basis function network), and all experts have the same input and the same number of outputs. The gating network is also feedforward, typically receives the same input as the expert networks, and has the number of outputs equal to that of

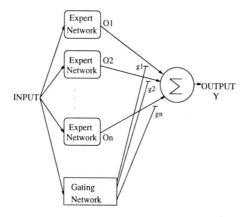

Figure 7.3: A system architecture of modular neural networks (Jacobs, Jordan, Nowlan, and Hinton 1991).

the expert networks. The overall output of the system $\mathbf{Y}$ is given by

$$\mathbf{Y} = \sum_i g_i \mathbf{O}_i \qquad (7.2)$$

where $\mathbf{O}_i$ is the output vector of expert i, and g_i is the corresponding gating strength produced by output unit i of the gating network:

$$g_i = \exp(X_i)/\sum_j \exp(X_j)$$

where X_i is the total weighted input received by output unit i of the gating network. Because of the normalization process,

$$\sum_i g_i = 1$$

Thus, g_i can be interpreted as the probability of selecting expert i. Note that g_i is produced in each inference cycle in contrast to other weights which are fixed during inference.

As long as the system behavior is described by a set of continuous functions, it can be trained by gradient descent. The overall output error is propagated backward to expert and gating networks. The weights inside both networks can be adjusted accordingly.

Multiple expert networks may cooperate or compete to solve a particular problem. Their interaction manner is influenced by the choice of the error criterion. Consider the error criterion given by

$$E = ||\mathbf{T} - \sum_i g_i \mathbf{O}_i||^2 \tag{7.3}$$

where $\mathbf{T}$ is the desired output vector, $\mathbf{O}_i$ is the actual output vector from the ith expert network, and g_i is the gating strength representing the proportional contribution of expert i to the combined output vector. The strong coupling between the experts due to the linear combination of their outputs causes them to cooperate and tends to produce solutions in which many experts are used for each case.

If, on the other hand, the gating network makes a stochastic decision about which single expert to use for each case, then the error is the expected value of the squared difference given by

$$E = \sum_i g_i ||\mathbf{T} - \mathbf{O}_i||^2 \tag{7.4}$$

This new error function tends to assign a single expert to each training case, since the best way to minimize the error is to pick the expert with the minimum error and set its gating strength to 1. Therefore, this error function encourages the experts to compete rather than to cooperate. In practice, the following error function works better:

$$E = -\log \sum_i g_i \exp(-\frac{1}{2}||\mathbf{T} - \mathbf{O}_i||^2) \tag{7.5}$$

because its derivative will reflect how well an expert does relative to other experts. This facilitates convergence in gradient descent.

The modularity of this approach can be further increased by introducing a hierarchical gating structure (tree), much like a decision tree, into the system (Jordan and Jacobs 1992). Then the training cases grouped under each node of the gating tree are processed by a local expert network.

7.4   Hybrid Models

In a hybrid network, each layer implements a certain network type and performs its function. The connection pattern in each layer is determined by the network type concerned.

7.4.1   Hamming Networks

The *Hamming network* is a hybrid of a perceptron-like net and MAXNET. This network has two layers. The lower layer calculates matching scores for predefined classes and the MAXNET as the upper layer picks the maximum. In the lower layer, the Hamming network operates by calculating a Hamming distance between the input pattern and each of the exemplar patterns for predefined classes. This distance is equal to the number of elements in the input pattern which are different in value from the corresponding nodes in the exemplar pattern.

In the MAXNET layer, each node feeds back to itself as well as to all its neighbors on that level so that each node will tend to reinforce itself while laterally inhibiting others.

7.4.2   Counterpropagation Networks

The *counterpropagation network*, developed by Robert Hecht-Nielsen (1987), is a hybrid of a Kohonen clustering network and a Grossberg outstar. The Kohonen network implements the winner-take-all strategy, and the Grossberg outstar maps the winning neuron into the desired output pattern. See Chapter 2 "Basic Neural Computational Models" for more discussions on competitive learning and counterpropagation. The following procedures summarize the counterpropagation network.

The Counterpropagation Network

- **Weight Initialization**
  Weights are initialized randomly, or heuristically so that the weight vectors of the Kohonen layer will be distributed according to the density of input vectors during training.

- **Calculation of Activation**

  1. The activation of an input unit is determined by the instance presented to the network.

  2. The activation of a unit in the Kohonen layer is calculated as in Kohonen's self-organizing network (described later), where the radius of the neighborhood is set to 0 so that for each instance, only one unit is activated (the winner).

  3. The activation of unit j in the Grossberg layer is given by

  $$O_j = \sum_i W_{ji} O_i$$

  where W_{ji} is the weight from unit i in the Kohonen layer to unit j and O_j and O_i are the activations of units j and i, respectively.

- **Weight Training**

1. The weights in the Kohonen layer are modified as in Kohonen's self-organizing network.

2. The weights in the Grossberg layer are modified by

$$\Delta W_{ji} = a(T_j - W_{ji})O_i$$

   where a is the learning rate ($0 < a < 1$) and T_j is the desired activation level at output unit j.

3. Repeat by presenting a new instance, calculating activations, and weight training.

This network can be taught to recognize inputs to different categories. Its performance is not as good as the backpropagation network, but it converges more rapidly. Because the Kohonen layer learns without supervision, counterpropagation is more incremental in nature than backpropagation.

This network model has found applications for image compression, data compression, and vector quantization.

7.5   Parallel Models

There are two approaches in which we can organize networks to operate in parallel:

- Different networks work in parallel, each network extracting different features from the same data.

- A complex problem is broken up into a number of subtasks, each solved by a separate network.

The parallel architecture is shown in Figure 7.4.

The first approach is useful for extracting more information by making different analyses of the same data. For instance, Gevins and Morgan (1988) applied different networks to detect different types of contaminants in EEG signals recorded from the brain. When data are not easy to obtain, this approach is especially valuable. Sometimes, different types of features need to be extracted in order to make different distinctions, and we may not know beforehand what features will be needed. In this case, the use of multiple networks may give rise to unexpected but important discoveries.

In the second approach, the results of the different networks employed can be combined to obtain desired results. Casselman and Acres (1990) applied multiple backpropagation networks in parallel to solve different diagnostic tasks involving satellite spectral data. It was found that a system of networks could solve a problem that was difficult for a single network of equivalent size

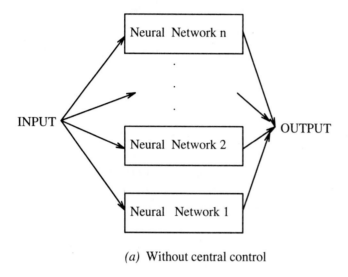

(a) Without central control

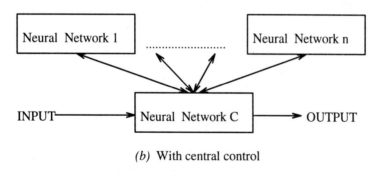

(b) With central control

Figure 7.4: Parallel network models. (*a*) Information is distributed to different networks for processing in parallel. (*b*) There exists a control network which coordinates parallel computing among multiple networks. This model can be adapted to the situation more dynamically than the former model.

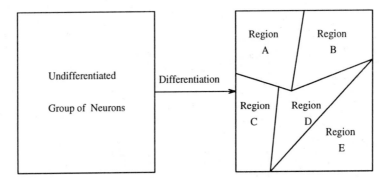

Figure 7.5: Differentiation network models.

(Hering, Khosla, and Kumar 1990). A parallel system can become more efficient and capable by incorporating a control structure. This issue is addressed in the section on control networks.

7.6   Differentiation Models

A system with multiple functions for solving complex problems can be generated in two ways. One is to integrate existing networks with different functions. The other is to let a large network "differentiate" into multiple networks with different functions. This concept is illustrated in Figure 7.5.

7.6.1   Kohonen's Self-Organizing Nets

In Kohonen's (1988) self-organizing feature maps, a network differentiates into multiple regions, each responsive to a specific stimulus pattern or feature, just as in the auditory pathway, nerve cells and fibers are arranged anatomically in relation to the frequency response. If a specific input pattern requires a specific processing function, then this self-organizing heuristic may lead to a network with functionally differentiated regions (subnetworks). The Kohonen network consists of an input and an output layers, and uses the following procedure to produce self-organizing feature maps. Refer to Chapter 2 for more discussions on this network.

Kohonen's Self-Organizing Network (adapted)

- **Weight Initialization**

  - Weights are initialized to small random values.
  - The initial radius of the neighborhood is set properly.

- **Calculation of Activation**

  1. The activation X_i of input unit i is determined by the instance presented to the network.
  2. The activation O_j of output unit j is calculated by

  $$O_j = F_{\min}(d_j) = F_{\min}(\sum_i (X_i - W_{ji})^2)$$

  where $F_{\min}$ is the unity function (returning 1) if unit j is the output node with minimum d_j or its neighbor, and the zero function (returning 0) otherwise. (Note that if the weight vectors are normalized to constant length, then we may calculate the inner dot product of the input and the weights to find the node with a maximum value.)

- **Weight Training**

  1. Weight modification is given by

  $$\Delta W_{ji} = O_j \eta (X_i - W_{ji})$$

  where η is a gain term ($0 < \eta < 1$) that decreases over time. Note that the radius of the neighborhood also does so.

  2. Repeat by presenting a new instance, calculating activations, and modifying weights until $\eta = 0$.

7.7   Control Networks

A complex network system may contain a neural network which controls or influences its process. This network is termed a *control neural network*. It can be built out of a domain model or based on domain knowledge. More than one network can be involved in the control structure.

Barto, Sutton, and Anderson (1983) developed an early neurocontrol scheme. Their system involved two networks, both of which were simple table lookups.

They made distinctions between action and critic networks in their neurocontrol theory. Their approach has nourished a substantial line of research on neurocontrol.

Lapedes and Farber (1987) developed another scheme which consisted of a master network and a slave network; the former set the weights for the latter. Both networks were Hopfield nets. The key issue concerned how to use one network to control the weights of another.

In the following subsections, we show how to design control networks. The main idea involves the merging of knowledge-based and neural network principles. A control neural network can be used as:

- An independent unit to solve a single task

- A control unit in a complex network system to control the system process

"Control" concerns what is the next action. This decision is based on the current situation and goals to be pursued. Such information is described in the data base or the working memory. The data base is nonmonotonic since an action when executed may change it.

When there are more than one goal to be accomplished, the controller must determine the dependencies among goals and order them properly. The ordering could be partial or complete. Partial order implies that some goals can be attained in parallel. Goals are then selected according to their order.

In planning systems, there are several ways to order goals. An old approach is to use a linear *stack*, which processes goals by the last-in–first-out order. Goals are pushed onto the stack. During processing a selected goal, which is always the top goal on the stack, a new goal may be generated, and it is placed at the top of the stack. The system's operation ceases when the stack becomes empty. Another approach is to assume that goals can be pursued in parallel first. If conflicts arise, the system resolves them by placing a goal order.

A *blackboard-based* model deals with goals in an asynchronously parallel manner. There are a set of heuristics for ordering goals. The goal with the highest priority score is visited first. This model is often applied to a problem which is so complex or difficult that the opportunistic (versus deterministic) use of available knowledge is the only means.

In the data-driven control, the action is selected based on the current situation; in the goal-directed control, based on the currently processed goal; and in the mixed approach, based on both the situation and the goal. The mixed control strategy would be more efficient than the other two by offering *bidirectional search* for the solution.

7.7.1   The Feedforward Model

Figure 7.6 shows a feedforward control network, in which the input layer contains situational and goal variables, and the output layer, action variables. In this model, the current situation and goal infer the action to be taken next.

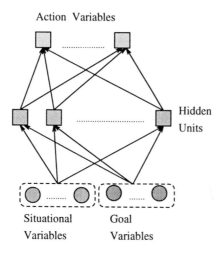

Figure 7.6: A feedforward neural network for control.

To reach optimal decisions, variables related to cost analysis should be added to the input as well. Building in some hidden layers can increase the inference power of the network through nonlinearity. Backpropagation is a reasonable choice for the computational mechanism underlying such control structure. It can learn to make actions by example mapping. However, this control model is quite limited, since it addresses neither the interactions among goals nor the temporal aspect of the control process.

7.7.2   The Recurrent Model

The recurrent control model addresses the issue of goal interaction. As discussed above, when goals interact, there must be a mechanism for inferring the goal order in order to solve the problem. A goal order, in fact, is a temporal order. Since recurrent neural networks have been shown capable of learning temporal patterns by identifying temporal relationships, it is natural to apply such networks to learn goal orders. Figure 7.7 shows how a recurrent control model can be designed based on this consideration. Goal interactions are modeled by recurrent connections among goal variables. In the absence of initial knowledge, goals are fully and recurrently connected. Some *hidden* recurrent units can be added. A goal order is learned by adjusting the connection weights according to training examples. Stack-based control is a special case of this model. A discussion regarding the derivation of a temporal order from recurrent weights

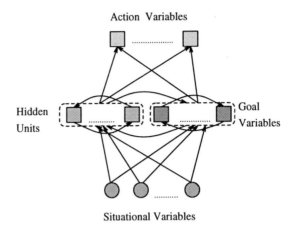

Figure 7.7: A recurrent neural network for control.

is made in Chapter 15 "Learning Grammars." Recurrent control networks can be trained by *recurrent backpropagation* (described in Chapter 10 "Learning Spatiotemporal Patterns.")

7.7.3   The Temporal Model

The recurrent control model just introduced is a time-implicit model because it does not represent the time parameter explicitly but rather implicitly. Moreover, the recurrent model as well as the feedforward model only gives a one-shot decision on actions. In order to generate a sequence of actions, they start with time = 0, generate the action for time = 1, update the situational and goal variables, generate the action for time = 2, and so on. However, the main concern with the nontemporal approach is that when training the network, we need to supply input/output information at each time cycle for each training example. We cannot, instead, just specify the initial situation and goals. The temporal control model addresses the question of whether a network can learn to generate a sequence of actions for achieving certain goals, given initial descriptions about the world. The network model of Figure 7.8 shows the control process over time.

If the desired action sequence is specified for each training example, then the learning problem is that addressed by either the feedforward or the recurrent model mentioned above. Relative to these two models, the learning problem of the temporal model is much less constrained. Both unsupervised and

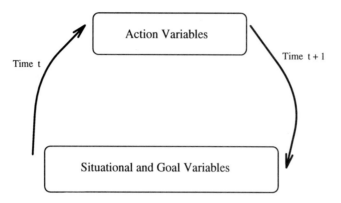

Figure 7.8: A temporal neural network for control.

supervised learning strategies can be considered.

When no hint about the desired sequence is given, learning can only proceed without supervision. The model will generate many action sequences to solve given goals by trial and error, and always keep the best sequence ever generated. Search in this approach is undoubtedly inefficient.

A supervised learning scheme can be devised if we know or can estimate the desired number of steps to realize goals. With recurrent connections involving time, we may consider using a temporal neural network procedure known as *backpropagation through time* (BPTT) (Rumelhart, Hinton, and Williams 1986) for training the network. In Figure 7.9, learning works backward through time, starting at time = k (k is the desired number of steps) when every goal variable is set to an activation of 0 (i.e., solved). A multilayer temporal network can be created in this way. It is an iterative expansion of the recursive model shown in Figure 7.8. Since the number k may vary with examples, so does the depth of the temporal network. The link weights from action variables to situational and goal variables are assumed fixed because we know the effect of each action. Those from the latter to the former variables are open to be adjusted so that the network learns to decide on actions. This network is then trained using standard backpropagation (see Chapter 3 "Learning: Supervised and Unsupervised").[1] The constraint is that all weights are equal at all levels (each level designating a different time). This constraint is maintained by changing each of the weights at the end of each iteration according to the sum of the weight changes computed

---

[1] The complexity of BPTT is $O(kN^2)$ where N is the number of units and k is the number of steps in time.

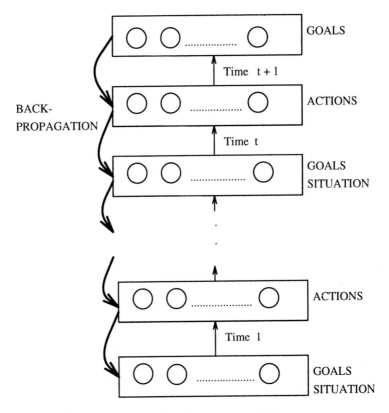

Figure 7.9: Backpropagation through time for training a control neural network. The recursive use of the same network which infers the desired actions based on goals and the situation is functionally equivalent to a feedforward network extending over time. The weights connecting each layer of units to the next are time-invariant during the inference phase, but vary with time during learning backward through time. Note that the error is propagated from the present to the past through the time network.

at each level. Each iteration involves backpropagation through the entire time sequence.

7.8   Summary

Attention has been shifting from the design of a single neural network to that of a system of networks, or a hybrid architecture. This is especially important when the problem to be solved is so complex that no single existing neural network can effectively manage it. On one hand, we may continue to explore a new computational model. On the other hand, we should exploit existing models which have been thoroughly investigated and create hybrids of them or integrate them properly in order to meet growing problem demand. And this was the central focus of this chapter.

For complex problems, the expert system technology base, which contains a rich set of heuristics, can be reimplemented in the framework of neural networks. For example, problem abstraction can be realized by a hierarchical system of networks configured as a linear or tree structure. The divide-and-conquer strategy can be implemented by a parallel-distributed system of networks.

We classify complex network systems into the *hierarchical, differentiation,* and *parallel* models. The hierarchical model is exemplified by the neocognitron and hybrid networks such as counterpropagation. It consists of multiple layers or networks related hierarchically in their functionalities, each connected to a subproblem. The differentiation model is represented by Kohonen's self-organizing network. The idea behind this model is that a network differentiates into multiple regions by self-organization, each region covering a certain aspect or part of the problem. The parallel model involves multiple networks working in parallel. This is useful when a problem is preferably analyzed from multiple perspectives or decomposed appropriately.

A control structure is very beneficial in a complex system architecture. It coordinates all of the system's activities and monitors its process. It dispatches jobs to suitable neural networks and combines their results. Although some problems can be decomposed in such a way that pure parallel-distributed processing without central control is adequate, in many others this is not so. A control neural network basically uses situational and goal parameters as input to infer the desired action or action sequence. Difficult aspects of the control process include goal interaction and nonmonotonicity of the data base. Temporal constraints among goals can be effectively dealt with by recurrent networks. The task of learning a sequence of actions can be accomplished by temporal networks.

7.9   References

1. Barto, A.G., Sutton, R.S., and Anderson, C.W. 1983. Neuron-like adaptive elements that can solve difficult learning control problems. *IEEE Transactions on Systems, Man, and Cybernetics*, SMC-13, pp. 834–846.

2. Carpenter, G., and Grossberg, S. 1990. ART 3: Hierarchical search using chemical transmitters in self-organizing pattern recognition architectures. *Neural Networks*, 3, pp. 129–152.

3. Casselman, F., and Acres, J.D. 1990. DASA/LARS, a large diagnostic system using neural networks. In *Proceedings of IJCNN* (Washington, D.C.), pp. II-539–542.

4. Fukushima, K., Miyake, S., and Ito, T. 1983. Neocognitron: A neural network model for a mechanism of visual pattern recognition. *IEEE Transactions on Systems, Man, and Cybernetics*, 13(5), pp. 826–834.

5. Gevins, A.S., and Morgan, N.H. 1988. Application of neural-network (NN) signal processing in brain research. *IEEE Transactions on Acoustics, Speech, and Signal Processing*, 36, pp. 1152–1166.

6. Hayes-Roth, B. 1985. A blackboard architecture for control. *Artificial Intelligence*, 26, pp. 251–321.

7. Hecht-Nielsen, R. 1987. Counter-propagation networks. *Applied Optics*, 26, pp. 4979–4984.

8. Hering, D., Khosla, P., and Kumar, B.V.K.V. 1990. The use of modular neural networks in tactile sensing. In *Proceedings of IJCNN* (Washington, D.C.), pp. II-355–358.

9. Hirsch, M.W. 1989. Convergence in cascades of neural networks. In *Proceedings of IJCNN* (Washington, D.C.), pp. I-207–208.

10. Jacobs, R.A., Jordan, M.I., Nowlan, S.J., and Hinton, G.E. 1991. Adaptive mixtures of local experts. *Neural Computation*, 3, pp. 79–87.

11. Jordan, M.I., and Jacobs, R.A. 1992. Hierarchies of adaptive experts. In *Advances in Neural Information Processing Systems*, 4. Morgan Kaufmann, San Mateo, CA.

12. Kadaba, N., Nygard, K.E., Juell, P.L., and Kanga, L. 1990. Modular backpropagation neural networks for large domain pattern classification. In *Proceedings of IJCNN* (Washington, D.C.), pp. II-551–554.

13. Kohonen, T. 1988. *Self-Organization and Associative Memory*. Springer-Verlag, New York.

14. Lapedes, A., and Farber, R. 1987. Programming a massively parallel, computation universal system: Static behavior. In *Proceeding of Neural Information Processing*, pp. 283–298.

15. Rumelhart, D.E., Hinton, G.E., and Williams, R.J. 1986. Learning internal representation by error propagation. In *Parallel Distributed Processing: Explorations in the Microstructures of Cognition*, Vol. 1. MIT Press, Cambridge, MA.

7.10 Problems

1. The Hamming network can be applied to code correction. In this application, Grossberg's outstar layer is placed on top of the Hamming net in order to produce a correct code pattern. Given an incorrect input pattern, the Hamming net will determine which is the nearest exemplar code pattern. The outstar uses the following learning rule to make weight adjustment:

$$\Delta W_{ji} = \eta(T_j - W_{ji})$$

where T_j is the correct bit value for output unit j in the outstar, W_{ji} is the weight from unit i in the MAXNET to unit j, and η is a learning rate that starts near 1 and is gradually reduced to zero during training. Assume the code is of 6 bits and there are 8 codes to be transmitted.

   (a) Specify the network structure.
   (b) Show how to set the connection weights.

2. The counterpropagation network can be applied to vector quantization. Suppose an image is to be transmitted. It can be divided into subimages. The set of subimage vectors is used as input to train the Kohonen layer so that only a single Kohonen neuron will get activated given a subimage. The Grossberg layer weights are trained to produce the binary code of the *index* of the Kohonen neuron that is 1. For example, if the ninth Kohonen neuron is active, then the Grossberg layer will generate 000. . .01001. Note that the output string of n bits allows the transmission of the information of up to 2^n Kohonen neurons. Suppose an image is divided into 128×128 subimages.

   (a) What is the length of the bit string to be transmitted?
   (b) Specify the network structure. How many output units are required?
   (c) Specify the connection weights.

3. The learning mode of the neocognitron is unsupervised in its early version. Later, the supervised mode is also used.

   (a) What are relative advantages of the supervised and unsupervised learning algorithms to train a neural network for pattern recognition?

(b) What is the proper way to integrate the supervised and unsupervised learning modes in a hierarchical neural network for pattern recognition?

4. Kohonen's self-organizing net can learn the statistical distribution of input patterns. Explain how and why.

5. A recurrent neural network has two units, 1 and 2. Each unit connects to the other and connects back to itself. So, there are four weights: W_{11}, W_{12}, W_{21}, W_{22}. For a particular inference, the network converges after three iterations. Draw an equivalent feedforward neural network.

Chapter 8

Discovery

8.1 Introduction

The advancement of science relies on the discovery of new principles. Scientific discovery is the crossroads of scientists', philosophers', and computer scientists' interest from different perspectives. For many years, researchers have been attempting to develop programs which make discoveries. It has become a main line of research in artificial intelligence.

"Discovery" involves more inference than any other approach to machine learning. Learning by discovery begins with completely unorganized data where instances are not classified by any teacher. This form of learning is a typical example of unsupervised learning. Though a discovery program is given as input disorganized information, it is also given a set of heuristics which implicitly organize the information. Supplied heuristics somehow direct the learning process toward the discovery of interesting concepts. It is often asked how far a discovery program can go under the heuristics. The program will be very powerful if the heuristics can continuously generate new hypotheses for evaluation. The concern is whether the program can indeed discover something new since those heuristics may have set general boundaries, and the discovery could be just logically implied by what is known. However, many successful examples of machine discovery have weakened this concern.

In the sections which follow, we review symbolic methods for machine discovery, including conceptual clustering, heuristic discovery, and search for laws, and then we present neural network methods. Various neural network architectures for discovery are introduced and related to their symbolic counterparts.

223

Table 8.1: Differences between numerical and conceptual clustering.

	Numerical Clustering	**Conceptual Clustering**
• Approach	Numerical, quantitative	Symbolic (dominant), qualitative
• Cluster formation	Numerical similarity	Generalization and discrimination
• Cluster evaluation	Numerical criterion	Conceptual criterion
• Comprehensibility	Poor	Good

8.2   Symbolic Methods

In the past, symbolic methods have been developed for discovering categories, domains, and laws. In this section, we examine and discuss these important methods.

8.2.1   Conceptual Clustering

Constructing a classification (taxonomy) of given objects or events is an important form of "learning from observation." A new class or subclass can be "discovered" in this process. Such classifications not only facilitate our comprehension of observations but may also lead to the discovery of new theories or laws. In the aspect of problem solving, a taxonomy tree embeds the knowledge of how to decompose a large-scale system into smaller, easier components.

Traditional techniques for this purpose such as cluster analysis and numerical taxonomy organize objects into classes on the basis of a numerical measure of object similarity. These techniques have been investigated for a long time and applied to many kinds of problem solving. With the emergence of artificial intelligent systems, there has been a concern whether such techniques can adequately handle many-valued, nominal variables which occur often in human classifications. In addition, the classes obtained from numerical analysis may have no simple conceptual description and may be difficult to interpret. To address these issues, Michalski and Stepp (1983) developed an approach called *conceptual clustering*, in which objects form a class only if they satisfy a certain conceptual criterion. Table 8.1 summarizes key differences between numerical and conceptual clustering.

In both the numerical and conceptual approaches, the objects (or events) assigned to the same cluster (class) must share some sort of similarity. The term "similarity" is a vague term. In the numerical approach, two objects are called similar if they are close in an assumed physical space. In the conceptual (symbolic) approach, two similar objects share some symbolic descriptions. It can be argued that symbolic descriptions are just a higher-level interpretation of numerical descriptions. For example, a symbolic description "height is tall" may correspond to a numerical description "height is greater than 2 meters." Thus, to view these two approaches as the same process but at different levels of abstraction would be more powerful, since we can now integrate them in a single framework and combine their advantages—the conceptual approach is more understandable but the numerical approach is more precise. Later, we address the translation mechanism between these two levels.

A program which discovers new laws or theories might also discover concepts (categories, clusters, or classes) to which those laws apply. Knowledge and methods which apply to one situation (object) may well apply to another situation (object) in the same category. Clustering is thus an important approach for machine discovery. A discovery program often looks for regularities. In fact, "regularity" is closely related to "similarity." However, the former term is a more general notion than the latter. "Regularity" is often defined by satisfaction of certain constraints which are predicates in symbolic languages or mathematical relations in numerical languages.

Conceptual clustering is best exemplified by CLUSTER/2 (Michalski and Stepp 1983). This program takes a collection of examples and produces a taxonomic organization which arranges the examples into disjoint clusters at several levels. CLUSTER/2 receives as input a set of objects (physical or abstract), a set of attributes for characterizing the objects, and a body of background knowledge including problem constraints, properties of attributes, and a quality criterion for evaluating constructed classifications. This program can accept abstract descriptions which characterize a class of objects, and so it can be applied recursively to generate a taxonomic hierarchy.

CLUSTER/2 consists of two modules: a clustering module and a hierarchy-building module. The clustering algorithm begins with a set of k seed events (where k is given), forms clusters, evaluates them, and repeats until a satisfactory clustering configuration is found. Over iterations, the program refines the cluster structure to optimize the quality criterion. The process can be viewed as a kind of "hill-climbing" search. In the next iteration, k seeds will be selected from the centers or the borders of clusters, depending on whether the clustering quality improves or not. An important notion in the formation of clusters based on seed events is a "star," which is defined as the set of all maximally general descriptions of a certain event which do not intersect with some other events. The quality criterion is referred to as LEF (lexicographical evaluation function), which takes into account the following properties of an abstract clustering:

- The fit between the clustering and the events

- The simplicity of cluster descriptions

- The intercluster difference

- The discrimination index, which is the number of variables having different values in every cluster description

- Dimensionality reduction, which is the negative of the essential dimensionality, defined as the minimum number of variables required to distinguish among all clusters

The hierarchy-building module recursively applies the clustering algorithm. The abstract descriptions concerning the clustering configuration at one level become data for clustering at the next level. The algorithm of CLUSTER/2 is formulated below.

The CLUSTER/2 (Conceptual Clustering) Algorithm

- The clustering algorithm
  Given a set of input events and a number of clusters k:

  1. Choose k seed events.

  2. Construct clusters based upon seed events.

  3. Modify clusters into disjoint clusters that optimize the LEF criterion.

  4. If clustering quality is satisfactory, exit; else go to the next step.

  5. If clustering quality improves, select k new seeds from centers of clusters and go to step 2; else select k new seeds from borders of clusters and go to step 2.

- The hierarchy-building algorithm
  Given a set of events E:

  1. Initialize the variable L to 1.

  2. Compute a set of clusterings (a clustering is a set of clusters).

  3. Select the best clustering (in terms of the LEF criterion) and call it C. Record C as the clustering at level L.

  4. If C has a single cluster, then exit; else increment L by 1, set $E = C$, and go to step 2.

COBWEB (Fisher 1987) is another conceptual clustering program, which is described in Chapter 5 "Incremental Learning."

8.2.2   The Role of Heuristics

AM (Lenat 1976) demonstrated that new domains of knowledge can be developed mechanically by applying heuristics. EURISKO (Lenat 1983) further showed that heuristics can in turn be used to discover new heuristics. Thus, the recursive use of heuristics endows a machine learning program with enormous capability of discovering domain knowledge (concepts, relations, and principles).

In these systems, a large corpus of heuristics, organized at varying levels of generality and in conjunction with some initial hypotheses about the nature of domain, is employed to suggest plausible and implausible hypotheses. Confirmation of plausible ones results in new knowledge which is then distributed to the whole system. As new domains of knowledge emerge and evolve, new heuristics are needed. Each time a field changes, the corpus of heuristics useful for dealing with that field may also change.

New representations can be developed by using heuristics. Since "how to represent" is also a kind of knowledge, the development of new representations can be managed by heuristics. Like heuristics, representations must evolve as domain knowledge accrues.

An important lesson learned is that new heuristics can be developed by using heuristics. Since "heuristics" are a domain of knowledge, they too can be discovered via heuristic guidance. To achieve this would require so-called metaheuristics, which deal with the discovery or transformation of *domain heuristics*, which are applied to learn domain knowledge. A hierarchy of heuristics of whatever levels can be built, or they can interact in a multidirectional manner. Sometimes, a heuristic can be both a metaheuristic and a domain heuristic, and a heuristic may recursively apply to itself.

Heuristics are often regarded as though they were incomplete or uncertain. This is not always true. Some heuristics have a sound mathematical basis. Some are precise knowledge with high utility. Some are derived from statistical observations. In any case, the standard use of heuristics is to pretend that they are true and let them guide the system behavior.

The domain of heuristics can be controlled by a single loop just as in a rule-based system. Heuristics are triggered by certain situational parameters defined for the learning system. For example, there is a set of heuristics for choosing representations. From time to time, some of these heuristics evaluate how well the current representation is performing. If it performs below the standard, some heuristics will be triggered to change the representation. Similarly, there are several heuristics which monitor the adequacy of the existing stock of heuristics. If needed, new heuristics can be created by metaheuristics, or old heuristics can be transferred to a new domain based on *analogy*. It is assumed that these representation heuristics and metaheuristics have run for a while, and the system then reaches a kind of equilibrium. As the domain knowledge evolves, those heuristics may need to be reactivated to establish a new equilibrium. Thus, the whole system operates in an event-driven fashion. Since the power of such systems is derived from heuristics rather than inference engines, employing a more sophisticated control is not a major concern.

The utility of an entire set of heuristics is hard to estimate from those of individual ones. Interactions among heuristics are often the rule rather than the exception. They may interact synergistically, redundantly, or even contradictorily. In fact, the system will not be so interesting if its overall utility is simply the linear superposition of individual heuristics.

Small heuristics can aggregate into large ones. The grain size of heuristics should be chosen properly for a given domain. If the heuristics are too small, they do not represent chunks of wisdom to the human expert, and risk having many undesired interactions. If the heuristic rules are large, the degree of their synergism is decreased and thus the benefit of the heuristic-, or rule-, based approach is lost.

Suppose we arrange all the world's heuristics in a generalization-and-specialization hierarchy. The most general ones are so-called weak methods, such as generate and test, hill climbing, means-ends analysis, and so on. The most specific ones involve domain-specific concepts.

Consider the tree of only those heuristics which have positive utility at least in some domains. One can take a specific heuristic and generalize it gradually, in all possible ways, until all the generalizations are weak methods. It may become apparent that most generalizations are no less powerful (useful) than the heuristics deriving them. In this sense, the specific heuristics can be eliminated from the tree. The resulting tree may be shallow and bushy. This argument is against the approach which synthesizes new heuristics via specialization, since it produces something no more useful than the rule at beginning. This problem is termed the "shallow tree problem" by Lenat (1983). He gave two ways out of this dilemma. One is to consider the utility of a heuristic from several distinct dimensions such as efficiency, flexibility, and so on. A specific heuristic may be better than its generalizations along one or more of these dimensions. The second way is to connect two heuristics using multiple useful relationships. In cases where the depth of the tree of heuristics related by a relation is great, that relation is a good one to generalize and specialize along; in cases where the resulting tree is shallow and broad, other methods such as analogy may be more productive ways of getting new heuristics.

The AM algorithm is described in Chapter 3 "Learning: Supervised and Unsupervised."

8.2.3   Search for Laws

Laws might be conceived as ways of connecting concepts, variables, or objects in the universe. A law enables one to infer about the world. For example, a gravity law allows one to predict what will happen if a pen falls. Discovery of laws is a much more difficult process than use of them. The former is inductive, whereas the latter is deductive. BACON (Langley, Bradshaw, and Simon 1983) demonstrated that a machine learning program can rediscover empirical laws that summarize data. Like AM and EURISKO, the success of BACON can be attributed to the use of a body of heuristics.

BACON has one set of heuristics for discovering laws and another for inventing new terms. However, these two processes (inventing terms and inventing laws) are not independent of each other. The heuristics for discovering laws identify constant, linear, and other relations between terms. For example, "If two terms Y and X are linearly related with slope M and intercept B across all data, then infer that $Y = MX + B$ for constant M and B." The heuristics for forming new terms compare how terms vary with respect to one another. For example, "If the term X rises whenever the term Y rises, then define the term X/Y"; "If the term X rises whenever the term Y falls, then define the term XY." Thus, the central activities of BACON are to detect regularities of data.

The control structure of BACON is a simple, forward-chaining production system, where all the rules applicable to a given situation are collected and one rule is selected. This rule is applied to the situation to produce a new situation by filling in new values or defining a new term. Rules are selected on the basis of "recency" of data in the situation so that a rule which is applicable to more recent changes will fire first.

In the earliest version, the program could not use the inference of a linear or constant relation to define new terms, and complicated relations between more than two terms could not be discovered. Later versions resolved this problem by introducing *levels of description*, at which regularities at one level of data become dependent terms at the next level. For example, if two terms are linearly related, then the slope and intercept of this linear relation are defined as new dependent terms on the next level. To recognize regularities in subsets of terms, BACON performs an exhaustive search. It looks for regularities for every possible combination of two terms while keeping others constant. The level-by-level approach allows the detection of regularities involving more than two terms.

The BACON approach leads one to wonder, "Is this the true process whereby scientists make discoveries?" Human scientists seem to be more model-driven than data-driven. They are quite intuitive and subjective when they formulate a scientific hypothesis. As the domain theory accrues, it seems too naive to perform a data-driven search. One can argue that laws discovered by BACON are limited to simple mathematical relations (perhaps, laws are simple). Can BACON discover a very complicated relation which can be derived only by solving a formidable set of equations in quantum physics? The answer is likely to be no, since in this case a theory-based, analytical approach will be much more accurate and efficient than heuristic search. Data-driven search for laws is reminiscent of *curve fitting*—an old practice in data analysis. However, the use of heuristics in BACON (later versions) will lead to a substantially different result than what can be obtained by a purely statistical procedure.

A related system named FAHRENHEIT (Zytkow 1987) addresses some limitations of BACON: (1) BACON does not have a concept of the limits within which a given law can be applied, (2) BACON is sensitive to the order in which independent terms are varied, and (3) BACON does not recognize irrelevant terms and may thus create spurious laws.

Despite some negative criticisms, BACON's impressive performance points to an important position for BACON as an assistant to scientists. Programs like BACON can be used to suggest patterns and regularities which can then be further investigated by scientists.

8.3   Neural Network Methods

In the previous section, we saw that the power of a machine discovery program stems from the heuristics embedded in it. The program will crumble upon removal of these heuristics. However, it is not a trivial matter to find good and workable heuristics. Existing heuristics have been achieved through ingenuity and expertise that are always in short supply. A question naturally arises of whether there exists an approach which can automatically form heuristics and obviate artificial ones. The neural network approach offers an immediate answer. By self-reorganization, neural networks are able to detect patterns and regularities of input data. If we treat a single neuron as a heuristic unit, the *grain size* of each unit may be too small. Recall that the human brain has billions of neurons. It is hard to imagine that neural networks available nowadays can make amazing discoveries.

Two solutions might get around this worry. One is to construct a hierarchy of neural networks where networks at each level can learn heuristics or knowledge at some level of abstraction. The principle of abstraction has been shown extremely powerful for solving complex problems. The other is to integrate symbolic heuristics and neural network heuristics where appropriate. In this section, we delineate several neural network architectures for discovery and also show how to extract symbolic knowledge from clustering networks.

8.3.1   Adaptive Clustering

Some clustering procedures assume that the number of clusters to be formed is given, while others do not. We refer to the latter case as *adaptive clustering*. For machine discovery, an adaptive clustering program can flexibly create a new concept or category as it sees fit.

Neural networks have been applied to cluster analysis for some time. In adaptive clustering, the ART network (Carpenter and Grossberg 1988) (described in Chapter 3) is representative. Common to clustering neural networks is the employment of the *winner-take-all* strategy (a competitive learning strategy). In addition, adaptive learning applies some kind of thresholding mechanism for cluster formation. Only when a new event is very different from existing clusters by more than a threshold value will a new cluster form.

In general, a clustering network comprises two layers: the input and the output (cluster) layers, as shown in Figure 8.1. A basic equation underlying the competitive learning mode for clustering is given by

$$\frac{dW_{ji}}{dt} = rO_j(-W_{ji} + O_i)$$

where W_{ji} is the weight of the connection from input unit i to output unit j, r is the learning rate, and O_i and O_j are the activations of unit i and unit

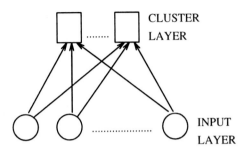

Figure 8.1: The basic architecture of a clustering network.

j, respectively. Under the winner-take-all strategy, O_j is either 0 or 1. It is clear that only when unit j is a winner can its weights be modified. The above equation, however, does not address the adaptive nature of clustering. In adaptive clustering, the weights associated with the winner node will be adapted to the input event if and only if it has been determined that the event is similar enough to the properties of the winner node.

8.3.2 Pattern Extraction

The neural network clustering procedure uses a numerical rather than symbolic function to compute the activation levels of cluster nodes and update their weights. The same kind of criticism against traditional cluster analysis can be cited against the neural network. Yet, the neural network may be even harder to interpret than clusters resulting from traditional techniques. Understanding what a clustering network learns is again an important issue. Here, we explore possibilities to decode a clustering network into symbolic form (if-then rules).

The difference between backpropagation and clustering networks should be noted first. In the backpropagation network, each concept node is associated with a threshold; in the clustering network, there is no such threshold, and cluster nodes are activated in a competitive mode. Therefore, in the back-propagation network, possible patterns (rules) of a concept are combinations of weights greater than the threshold; however, in the clustering network, possible patterns of a cluster are combinations of weights which are maxima among all cluster nodes. Assume that the activation range of each node in the network is from 0 to 1. Based on the above discussion, the procedure for extracting patterns from a clustering network is given below. This *direct* approach is depicted in Figure 8.2.

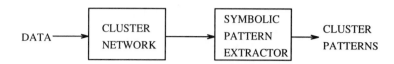

Figure 8.2: Direct translation of a clustering network.

Rule Extraction from a Clustering Network (Direct Method)

For each cluster node j, search for a set S_p of patterns with each pattern p (a pattern is a set of attributes, each in either positive or negative form) satisfying any of the following conditions: (Let A_p be the set of attributes involved in p and A_T all attributes.)

1. The summed weights of p are the maximum among all clusters for cluster j, and $W_{ji} \geq W_{ki}$ for every $i \in A_T - A_p$ and for every $k \neq j$.

2. The summed weights of p in conjunction with any pattern defined based on all the attributes in $A_T - A_p$ are the maximum among all clusters for cluster j.

For a given cluster node, a valid pattern is one which maximally activates it in all circumstances. The search task is very complicated because all cluster nodes should be considered. A sufficient condition for a valid pattern of a cluster is when both the summed weights of the pattern and every weight not mentioned by the pattern are maxima among all clusters. This condition is by no means a necessary condition. In most cases, this sufficient condition cannot be satisfied, and few other sufficient conditions can be found. Consequently, expensive search efforts are often demanded. By contrast, in the backpropagation network, interactions between different concept nodes are sorted so that we can consider one node at a time, and this effectively reduces the size of the search space.

Another alternative for translation of a clustering network is by means of a mapping network, such as the backpropagation network. Since a neural network is able to perform example-based mapping, it follows that we can first transfer the knowledge of a clustering network into a mapping network and then read out the knowledge of the latter network. As diagrammed in Figure 8.3, this approach involves training a mapping network on the training

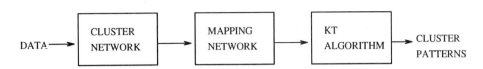

Figure 8.3: Indirect translation of a clustering network via a mapping network.

instances, each labeled with the cluster assigned by the clustering network. The mapping network is constructed like the clustering network but with additional hidden layers.

To develop a new algorithm for translating each different kind of network is time-consuming and laborious. The above *indirect* approach can save many such efforts by reusing the same software for translation.[1] Moreover, this approach is theoretically sound, because a mapping network can accurately approximate any continuous function, with adequate training samples.

In summary, the procedure for learning rules by clustering includes two steps:

1. Clustering: Train the clustering network on a set of instances without class labels.

2. Rule extraction:

   - Direct extraction from the clustering network
   - Indirect extraction by means of a mapping network

8.3.3 Mixed Unsupervised and Supervised Architectures

"Discovery" often implies that there is an unsupervised component in the process since nothing can be discovered if everything is known. Experience shows that completely unsupervised learning seldom leads to meaningful discovery. The heuristics employed by programs like AM or BACON actually guide the learning process in an implicit manner. The point of the arguments here is that combining unsupervised and supervised learning strategies should be a legitimate and important approach for machine discovery.

Figure 8.4 presents a possible architecture for combining unsupervised and supervised networks. In this architecture, the unsupervised network automatically forms categories, and through such a process, it transforms original physical data into abstract descriptions, which are in turn accepted

---

[1]See the KT algorithm in Chapter 14 "Rule Generation from Neural Networks."

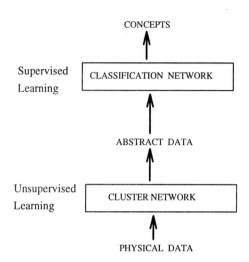

Figure 8.4: A hierarchical network architecture combining unsupervised and supervised learning.

as input by the supervised network. This design is based on the following considerations:

- The clustering (unsupervised) network is used to filter out data noise by performing abstraction.

- The raw data may be too complex to be analyzed directly by the supervised network. What the unsupervised network does is "data compression" and data reorganization.

- Since the supervised network learns much more slowly than the unsupervised network, this design provides better efficiency than the supervised network alone.

Several kinds of discoveries are made possible by such learning architecture:

- Discovery of new useful attributes

- Discovery of new classification rules based on new attributes

- Discovery of new taxonomies (In this case, a clustering network with hierarchy-building capability is needed.)

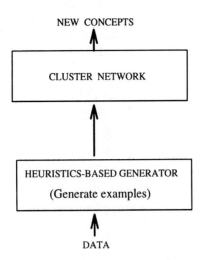

NEW CONCEPTS

CLUSTER NETWORK

HEURISTICS-BASED GENERATOR

(Generate examples)

DATA

Figure 8.5: A heuristic generator coupled with a clustering network.

8.3.4 Heuristics-Supported Architectures

The main activities of the AM program are to generate examples of certain concepts and then look for regularities. One way to integrate neural networks into the AM system is to let them handle something which is fuzzy, for example, how to measure interestingness and how to define regularities. However, the fundamental spirit of the heuristics should remain intact since they are the essential ingredients of the system.

With this thought, the first architecture is shown in Figure 8.5. In this design, examples heuristically generated are processed by a clustering network. A new concept or category may be formed in this way. If the examples are originally of the same concept, then a new concept is a subconcept (i.e., a specialization) of that concept. On the other hand, if the examples are generated from different concepts, then a new concept may be a more interesting, hybrid concept of them. In either case, this architecture can discover new concepts but still cannot evaluate how important they are.

This concern motivates another architecture, given in Figure 8.6. In this architecture, examples are generated as before but then analyzed by a supervised rather than unsupervised network. The supervised network can be trained to learn what is interesting and what is regular. To do this, it should be presented with a set of examples which are interesting or regular in some aspect. Specifically:

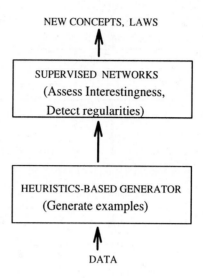

Figure 8.6: A heuristic generator integrated with a supervised network.

- The network can be trained to "score" interestingness of given observations.

- The network can be trained to model a set of predicates or mathematical relations for defining regularities.

By self-learning, the neural network can generalize the features of interestingness and regularity associated with specific sets of instances. Thus, the neural network augments the capability of discovering new concepts or relations. Also, new concepts discovered by the first architecture can be further evaluated by the supervised network for their interestingness.

8.3.5   Law-Discovery Architectures

Despite the successes of AM and BACON, the nature of processes by which human scientists make discoveries remains fuzzy. In BACON, laws are discovered by detecting certain regular relationships between variables. Since neural networks are adept at learning patterns or regularities implicit in given data, one wonders whether they can be employed to discover laws. At first, we examine what neural networks can do.

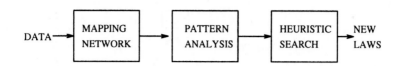

Figure 8.7: Integration of neural networks into a law-discovery system.

Suppose a law defines the relationship between two variables X and Y as follows:

$$XY = k$$

where k is a constant. This relation can be formulated from the "functional" point of view as

$$Y = F(X) = k/X$$

where F is a function such that $F(a) = k/a$. Since neural networks can accurately learn any continuous function (Kolmogorov's theorem) (Hecht-Nielsen 1990), this perspective suggests a possible role of neural networks in learning laws. However, the problem is not that simple. Even if a neural network can learn to approximate a function, the function encoded in terms of connection weights stands intangible. Now, the problem becomes understanding the neural network. If we can extract patterns from the network, then we can apply the law search module of BACON on those patterns. This process narrows down the search space and minimizes the likelihood of spurious laws. So, in the above example, the neural network may first learn the pattern,

$$1/X \longrightarrow Y$$

and the precise mathematical relation is learned later. This approach can be extended to learning laws involving many variables, for example,

$$Y = F(X_1, X_2, ...)$$

In the architecture shown in Figure 8.7, pattern analysis results in qualitative descriptions about the relationships among variables concerned.

A neural network procedure for law discovery thus includes the following steps:

1. Qualitative analysis on qualitative data:

   - Use a mapping network such as the backpropagation network to model the relationships among variables.

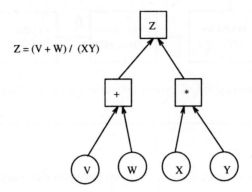

$$Z = (V + W) / (XY)$$

Figure 8.8: A network view of a mathematical law.

- Extract patterns (rules) from the network.

2. Quantitative search for laws on quantitative data:

  - Identify mathematical relationships among variables involved in those patterns.

An even bolder attempt is to let neural networks discover mathematical laws directly. Figure 8.8 shows how a mathematical law or relation can be mapped into a network, in which the activation functions of hidden and output units represent corresponding mathematical operators. In learning laws, since the variables involved are unknown beforehand, a more general learning architecture should include many other variables and operators. Then, the neural network learns to identify key elements which play in the law. The philosophy taken here is that if a problem can be mapped into a neural network, then it can be solved accordingly.

This approach, however, runs into some problems. First, operators along with their arguments may be nested in multiple levels. For an unknown law, it is not known how variables are nested, so there is no idea of exactly how the network should be designed. Note that a neural network can still learn to approximate a function without such direct correspondence between the functional components and the network components. In this circumstance, however, we cannot translate the network knowledge into symbolic laws directly.

There is another problem with this approach. If all network weights are randomized initially, then the discovered law may well be a local minimum.

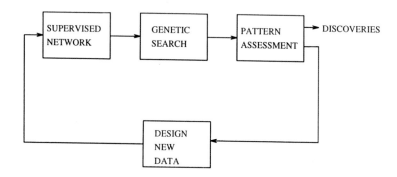

Figure 8.9: Combining neural networks and genetic search in discovery.

Moreover, even if it best fits the given data, it is not necessarily the underlying law. In fact, this criticism applies to any data-driven approach to discovery, including BACON.

To overcome these problems, partial knowledge about the law should be embodied in the network before it starts to learn from examples. This knowledge can be used to determine the connection topology and initialize weights as in the rule-based connectionist networks (RBCNs).

8.3.6 Genetic Search

The idea of genetic search (Goldberg 1989) lends to many kinds of problems related to optimization and machine learning. Figure 8.9 displays an architecture which combines neural networks and genetic search in the process of scientific discovery. This architecture has several components:

- The neural network, which learns patterns associated with selected variables

- The genetic component, which combines or modifies patterns

- The critic, which evaluates the merits of patterns

- The design component, which designs new experiments or new data for further analysis

This architecture assumes that there is a design goal in mind and that performance can be assessed. It mixes supervised and unsupervised learning modes. The learning of the neural network is supervised since it receives feedback from the critic. The neural network will learn patterns associated with what is called "good." In contrast, the genetic component combines and mutates the patterns in an unsupervised manner. The system is connected to an external component, namely the design component, which designs new experiments or data on the basis of good patterns. Thus, it uses the hindsight gained from pattern analysis as foresight to design. Because of this external link, the system knowledge, explicit or implicit, is not fixed. The critic needs to raise the standard of quality, as time progresses. So, the system will continue to improve its knowledge if possible. The ability of discovery is attributed to the genetic and the design components. Possible applications include drug design and circuit design. The whole procedure is summarized below.

The Design and Discovery Procedure

1. Train the backpropagation network on a set of examples classified as good or bad.

2. Extract patterns.

3. Combine and mutate the patterns.

4. Assess the patterns. Raise the standard of good patterns.

5. Design new experiments and data, and go to step 1.

8.4   Summary

Several computer programs for machine discovery such as CLUSTER/2, AM, and BACON were examined. The successes of AM, EURISKO, and BACON in discovering new concepts or new laws can be attributed to the heuristics embedded in the programs. Since these programs made discoveries by seeking regularities from observations, neural networks naturally endowed with such capability show promise in this field. Various neural network architectures for this purpose have been described. They all share the same idea—to let neural networks discover regularities. However, heuristic guidance is still necessary, since neural networks nowadays are not complex enough to learn everything from scratch. Therefore, most of the architectures introduced are either partially supervised or guided heuristically. Discovery of mathematical relations remains a great challenge to neural networks, despite the fact that they can learn to approximate any continuous function. Finally, the idea of genetic search plays a role in design and discovery.

8.5 References

1. Carpenter, G.A., and Grossberg, S. 1988. The ART of adaptive pattern recognition by a self-organizing neural network. *Computer*, March, pp. 77–88.

2. Fisher, D.H. 1987. Knowledge acquisition via incremental conceptual clustering. *Machine Learning*, 2, pp. 139–172.

3. Goldberg, D.E. 1989. *Genetic Algorithms*. Addison-Wesley, Reading, MA.

4. Hecht-Nielsen, R. 1990. *Neurocomputing*. Addison-Wesley, Reading, MA.

5. Langley, P., Bradshaw, G.L., and Simon, H.A. 1983. Rediscovering chemistry with the BACON system. In *Machine Learning*. Tioga Publishing Company, Palo Alto, CA.

6. Lenat, D. 1976. AM: An Artificial Intelligence Approach to Discovery in Mathematics as Heuristic Search. Ph.D. thesis, Stanford University.

7. Lenat, D. 1983. The role of heuristics in learning by discovery: Three case studies. In *Machine Learning*. Tioga, Palo Alto, CA.

8. Michalski, R.S., and Stepp, R.E. 1983. Learning from observations: Conceptual clustering. In *Machine Learning*. Tioga, Palo Alto, CA.

9. Zytkow, J.M. 1987. Combining many searches in the FAHRENHEIT discovery system. In *Proceedings of the Fourth International Workshop on Machine Learning*, pp. 218–287. Morgan Kaufmann, Los Altos, CA.

8.6 Problems

1. In discrete time implementation for adaptive clustering, we use the following formula for weight updating ($\Delta t = 1$):

$$\Delta W_{ji} = \frac{1}{n_{jk}} O_{jk}(-W_{ji} + O_{ik}) \qquad (8.1)$$

where n_{jk} is the size of cluster j incremented by 1, O_{ik} and O_{jk} are the activations of unit i and j, respectively, when instance k is presented. Let $W_{ji}(n)$ be the W_{ji} when the size of cluster j is n. Show that W_{ji} is the average of O_{ik} over all the patterns assigned to cluster j. That is,

$$W_{ji}(n) = \frac{\sum O_{ik}}{n}$$

2. In the design and discovery procedure, suppose good patterns in each design cycle represent the upper α fraction of all patterns arranged in the decreasing order of their merit. Assume that new patterns designed based on old patterns always improve. Suppose the good patterns in the nth design cycle represent the upper β fraction of the entire population.

   (a) What is the relationship between α and β?

   (b) Link this result to the genetic algorithm described in Chapter 3.

3. A clustering neural network has two cluster nodes X and Y in the output layer and six attribute nodes A, B, C, D, E, and F in the input layer. Each attribute takes on a binary value (0 or 1). The trained weights are shown below:

   $$W_{XA} = 6, W_{XB} = 4, W_{XC} = 3, W_{XD} = 1, W_{XE} = 1, W_{XF} = 3,$$
   $$W_{YA} = 1, W_{YB} = 2, W_{YC} = 1, W_{YD} = 1, W_{YE} = 2, W_{YF} = 7$$

   Find valid rules for clusters X and Y, respectively.

4. In leukemic diagnosis, specific antibodies are used to detect specific types of leukemic cells. The technique requires cluster analysis of flow cytometric measurements of leukemic cells. The appearance of abnormal clusters suggests a specific leukemic disorder.

   (a) Discuss how to discover new leukemic disorders with this approach.

   (b) Design a neural network for classification in this domain.

Chapter 9

Structures and Sequences

9.1 Introduction

One of the major issues in the application of connectionism to higher-level learning tasks has been the inadequacy of its representations. Elements of the task domain must be represented, a network architecture must be designed, and a learning algorithm must be specified. If the knowledge in the model is to be provided by the designer, the network must be designed to materialize the knowledge. If the model is to acquire its knowledge through learning, a learning algorithm for network adaptation must be specified, and a training set must be designed. The proper representation of training examples is a major factor for successful learning. A poor representation will often doom the model to failure. Representation is also critical to bridge connectionist learning and symbolic computation. There exists considerable literature on knowledge representation in symbolic artificial intelligence. The general issue addressed here is how to rerepresent structures which are symbolically encoded in the framework of connectionist networks.

In some language, an object or instance is described by a set of attributes such as "color" and "size." It is desirable that a connectionist network be able to represent what a more general language like predicate calculus can describe, including such structural relationships as "ontop" and "beside." In the description of a chemical molecule, for example, we specify not only what types of atoms occupy what positions but also how atoms are next to each other.

The following sections explore various connectionist representations and introduce a hybrid network approach for learning from structured data.

9.2 Connectionist Representation

The long-term knowledge of a connectionist network is stored as a set of weights on connections between units. This general scheme admits many

Representation of atomic relationship, linkage (X,Y):

For example, linkage (C,N) is given by

(a) Local representation

(b) Distributed representation

Figure 9.1: Connectionist representation of structural relationship.

kinds of representations. Connectionist representation is traditionally divided into two classes: local and distributed representations. However, it has been noticed that there is substantial difference between representing fixed-sized and variable-sized structures.

9.2.1   Local Representation

In a local representation, one node designates one object or concept, as illustrated in Figure 9.1(*a*). When a concept is true in the given context, the corresponding unit is activated. An example is NETL (Fahlman 1979). Each node in a NETL network stands for one concept in a semantic network. When the network is referring to a concept, the corresponding unit becomes active. This unit then activates neighboring units.

Another example is the representation of the input of the NETtalk system of Sejnowski and Rosenberg (1987). Each NETtalk input consists of a letter to be pronounced together with the three preceding and three following letters to provide some context. For each of these seven letters there is a separate set of input units in the network, and within each set there is a separate unit for each letter. There is no overlap of the activity representing alternative values for each letter in the input. The input representation in NETtalk illustrates how to handle variable binding in connectionist networks. The input is a string of seven letters. Each input position can be viewed as a slot in the structure or as a variable. And each possible value of the variable is encoded by an input unit.

9.2.2 Distributed Representation

In a distributed representation (Hinton, McClelland, and Rumelhart 1986), concepts are represented by patterns of activations over many rather than individual units, as shown in Figure 9.1(*b*). For example, a Hopfield network provides a distributed representation for an associative (content-addressable) memory, in which each structure is stored as a collection of active units.

Another example is the representation of the output of the NETtalk system. Each output of this network is a phoneme, e.g., the "p" of "pit." Each phoneme is represented in terms of phonetic features. There is one output unit in the network for each of the phonetic features, and its numerical value indicates whether that feature is present (1) or absent (0). Each phoneme is therefore represented by a pattern of activity over multiple output units.

Distributed representations are more fault-tolerant. A local representation will lose its entire memory about a certain concept once the unit denoting that concept is damaged. In contrast, the memory loss in a distributed representation is partial unless all units representing that concept are lost. The ability of graceful (rather than abrupt) degradation is desirable if our goal is to build a very large system from unreliable parts. It has also been suggested that human and animal memory is organized in a distributed fashion.

In addition to being more robust than local representations, distributed representations can also be more spatially economical. One set of units can store many different objects. For example, suppose we use 10 units (10 bits) for representation. A local representation can represent 10 objects, whereas a distributed representation can represent $2^{10} - 1$ objects.

Distributed representations have another important property; namely, stored objects may be superimposed on one another. When two different sets of objects result in the same superimposed pattern of activations over units, it is impossible to tell which set corresponds to actual objects. There is a distributed representation for solving this problem, namely, *coarse coding* (Hinton, McClelland, and Rumelhart 1986; Touretzky 1990). Imagine that the space of possible object locations is divided into a number of large, overlapping, circular zones. Each zone is monitored by a unit; the zone is called the unit's receptive field. The unit becomes active if any object falls within its receptive field. Looking at a single active unit gives little information about which objects are active in the context. Only the pattern of activity across all the units can be more precise about it. For example, suppose unit X covers objects A and B and unit Y covers objects A and C in their receptive fields. If only one unit is *on*, we are not certain which object is active. However, if both units X and Y are *on*, it is suggested that object A is active. This idea is shown schematically in Figure 9.2. In essence, the technique of coarse coding represents multiple objects with some precision without paying the price of the local representation

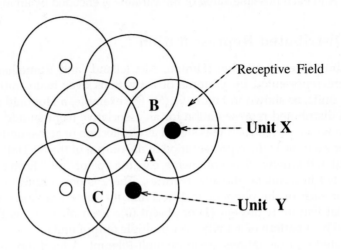

Figure 9.2: Coarse coding.

scheme.

One disadvantage of distributed representations is that they cannot store many densely packed objects. In this case, the intersection area of multiple receptive fields is not small enough to discriminate an object from its neighbors. A similar interference effect very likely accounts for forgetting in human memory (Gleitman 1981). Another drawback concerning distributed representations is the difficulty of interpreting accurately the knowledge encoded in them. The difficulty lies in the fact that the decoding process involves a one-to-many mapping.

9.2.3   Representation of Variable-Sized Structures

How to represent variable-sized structures in a fixed connectionist network has been a longstanding difficulty. Then, why not just use a variable-sized network? Consider processing character strings for example. Suppose we encode each character by one input unit. If a string is nonperiodic and infinitely long, then it cannot be represented physically. In addition, learning and information processing become complicated if the network size changes from time to time.

A structure can be described in terms of a set of slots and fillers. Slots correspond to roles or attributes or variables and fillers to values. The technique of tensor product representation is a formalization of the idea that a set of variable-value pairs can be represented by accumulating activity in a collection of units (Smolensky 1990). In this formalism, a set of variable-value pairs {value-1/variable-1, value-2/variable-2, value-3/variable-3} is represented by

value-1 $\otimes$ variable-1 + value-2 $\otimes$ variable-2 + value-3 $\otimes$ variable-3

where $\otimes$ denotes the tensor (matrix) product. If a variable is encoded as an n-dimensional vector and a value as an m-dimensional vector, then their tensor product results in an $m \times n$ matrix, which can be encoded by an $m \times n$ array of input units. The whole structure is encoded by linear superimposition of these variable-value products. This approach permits recursive construction of complex representations from simpler ones and representation of structures of unbounded size in a fixed connectionist network with graceful saturation.

We can extract the value for a particular variable from the tensor product representation of a structure through an *unbinding* process. The unbinding process involves taking an inner product of the encoded structure with an unbinding vector (which could be the variable vector itself). If the vectors representing the variables bound in a structure are linearly independent, then each variable can be unbound with complete accuracy. To meet this condition, we may need a large network to encode a complex structure. On the other hand, we may choose to lose some accuracy in exchange for a smaller network.

Another technique for representing variable-sized structures is seen in RAAM (recursive auto-associative memory) (Pollack 1990). In this approach, recursive data structures such as trees and lists are represented in fixed-width patterns in the hidden layer through the recursive use of backpropagation.

9.3 A Hybrid Network Approach

Reasoning with structures often involves matching patterns. The capability of pattern matching is one of the main features characterizing a knowledge-based system. To match a pattern like "p(W,X) $\wedge$ q(X,Y) $\wedge$ R(Y,Z)" ($\wedge$ denoting conjunction) is a simple matter in such a system but would present a difficulty to a neural network. Although one may devise a sophisticated neural network where each processing element can conduct complicated pattern matching, it would be easier just to integrate a symbolic pattern-matching machinery into the existing neural framework.

In a hybrid network approach, we link predicates into a graph termed a *predicate graph* according to rules, as seen in Figure 9.3. Unary predicates (with a single argument) are used to represent attributes, while nonunary predicates (with multiple arguments) are used to specify structural information. The predicate graph is then mapped into a connectionist (neural) network termed a *predicate connectionist network* where each predicate is encoded by an array of nodes, each for one possible tuple value.[1] The array is n-dimensional where n is the arity of the predicate. This array serves as a data structure for recording

---

[1] A tuple value in the predicate language is like an attribute value in the attribute-based language.

R1: If grade(mid,A) and grade(final,A), then class A.

R2: If grade(proj,A) and grade(final,A), then class A.

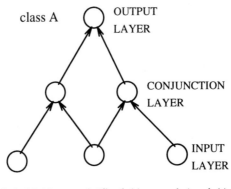

Figure 9.3: A predicate connectionist network based on rules.

given or derived tuple values bound to the predicate. There are different treatments for inference and for learning in such a network.

In the inference phase, the ground (activation) level of a tuple node is zero; i.e., no activation. When a tuple value is true, the corresponding node is activated with the activation level raised above zero. The predicate network is coupled with a data-driven, pattern-matching network such as a Rete network[2] (Brownston, Farrell, Kant, and Martin 1985) so that the latter network actually computes tuple values and transmits them to the former network. It is clear that in the inference phase, the predicate network does nothing but bookkeeping.

In the learning phase, we use the backpropagation heuristic for learning and revising rules. In terms of error propagation, there is not much difference in structured domains as compared with nonstructured ones. However, in postprocessing rules decoded from the neural network, there exist some differences. In a nonstructured domain, we use an attribute-based language to describe rules in the form of

If attribute-1=value-1, attribute-2=value-2, . . ., then a concept.

---

[2] A Rete network is transformed from a rule base using an algorithm known as the Rete algorithm in order to improve the efficiency of rule processing. The algorithm is based on the concepts of structural similarity between rules and temporal redundancy in the data base.

A rule can be refined by adding or dropping a condition as well as by replacing a value with a more specific or more general value. In a structured domain, we use a predicate language (e.g., predicate calculus) to state a rule in the form of

If pred-1(value-1, value-2), pred-2(value-3, value-4), . . ., then a concept.

In this case, there are more varieties to refine a rule. Besides adding and deleting some conditions, we can apply "changing constants into variables" to generalize a rule.

It appears that local representation is more advantageous than distributed encoding of instance information in the aspect of learning symbolic patterns. In a local representation, patterns directly decoded from the neural network are described by the same set of predicates and tuple values used to describe instances. In a distributed representation, different pieces of structural information are distributed and superimposed over a set of units. A pattern translated from the encoding space into the original space is often noisy.

However, local representations demand more network units for storing the same amount of information than distributed ones. If we choose a local representation, the issue is how to reduce the dimensionality of representation. A technique called *abstract value representation* is introduced, in which instances are described by abstract values that are as general as possible. For example, about a molecule, suppose we want to say, "The atom at position-10 is a carbon." Formally, it can be stated as "at-position-10(a) $\wedge$ carbon(a)." The problem with this representation is that since the symbol "a" can be arbitrary and different instances may use different symbols, a large number of network units would be needed to encode them. A more efficient way under abstract value representation is to rephrase the statement as "at-position-10(carbon)." The symbolic value "a" is replaced by a more general value "carbon." In this way, the number of network units for this encoding purpose will not depend on the number of specific atoms. To deal with a complex structure, we may use a *matcher* to convert a specific structural description into a general one. This technique addresses the question of how to represent a problem properly before it can be solved.

When learning involves variable-sized structures, the local representation scheme will fall short. In this case, recursive representation using recursive neural networks can offer a useful solution. See Chapter 10 "Spatiotemporal Learning" and Chapter 15 "Learning Grammars."

9.4 Summary

A hybrid network approach was introduced for learning patterns from structures. This approach integrates the technique of symbolic pattern matching for making inference and the heuristics of the neural network for learning. Broadly, there are two classes of connectionist representations: local and distributed representations. In learning symbolic patterns, a serious deficiency concerning distributed representations is the difficulty of precisely interpreting the knowledge learned and encoded in them. Local representations are more advantageous in this respect. However, they demand more space for storing the same amount of information than distributed ones. A technique known as abstract value representation addresses this issue. When learning involves variable-sized structures, recursive representation using recursive neural networks is a useful approach.

9.5   References

1. Brownston, L., Farrell, R., Kant, E., and Martin, N. 1985. *Programming Expert Systems in OPS5*. Addison-Wesley Publishing Company, Inc., Reading, MA.

2. Fahlman, S.E. 1979. *NETL: A System for Representing and Using Real-World Knowledge*. MIT Press, Cambridge, MA.

3. Gleitman, H. 1981. *Psychology*. W.W. Norton, New York.

4. Hinton, G.E., McClelland, J.L., and Rumelhart, D.E. 1986. Distributed representation. In *Parallel Distributed Processing*. MIT Press, Cambridge, MA.

5. Pollack, J.B. 1990. Recursive distributed representations. *Artificial Intelligence*, 46, pp. 77–105.

6. Sejnowski, T.J., and Rosenberg, C.R. 1987. Parallel networks that learn to pronounce English text. *Complex Systems*, 1, pp. 145–168.

7. Smolensky, P. 1990. Tensor product variable binding and the representation of symbolic structures in connectionist systems. *Artificial Intelligence*, 46, pp. 159–216.

8. Touretzky, D.S. 1990. BoltzCONS: Dynamic symbol structures in a connectionist network. *Artificial Intelligence*, 46, pp. 5–46.

9.6   Problems

1. In a coarse coding scheme, suppose a receptor consists of 3 triples (a triple here means an object-attribute-value), there are 1000 possible triples, and memory contains 1000 units. Note that each unit has a receptor.

   (a) What is the percentage of the triple space covered by each receptor?

   (b) What is the average number of receptors involved by a triple?

(c) The receptors of the following units are
Unit A: (a, b, c) (d, e, f) (g, h, i)
Unit B: (k, l, m) (o, p, q) (d, e, f)
Unit C: (g, h, i) (a, b, c) (x, y, z)
Supposing that units A and B are *on*, which triple is most likely to be present?

2. Design a neural network which represents a semantic net using tensor product representation. A semantic net is a knowledge structure in which a node represents an object and a link (arrow) represents the relationship between two linked objects. For example, Tom—owns→ a Volvo—isa→ Car. (Hint: A value is specified by two variables.)

3. Use a BAM (bidirectional associative memory) to store the following pairs of associated strings:

Original string	Associated string
aabaac	ccd
bbaa	dccccc
ababa	cddd
bbbbbb	cdcdcd

(a) Describe how to encode the above variable-length strings.

(b) Specify the BAM structure.

(c) Specify the connection weights.

4. That a specific object inherits some properties from a more general object is referred to as property inheritance, which is an important inference mechanism in semantic nets. For example, Clyde is a bird and birds can fly, so Clyde can fly. However, property inheritance is just a kind of default reasoning. The inherited property may be overridden as more specific information arrives. For example, if we know later that Clyde is an ostrich, then Clyde cannot fly.

(a) Design a general neural network which implements the mechanism of property inheritance.

(b) Describe how to set the connection weights.

Chapter 10

Learning Spatiotemporal Patterns

10.1   Introduction

Artificial intelligence systems which deal with real-world problems often require reasoning with time and space. Some temporal reasoning systems model time using a state-space approach. In this approach, the world is described as a sequence of states (snapshots). A state is what occurs at a time instant. Some systems model time using an event-based approach. An event is associated with a time interval rather than a point. Either approach has found different applications. The time parameter can be explicitly stated or implicitly assumed.

Geometric reasoning is a research topic mainly in the context of robotics and computer vision. It bears on the deduction of spatial relationships of objects in three-dimensional space.

Temporal data are one-dimensional and can be treated as a kind of sequence, while spatial data has a three-dimensional structure. However, there is a direct isomorphism between temporal reasoning and spatial reasoning in one dimension. The former concerns the precedence relationships between events and the latter between objects. Precedence relationships are a key element of spatiotemporal patterns. In fact, the most difficult part of learning spatiotemporal patterns could be how to identify, represent, and store such relationships.

In this chapter, we address the problem of learning temporal or spatiotemporal patterns in the framework of neural networks. Symbolic inductive techniques have been applied to learn temporal knowledge with success. Our motivation to explore the neural network approach to this learning problem is again based on our contention that neural networks are better to model some of the intricacies of the problem, such as uncertainty. Moreover, neural networks are inherently more advantageous in dealing with low-level signal processing and control tasks than are symbolic approaches. However, it would still be true that knowledge combined with neural heuristics presents the most promising solution, and we show how to infuse knowledge into neural networks for this learning task.

Learning snapshot or static patterns is much easier than learning patterns involving dynamics, previous history, and context. The first problem can be solved by feedforward networks like backpropagation in quite a straightforward way. The second problem may require a special kind of network which can recognize temporal features from given temporal data. However, it should be noted that the design of the network for a particular problem depends on how the problem is formulated and represented. A good example of the second problem is speech recognition (see Lippmann 1989).

The following sections explore various spatiotemporal neural networks, describe important learning procedures, and show how to apply knowledge to neural networks.

10.2   Spatiotemporal Neural Networks

We can view spatiotemporal neural networks in the following aspects:

- Input representation

  - Spatial representation: Turn a temporal sequence into a spatial pattern encoded on the input layer, for example, of static and time-delay neural networks. Here, time is discrete.

  - Temporal representation: A temporal sequence arrives to the network one data element at a time, for example, in temporal summation and recurrent neural networks. Time can be discrete or continuous.

- Network architectures

  - Feedforward: There is no recurrent connection (back connection), for example, static and time-delay neural networks.

  - Recurrent: There are recurrent connections.

- Duality

  - Spatiotemporal domain: Information is processed in the spatiotemporal domain, for example, in most types of spatiotemporal neural networks.

  - Frequency domain: Information is processed in the frequency domain, for example, in frequency coding neural networks.

Spatiotemporal neural networks are also classified in terms of how they memorize (store) past inputs. Each past input can be weighted by a constant or by a factor exponentially decaying with time. One approach is to view the memory (short-term memory) as the *convolution* of the input sequence with a kernel function, which varies with the memory mechanism:

$$\int_0^t K(t-\tau)X(\tau)$$

where $K(t)$ and $X(t)$ are the kernel and the input functions, respectively. Principe et al. (1992) show that it is possible to adapt the memory structure to a particular problem.

The dynamical equations of spatiotemporal neural networks have the following general form:

$$T\frac{dy(t)}{dt} = -y(t) + \text{MST}$$

where T is the time constant and MST is the model-specific term. In the time-delay approach, the MST is a function of delayed signals. In the recurrent network approach, the MST is a function of weighted internal (recurrent and nonrecurrent) inputs plus external input. In static representation, we assume

$$\frac{dy(t)}{dt} = 0$$

and

$$y(t) = \text{MST}$$

10.2.1   Static Neural Networks

A simple strategy for processing temporal information is to represent a sequence of incoming temporal data "simultaneously" on the input layer of the neural network. This is a *static* strategy since it does not explicitly address the dynamic or temporal nature of the data. As shown in Figure 10.1, the network typically used is a feedforward backpropagation network, which classifies an input pattern into a predefined category.

The input layer is a buffer which holds the current temporal data for processing. Suppose each input unit encodes a data element received at a time instant (or interval). There are two basic ways to change the contents of the buffer:

- The buffer acts like a shift register. When a new data element arrives, the oldest data element in the buffer is dropped, the remaining ones are shifted to the next position in line, and the new element is inserted at the first position.

- The buffer contains the data sampled within the current time window. Windows may overlap.

This approach has been taken in a number of investigations. For example, Gorman and Sejnowski (1986, 1988) took this approach for classifying sonar

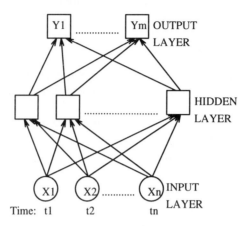

Figure 10.1: A static neural network where temporal information is represented by a set of spatial units.

targets. Bengio et al. (1989) used it for automatic speech recognition. Lippmann (1989) reviews a number of other applications of similar approaches to this area. Goldberg and Pearlmutter (1989) applied it to the problem of learning dynamics for a robotic arm. Tom and Tenorio (1989) used the same approach to extract words from temporal data.

Elman (1990) discusses several disadvantages with this approach: It needs to know how often to examine the buffer, it imposes a fixed duration for patterns, it does not distinguish between absolute and relative temporal positions, and the backpropagation network usually does not handle novel inputs well.

Accurate pattern recognition requires that the buffer size must be large enough to hold sufficient data. The absolute positions of data elements should play a minor role in matching an input pattern against a predefined pattern. Preliminary feature extraction of raw data can facilitate pattern recognition. In real-time cases, the data arrival or sampling rate should not exceed the processing rate.

10.2.2   Time-Delay Neural Networks

"Time delay" is an old concept in adaptive signal processing. If we delay the input signal by one time unit and let the network receive both the original and the delayed signals, we have a simple time-delay neural network. Of course, we can build a more complicated one by delaying the signal at various lengths. If

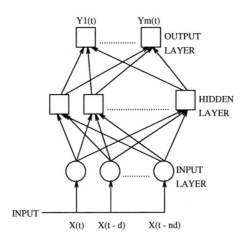

Figure 10.2: A time-delay neural network whose input contains a number of tapped delay lines.

the input signal is n bits and delayed for m different lengths, then there should be nm input units to encode the total input. When new information arrives, it is placed in nodes at one end and old information shifts down a series of nodes like a shift register controlled by a clock. A general architecture of time-delay networks is drawn in Figure 10.2.

A time-delay neural network assumes that its output depends on its current and previous inputs. The network design reflects this dependency relationship. For example, if the output at time t, $Y(t)$, is determined by the input $X(t)$ and the last input $X(t-1)$, then the network input layer should receive the current and one delayed signal line. This is somewhat reminiscent of the concept of Markov chain. If the next-to-last input $x(t-2)$ is also involved, then another delayed line should be added. Tank and Hopfield (1987) suggested greater broadening for longer delayed signals so that delayed signals need not arrive at exact rates. They used an analog neural net with dispersive delay kernels (concentration-in-time net):

$$Y(t;k) = \int_{-\infty}^{t} G(t-\tau;k)X(\tau)\, d\tau \qquad (10.1)$$

where

$$G(t;k) = (\frac{t}{k})^{\alpha} e^{\alpha(1-t/k)}, \ k = 1, 2, \dots \qquad (10.2)$$

That is, the output $Y(t)$ is the convolution of the input $X(t)$ with the delay kernel $G(t; k)$ (k is its order). The kernel is normalized to have maximum value 1 when $t = k$. The parameter α regulates the degree of dispersion. This technique makes the scheme more robust.

There may be some confusion between static neural networks and time-delay ones since both consider the input information spread over a certain time period. At a closer look, the former type considers a sequence of temporal data simultaneously, whereas the latter does so dynamically. Static neural networks relate their input and output by

$$Y = F_{nn}(X_1, X_2, ..., X_n)$$

where Y is the output, X_i is the ith data element, and F_{nn} is the overall function equivalent to the network operation. Note that X_i is a data value collected at a certain time, but the time notion is implicit. Time-delay networks, on the other hand, define their input/output behavior by

$$Y(t) = F_{nn}(X(t), X(t - \tau_1), ..., X(t - \tau_n)) \qquad (10.3)$$

where $Y(t)$ and $X(t)$ are the output and input, respectively, at time t and $X(t - \tau_i)$ corresponds to the signal delayed by τ_i time units.[1] In this representation, the time notion is explicit.

In both static and time delay neural networks, the output is assumed to depend on the information collected within a fixed time window, and there is no explicit integration of information along the time axis. Marcus and Westervelt (1989) found that chaotic behavior might be observed when small time delays were introduced into a neural network. Principe et al. (1992) developed the gamma network in which the window width can be adapted in order to optimize the system performance. The advantage with this approach is obvious since a fixed window width may cut off some past information useful for current information processing.

Tam and Perkel (1989) introduced the concept of time-delay into a back-propagation network for recognizing sequences of spike trains. Lang, Waibel, and Hinton (1990) used a time-delay neural network to distinguish among a difficult class of words, with performance comparable to humans. Hampshire and Waibel (1990) worked further on the same problem. They developed a better solution which employed three similar networks, each trained using a different objective function. A simple criterion was used to resolve conflicts between the decisions of the three networks. Bottou et al. (1990) applied a time-delay neural network to the task of speaker-independent isolated digit recognition with very good results.

---

[1] When F_{nn} is a weighted linear sum, this architecture is equivalent to a linear finite impulse response (FIR) filter in signal processing.

10.2.3 Temporal Summation Neural Networks

As mentioned above, neither static nor time-delay networks integrate temporal information over time explicitly in the sense that they perform their operations in a single network cycle. However, they integrate the information obtained during a fixed time period, the information being represented spatially on the input layer. Thus, with these approaches, the capability of temporal integration is quite limited and, hence, so is the ability of learning temporal patterns. One way to overcome this limitation is by endowing neurons with the faculty of temporal summation. This approach is biologically plausible since biological neurons are able to integrate both spatial and temporal information.

In neural information processing, *spatial summation* refers to summing up all input information transmitted from different sites. Calculating the activation of an output unit based on those of its input units is an example of spatial summation. In fact, this is the basic behavior of all artificial neural networks.

Temporal summation is a relatively strange concept for artificial networks. It means the summation of input information along the time axis and relies on memorization of previous information.

In temporal summation neural networks, computing neurons are able to sum time-varying data over time. The network responds to data presented across cycles rather than at each cycle of operation. The neurons keep some memory of previous signals and may allow slow decay of historical information. Temporal summation can be implemented by

- The use of recurrent connections which sustain or perpetuate induced activations by creating hysteresis in neurons (Norrod et al. 1989; Yanai and Sawada 1990)

- The use of a time-dependent activation function in neurons so that the activation decays over time (Uchiyama et al. 1989)

In our terminology, however, a *temporal summation* network refers to one incorporating the second alternative. Cohen et al. (1987) have applied this approach to speech analysis and synthesis. Recurrent neural networks are described in the next subsection.

The speed of information decay depends on the selected decay constant. Using two different constants can provide a network with short-term and long-term memory.

10.2.4 Recurrent Neural Networks

Does "temporal summation" solve all problems associated with temporal pattern recognition and learning? Recall that a critical element in learning spatiotemporal patterns is the identification of temporal relationship. It has been found that a feedforward network is unable to learn this relationship and it must be programmed in advance. On the other hand, recurrent neural networks hold a great promise in this aspect. They can store temporal information and

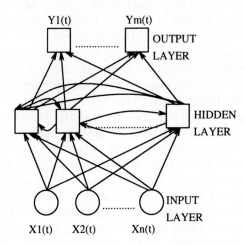

Figure 10.3: A recurrent neural network in which temporal information is recursively encoded.

somehow manage to learn temporal relationship. The latter ability should be ascribed to recurrent connections plus temporal summation. An account of how this is achieved is given in Chapter 15 "Learning Grammars." Notice that recurrent networks can learn complex structures involving a precedence (not necessarily temporal) relationship, for example, a taxonomy of objects.

The avalanche network of Grossberg (1969, 1970) is an early example of a recurrent neural network. It can store a motor sequence, for example, for robotic control.

Recurrent neural networks for processing temporal information generally have the structure depicted in Figure 10.3. Recurrent connections are introduced into processing elements, input or hidden or output units.[2] Such networks actually receive two types of input: One is from the current incoming data and the other from the state information at the preceding time which is fed back to the network. In this way, the neural network can integrate temporal information dating back to the starting point using a limited number of neurons. Thus, the memory capacity is *nonlinear* with respect to memory units. This

---

[2] The architecture with the following system function is equivalent to an infinite impulse response (IIR) filter in signal processing:

$$Y(k) = F_{nn}(X(k), X(k-1), ..., X(k-n), Y(k-1), Y(k-2), ..., Y(k-m))$$

where F_{nn} is a weighted linear sum.

fact makes recurrent neural networks very attractive because of *dimensionality reduction* in representation. In contrast, static and time-delay neural networks discussed earlier use linear memory. Brown (1990) studied the short-term memory capacity limitations in recurrent networks. Elman (1990) has explored the use of recurrent networks for representing structure in time. One point is that time-varying error signals can hint at temporal structures. He found that representation of time is highly task-dependent.

Almeida (1987) and Pineda (1987) pointed out that the backpropagation training procedure, conventionally for feedforward networks, can be extended to recurrent network architectures. It is called *recurrent backpropagation*. However, it generally requires a long training time—a major disadvantage. Considerable improvement in convergence speed can be attained by knowledge-based design. These networks have performed well on certain applications related to speech recognition and robotic control.

10.2.5 Frequency Coding Neural Networks

In signal processing, transformation of a spatiotemporal signal into its frequency spectrum through techniques like *Fourier transform* is a standard practice. Frequency domain analysis complements spatiotemporal domain analysis, providing additional insight into the problem. This transformation may also make the problem computationally feasible or easier. Thus, it is natural to bring this idea into the realm of neural computing. Moreover, frequency coding is a phenomenon observed in biological neurons. Neural networks have been developed which respond to frequency-encoded or pulse-coded information rather than time series.

In frequency-coding neural networks (see Figure 10.4), each input unit encodes a frequency instead of a time unit. The activation of an input unit is based on the intensity (e.g., log magnitude) of the encoded frequency. The network can be a feedforward or a recurrent type. The latter is useful for analyzing frequency or pulse structures.

Goerke et al. (1990) have developed a network that can generate different temporal sequences using pulse processing neurons. Beerhold et al. (1990) have developed neural net hardware for processing pulse-coded information.

10.2.6 Complex Neural Networks

Neural networks with different temporal capabilities can be further combined to meet the problem's need. Combination strategies include:

- Creating a hierarchical system of networks. For example, a backpropagation network can be concatenated to an autoassociative network, as suggested by Rossen and Anderson (1989). This system can map a temporal sequence into another sequence by backpropagation, which is then completed by autoassociation.

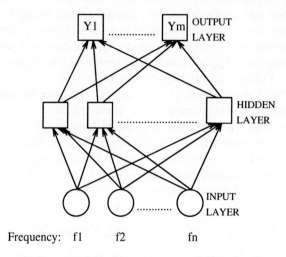

Figure 10.4: A neural network whose input encodes frequency information.

- Creating a parallel system of networks. For example, a network for spatiotemporal domain analysis operates in parallel with another network for frequency domain analysis; the results are then combined.

- Creating a multitype input network. For example, the network input consists of both time series and frequency spectrum data.

These combined approaches are shown in Figure 10.5. Also, see Chapter 7 "Complex Domains."

10.3   Learning Procedures

Standard backpropagation is the learning algorithm commonly used in feedforward spatiotemporal networks such as static and time-delay neural networks. For recurrent spatiotemporal networks, three important learning procedures have been developed. They are

- Recurrent backpropagation,

- Real-time recurrent learning, and

- Backpropagation through time.

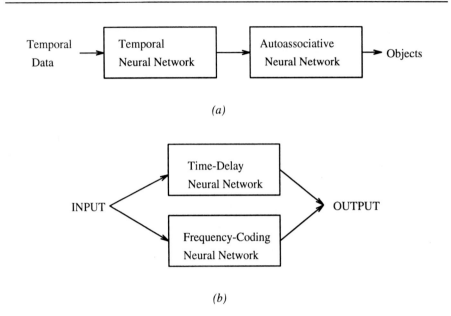

Figure 10.5: Two examples of complex neural networks which combine multiple paradigms for processing temporal information.

The second procedure, suitable for training real-time dynamic nets, is described in Chapter 15; the third is described in Chapter 7; and only the first is dealt with here.

10.3.1 Recurrent Backpropagation

The main issue of recurrent networks is *stability*. In recurrent backpropagation, we assume that there exists a stable attractor. Recurrent backpropagation, like its counterpart in feedforward networks, is a gradient descent technique. Because of recurrent connections, the network requires more than one cycle to stabilize. Its dynamic equation is recursive in nature and associated with more complicated error gradients than the feedforward version. In recurrent networks, some units accept inputs and are called input units, some are defined as output units, and the rest are hidden units. Note that a unit can be both an input and output unit. Omitting detailed derivation, we summarize the recurrent backpropagation procedure below.

Recurrent Backpropagation (adapted from Hertz, Krogh, and Palmer 1991)

- **Weight Initialization**
  Initial weights are set to small random values.

- **Calculation of Activation**
  Relax the network to find the activation O_j for unit j according to

$$\tau \frac{dO_j(t)}{dt} = -O_j(t) + F(\sum_i W_{ji}O_i(t) + X_j(t))$$

where the function F is the activation function, W_{ji} is the weight of the connection from units i to j, and X_j is the input value specified for unit j (if not, then $X_j = 0$). At equilibrium (i.e., $dO_j/dt = 0$), O_j is found by applying the recursive formula

$$O_j(t) = F(\sum_i W_{ji}O_i(t-1) + X_j(t-1))$$

- **Weight Training**

  1. Calculate activations for O_j's.

  2. Calculate errors by

$$E_j = \begin{cases} T_j - O_j & \text{if } j \text{ is an output unit} \\ 0 & \text{otherwise} \end{cases}$$

  where T_j is the desired activation.

  3. Relax the following equation to find Y_j's:

$$\tau \frac{dY_j(t)}{dt} = -Y_j(t) + \sum_k F'(\sum_l W_{kl}O_l(t) + X_k(t))W_{kj}Y_k(t) + E_j(t)$$

  4. Update the weights using

$$\Delta W_{ji} = \eta \delta_j O_i$$

  and

$$\delta_j = F'(\sum_l W_{jl}O_l + X_j)Y_j$$

10.4 Knowledge-Based Approaches

As we know, neural network learning procedures based on gradient descent search only look for local optimum solutions. Without proper design, the network may not even converge. A powerful solution to these problems is "knowledge." Domain knowledge is useful for

- Feature extraction and problem abstraction

- Design of the network topology and weight initialization

- Model-based and context-directed learning

In this section, we show how domain knowledge can be integrated into the process of learning spatiotemporal patterns. Although the knowledge-based approach is often conceived as limited to a high symbolic level, this is not true. Applying it to a low signal level is also possible.

10.4.1 Signal-to-Symbol Transformation

In knowledge-based systems, knowledge is represented symbolically. Application of knowledge to signal processing may involve a process called *signal-to-symbol transformation*. Here, we assume that the signal processing system contains a set of variables, some of which can be symbolized, observable, and controllable. This is how we can incorporate symbolic knowledge into signal processing. And the symbolic level represents a higher level of abstraction than the signal level.

Signal-to-symbol transformation is somewhat analogous to analog-to-digital conversion. However, the difference is that the former is intended to assign some semantics to generated symbols so that they can be combined in a meaningful way. HEARSAY-II (Erman et al. 1980) is a well-known speech recognition system using artificial intelligence techniques. It demonstrates how to apply knowledge to process signals. In this system, incoming sound signals are segmented and recognized as phonemes, which are then subsequently aggregated into larger units of language, as shown in Figure 10.6. Here, signal-to-symbol transformation refers to the process of classifying a signal segment into a certain phoneme. This can be done by, for example, spectrum analysis; however, the technical detail is beyond the scope of this text. The important idea is that once signals are transformed into symbols, then knowledge can come into play.

Temporal neural networks mentioned previously access and process raw signals directly. In speech recognition, most neural networks developed by now can recognize only up to the "word" level. It will be very difficult for a neural network to comprehend higher language units without symbolic abstraction. A short-cut solution is to make neural networks more knowledgeable by infusing existing knowledge into them. Signal-to-symbol transformation is

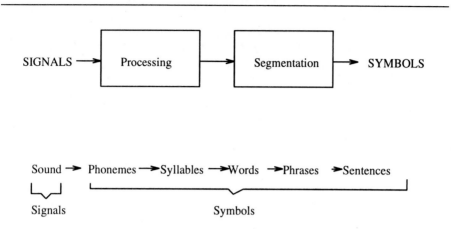

Figure 10.6: The process of signal-to-symbol transformation illustrated by speech recognition.

a preliminary step for this approach. Other benefits of such transformation include noise filtering and reduction of problem complexity via abstraction.

10.4.2   Feature Extraction and Problem Abstraction

Multilayer neural networks are more powerful than single-layer ones mainly because they possess hidden units capable of extracting useful features from training examples. However, there is no guarantee that the network has extracted all useful features since the features extracted depend on the training examples used and the layered architecture. Suppose we already know what features are important in the domain concerned; then why not encode these features into the network? This simple and straightforward approach saves a lot of learning efforts by the network. Moreover, the network may be prevented from learning some features which turn out to be useless in the future.

If known features have been programmed into the network, then it will discover additional new features and extract features from known features. Hence, more levels of abstraction can be created in the architecture with the same number of hidden layers. Figure 10.7 shows this design principle.

The problem at different levels of abstraction can also be mapped into a hierarchical system of networks, each dealing with a certain level of abstraction. How to abstract the problem is just a kind of knowledge.

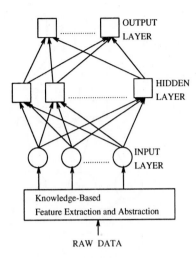

Figure 10.7: A neural network whose input encodes knowledge-based features.

10.4.3 Knowledge-Based Network Architectures

In Chapter 4 "Knowledge-Based Neural Networks," we see how domain knowledge can be used to determine the network topology and weights. The same principle can be applied to the design of spatiotemporal neural networks.

At the signal level, the network design is based on a set of mathematical equations in the domain. This idea can be further elaborated for different kinds of temporal networks:

- Static neural networks: Knowledge determines the size of the time window for the input buffer and how the window shifts over time.

- Time-delay neural networks: Knowledge determines the number of delayed lines and lengths.

- Temporal summation neural networks: Knowledge determines the decay constant of the activation function.

- Recurrent neural networks: Knowledge estimates the number of hidden units, which is related to that of patterns or subpatterns.

- Frequency-coding neural networks: Acting like a filter, knowledge determines which frequency ranges are important.

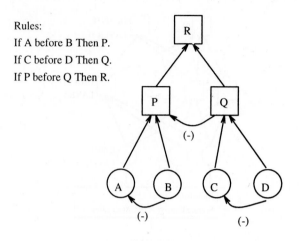

Rules:
If A before B Then P.
If C before D Then Q.
If P before Q Then R.

(-): Inhibitory connection.

Figure 10.8: Knowledge-based design of neural networks for encoding temporal relationships.

At the symbolic level, the network design is based on a set of domain rules. Again, we can examine this for different types of networks as follows:

- Static neural networks: Knowledge indicates which temporal features are important, each being encoded by an input unit. Knowledge also determines the connection topology and weights.

- Time-delay neural networks: Features related to history and causal relationship are encoded on the network input.

- Temporal summation neural networks: These correspond to real-time expert systems with nonmonotonic data bases.

- Recurrent neural networks: Forward connections and weights are based on the knowledge about dependency relationships. Recurrent connections and weights are based on precedence relationships. Since a temporal order can be derived from a set of recurrent connections (as suggested in Chapter 15), knowledge concerning such orders can be programmed into the network. This approach is useful for syntactic pattern recognition, in which known features are encoded as primitives or symbols. An example is provided in Figure 10.8. In addition, Frasconi et al. (1991) describe a linear programming technique as a means to inject knowledge into a recurrent neural network for pattern recognition.

- Frequency-coding neural networks: Useful features related to frequency analysis are connected according to knowledge.

10.4.4   Model-Based and Context-Directed Learning

A domain model consists of a set of domain concepts and their relationships which are represented in a certain formalism such as rules, semantic nets, or constraint graphs. Inasmuch as a domain model is a knowledge structure, "model based" is sometimes used interchangeably with "knowledge based." However, a model is often defined as a subset of domain knowledge which may be too open to formulate. A domain model can be converted to a neural network. For example, a rule-based model can be converted to a neural network called a rule-based connectionist network; a constraint model to a recurrent network.

Suppose there are multiple models defined and they can be related in certain ways. An activated model can instantiate another via a model interface. Model interface refers to commonly shared variables or relationships between two models in terms of related variables. If each model is implemented as a neural network (feedforward or recurrent), then the model interface is a set of variables or connections or a mixture. A cascade of networks allows the information to flow from one model to another. When a new model is instantiated, additional information is learned and can be used for problem solving.

In Elman's (1990) neural network model, the network state information at time $t-1$ is fed back to the network and sets a context for processing at time t. A special set of *context units* are defined that receive feedback signals from the hidden layer. The activation C_j of a context unit j is given by

$$C_j(t) = \alpha C_j(t-1) + N_j(t-1)$$

where N_j is the feedback received from noncontext units and α is the strength of self-connections ($\alpha < 1$). Thus, past memory is kept but gradually decayed over time. In comparison, Jordan's (1989) model has the context units fed from the output layer and also from themselves.

In a more general sense, "context" refers to *temporal* or *spatial adjacency*. Context information is essential for pattern recognition and learning. For example, in medical images, the criterion for detecting a cancer in a solid structure such as the liver will be quite different from that in a hollow organ such as the intestine because of different contexts. Context information can be static in nature or generated dynamically as necessary. In recurrent neural networks, context information is implicit and dynamically set. It is possible to make this information explicitly represented by knowledge-based context units along with their connections with other units, as suggested by Figure 10.9. Recruiting appropriate context units into a learning network makes learning more context-dependent and hence more sensible and accurate.

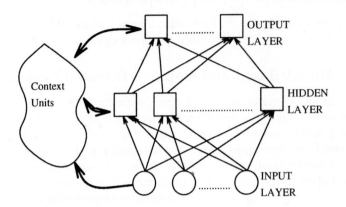

Figure 10.9: A neural network with built-in context information encoded by context units. These units communicate with the network and influence its processing.

10.5 Summary

Several neural networks are available for learning spatiotemporal patterns. The selection of neural networks depends on how the problem is formulated. Static and time-delay neural networks use spatial representation of temporal sequences on their input layers. In these networks, the size of the input buffer is fixed, and data entry is controlled by a clock. Static networks are useful for pattern classification. Time-delay networks have shown great promise in such applications as speech recognition. However, spatial representation has an inherent limitation with scaling in terms of how large a temporal pattern can be encoded since this representational method uses a linear memory to store temporal information acquired from an external source. In contrast, recurrent neural networks use temporal representation, which means that a temporal sequence enters the network one data element at a time. Recurrent networks are intrinsically more powerful and scalable than spatial networks by using a nonlinear memory to store temporal information. Recurrent networks have been applied to speech recognition and robotic control. Other alternative types of networks exist, such as temporal summation and frequency-coding networks. The combination of networks with different temporal capabilities is needed for complex problems.

Neural networks in most cases seek local optimum solutions and generally require a long training time. These problems can be effectively dealt with by infusing knowledge into the networks. Since knowledge is often represented symbolically, signal-to-symbol transformation is often a preliminary step for such an approach. Knowledge can indicate which features are useful for a particular problem domain and how to decompose the problem and form abstraction. Furthermore, knowledge can be applied to guide network design at both the signal and the symbolic levels and can be used for model-based and context-directed learning.

10.6 References

1. Almeida, L.B. 1987. A learning rule for asynchronous perceptrons with feedback in a combinatorial environment. In *Proceedings of ICNN* (San Diego, CA), pp. II-609–618.

2. Beerhold, J.R., Jansen, M., and Eckmiller, R. 1990. Pulse-processing neural net hardware with selectable topology and adaptive weights and delays. In *Proceedings of IJCNN* (San Diego, CA), pp. II-569–574.

3. Bengio, Y., Cardin, R., de Mori, R., and Merlo, E. 1989. Programmable execution of multi-layered networks for automatic speech recognition. *Communications of the ACM*, 32, pp. 195–199.

4. Bottou, L., Fogelman Soulie, F., Blanchet, P., and Lienard, J.S. 1990. Speaker-independent isolated digit recognition: Multilayer perceptrons vs. dynamic time warping. *Neural Network*, 3, pp. 453–465.

5. Brown, G.D.A. 1990. Short-term memory capacity limitations in recurrent speech production and perception networks. In *Proceedings of IJCNN* (Washington, DC), pp. I-43–46.

6. Cohen, M.A., Grossberg, S., and Stork, D. 1987. Recent developments in a neural model of real-time speech analysis and synthesis. In *Proceedings of ICNN* (San Diego, CA), pp. IV-443–453.

7. Elman, J.L. 1990. Finding structure in time. *Cognitive Science*, 14, pp. 179–211.

8. Erman, L.D., Hayes-Roth, F., Lesser, V.R., and Reddy, D.R. 1980. The Hearsay-II speech understanding system: Integrating knowledge to resolve uncertainty. *Comput. Surveys*, 12, pp. 213–253.

9. Frasconi, P., Gori, M., Maggini, M., and Soda, G. 1991. A unified approach for integrating explicit knowledge and learning by examples in recurrent networks. In *Proceedings of IJCNN* (Seattle, WA), pp. I-811–816.

10. Goerke, N., Schone, M., Kreimeier, B., and Eckmiller, R. 1990. A network with pulse processing neurons for generation of arbitrary temporal sequences. In *Proceedings of IJCNN* (San Diego, CA), pp. III-315–320.

11. Goldberg, K.Y., and Pearlmutter, B.A. 1989. Using backpropagation with temporal windows to learn the dynamics of the CMU direct-drive arm, II. In *Advances in Neural Information Processing Systems I*. Morgan Kaufmann, San Mateo, CA.

12. Gorman, R.P., and Sejnowski, T.J. 1986. Learned classification of sonar targets using a massively parallel network. *IEEE Transactions on Acoustics, Speech, and Signal Processing*, 36, pp. 1135–1140.

13. Gorman, R.P., and Sejnowski, T.J. 1988. Analysis of hidden units in a layered network trained to classify sonar targets. *Neural Networks*, 1, pp. 75–89.

14. Grossberg, S. 1969. Some networks that can learn, remember, and reproduce any number of complicated space-time patterns, I. *J. Math. and Mechanics*, 49, pp. 53–91.

15. Grossberg, S. 1970. Some networks that can learn, remember, and reproduce any number of complicated space-time patterns, II. *Studies in Applied Math.*, 49, pp. 135–166.

16. Hampshire II, J.B., and Waibel, A.H. 1990. A novel objective function for improved phoneme recognition using time-delay neural networks. *IEEE Transactions on Neural Networks*, 1, pp. 216–228.

17. Hertz, J., Krogh, A., and Palmer, R.G. 1991. *Introduction to the Theory of Neural Computation*. Addison-Wesley, Reading, MA.

18. Jordan, M.I. 1989. Serial order: A parallel distributed processing approach. In *Advances in Connectionist Theory: Speech*. Erlbaum, Hillsdale, NJ.

19. Lang, K.J., Waibel, A.H., and Hinton, G.E. 1990. A time-delay neural network architecture for isolated word recognition. *Neural Networks*, 3, pp. 23–43.

20. Lippmann, R.P. 1989. Review of neural networks for speech recognition. *Neural Computation*, 1, pp. 1–38.

21. Marcus, C.M., and Westervelt, R.M. 1989. Dynamics of analog neural networks with time delay. In *Advances in Neural Information Processing Systems 1*, pp. 568–576. Morgan Kaufmann, San Mateo, CA.

22. Norrod, F.E., O'Neill, M.D., and Gat, E. 1989. Feedback-induced sequentiality in neural networks. In *Proceedings of IJCNN* (San Diego, CA), pp. II-251–258.

23. Pineda, F.J. 1987. Generalization of back-propagation to recurrent neural networks. *Physics Review Letters*, 59, pp. 2229–2232.

24. Principe, J.C., Vries, B., Kuo, J.M., and Oliveira, P.G. 1992. Modeling applications with the focused gamma net. In *Advances in Neural Information Processing Systems, 4*, pp. 143–150. Morgan Kaufmann, San Mateo, CA.

25. Rossen, M.L., and Anderson, J.A. 1989. Representational issues in a neural network model of syllable recognition. In *Proceedings of IJCNN* (Washington, DC), pp. I-19–25.

26. Tam, D.C., and Perkel, D.H. 1989. A model for temporal correlation of biological neuronal spike trains. In *Proceedings of IJCNN* (Washington, DC), pp. I-781–786.

27. Tank, D., and Hopfield, J.J. 1987. Concentrating information in time: Analog neural networks with applications to speech recognition problems. In *Proceedings of ICNN* (San Diego, CA), pp. 455–468.

28. Tolat, V.V., and Peterson, A.M. 1989. A self-organizing neural network for classifying sequences. In *Proceedings of IJCNN* (Washington, DC), pp. II-561–568.

29. Tom, M.D., and Tenorio, M.F. 1989. A spatio-temporal pattern recognition approach to word recognition. In *Proceedings of IJCNN* (Washington, DC), pp. I-351–355.

30. Uchiyama, T., Shimohara, K., and Tokunaga, Y. 1989. A modified leaky integrator network for temporal pattern processing. In *Proceedings of IJCNN* (Washington, DC), pp. I-469–475.

31. Yanai, H., and Sawada, Y. 1990. Associative memory network composed of neurons with hysteretic property. *Neural Networks*, 3, pp. 223–228.

10.7 Problems

1. In digital implementation, pulse trains can be used to represent weights and signal strengths. Pulse trains reflect the frequency or probability that a neuron fires, simulating frequency modulation observed in biological neural networks. Multiplication of two pulse trains is equivalent to taking their logic-AND, and summation is equivalent to the logic-OR operation. Show how the sigmoid activation function can be implemented in this technique?

2. Use an adaline as an adaptive filter to predict signal values. The adaline has three tapped delay lines connected to the output unit which uses the "identify" function as the activation function. The following signal trend is used to train the network:

$$2, 5, 6, 4, 3, 4, 5, 7, 6, 4, 2, 5, 6, 7$$

    (a) Specify the network structure.

    (b) Specify the connection weights after training. (The adaline learning algorithm is described in Chapter 2 "Basic Neural Computational Models.")

    (c) Given the above signal trend, what is the next signal value predicted by the network?

3. Discuss the computational complexity of the real-time recurrent learning and the backpropagation-through-time algorithms. Which algorithm is more efficient under what circumstances?

4. Hecht-Nielsen (1990) indicated that the recurrent backpropagation network error function makes little sense if an input sequence depends strongly on the past outputs of the network and the network has poor mapping capability. Give an explanation, and identify situations where this problem would or would not occur.

5. Differential equations are often used for system modeling. A differential equation like

$$T\frac{dx(t)}{dt} = -x(t)$$

where T is a constant can be implemented in discrete time as a difference equation given by

$$x(t) = (1 - \frac{1}{T})x(t-1)$$

    (a) Solve both the differential and the difference equations analytically, and see how the solutions relate to each other.

    (b) Design a simple recurrent neural network to model the above differential equation.

    (c) Let $T = 5$. Use the following time series to train the neural network, and give the final connection weights

$$10, 8.2, 6.7, 5.4, 4.5, 3.7, 3.0, 2.5, 2.0, 1.7$$

    (d) Compare the numerical and the analytical results (the neural network is a numerical approach). How can you interpret the connection weights?

Part II

Neural Networks and Expert Systems

Chapter 11

Expert Systems

11.1 Introduction

An expert system refers to a computer system which exhibits the human expert's intelligence. An expert system handles real-world problems requiring the expert's involvement, uses a computer model of expert knowledge and expert reasoning, and is comparable with or even superior to a human expert in performance (accuracy and efficiency). MYCIN and DENDRAL (Buchanan and Shortliffe 1984) are two important expert systems in history. MYCIN addresses the problem of diagnosing and treating infectious blood diseases and meningitis, DENDRAL the problem of chemical structure elucidation. PROSPECTOR (Duda, Gaschnig, and Hart 1979), R1/XCON (McDermott 1981), and CADUCEUS (Pople 1982) are some important examples of other successful expert systems. The number of real-world expert systems has increased so rapidly in the past decade that it would be impossible to enumerate all of them here.

As shown schematically in Figure 11.1, an expert system typically consists of a knowledge base, an inference engine, a user interface, and an explanation facility. The knowledge base stores the domain knowledge, and the inference engine reasons with this knowledge for solving problems. Also, there is increasing emphasis on the connection of an expert system with conventional software such as a data base management system.

Feigenbaum (1977) indicated that the power of an expert system derives from the knowledge it possesses rather than from the inference method it employs. For difficult problems lacking tractable algorithmic solutions, the use of the human expert's knowledge is the most obvious solution if it is available. Explicit representation of knowledge facilitates not only the use but also the dissemination of knowledge. The latter is important for the purpose of education. It turns out that the emphasis on "knowledge" has significantly advanced the technology bases in science and engineering and also stimulated a great deal of research on *knowledge-based systems*. The terms "expert systems"

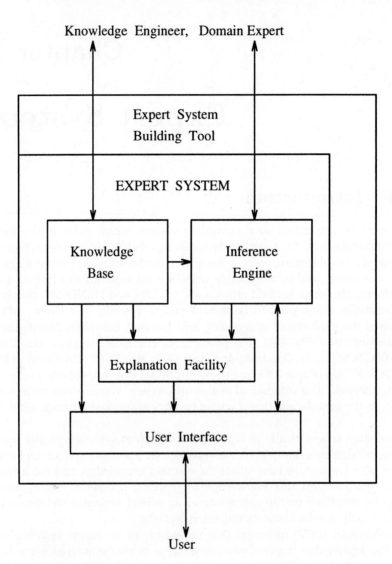

Figure 11.1: The basic elements of an expert system.

and "knowledge-based systems" are sometimes used interchangeably.

Artificial intelligence (AI) applications are characterized by such features as heuristic search, symbolic representation, and symbolic inference. Expert systems have emerged as a successful branch of AI but differ from the broad class of AI tasks in several important ways. Expert systems deal with expert-level tasks, use domain-specific knowledge and strategies, separate out the control structure as the inference engine, and provide explanations for conclusions reached. Conventional data processing systems generally lack these features.

Building expert systems is justified by a number of facts. Human experts are often expensive to consult. Their knowledge is often abstract and difficult to obtain. Also, expert systems have demonstrated their usefulness in many cases. For example, PROSPECTOR has discovered a valuable molybdenum deposit; DENDRAL is used routinely by many chemists in the world.

Expert systems increase the availability of expert knowledge, reduce the cost and risk involved in solving particular problems, allow integration of multiple experts' knowledge, provide good reliability and permanent expertise, and can serve as intelligent tutors and data bases. It is desirable but unnecessary that expert systems outperform human experts. As more expert tasks are taken over by expert systems, human experts can divert more of their efforts to research in an attempt to develop better systems. This is an optimistic view of the future relationship between human experts and expert systems.

Expert systems have been developed for such problems as interpretation, diagnosis, monitoring, prediction, planning, design, control, and so on. In general, a domain is appropriate for taking the expert system approach if the problem cannot be solved by conventional programming, the domain is ill-structured but well-bounded, and the problem-solving knowledge is heuristic and uncertain.

It appears that research on expert systems has slowed down relative to their development since the mideighties. This is in part due to the fact that powerful knowledge-based techniques like the rule-based technique have been mature and the concept of expert systems has merged into many disciplines. On the other hand, the neural network approach, which resurged in the last decade, seems to have opened a new direction for expert system development, namely, the integration of neural networks and conventional expert systems. A main focus of this chapter is to explore such integration architectures.

In the remaining sections, we examine the issues of knowledge acquisition, knowledge representation, and inference structures and describe methods for reasoning under uncertainty. Both the conventional and the neural network approaches are discussed. Then, we explore the integration of neural networks and expert systems.

11.2   Knowledge Acquisition

The domain expertise that needs to be transferred to an expert system is a collection of definitions, relations, specialized facts, procedures, heuristics, strategies, and assumptions. The transfer of knowledge from some knowledge source to a computer system is called *knowledge acquisition*. There are many sources we may turn to, such as human experts, literature, textbooks, and data bases. Among these, acquiring knowledge from human experts is known as *knowledge engineering*. And the well-known bottleneck is extracting the human expert's knowledge via interviews or tools, a process called *knowledge elicitation*.

Two basic issues involved in knowledge acquisition are incrementability and transparency. First, since it is often impossible to acquire perfect knowledge in one step, incremental acquisition is necessary. On this issue, *modularity* is important, which refers to the ability to modify individual elements more or less independently of others in the system. Second, transparency makes the system understandable. Only when the system is transparent, can its knowledge be criticized, edited, and incrementally refined.

Buchanan and Shortliffe (1984) identify three modes of knowledge acquisition as follows:

- Handcrafting: Code knowledge into the program directly.

- Knowledge engineering: Work with an expert to organize his/her knowledge in a suitable form for an expert system to use.

- Machine learning: Extract knowledge from training examples.

"Handcrafting" is feasible only if an expert happens to be a programmer. It is generally slow to build and debug a program in this way. Also, it is difficult to make the system consistent when it grows by small increments. "Machine learning" has long been advocated for knowledge acquisition. It dispenses with human experts but requires good examples. It is a potentially economical and efficient way for building an expert system. Chapter 3 "Learning" reviews a number of important learning algorithms developed to date. Only the knowledge engineering approach is elaborated further.

Knowledge acquisition (engineering) can be divided into the following five stages (Hayes-Roth, Waterman, and Lenat 1983):

1. *Identification*: Define an appropriate problem and determine its characteristics.

2. *Conceptualization*: Find concepts (objects, relations, information flow, etc.) to represent knowledge.

3. *Formalization*: Choose a knowledge representation method and an inference mechanism.

4. *Implementation*: Formulate knowledge in the chosen formalism (rules, frames, semantic nets, etc.).

5. *Testing*: Verify the knowledge and validate the system.

The whole process is iterative. The results of testing may indicate reformulating the problem, redefining the concepts, redesigning the knowledge structures, or refining the knowledge. Throughout the process, the *knowledge engineer* (a person who assists in knowledge engineering) works with the domain expert closely. A qualified knowledge engineer is typically a computer engineer or scientist who has sufficient experience in building practical expert systems.

Knowledge engineering tools automate knowledge acquisition. With a good tool, an expert can built an expert system and bypass a knowledge engineer. Another advantage of using tools is *rapid prototyping*. Building a practical expert system often takes many man-years without tools. The time, however, can be considerably shortened with tools to, say, a few man-months.

TEIRESIAS (Davis 1976), dealing with interactive transfer of expertise, is a classical example of a knowledge acquisition tool. TEIRESIAS assists human experts in editing the knowledge base by tracking down the relevant rules and allowing the experts to correct the faulty rules or add missing rules. In order to accomplish this, TEIRESIAS uses the information embedded in the old rules.

Today, there have been a lot of expert system tools on the market, such as ART, KEE, Knowledge Craft, S.1, M.1, LOOPS, OPS5, Personal Consultant, and so forth. Tools at the high end (e.g., KEE, ART) provide a mixed environment (combination of different knowledge representation languages) and nice graphical interfaces, and are suitable for large-scale applications. Tools at the low end are much less versatile and are often for small-scale applications. A good survey of expert system tools can be found in Firebaugh (1988).

To choose a tool, the important thing is the match between the tool features and the problem characteristics including the type of the problem, the size of search space, the form of data (time varying, uncertain, monotonic, etc.), control (top-down or bottom-up, with or without backtracking). Features such as generality, testing accessibility, and development speed should be considered as well. A tool that provides more generality than is needed will incur unnecessary programming efforts. A tool should be currently maintained by the developer. Also, a tool should have built-in explanation and interaction facilities to speed up the system development.

In designing a tool, considerations should be placed on generality, completeness, language features, data base structures, and control methods. Specialized tools such as EMYCIN (the core of MYCIN) provide good user interfaces and a rather complete skeleton of an expert system but a limited range of applications. Tools such as OPS5 have language generality but no sophisticated user interfaces. Natural-language interface is desirable for consultation as well as for knowledge acquisition. Accessibility to local operating systems enables the system to control other jobs in parallel and to call external subroutines written in C, PASCAL, or FORTRAN. The data representation scheme should be as general as possible. If generality is more important than efficiency, a tool should provide an accessible control mechanism so that the desired flow of control can be implemented. If learning and self-modification are required, a tool should provide a constrained control mechanism.

11.3   Knowledge Representation

Knowledge representation is a major issue in building expert systems. It is concerned with both the storage of knowledge in proper data structures and the use of knowledge in intelligent processes. It would be incomplete to mention either aspect alone.

We start with the *knowledge representation hypothesis* of Smith (1982), which states that any intelligent process contains structural ingredients which external observers naturally take to represent the knowledge exhibited by the process. In other words, any intelligent system possesses a knowledge base underlying its intelligent behavior. Expert systems are a good example of this hypothesis.

Reichgelt (1991) describes four levels of knowledge representation:

- The first level is the *implementational* level, which concerns the possibility of building a computer program for the knowledge representation language.

- The second level is the *logic* level, which concerns the logic properties of the knowledge representation language, such as the meanings of expressions and the soundness of the associated inference procedure.

- The third level is the *epistemological* level, which concerns the knowledge structure (e.g., semantic nets) and the inference strategy of the knowledge representation language.

- The fourth level is the *conceptual* level, which concerns the actual primitives (concepts, objects, etc.) of the knowledge representation language.

This knowledge representation hierarchy roughly corresponds to the process of knowledge acquisition described in the last section: the conceptual level versus conceptualization, the epistemological level versus formalization, and the implementational level versus implementation. One thing that should have been mentioned in knowledge acquisition is *knowledge analysis*, which corresponds to the logic level of knowledge representation.

Four criteria can be used to evaluate a knowledge representation language for a given problem domain, as described by Rich (1983):

- Representational adequacy: the ability to represent all kinds of knowledge in the domain

- Inferential adequacy: the ability to make inferences and solve problems in the domain

- Inferential efficiency: the ability to deduce information efficiently

- Acquisitional efficiency: the ability to acquire new knowledge easily

If possible, one should use only a single representation (homogeneous representation) because of simplicity. However, it is often true that no single language optimizes all the capabilities mentioned above. In this case, one may consider using multiple languages (heterogeneous representation). The trade-off is between simplicity and capability.

In the following subsections, we briefly review important knowledge representation paradigms and mention only their key features.

11.3.1 Logic

In propositional logic, the most fundamental notion is that of *truth*. There are propositions which are things we can call true or false, axioms which describe relationships and implications we can formalize, rules of inference for deducing new information, and sentential connectives for combining simple sentences.

Because propositional logic is inadequate for describing objects and relations, predicate calculus was invented. In predicate calculus, predicates, quantifiers (universal and existential), and more inference rules are added. Five types of symbols can be distinguished: object symbols, object variables, function symbols, relation symbols, and operators. A logic is called first-order (first-order logic, or FOL) if it does not permit quantification over relation (predicate) and function symbols; else it is of second order.

In logic, two commonly applied rules of inference are:

- *Modus ponens*: If "A implies B" and "A is true," then "B is true."

- *Resolution*: If "A is false or B is true" and "A is true," then "B is true."

In predicate calculus, the concept of matching or unification (a special matching procedure) is introduced into the above rules in order to handle variables. The advantages of logic representation include generality, naturalness, preciseness, flexibility, and modularity. The major disadvantage lies in the separation of representation and utilization and the consequential inefficiency for inference.

11.3.2 Production Rules

Production systems were developed by Newell and Simon (1972). The knowledge base of such systems consists of rules called productions. Each production rule is put in the form of a condition-action pair, e.g., "If A and B, then C." When the condition (antecedent) is satisfied, the action (consequent) is executed. Production systems have been successfully applied to psychological modeling and expert systems. The inference procedures will be described in Section 11.4.

The advantages of production systems include modularity, uniformity, and naturalness. Rules have been found quite useful for providing explanations as to why a question is asked, how a conclusion is reached, and what strategy is used by an expert system. The disadvantages are the inefficiency of execution if good control knowledge is unavailable and the difficulty of representing algorithmic knowledge.

The validity of the production rule representation has been demonstrated in many expert systems such as DENDRAL and MYCIN. The ease of this scheme to capture and to use expertise accounts for its successful applications. Domains in which theory is diffuse, control flow is simple, and the use of knowledge is not predetermined are particularly suitable. Medicine is a good example, while physics is a counterexample.

11.3.3   Semantic Nets

Semantic nets were developed by Quillian (1968) and others. A net consists of nodes and links between nodes. Nodes may be objects, events, or concepts. Links specify the relationships between connected nodes. Despite the simplicity of this scheme, ambiguity often occurs. For instance, it is a common error to use the link "is-a" to represent both the "member" and the "subset" relations.

Inference can be made in semantic nets by:

- *Intersection search*: This is an inference procedure which propagates information from nodes under query through the network and sees where the propagations intersect. The relationships among objects can be found in this way.

- *Property inheritance*: The semantic net allows *property inheritance*, in which specific objects inherit properties from more general objects or classes. For example, if Clyde is a bird, then Clyde can fly since birds can fly. However, this inference rule may lead to incorrect conclusions for exceptional cases.

- *Graph-based matching*: Semantic nets have been used as labeled digraphs (directed graphs) to represent structural objects in machine learning research. In this representation, two objects can be compared for similarity or dissimilarity.

The advantage of the semantic net representation lies in the explicit and succinct associations between objects and concepts. However, without extending its formalism, it is difficult to represent quantification, disjunction, implication, and second-order statements.

Woods (1975) raised several criticisms against the semantic net formalism. For example, semantic nets are unable to represent propositions without commitment to their truth value and unable to represent intensional descriptions without commitment to their existence. His points address some subtle yet important aspects of knowledge representation.

11.3.4 Frames

A frame is a collection of slots (attributes) that characterize an object. Each slot may be filled with a value, a default, another frame, or procedures. Embedding procedures within a frame (or an otherwise declarative structure) is called *procedural attachment*. If stored with a slot, procedures that are triggered whenever the slot is changed are known as *demons*. Since both *procedural* representation and *declarative* representation have pros and cons, frames are intended to combine their advantages.

A slot in a frame is equivalent to a link in a semantic net. So, frames and semantic nets are mutually convertible.

Frames reason with the following mechanisms:

- *Selection and instantiation*: Select frames that best match the current situation, and then use them to provide more information.

- *Property inheritance*: In the case of *multiple inheritance*, multiple paths in the generalization hierarchy need to be explored, and conflicts need to be resolved.

- *Default reasoning*: It proceeds by using default values or by property inheritance. Default values are overridden by specific values on arrival.

- *Procedural attachment*: During problem solving, frames can generate messages, actions, and post new tasks through embedded procedures.

The frame representation has several advantages. It is natural for representing structural objects. It is more efficient than logic and is computationally tractable. The default reasoning in frames is *decidable*. In logic, however, default and nonmonotonic reasoning may be semidecidable or undecidable.

The frame representation suffers from some weaknesses. It lacks a clear semantics. It has the same expressive limitations as the semantic net representation. Also, default inheritance may jeopardize definition capability.

Knowledge represented in different schemes is illustrated in Figure 11.2.

11.3.5 Object-Oriented Languages

An object-oriented language not only uses object-oriented representation like frames but also defines computational objects. Objects are active, having characteristics of both data and programs. *Methods* are associated with objects and invoked by sending messages to objects. Each method-bearing object (class) in a hierarchy of method-source properties is called a *flavor*. That is, a flavor is a class of objects which use the same procedure to do the same thing. Objects communicate by sending messages.

In contrast to flavors, property inheritance in a frame-based system is directed at finding values rather than methods. In addition, objects execute methods, whereas frames are acted on by external procedures.

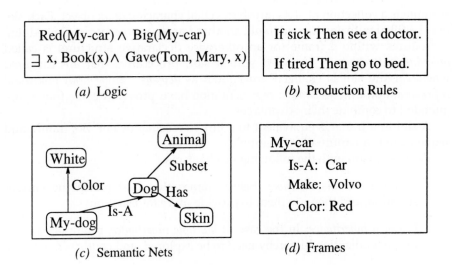

(a) Logic

(b) Production Rules

(c) Semantic Nets

(d) Frames

Figure 11.2: Examples of knowledge representation.

Advantageous features of object-oriented languages include modularity, strong typing of operators without global type checking on the operands, overloading of operators (an operator is interpreted differently according to the objects involved), and information hiding (encapsulation, i.e., preventing users from seeing internal behavior).

On the negative side, the implementation of an object-oriented language often varies with software designers. It lacks clear semantics. Also, its ability to model events may be limited.

11.3.6   Mixed Representation

Sophisticated expert system tools such as KEE and ART provide a variety of representational schemes and inference techniques. These schemes are more or less integrated. For example, rules can access information stored in frames; rules can be attached to an object class with some control strategy.

KRYPTON (Brachman, Fikes, and Levesque 1983) is a hybrid language, which provides a functional view of knowledge representation, and makes distinctions between definitional and assertional information. It emphasizes what functions, rather than what structures, a system should provide and addresses the problem with semantic nets and frames; namely, they cannot distinguish between definitions (intensional) and assertions (extensional), as raised by Woods (1975).

11.3.7   Analogical Representation

In analogical (direct) representation, the structure of representation resembles and corresponds to the structure of the object being represented. Examples include maps, electrical circuits, and photographs. Its advantages include naturalness, ease of interpretation, and observability of complex relationships. The disadvantage lies in the limitation to express all domain knowledge.

11.3.8   Connectionists

The long-term knowledge of a connectionist network is encoded as a set of weights on connections between units. The *connectionist* (neural network) representation can be broadly divided into *local* representations and *distributed* representations. This topic is treated in Chapter 9 "Structures and Sequences."

11.4   Inference Engines

We divide inference engines into two kinds: *categorical* and *noncategorical*. A noncategorical inference engine calculates the confidence level for each conclusion it reaches, whereas a categorical engine does not. The next section describes the techniques which noncategorical engines can use to manage uncertainty.

As the complexity of the problem increases, special strategies of a reasoning model are required. Hayes-Roth et al. (1983) present a clear view on this issue, which can be summarized as follows:

- When search space is small and data and knowledge are reliable, exhaustive search, monotonic reasoning, and single line of reasoning can be used.

- When data or knowledge is unreliable, combining evidence from multiple sources is justified and probabilistic or other fuzzy models can be used.

- For time-varying data, state-triggered expectations are useful.

- In the case of a large search space, hierarchical generate and test and abstraction are useful.

- When subproblems interact, the least-commitment strategy and constraint propagation can be applied.

- When guessing is needed, plausible reasoning and backtracking are useful.

- When a single model is too weak, use multiple lines of reasoning.

- In the case of diverse specialists, try heterogeneous models, opportunistic scheduling, and variable-width search.

- If the knowledge base is too inefficient, then compile the knowledge structure into a more efficient form.

In the following subsections, we examine important control strategies and inference techniques.

11.4.1   Event-Driven Systems

Under the event-driven strategy, input or previous events guide the generation of future events. The goal state can be reached by applying suitable operators successively, starting from the initial state. In a rule-based system, the rules whose antecedents match the input data are first chosen, and rules whose antecedents match the consequents of the initially or previously chosen rules are invoked. This invocation is performed recursively until the goal is concluded or no rules can be further invoked. Thus, this strategy is also termed *forward-chaining* because it reasons forward from the data and the rules are chained together to draw conclusions. For instance, given the rule "If A, then B," we reason that "if A is true, then B is true."

When more than one rule can be invoked, the strategy of selecting one rule to execute its actions is known as *conflict resolution*. Some criteria are required for conflict resolution. Several are described by Davis and King (1984) as follows:

- Rule order: Select the rule with the highest priority (assume that there is a complete ordering of all rules in the system).

- Data order: Select the rule which matches the data base element with the highest priority.

- Generality order: Select the most specific rule.

- Precedence order: Select the rule with the highest precedence based on a network or hierarchy.

- Recency order: Select the rule which is most recently executed or matches the most recently updated data base element.

11.4.2   Goal-Oriented Systems

Under the goal-driven strategy, a goal statement (the problem to be solved) is converted to a set of subgoals whose solutions together can solve the original goal. The conversion of a goal into its subgoals is done recursively until each of them has been solved. In a rule-based system, this means that it chooses rules whose consequents deal with the goal concerned (called goal rules) and invokes all rules whose consequents are referenced by the antecedents of goal rules. This conversion is performed recursively until rules whose antecedents reference only the input data are reached or until no rules can be further invoked. In the latter case, the system may query the user for information required. Thus, this strategy is also named *backward-chaining* since it reasons backward from the goal. So, given the rule, "If A, then B," we reason that "to conclude B, we need to conclude A."

11.4.3   Expectation-Driven Systems

In expectation-driven control, the system matches the current state (or data base) against existing models to generate expectations, which in turn drive future actions. The initial hypothesis forming rules make an initial, broad hypothesis by focusing on a limited number of data elements of primary importance. On the basis of this initial hypothesis and existing models, the system generates expectations, which are then compared with the input data to see if the initial hypothesis is reinforced or weakened.

11.4.4   Metalevel Reasoning Systems

Metalevel reasoning models make distinctions between domain actions and metalevel actions. The basic control loop is:

1. Execute all metalevel actions.

2. Based on the results of step 1, execute the ideal domain actions.

Metalevel knowledge expedites the convergence upon the desired solution by selecting pertinent domain knowledge. It is assumed that the metalevel knowledge exists in much smaller quantity than the domain knowledge.

11.4.5   Blackboard Systems

The blackboard model (Hayes-Roth 1985) is a problem-solving framework initially developed in the HEARSAY-II speech understanding system. This model has three basic elements:

- A *blackboard* is a global data base which records all solution elements generated during problem solving.

- *Knowledge sources* (KSs) generate solution elements. Only those knowledge sources whose conditions are satisfied can execute their actions. Most blackboard systems use the event-driven strategy. Each change to the blackboard constitutes an event. By combining other specific information on the blackboard, a new event can trigger one or more knowledge sources. Each such triggering process results in a unique *knowledge source activation record* (KSAR). Each KSAR is characterized by the KS, the triggering cycle, the triggering event, and condition values.

- A *scheduler* chooses a single KSAR to execute its actions during each problem-solving cycle.

The blackboard model allows multilevel, heterogeneous abstraction spaces. It is a good model for integrating diverse specialties and coping with the conflicting demands of searching a large space and using limited computational resources. To achieve this, the model executes the knowledge sources in an opportunistic manner.

11.4.6 Neural Networks

A neural network is organized as a feedforward or recurrent, single-layer or multilayer structure. A feedforward neural network is used if the inference behavior is characterized by propagating and combining activations successively in the forward direction from the input to the output. A recurrent network is used instead if the inference behavior involves collateral inhibition and feedback. For instance, the winner-take-all strategy can be implemented with collateral inhibition circuits.

As for the layered arrangement, multilayer neural networks are more advantageous than single-layer networks in performing nonlinear classification. This advantage stems from the nonlinear operation at hidden units. Important neural network algorithms are described elsewhere.

11.5   Reasoning under Uncertainty

"Uncertainty" refers to the lack of adequate and correct information to make decisions.[1] Reasoning (or inference) under uncertainty is always a major issue in designing a practical AI system. This section examines important methods on this issue. For each method, how the information is combined and propagated under uncertainty is addressed.

11.5.1 Probabilistic Approaches

PROSPECTOR is representative of systems which use probabilities to handle uncertainty. The description below centers around this system. A probabilistic model presented by Pearl (1986) is examined in Chapter 12 "Causal Learning and Modeling."

We starts with Bayes' theorem:

$$P(H|E) = \frac{P(E|H)P(H)}{\sum_i P(E|H_i)P(H_i)} \tag{11.1}$$

---

[1] In the logic approach, so-called truth maintenance systems (TMS) (Doyle 1979) revise beliefs or assumptions when contradictions arise.

where the function P is the probability function. Evidence can be combined under the assumption of conditional independence by

$$P(H|E1, E2) = \frac{P(E1|H)P(E2|H)P(H)}{\sum_i P(E1|H_i)P(E2|H_i)P(H_i)}$$

Suppose we define *odds* by

$$O(H) = \frac{P(H)}{P(\neg H)} = \frac{P(H)}{1 - P(H)}$$

which is the odds of H. And we define a *likelihood ratio* by

$$\lambda(E, H) = \frac{P(E|H)}{P(E|\neg H)}$$

which is the likelihood ratio of E with respect to H. It can be derived that

$$O(H|E) = \lambda(E, H)O(H) \tag{11.2}$$

which is called the *odds-likelihood formulation* of Bayes' rule. Now, evidence can be combined by

$$O(H|E1, E2) = \lambda(E2, H)\lambda(E1, H)O(H)$$

Obviously, it is easier to update odds than probabilities. Probabilities can always be recovered easily by

$$P(H) = \frac{O(H)}{1 + O(H)}$$

Moreover, human experts seem to prefer odds to probabilities.

When information is propagated along a chain of rules, the evidence based on the rule's conclusion is often uncertain. Besides, the initially given evidence can be uncertain. In these cases, we assume that

$$P(H|E') = P(H|E)P(E|E') + P(H|\neg E)P(\neg E|E') \tag{11.3}$$

where E' is the observed evidence and E the actual, absolute evidence. As suggested in PROSPECTOR, $P(H|E')$ can be calculated by using a linear interpolation between two extreme cases, $P(H|E)$ (E known to be true) and $P(H|\neg E)$ (E known to be false). This interpolation scheme uses three reference points:

- When $P(E|E') = 0$, $P(H|E') = P(H|\neg E)$.
- When $P(E|E') = P(E)$, $P(H|E') = P(H)$.
- When $P(E|E') = 1$, $P(H|E') = P(H|E)$.

For the case $0 \leq P(E|E') < P(E)$,

$$P(H|E') = P(H|\neg E) + \frac{P(H) - P(H|\neg E)}{P(E)} P(E|E') \qquad (11.4)$$

And for the case $P(E) \leq P(E|E') \leq 1$,

$$P(H|E') = P(H) + \frac{P(H|E) - P(H)}{1 - P(E)}[P(E|E') - P(E)] \qquad (11.5)$$

In a rule-based system, the rule's premise may involve conjunction and disjunction. The conjunction (disjunction) of probabilities in the rule's premise is defined as the minimum (maximum) of the probabilities unless given otherwise.

The probabilistic approach is precise but needs much statistical knowledge.

11.5.2   Certainty Factors

Certainty factors (CFs) are reals ranging from -1.0 to 1.0. A minus number indicates disbelief, whereas a positive number indicates belief. The degree of belief or disbelief parallels the absolute value of the number. The extreme values -1.0 and 1.0 represent "no" and "yes," respectively. An object is associated with a CF indicating the current belief in the object. A rule is assigned a CF representing the degree of belief in its conclusion given that its premise is true. The CF of a conclusion based upon a rule can be computed by multiplying the CF of the premise and the CF of the rule. Each condition in the premise on evaluation will return a number ranging from 0 to 1.0 representing the CF of the condition. The CFs of all conditions in the premise are combined to result in the CF of the premise. The conjunction operator ($AND) returns the minimum of the CFs of its arguments. The CFs of a fact due to different rules are combined according to the formulae described below.

In the certainty factor model, evidence is divided into confirming evidence and disconfirming evidence. The basic formula is

$$CF[H, E+ \, \& \, E-] = MB[H, E+] - MD[H, E-] \qquad (11.6)$$

where CF is the certainty factor function, MB the measure of belief, MD the measure of disbelief, and $E+$ and $E-$ confirming and disconfirming evidence, respectively. One observation with this formula is that a single piece of negative evidence could negate the combined evidence of any number of supporting rules. For this reason, the current version of the CF-combining function (Buchanan and Shortliffe 1984) is changed to

$$\text{CF}_{\text{combine}}(X, Y) = \begin{cases} X + Y(1 - X) & X, Y \text{ both } > 0 \\ \frac{X+Y}{1-\min(|X|,|Y|)} & XY < 0 \\ -\text{CF}_{\text{combine}}(-X, -Y) & X, Y \text{ both } < 0. \end{cases} \qquad (11.7)$$

The CF model is simple and does not require much statistical knowledge. However, it converges rapidly on the asymptote of 1 and occasionally yields inconsistent results if CFs are not assigned properly. This model has been validated in the MYCIN system.

11.5.3   Dempster-Shafer's Theory

Dempster-Shafer's theory of evidence is based on set theory. A description of its application to expert systems is given by Buchanan and Shortliffe (1984).

Suppose there are four possible hypotheses in the hypothesis space θ:

$$\theta = [h_1, h_2, h_3, h_4]$$

The hypotheses in θ are assumed to be mutually exclusive and exhaustive. For each piece of evidence, we try to assign a probability to each element of the power set of θ. This is called a *basic probability assignment* (bpa). The quantity $m(A)$ is the measure of the probability (or belief) assigned to the element A. Now, the quantity $m(\theta)$ is defined as the measure of that portion of total belief that remains unassigned for a specific bpa. A belief function (denoted as Bel) assigns to every subset S of θ the sum of beliefs assigned to every subset of S by a specific bpa. For example,

$$Bel([h_1, h_2]) = m([h_1, h_2]) + m([h_1]) + m([h_2]).$$

The *belief interval* for A is defined to be the interval $[Bel(A), 1 - Bel(A^c)]$ where A^c is the complement of A.

Next, consider how to combine evidence. Suppose there are two pieces of evidence each causing a specific bpa, m_1 and m_2. Then,

$$m_1 \oplus m_2(S) = \sum_{i,j} m_1(S_i) m_2(S_j)$$

where $\oplus$ is the combining operator, $S_i \cap S_j = S$, and $m_1(S_i) m_2(S_j) \neq 0$. If $m_1 \oplus m_2(\phi) \neq 0$ (ϕ is an empty set), then normalize the assigned values to make $m_1 \oplus m_2(\phi) = 0$ by proportionally distributing the value of $m_1 \oplus m_2(\phi)$ to other subsets.

Dempster-Shafer's scheme is computationally complex. However, it handles disjunction of hypotheses and can provide hierarchical diagnosis.

11.5.4   Fuzzy Set Theory

Fuzzy set theory was developed by Zadeh (1965). A fuzzy set differs from a traditional set in that each element in it has a membership grade ranging from 0 to 1. A fuzzy set F is expressed as follows:

$$F = \mu_1/e_1 + \cdots + \mu_n/e_n$$

where μ_i represents the grade of membership of e_i in F. F can also be expressed as

$$F = \int_U \mu_F(e)/e$$

where U is the universe. The union of two fuzzy sets F and G is defined to be

$$F \cup G = \int_U \max(\mu_F(e), \mu_G(e))/e$$

Their intersection is defined by

$$F \cap G = \int_U \min(\mu_F(e), \mu_G(e))/e$$

As in MYCIN and PROSPECTOR, conjunction and disjunction correspond to the functions min and max, respectively.

Rules involving fuzzy sets are called *fuzzy rules*. The grades of membership of a fuzzy set in the consequent of a fuzzy rule are bounded from above by the truth value of its antecedent (premise). So, for example, consider the rule

If X is A and Y is B, then Z is C

where A, B, and C are all fuzzy sets:

$A = 0.1/a + 0.5/b + 0.6/c$
$B = 0.7/d + 0.3/e$
$C = 0.4/f + 0.9/g$

Given $X = b$ and $Y = d$, what is Z? From the above definitions, the truth value of the rule's premise is 0.5 and $Z = 0.4/f + 0.5/g$.

Suppose the membership grade of an object x in a certain fuzzy set based on the ith fuzzy rule is $\mu_i(x)$. Then the grade of membership of the object based on all n rules is given by

$$\mu(x) = \max(\mu_1(x), ..., \mu_n(x))$$

Defuzzification refers to translating the membership grades of a fuzzy set into a crisp value. Two methods are available for this task:

- The *maximum method*: Choose the element with the maximum membership grade.

- The *moments method*: Calculate the first moment of inertia, I:

$$I = \frac{\sum_i \mu(x)x}{\sum_i \mu(x)}$$

where μ is the membership function. In the case of continuous elements, summation is replaced by integration.

While fuzzy set theory has no statistical basis, it has found a number of successful applications already.

11.5.5   Neural Networks

Recent research has indicated that neural networks are capable of not only deducing useful information but also inducing knowledge from the data. This capability is especially prominent compared with other techniques when uncertainty is involved. It appears that this capability is due to the storage of information in a large number of connection weights and the use of clever heuristics to adjust weights properly. This capability also seems related to the ability of modeling unknown systems. Suppose a neural network can approximate the underlying probability density functions more accurately than any other means; then, of course, the neural network can offer better decisions. See also Chapter 6 "Mathematical Modeling."

The way the information is combined and propagated depends on the neural network algorithm. Important neural network algorithms can be found in other chapters.

11.6   Hybrid Expert Systems

While symbolic AI and neural networks represent two different approaches to artificial intelligence, the former can be related to the latter in functionality. Though some think of knowledge-based systems and neural networks as separate AI tools, viewing them simply as different levels of description about the same mechanism would be more insightful. This view has been supported by the success of the KT algorithm, which translates the neural network knowledge into symbolic rules (see Chapter 14 "Rule Generation from Neural Networks").

Another view of combining connectionists and symbolic models is based on the observation that the former are well-suited for perceptual reasoning and the latter for cognitive reasoning. An architecture corresponding to this view can be designed in which information is processed at different levels of abstraction by different models. A number of hybrid system architectures are collected in the book by Kandel and Langholz (1992).

Expert networks refer to neural networks used as experts in a particular domain. A major weakness of these systems is that they cannot justify their responses as traditional expert systems do. Some solutions have been proposed. For example, Gallant's (1988) connectionist expert system is able to explain itself. A recent article by Caudill (1990) describes that rules can be formulated from a neural net by determining the features the net is using to make decisions (reverse engineering of the trained net). The idea here is to build a hybrid system combining neural networks and rule-based techniques so that it can explain its own behavior.

The integration or synergism of knowledge-based components and neural networks in a system can be explored from their functional and structural relationships in the system. Five integration architectures can be identified as follows (see Figure 11.3):

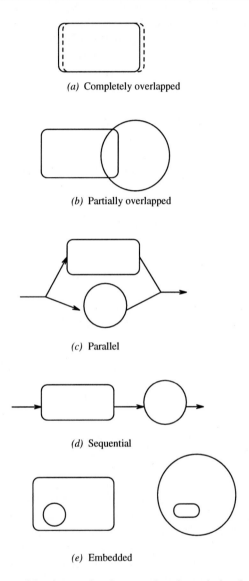

(a) Completely overlapped

(b) Partially overlapped

(c) Parallel

(d) Sequential

(e) Embedded

Figure 11.3: Five architectures for integrating knowledge-based systems and neural networks.

- *Completely overlapped*: In this architecture, the system is both a knowledge-based system and a neural network. It has a *dual* nature. The system optimizes its performance by combining the strengths of the two forms. Depending on the need, it can be presented to the user as a traditional expert system or as a neural network. One form can be converted to the other through inherent translation mechanisms. Therefore, only one form needs to be stored. The KBCNN model described in Chapter 4 "Knowledge-Based Neural Networks" is representative of this architecture.

- *Partially overlapped*: The system is a *hybrid* of a knowledge-based system and a neural network, exhibiting features of both. The two components share some but not all of their own internal variables or data structures. They often communicate through computer internal memory rather than external data files. An expert network augmented with explanation capability is a partially overlapped system. Gallant's connectionist expert system serves as another example.

- *Parallel*: A knowledge-based system and a neural network work in parallel to solve a common problem. Both can be stand-alone systems. The two components do not share their own internal variables or data structures. They communicate through their input/output devices, such as data files. For example, in a medical diagnostic system, a neural network analyzes signals and images, and a knowledge-based system interprets clinical symptoms and signs. The results are then combined.

- *Sequential*: A knowledge-based system and a neural network operate in sequence to solve a particular problem. Again, both can be stand-alone systems, and they do not share internal variables. The output of one component is passed on to the other for further processing. For example, a neural network is used as a front-end (preprocessor) for filtering noise and transforming signals to symbols, which are subsequently processed by an expert system. Handelman, Lane, and Gelfand (1989) present an approach that integrates knowledge-based systems and artificial neural networks for robotic control. In this approach, a rule-based system supervises the training of a neural network and controls the operation of the network during the learning process. The rule-based system initially finds acceptable first-cut solutions to the given task, then teaches the neural network how to accomplish the task by having the network observe and generalize on rule-based task execution.

- *Embedded*: In this integration, either a knowledge-based component is embedded within a neural network or vice versa. By saying that X is embedded in Y, we mean that X (a guest) becomes an element of Y (a host). Internal information exchange is expected. However, this architecture differs from the partially overlapped architecture in that the system's external features are determined by the host component only. It is arguable that many neural networks already use knowledge in specifying their inputs/outputs and structures. On the other hand, it is worthwhile to embed a neural network within an expert system. In a blackboard system, a trained neural network can be a useful knowledge source. In a speech understanding system, for example, the neural network can be used to analyze low-level signals and time-dependent behavior.

In another perspective, we can categorize integration paradigms according to the nature of coupling:

- *Fully coupled*: corresponding to the completely overlapped architecture

- *Tightly coupled*: including the partially overlapped and the embedded architectures

- *Loosely coupled*: including the parallel and sequential architectures

Note that the parallel and the sequential relationships can be combined and nested in any desired fashion, yielding a hierarchical, integrated system. See also Chapter 7 "Complex Domains."

11.7   Fuzzy Logic and Neural Networks

Based on Zadeh's fuzzy set theory, fuzzy logic views each predicate as a fuzzy set. The relationship between fuzzy systems and neural networks has drawn much attention recently, since both are trainable systems capable of handling uncertainty and imprecision and both have found may successful applications. Their complementary roles have been suggested by Pao (1989) and Kosko (1992). Recent work on this subject has been collected by Bezdek (1992). In this section, we focus on a major development along this line, namely, how to integrate the basic elements of fuzzy set theory into neural networks to yield computational structures known as *fuzzy neural networks*.

11.7.1   Fuzzy Neural Networks

As it is still an ongoing research topic, the fuzzy neural network may have different implementations. Despite this fact, a general approach can be identified. Assume that fuzzy knowledge is represented as a set of fuzzy rules. We concern ourselves with the construction of a fuzzy neural network based on these rules.

Fuzzy neural networks are well known for their ability to handle the fuzzy (inexact) nature of inference involving symbols (symbolic inference). In fuzzy logic, a linguistic variable like "size" can have several linguistic values like "small," "medium," or "large." Each linguistic value is viewed as a fuzzy set associated with a membership function, which can be triangular, bell-shaped, or of another form. The degree of membership can be interpreted as the degree of *possibility*, which evades the requirement of satisfying the probability

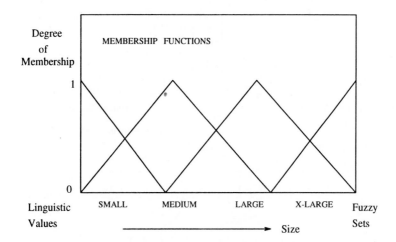

Figure 11.4: Membership functions associated with the linguistic variable "size."

axioms. An example is shown in Figure 11.4. Given a numerical value, we can obtain its degree of membership in each linguistic category (fuzzy set) from the membership function. Reversely, given a degree of membership in each set, we may decide on a proper numerical value (i.e., defuzzification).

In the RBCN approach (described in Chapter 4), we see that a rule is mapped into a connectionist structure of three layers (levels). For fuzzy rules, additional layers are used to store fuzzy set units. It would be reasonable to use a connection of five layers to implement one-level fuzzy rules, as illustrated in Figure 11.5. A similar approach is also suggested by Lin and Lee (1992). We call these five layers:

- The input layer

- The input fuzzy layer

- The conjunction layer

- The output fuzzy layer

- The output layer

The activation level of an input unit is the value of a certain input variable in the given instance. The input value is passed on to fuzzy set units, which then translate the value into a degree of membership as the activation level of a fuzzy set unit. The conjunction unit will take the minimum of the inputs

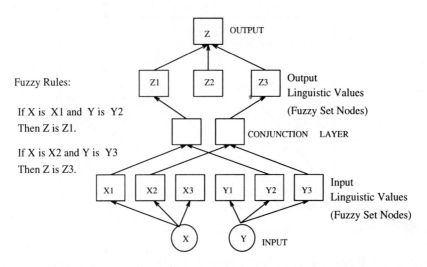

Fuzzy Rules:

If X is X1 and Y is Y2
Then Z is Z1.

If X is X2 and Y is Y3
Then Z is Z3.

Figure 11.5: A fuzzy neural network based on fuzzy rules.

(degrees of membership) it receives from the input fuzzy set units below. Now, the output fuzzy set unit will collect information from one or more conjunction units (each corresponding to a fuzzy rule). There exist variations at this point. An output fuzzy set unit may take the maximum or sum of its inputs or may employ the CF-based combination function. The last alternative ensures the combined value in the range from 0 to 1. Then, the output unit generates the final result by integrating the information from the output fuzzy set units. How the output unit calculates its activation level depends on the defuzzification scheme adopted. In the case of the bell-shaped membership function, Lin and Lee (1992) suggest the following formula:

$$O_j = \frac{\sum_i X_i(m_{ji}\sigma_{ji})}{\sum_i X_i\sigma_{ji}} \qquad (11.8)$$

where O_j is the activation level of output unit j, X_i is the input from output fuzzy set unit i, and m_{ji} and σ_{ji} are, respectively, the center and variance (width) of the membership function of fuzzy set unit i linking to output unit j. This is known as the *center-of-area* defuzzification method, which is related to the moments method described earlier.

Each link weight can be set to 1 except the output layer in which we set the weight linking output fuzzy set unit i to output unit j to $m_{ji}\sigma_{ji}$.

We may summarize the activation function used in each layer as follows:

- The input layer: no activation function

- The input fuzzy layer: the membership function

- The conjunction layer: the min function

- The output fuzzy layer: the max function or the CF-based function

- The output layer: $F(a) = a / \sum_i X_i \sigma_{ji}$

The fuzzy neural network can learn by adjusting weights. Not only the parameters of the membership function like the mean and the width, but also connection weights can be left open for change. When connections are deleted or created, it means structural change. Both structural change and parameter tuning are important in network learning. Training strategies include

- Backpropagation

- Reinforcement (e.g., Machado and da Rocha 1992)

- Statistical methods such as random weight change combined with annealing

Compared with the other two alternatives, the third approach is advantageous in finding global minima but at higher cost.

Inasmuch as backpropagation requires the calculation of error gradients, direct application of backpropagation to fuzzy neural networks involving the undifferentiable, min function is ad hoc. One way to approximate such functions is by using (Derthick 1990)

$$M_k(a) = \left(\frac{1}{n} \sum_{i=1}^{n} a_i^k\right)^{1/k} \tag{11.9}$$

where n is number of arguments a_i's. When $k = 1$, it is the ordinary arithmetic mean; as $k \to -\infty$, it approximates the min function; and as $k \to \infty$, it approximates the max function. With proper substitution, it would then be a straightforward matter to extend the training procedure for the KBCNN model (described in Chapter 4) to the fuzzy neural network.

11.8 Summary

The recent confluence of expert system and neural network technologies leads to a new direction for the research and development of intelligent systems. That is, these two different types of models can be combined in a way that exploits their strengths. In this chapter, we reviewed important knowledge acquisition techniques and knowledge representation methods in an attempt to provide some insight into how expert systems and neural networks can be related and integrated.

Reducing uncertainty is one of the most prominent capabilities of expert systems. Pros and cons for each well-known technique has been examined. These include the probabilistic model, the certainty factor model, Dempster-Shafer's theory of evidence, and fuzzy set theory. The neural network approach holds great promise on this area of research, since it can be used to estimate probabilities, certainty factors, or even fuzzy membership grades simply by example mapping.

The classification of the integration of knowledge-based systems and neural networks has been made. The two types of models can be completely overlapped, partially overlapped, or not overlapped. In the last case, they can be connected in parallel and/or in sequence. The completely overlapped architecture is the most advanced form of integration, and has been successfully implemented by the KBCNN model.

The combination of fuzzy logic and neural networks has resulted in an extremely powerful computational model known as a fuzzy neural network. Representing a linguistic value as a fuzzy set has enabled the system to deal successfully with many expert problems. Neural heuristics further provide the fuzzy network with the capability of learning by self-adaptation and self-organization.

11.9   References

1. Bezdek, J. (ed.). 1992. Fuzzy logic and neural networks. *IEEE Transactions on Neural Networks*, 3(5), special issue, 1992.

2. Brachman, R., Fikes, R., and Levesque, H. 1983. KRYPTON: A functional approach to knowledge representation. *IEEE Computer*, 16(10), pp. 67–73.

3. Buchanan, B.G., and Shortliffe, E.H. (eds.). 1984. *Rule-Based Expert Systems*. Addison-Wesley, Reading, MA.

4. Caudill, M. 1990. Using neural nets: Hybrid expert networks. *AI Expert*, November, pp. 49–54.

5. Davis, R. 1976. Applications of Metalevel Knowledge to the Construction, Maintenance, and Use of Large Knowledge Bases. Ph.D. thesis, Computer Science Department, Stanford University.

6. Davis, R., and King, J.J. 1984. The origin of rule-based systems in AI. In *Rule-Based Expert Systems*. Addison-Wesley, Reading, MA.

7. Derthick, M. 1990. Mundane reasoning by settling on a plausible model. *Artificial Intelligence*, 46, pp. 107–157.

8. Doyle, J. 1979. A truth maintenance system. *Artificial Intelligence*, 12(3), pp. 231–272.

9. Duda, R., Gaschnig, H., and Hart, P. 1979. Model design in the PROSPECTOR consultant system for mineral exploration. In *Expert Systems in the Micro-electronic Age*. Edinburgh University Press.

10. Feigenbaum, E.A. 1977. The art of artificial intelligence: Themes and case studies of knowledge engineering. In *Proceedings of IJCAI-77*, pp. 1014–1029.

11. Firebaugh, M.W. 1988. *Artificial Intelligence*. Boyd & Fraser, Boston.

12. Gallant, S.I. 1988. Connectionist expert systems. *Communications of the ACM*, 31(2), pp. 152–169.

13. Handelman, D.A., Lane, S.H., and Gelfand, J.J. 1989. Integration of knowledge-based systems and neural network techniques for autonomous learning machines. In *Proceedings of IJCNN*, pp. I-683–688.

14. Hayes-Roth, B. 1985. A blackboard architecture for control. *Artificial Intelligence*, 26, pp. 251–321.

15. Hayes-Roth, F., Waterman, D., and Lenat, D. (eds.). 1983. *Building Expert Systems*. Addison-Wesley, Reading, MA.

16. Kandel, A., and Langholz, G. 1992. (eds.). *Hybrid Architectures for Intelligent Systems*. CRC Press, Boca Raton, FL.

17. Kosko, B. 1992. *Neural Networks and Fuzzy Systems*. Prentice-Hall, Englewood Cliffs, NJ.

18. Lin, C.T., and Lee, C.S.G. 1992. Real-time supervised structure/parameter learning for fuzzy neural networks. In *Proceedings of IEEE Conference on Fuzzy Systems*, pp. 1283–1290.

19. Machado, R.J., and da Rocha, A.F. 1992. Evolutive fuzzy neural networks. In *Proceedings of IEEE Conference on Fuzzy Systems*, pp. 493–500.

20. McDermott, J. 1981. R1: The formative years. *AI Magazine*, 2(2), pp. 21–29.

21. Newell, A., and Simon, H.A. 1972. *Human Problem Solving*. Prentice Hall, Englewood Cliffs, NJ.

22. Pao, Y.H. 1989. *Adaptive Pattern Recognition and Neural Networks*. Addison-Wesley, Reading, MA.

23. Pearl, J. 1986. Fusion, propagation, and structuring in belief networks. *Artificial Intelligence*, 29, pp. 241–288.

24. Pople, Jr., H.E. 1982. Heuristic methods for imposing structure on ill-structured problems: The structuring of medical diagnostics. In *Artificial Intelligence in Medicine*. Westview Press, Boulder, CO.

25. Quillian, R. 1968. Semantic memory. In *Semantic Information Processing*, Minsky, M. (ed.). MIT Press, Cambridge, MA.

26. Reichgelt, H. 1991. *Knowledge Representation*. Ablex, Norwood, NJ.

27. Rich, E. 1983. *Artificial Intelligence*. McGraw-Hill, New York.

28. Smith, B. 1982. Reflection and Semantics in a Procedural Language. Ph.D. thesis, Massachusetts Institute of Technology, Cambridge.

29. Woods, W.A. 1975. What's in a link: Foundations for semantic networks. In *Representation and Understanding*. Academic Press, New York.

30. Zadeh, L.A. 1965. Fuzzy sets. *Information and Control*, 8, pp. 338–353.

11.10   Problems

1. For each of the following problems, which inference strategy (forward or backward reasoning) would be appropriate? Give a brief justification.

   (a) Diagnosis of computer faults

   (b) Alarm monitoring of hazards in a plant

   (c) Circuit design

   (d) Robotic planning

   (e) Natural language understanding

2. In PROSPECTOR's approach, what is the posterior probability of X given the following rules and facts:

   - If A, then B. ($\lambda[A, B] = 20$)
   - If B, then C. ($\lambda[B, C] = 100$)
   - If C, then X. ($\lambda[C, X] = 500$)
   - If D, then X. ($\lambda[D, X] = 400$)
   - $P(B) = P(C) = P(X) = 0.01$
   - Both A and D are true.

3. In MYCIN's approach, what is the certainty factor (CF) of X given the following rules and facts:

   - If A, then B. (CF = 0.4)
   - If B and C, then D. (CF = 0.9)
   - If D, then X. (CF = 0.8)
   - If E, then X. (CF = -0.3)
   - If F, then X. (CF = -0.4)

- CF[A] = 1, CF[C] = 0.8, CF[E] = 1, and CF[F]= 0.7

4. In Dempster-Shafer's approach, what is the belief value (*Bel*) of $\{h_1, h_2\}$ given the following assignments and facts:

   - $\theta = \{h_1, h_2, h_3, h_4\}$
   - $m_1(\{h_1\}) = 0.2, m_1(\{h_1, h_2, h_3\}) = 0.4$
   - $m_2(\{h_2, h_4\}) = 0.3, m_2(\{h_1, h_2\}) = 0.5$
   - The evidence corresponding to m_1 and m_2 is true.

5. Suppose the membership function of a fuzzy set is defined by the following:

$$\mu(x) = \begin{cases} 1 - \frac{(x-m)^2}{\sigma^2}, & |x - m| \leq \sigma \\ 0, & \text{else} \end{cases}$$

where m and σ are the center and the width of the function. A fuzzy system has the following two rules:

If X is X_1 and Y is Y_1, then Z is Z_1.
If X is X_2 and Y is Y_2, then Z is Z_2.

All X_1, X_2, Y_1, Y_2, Z_1, Z_2 are fuzzy sets with the membership functions whose centers and widths are given by

Fuzzy set	Center	width
X_1	5	4
X_2	8	3
Y_1	12	4
Y_2	16	5
Z_1	22	2
Z_2	32	3

Given the inputs $X = 6$ and $Y = 15$, what is Z as calculated by a fuzzy neural network?

Chapter 12

Causal Learning and Modeling

12.1 Introduction

Scientists are interested in discovering functional relationships among physical phenomena in order to explain the behavior. Over the years, scientists have studied two aspects of causality: isolation of variables which represent cause phenomena and those which represent effect phenomena, and determination of the magnitude and direction of change in the latter corresponding to a change in the former. The identified variables in conjunction with their functional relationships can serve as a useful computational model for making inferences.

The study of causal modeling can be traced back to the middle 1950s when Simon (1954) first addressed the question, "Is correlation proof of causation?" Blalock (1962, 1964) further investigated this issue. Their insights have inspired a great deal of interest on this subject matter.

However, many criticisms of causal modeling practices arose, which can be found in Glymour, Scheines, Spirtes, and Kelly (1987). Some argued that linear causal models should be rejected because they are always literally false. Many advocates of causal models do not or cannot justify the assumptions of their models. Some believed that only experimental data can contribute to our knowledge of causal relationships. In fact, causal modeling of nonexperimental data has been controversial since its beginning. Despite these negative criticisms, the successful application of causal models to problem solving in knowledge-based systems has made a strong case for this approach. The main lesson learned seems to be that there is nothing wrong with causal modeling, but some approaches may be inappropriate in given domains.

The quantitative approach to causal modeling and inference involves computing the path coefficient or numerical relationship between the cause and the effect variables. However, in reality, there may not exist enough quantitative

knowledge to permit full quantitative modeling. Qualitative causal modeling has become one major line of research toward the representation of deep
models in knowledge-based systems (Bobrow 1985; Forbus 1984; Kuipers 1986;
Pearl 1986, 1987). Two well-known qualitative causal simulation techniques are
briefly reviewed here: Kuipers' QSIM and Pearl's stochastic simulation.

QSIM (Kuipers 1986) refers to the technique which predicts the possible qualitative behaviors of a system on the basis of the model comprising
predefined physical parameters and constraint predicates. These parameters
and constraints are abstracted from the mathematical equations (differential
equations) describing the system's dynamic behavior. This model provides a
snapshot of the qualitative characteristics of the system at each defined time
frame and is especially useful when we want to know the dynamic trends of
the cause and the effect.

In the approach by Pearl (1986, 1987), causal knowledge is modeled as
causal networks in which the nodes represent propositions (or variables), the
arcs signify direct dependencies between linked propositions, and the strengths
of these dependencies are quantified by conditional probabilities. He proposed
the method of stochastic simulation which computes probabilities by counting
the fraction of time in which an event occurs among a series of simulation
runs. A causal model can be used to generate random samples of hypothetical
scenarios that are likely to develop in the domain. This approach can arrive at
stationary estimates of posterior probabilities based on prior probabilities.

In the rest of this chapter, we describe a general causal modeling technique,
discuss approaches to causal simulation and inference, show how to design and
train causal neural networks, and present the general methodology of learning
causal knowledge with particular attention to learning causal patterns in the
connectionist framework.

12.2   Causal Modeling

Causal modeling attempts to resolve questions about possible causes so as to
provide explanations of phenomena (effects) as a result of previous phenomena
(causes). It is a technique for selecting variables which are potential determi-
nants of effects and then attempting to isolate separate contributions to the
effects by each cause (Asher 1983). For example, causal factors for cancer include heredity, diet, age, and so forth; causal factors for a student's performance
include the teacher's quality, the student's family, etc.

Many causal models have been described, such as in Cooper (1984), Kulikowski and Weiss (1982), Patil, Szolovits, and Schwartz (1981), Peng and
Reggia (1987), and Szolovits (1982). Without losing generality, a causal model
(structure) consists of a representation of the phenomena along with directions
indicating the cause-and-effect relationships among the phenomena. A causal
graph (a directed graph) is a means of how this causal structure can be visualized, in which a node is labeled by a domain concept (variable) and an arc

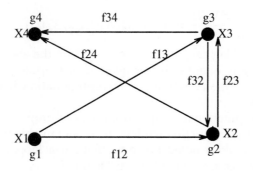

Xi : Variable

gi : Fusion function

fij : Influence function

Figure 12.1: A causal model (Fu 1991).

points from a cause node to an effect node. Since causal reasoning requires the knowledge of the quantitative and/or qualitative characteristics of causal relationships and the interaction manner among causal influences, we associate each arc with a function describing the characteristics of the designated causal relationship and associate each node with a function for combining causal influences from different sources.

In the causal model of Figure 12.1, each variable X_i assumes either symbolic or numerical values. A quantitative model refers to a model in which variable values are defined on the interval or ratio scale, whereas a qualitative model employs the nominal or ordinal scale. Each arc in the network is labeled (associated with) an *influence function*. If function f_{ij} is associated with arc $X_i \rightarrow X_j$, the influence of variable X_i on variable X_j is $f_{ij}(X_i)$. Each such influence function f_{ij} is specified by the quantitative and/or qualitative relationships between X_i and X_j. Each variable is labeled (associated with) a *fusion function*. Suppose fusion function g_j is associated with variable X_j, which receives influences from variables $X_1, X_2, ..., X_k$ with respective influence functions $f_{1j}, f_{2j}, ..., f_{kj}$, then

$$X_j = g_j(f_{1j}(X_1), f_{2j}(X_2), ..., f_{kj}(X_k)) \qquad (12.1)$$

Composing all the influence functions and the fusion function into G_j yields

$$X_j = G_j(X_1, X_2, ..., X_k) \qquad (12.2)$$

In a dynamic system, we further consider the time dimension and modify the above expression into

$$\frac{dX_j(t)}{dt} = G_j(X_1(t), X_2(t), ..., X_k(t)) \tag{12.3}$$

The notion of causal lag can also be integrated into the above form. Function G_j can represent any quantitative or qualitative mapping. Thus, the above mathematical formulation can be a general representation of a single or a set of equations or rules.

To reduce computational complexity, a causal graph is often defined as an *acyclic* graph. This restriction renders the model unable to represent causal loops directly. It should be noted, however, that causal loops can be represented by recurrent networks in a straightforward manner.

A multilevel hierarchy of abstraction can be introduced into causal models, as addressed by Patil, Szolovits, and Schwartz (1981). For example, we can represent medical knowledge at the clinical and the pathophysiologic levels. The traversal mechanism between levels must be defined, which should provide correspondence in knowledge between levels.

The model-representational methods can also be organized as a taxonomy (Zeigler 1984). Fishwick (1988) developed a technique of process abstraction, which allows simulationists to construct models composed of a set of interconnected levels. Each level in the network represents the process at some given level of abstraction and is encoded using a model type appropriate to that level. In causal modeling, if we treat the quantitative method and the qualitative method as two different levels of abstraction, we need to define how to translate quantitative knowledge into qualitative knowledge and vice versa. Kuipers (1986) provides a clue to this problem.

12.2.1   Causal Ordering

Causal ordering is an important part of causal modeling. It defines an asymmetrical relationship among variables of a set of simultaneous equations representing functional relationships. The objective of causal ordering is to establish direct causality or determine the number of intervening levels for indirect causality. The basic idea behind the causal ordering algorithm developed by Iwasaki and Simon (1986), as formulated below, is this: If a system has n independent equations and n variables, then a unique solution can be found for each variable. Suppose a subsystem has m equations but n variables and $n > m$. And suppose after some $n - m$ variables have been determined, the remaining m variables in the subsystem can also be uniquely determined. Then the m variables are directly (causally) dependent on the $n - m$ variables.

The Causal Ordering Algorithm (Iwasaki and Simon 1986)

Consider a self-contained system S.

1. Initialize the variable i to 0.

2. Let S_0 be the union of all minimal complete subsets of S. Call S_0 the set of ith order, V_i.

3. Solve the equations in S_0 to obtain the values of all the variables in S_0 (note that S_0 is also self-contained); and then substitute these values for all the occurrences of these variables in the equations of the set $S - S_0$ to obtain a new self-contained structure S_1.

4. Set $S = S_1$. If S is empty, go to the next step; else increment i by 1 and go to step 2.

5. A causal order is established by the fact that the elements in V_i are directly causally dependent on those in V_{i-1}.

A system of n equations is called self-contained if it has exactly n unknowns. A minimal complete subset refers to a proper self-contained subset that does not contain a similar subset.

12.2.2 Estimation of Model Parameters

Once we complete the model design, the task of estimating model parameters or coefficients ensues. Statistical techniques such as path analysis (Asher 1983) are traditionally used for this purpose. However, parameter values can be set by knowledge for a model which is completely theory-driven.

The backpropagation procedure presents to us an appealing alternative for parameter estimation. It can be applied to both cyclic and acyclic causal models. While backpropagation is originally developed for nonrecurrent architectures, this technique can be extended to arbitrary networks as long as they converge to stable states. See Hertz, Krogh, and Palmer (1991) for *recurrent backpropagation*. However, the concern is that this procedure often ends up with a local minimum. With the technique of *teacher forcing* (described later), this problem can be much alleviated.

12.3 Causal Simulation and Inference

Zeigler (1976) places modeling and simulation in a simple yet elegant perspective. Modeling is the bridge between a real system and a model, while simulation is the connection to a computational device that can activate the mechanism within the model. Many simulation attempts are based on models that have a time dimension. This makes the models and, in turn, the simulation dynamic. There has been some concern that the functional relationships established by simulation may be valid only for the set of data used in simulation and may not be generalized to the real system. A recent study shows that simulation is a reliable technique, and the results are valid in postsimulation analysis with almost the same certainty as with the simulation data (Weiser-Friedman and Pressman 1989).

There are two ways to conduct simulation based on causal models. One way is to propagate the given causal information from corresponding nodes through the causal graph until a steady state is reached. The other alternative is to examine each predefined possible answer and see whether it can be predicted from given causes. These alternatives simply correspond to forward and backward reasoning and are thus called *forward simulation* and *backward simulation*, respectively. It is generally agreed that if goals are numerous or ill-defined, then forward reasoning will be more appropriate; otherwise backward reasoning is a better choice. From this consideration, we distinguish between two different types of questions. The first type of question deals with "what the world will be if certain things are known to be true." In most practical cases, many things can possibly occur, so we choose forward simulation. The second type of question is concerned with "whether the thing under consideration will arise given that certain things have occurred." In this case, we would choose backward simulation because the goal is specified. Simulation can be quantitative or qualitative, depending on the type of model used.

In some causal models, time is an explicit factor. Simulation with these models assumes that the process goes on along a time axis, and each data point is associated with a time. We call these models *time-explicit* models. In other models, time is not explicitly represented but inevitably involved due to causality. They are named *time-implicit* models. For example, the probability causal model (qualitative) and the static equation model (quantitative) are time-implicit, whereas the QSIM (qualitative) and the dynamic equation model (quantitative) are time-explicit.

Inasmuch as causal influence is often complicated by many unidentified factors, it is often difficult to formulate a causal rule without introducing an amount of uncertainty. As a result, simulation based on causal knowledge often cannot escape uncertainty. Nevertheless, the environment projected by simulation should be consistent with our knowledge. Let us consider an example. Given A, we predict B at time t_1. Then, given B at time t_1, we predict C at time t_2. If we know B is not true at time t_1, it makes no sense to predict C at time t_2. Thus, in the course of simulation, if a projected fact is contradicted by certain evidence, it will not be considered as a basis for subsequent prediction. This problem occurs because we make a prediction on the basis of some given facts which may spread along the time axis. In addition, there should be a constraint-checking mechanism which ensures the consistency in simulation results. In the connectionist approach, a constraint is implemented as a weighted connection.

Causal simulation can be applied to solve two important kinds of problems: prediction and diagnosis. Prediction deals with inferring possible consequences from given situations such as weather forecasting. Likely scenarios are typically generated by instantiating parameter values in a parametric model according to the given situation. If A can predict B, we are inclined to believe that A is directly or indirectly involved in or associated with a cause of B. In fact, causal models have been employed to make predictions in many cases.

Diagnosis concerns inferring the cause of system malfunction from given observable manifestations. Recently, growing emphasis is placed on using causal knowledge to solve diagnostic problems. Diagnostic systems can benefit from causal simulation in the following ways: First, solutions generated based on heuristics can be further verified by causal simulation. This can increase the reliability of solutions provided by a diagnostic system. Second, if a diagnostic system uses a *generate-and-test* strategy to solve its problems, then a causal simulator is needed. In a dynamic system, diagnosis may often pose such a hard problem that there is no easy way to solve it directly. Under such circumstances, simulation techniques will be of great value.

12.3.1 The Bayesian Network

Pearl (1986) also devised a parallel-distributed approach for updating belief values in a causal network according to the Bayes theorem; hence it is called a Bayesian network. This scheme provides both forward (cause-to-effect) and backward (effect-to-cause) information propagation so that information can arrive at any node in the network and transmit to all other nodes in the network. In each node, the probability (belief value) of a variable value V after observing evidence E is computed by the Bayes theorem as follows:

$$P(V|E) = \alpha P(E|V)P(V)$$

where P is the probability function and α is a normalizing factor. Normalization makes the sum of the probabilities of all exhaustive and mutually exclusive values equal one.

To see information propagation, consider an example. In a simple network, suppose variable A is a causal variable connected to both variables B and C. The belief value of A can propagate to derive that of B by

$$P(B) = P(B|A)P(A) + P(B|\neg A)P(\neg A)$$

and

$$P(\neg B) = P(\neg B|A)P(A) + P(\neg B|\neg A)P(\neg A)$$

with subsequent normalization for ensuring

$$P(B) + P(\neg B) = 1$$

where "$\neg B$" reads "not B." The same is true for deriving the belief value of C. The link pointing from node A to node B is characterized by the conditional probabilities $P(B|A)$, $P(B|\neg A)$, $P(\neg B|A)$, and $P(\neg B|\neg A)$ (often they are represented as a matrix). The message passed from a parent node to a child node is called a π message. For example, the π message sent from node A to node B consists of $P(A)$ and $P(\neg A)$ modulated by the conditional probability matrix. This illustrates forward information propagation.

Suppose information $E1$ arrives at node B. The probability of B is updated by the Bayes theorem:

$$P(B|E1) = \alpha_1 P(E1|B)P(B)$$

and

$$P(\neg B|E1) = \alpha_2 P(E1|\neg B)P(\neg B)$$

This information can propagate to node A using the relation

$$P(E1|A) = P(E1|B)P(B|A) + P(E1|\neg B)P(\neg B|A)$$

and

$$P(E1|\neg A) = P(E1|B)P(B|\neg A) + P(E1|\neg B)P(\neg B|\neg A)$$

Then the probability of A is updated by the Bayes theorem. The message passed from a child node to a parent node is called a λ message. For example, the λ message received at node A from node B consists of $P(E1|A)$ and $P(E1|\neg A)$. Information propagates backwards this time.

The same evidence should not be used more than once in updating the belief value at the same node. For example, suppose new information $E2$ arrives at node C. This information is passed backwards to node A, and in turn passed forward to node B. To avoid counting information $E1$ twice at node B, the π message sent from node A to node B at this point should be divided by the λ message (on a term-by-term basis) sent from node B to node A earlier.

12.4   Causal Neural Networks

Through its amazing mapping and generalization capability, the neural network approach may outperform classical techniques, such as multiple regression or discriminant analysis, in terms of prediction success rates. However, this approach has been faulted for failing to model a set of causal factors in an intuitively satisfying manner. The main criticism against this approach has been that neural networks are black boxes. This issue is addressed in Chapter 14 "Rule Generation from Neural Networks."

In the context of causal modeling, we want to be more specific about what might be wrong with the neural network approach. In comparison with previous approaches, the main problem seems to be that such an approach does not generate a causal structure which indicates how causal factors interact. This causal structure may be implicitly encoded in the hidden layer but may be too complex for us to understand. Would it be possible to identify a proper causal order by interpreting trained network weights? Indeed, this could be a formidable task. However, one can dodge this task by building our knowledge into the neural network. That is, we can identify the causal order with the best technique available, and then put this knowledge into the network.

The *backpropagation* procedure is suitable for training a causal neural network, whether it is built from scratch or according to the domain causal model. With respect to the latter case, some specific considerations will influence the training algorithm. Among them, the activation function of each causal node in the network can be better determined by the causal equation involved than selected as a sigmoid. This function must be differentiable because backpropagation is a gradient descent technique.

Another consideration is that hidden units encoding certain intermediate causal variables may be observable. It means that their values may be known in training instances. A modification often found to be useful is *teacher forcing*. During training, this technique always replaces the activation level of a node by its target value if the latter is known. This must be done after computing error derivatives and weight adjustments for weights incident upon the node. Otherwise, the error will be zero, and no weight adjustment for that node is possible. The teacher-forcing technique allows the network to converge to the right tract by imposing constraints and thereby speeds up learning. It can be used in dynamic networks, including recurrent ones. A potential disadvantage, however, is that when the constraints are removed, a local minimum may not be so any more. See Hertz, Krogh, and Palmer (1991) for more discussion on this issue.

We set forth four different approaches to construct neural networks for causal reasoning and learning:

- Simple neural networks: a blind or brute force approach.

- Graph-based neural networks: based on the ordering and directionality of causal information flow.

- Function-based neural networks: based on mathematical functions which formalize variable relationships.

- Rule-based neural networks: based on the domain causal knowledge represented as rules.

The following network training algorithm (an adapted formulation of backpropagation) can be generally applied to all these networks. They all fall in the category of time-implicit models. Each of them is delineated subsequently. For time-explicit neural networks, see Chapter 10 "Spatiotemporal Learning."

The Causal Network Training (Learning) Algorithm

- **Weight Initialization**

  Weights are initialized according to the domain causal knowledge as in the RBCN (see Chapter 4 "Knowledge-Based Neural Networks"). Some are randomized in the absence of such knowledge.

- **Calculation of Activation**

  1. The activation level of an input unit is determined by the instance presented to the network.

  2. The activation level O_j of a hidden and output unit is determined by

  $$O_j = \begin{cases} T_j & \text{if given for hidden unit } j \\ F_j(W_{j1}O_1, W_{j2}O_2, ..., -\theta_j) & \text{else} \end{cases}$$

  where T_j is the desired (target) activation, W_{ji}'s and O_i's are input weights and inputs to unit j, respectively, θ_j is the threshold, and function F_j is the differentiable activation function on unit j.

- **Weight Training**

  1. Start at the output units and work backward to the hidden layers recursively. Adjust weights by

  $$W_{ji}(n+1) = W_{ji}(n) + \Delta W_{ji}$$

  where $W_{ji}(n)$ is the weight from unit i to unit j at iteration n and ΔW_{ji} is the weight adjustment.

  2. The weight change is computed by

  $$\Delta W_{ji} = \eta D_j \left(\frac{\partial O_j}{\partial W_{ji}}\right)$$

  where η is a trial-independent learning rate and D_j is the discrepancy (error) between the actual and the desired output activation at unit j.

  3. The discrepancy is given by

     - For output units and hidden units with given values:

     $$D_j = T_j - F(W_{j1}O_1, W_{j2}O_2, ..., -\theta_j)$$

     where T_j is the desired (target) output activation and O_j is the actual output activation at unit j. Note that $T_j = O_j$ for hidden unit j with a given value.

     - For other hidden units:

     $$D_j = \sum_k \left(\frac{\partial O_k}{\partial O_j}\right) D_k$$

     where D_k is the discrepancy at unit k to which a connection points from hidden unit j.

  4. Repeat iterations until stopping conditions are met.

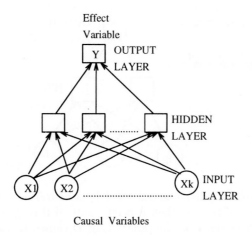

Figure 12.2: A simple causal neural network.

12.4.1   Simple Neural Networks

In many applications, neural networks are used as a mapping machine which maps inputs into outputs by examples. A straightforward construction of a causal neural network is to assign an input unit to each causal variable and an output unit to each effect variable and then to add a number of hidden units. Such a construction, called a *simple* causal neural network, is depicted in Figure 12.2. This network can often predict effects quite well from given causes after adequate training. Causal interaction and ordering are dealt with implicitly in the hidden layer. Figure 12.3 illustrates a possible mechanism of how this can be achieved. It turns out that a feedforward *simple* network is not capable enough to learn a complete causal order. Moreover, since each possible interaction may need to be encoded by a separate hidden unit, a cumbersome network would be required to learn complex causal influences. The indirectness of this blind approach not only leads to inefficiency but also provides little insight into the underlying causal model.

The simple neural network can be applied for both quantitative and qualitative purposes. When causal variables are independent of each other, the naive construction topologically reflects the causal structure as in the graph-based approach described next. The activation function (nonlinearity) typically selected is the sigmoid function for hidden and output units, and the qualitative interpretation of activations is: > 0.5 as "yes" and ≤ 0.5 as "no." However, if the purpose is for quantitative simulation, then the nonlinearity can be re-

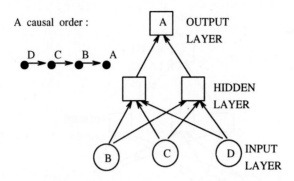

Figure 12.3: Learning a partial causal order by a neural network. Hidden units learn two patterns: "if B is *on*, then A is *on*"; and "if B is *off*, then A is *off*." So, the neural network learns a partial order "C or D causes B causes A."

moved from the output units. The activation level ranges from 0 to 1 for nodes involving nonlinearities and is otherwise unrestricted.

Garson (1991) proposed a way to understand the individual effects of causal factors by partitioning the output layer connection weights into input unit shares. Similar results can be obtained by the following procedure.

Suppose we use the equation below to capture the network behavior:

$$Y = b + F_{NN}(X_1, X_2, ..., X_k) + \epsilon$$

where Y is the effect variable, b is the bias, F_{NN} is a nonlinear function equivalent to the neural network, X_i's are causal variables, and ϵ is the error to be minimized. Assume that all variable values are defined in the range of 0 to 1. After error minimization, the causal effect of X_i on Y can be estimated by setting $X_i = 1$ and setting $X_j = 0$ (where $j \neq i$) to compute the value of

$$F_{NN}(X_1, X_2, ..., X_k).$$

These approaches seem to be able to distinguish between direct and indirect causes. Nevertheless, their role in analyzing a complex causal model would be very limited.

12.4.2   Graph-Based Networks

A causal graph is a qualitative (part of a) causal model which represents causal relationships between a set of variables. A direct correspondence can

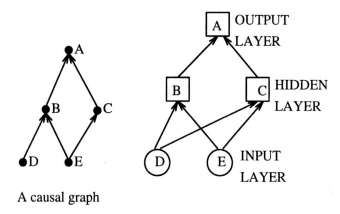

A causal graph

Figure 12.4: A neural network based on a causal graph. Additional hidden units and connections can be included.

be established between such a graph and a neural network by mapping each causal link into a connection so that the head node activates (causes) the tail node. Figure 12.4 shows such a construction. This is a special rule-based connectionist network (RBCN) where each rule has a single condition, and therefore conjunction units can be obviated. Since the causal graph has indicated the causal order, the problem of causal ordering is not dealt with by this neural network, and so, the network can be implemented much more efficiently than the brute force (blind) approach. To increase the freedom of learning, undefined hidden units (not corresponding to any variables in the graph) can be added properly. A graph-based neural network can be trained to simulate the quantitative effect of causal variables or qualitatively predict their outcome.

In quantitative simulation, we assume that each node encoding some variable in the causal graph employs the *identity* function as its activation function. That is, the activation level of such nodes is the linear sum of weighted inputs. If a more accurate function can be found, then it should be used instead (see the following text). For undefined hidden units, we simply use the sigmoid function as is the convention. The activation range of each "variable" node is not restricted but can be normalized as appropriate; that of an undefined hidden unit is squeezed in the range from 0 to 1 by the sigmoid function.

As for qualitative inference or prediction, the neural network employs the sigmoid function as the activation function for all noninput units. The activation

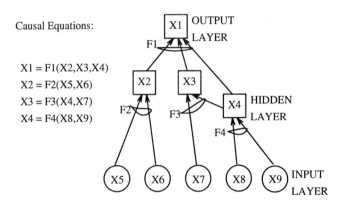

Figure 12.5: A neural network based on causal functions.

range is defined from 0 to 1 for all such units and is unrestricted for input units.

12.4.3   Function-Based Networks

A causal neural network can be constructed on the basis of the knowledge regarding the mathematical functions involved in the causal model. The linear assumption is often criticized as incorrect in modeling causal influences. The function-based approach deals with this issue by building more plausible functions into the network. This approach is intended for quantitative simulation rather than qualitative inference. If those functions are correct, then this approach should yield better quantitative results than the graph-based approach.

Suppose we put each causal equation in a canonical form as follows:

$$Y = F(X_1, X_2, ...)$$

In the network framework, X_i's nodes point to the Y node, and function F is selected as the activation function at Y node. In this way, we can transform a set of causal equations into a neural network, as illustrated in Figure 12.5. Often, the functional model does not guarantee 100 percent accuracy due to inevitable uncertainty, noise, and some ignorance. By its nature, the neural network appears to be an excellent candidate for modeling these unknown factors. There exists more than one way to implement this capability. One solution is to assign a weight to each argument in the functional form; for example,

$$Y = F(W_1 X_1, W_2 X_2, ...)$$

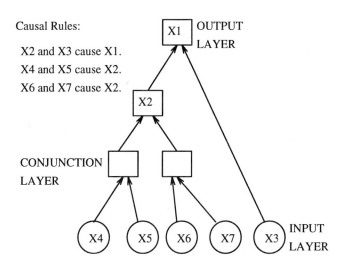

Figure 12.6: A neural network based on causal rules.

The weight W_i is adjustable during network training. Incorporating undefined hidden units into the functional model presents another option to this problem.

12.4.4   Rule-Based Networks

We often ask how true a causal relationship, such as "X causes Y," is. This statement is interpreted as "X possibly causes Y" more frequently than "X necessarily causes Y." In fact, this kind of statement may be too simple to be useful. There are so many relevant factors overlooked. In the least, we can recognize two important kinds of such factors. One is *enabling factors*, and the other is *disabling factors* (inhibitors). The validity of a causal relationship relies on including them, i.e., to specify the presence of enabling and the absence of disabling factors, if there are any. Thus, a more realistic formulation of a causal relationship has the form of

"X and E_i's and not D_j's" cause Y

where E_i's and D_j's are enabling and disabling factors, respectively. This argument is in favor of the rule-based approach to causal modeling.

A set of causal rules can be translated into a neural network. The RBCN approach, described in Chapter 4, shows how such translation can be performed. An example is given in Figure 12.6. Causal rules can be given, or learned as described later in this chapter. Rule-based causal neural networks are mainly for the use of qualitative inference.

A Summary of Causal Neural Networks

- *A Simple Neural Network*

  - A black-box approach
  - Activation function
    * For quantitative simulation: the sigmoid function for hidden units; the identity function for output units
    * For qualitative inference: the sigmoid function for hidden and output units
  - Activation range
    * For quantitative simulation: unrestricted for input and output units; from 0 to 1 for hidden units
    * For qualitative inference: unrestricted for input units; from 0 to 1 for all other units
  - Use: quantitative simulation or qualitative inference

- *A Graph-Based Neural Network*

  - Based on the domain causal graph
  - Activation function
    * For quantitative simulation: the identity function for defined hidden units (referring to those representing intermediate causal variables in the graph) and output units; the sigmoid function for undefined hidden units
    * For qualitative inference: the sigmoid function for hidden and output units
  - Activation range
    * For quantitative simulation: unrestricted for input, defined hidden, and output units; from 0 to 1 for undefined hidden units
    * For qualitative inference: unrestricted for input units; from 0 to 1 for all other units
  - Use: quantitative simulation or qualitative inference

- *A Function-Based Neural Network*

  - Based on domain causal functions
  - Activation function: the function in the corresponding causal equation

- Activation range: unrestricted (but depending on the range of the function involved)
- Use: quantitative simulation

- *A Rule-Based Neural Network*

    - A special case of KBCNN
    - Based on domain causal rules
    - Activation function: the CF-based function
    - Activation range: from −1 to 1
    - Use: qualitative inference

12.5   Learning Causal Knowledge

Approaches to learning (or discovering) causal knowledge can be broadly divided into two groups: induction and deduction. The former learning is concerned with the extraction of general causal principles from examples, the latter with the verification of causal hypotheses using prior causal theories.

The inductive approach works by detecting regularities among examples. However, "regularity" alone is not sufficient enough to establish causality, as discussed later. Inductive inference can be further constrained by causal attributes such as *direction of change* (increase or decrease), *delay*, and *duration* of causal influence.

The general strategy behind the inductive approach is "generate and test." Hypothesis generation heavily relies on heuristics. Anderson (1987) identified three well-documented factors underlying the human perception of causality in the absence of an existing theory:

- *Contiguity*: The cause tends to be contiguous with the effect in time and space with the strong discontinuous provision that effects cannot precede their causes.

- *Similarity*: Something is perceived as a cause the more similar it is to the effect.

- *Statistical association*: The cause is followed fairly regularly by the effect.

In the RX (Blum 1982) algorithm, causal hypotheses are generated based on a test for strength of association and time precedence.

In deductive learning, it is assumed that there is some *process* or *mechanism* underlying causal relations. Axiomatization of these mechanisms forms a domain theory, which can be used to prove a causal hypothesis or instantiated to understand a certain physical phenomenon.

In *explanation-based* learning, the domain theory is used to explain observed regularities and direct the derivation of general causal principles. Pazzani, Dyer, and Flowers (1986) describe how to integrate existing theories and correlational information to generate new causal knowledge. In their approach, a generalization confirmed by prior causal theories is called an explanatory generalization; if not confirmed, it is a tentative generalization, which will hold until contradicted by later examples.

Other learning strategies may well be applicable. For example, "learning by analogy" allows the transfer of causal principles from one domain to another.

There are two distinct process components in learning causal knowledge: discovery and validation. After discussing several approaches to discovery, we can now turn our attention to the issue of validation.

A causal hypothesis can be confirmed with prior causal theories or by experimentation. But can we do it using observational data? To answer this question, maybe we should define "causality" first. Blum (1982) used the following operational definition (criterion) of causality:

- Temporal precedence: The causal variable precedes the effect variable.

- Covariation or association: The intensity of the causal variable is correlated with that of the effect variable.

- Nonspuriousness: There is no known third variable responsible for the correlation.

These three properties should be shown over repeated observations. The above definition provides necessary rigor for establishing a new causal relationship.

A critical part of learning causal knowledge is the demonstration of *non-spuriousness*. Spurious correlation between two variables occurs when there exists a third variable which influences both of them while those two are not actually correlated. By definition, a confounding variable is any variable that (significantly) affects both the cause and the effect in the causal relationship under study. Let us define *causal antecedents* of a variable as the set of nodes that can reach it directly or indirectly in the causal graph. Then, the set of confounders for a hypothetical causal relationship "X causes Y" is the intersection of the causal antecedents of X and those of Y. In practice, however, it is neither efficient nor necessary to determine and control all confounders in the study. The essential task is to identify a set of confounding nodes through which all confounding influences flow. Control of these nodes is tantamount to control of all confounders. The smallest such set is known as *causal dominators*, for which Blum (1982) devised an algorithm, as formulated below.

The Algorithm for Selecting Confounding Variables (Blum 1982)

Assume that we are investigating whether X causes Y.

1. Initialize the set C to the empty set.

2. Let P designate the set of proximate causes of Y. That is, P is the set of nodes directly pointing to Y in the causal graph.

3. Check whether any node in P can reach X directly or indirectly in the causal graph. These nodes form set P_1, which is appended to set C so that C is a union of P_1 and the last version of C.

4. The nodes in P_1 are blocked by placing flags on them in order to prevent flow through them on subsequent iterations.

5. Consider the set of nodes $P_2 = P - P_1$. Generate the set of all proximate causes of the nodes in P_2 to obtain set Q.

6. If Q is empty, then exit, and current set C contains selected confounding variables for control; else, set $P = Q$ and go to step 3.

This algorithm identifies the smallest subset of confounding variables through which all known causal influences on both X and Y flow.

12.5.1   Learning Causal Patterns

A causal pattern is a conjunction of a set of causal variables along with their values or ranges of values, which can predict certain effect variables. Such relationships can be represented as if-then rules and stored in a rule-based expert system in the defined domain. Causal knowledge enables one to reason in a more general and fundamental way and is often referred to as *deep knowledge*, which complements empirical heuristic knowledge for problem solving. In other circumstances, causal patterns help one understand interactions among different variables; for example, how different genes interact for the manifestation of some disease trait and how different drugs potentiate or interfere in the human body. In the expert system application, rules are selected so that the system performance error can be minimized. In pattern analysis, the statistical significance of patterns is emphasized.

We treat learning causal patterns as a special case of rule learning with additional considerations on causality. Existing causal knowledge can be utilized to remove confounding causal factors. Even in the absence of this knowledge, some preliminary statistical analysis for identifying a complete or partial causal structure is useful for later learning.

Confounding variables are controlled by eliminating an entire instance involving them or controlling them statistically. The first method is infeasible when the remaining sample after elimination is too small for us to obtain any significant result. The second method relies on a statistical model. The rule-based connectionist network seems to serve as a good model for such statistical control. In this approach, the two bases of the final interpretation are the statistical P value and the connection weight between the pattern node and the effect variable node. They are related to the use of the multiple regression coefficient and its corresponding P value in determining the significance of a discovered causal relationship in the RX project. For a given P value, a higher validity is assigned to the result with a higher pattern weight. Chapter 13 "Validation and Verification" has a more detailed description on how to validate individual patterns.

Thus, the general procedure for learning causal patterns includes the following steps.

The Connectionist Procedure of Learning Causal Patterns

1. Build a causal neural network.

2. Set up training instances with confounding variables controlled (if possible).

3. Train the neural network to minimize the prediction error over the training set.

4. Extract patterns from the trained neural network.

5. Validate patterns:

   (a) Compute the statistical P value for each pattern.

   (b) Build a rule-based connectionist network (RBCN) according to the patterns.

   (c) Train the RBCN.

   (d) Interpret the results to determine the significance of each pattern on the basis of its P value and the connection weight between the pattern node (a pattern node is a conjunction node in the RBCN) and the effect variable node.

Steps 1 to 4 constitute the discovery component and step 5 the validation component of the general methodology for learning causality.

The *time* factor is not an explicit element in the above procedure since we assume that it has been handled in the prior or preliminary causal modeling process.

12.6 Summary

Domain causal knowledge can be modeled as a network. In this case, causal simulation becomes a process of propagating known causal information through the network to generate additional information. There is less concern about the issue of learning if there is a stronger theory behind the model. When the theory is weak, some questions may arise. At first, what is the correct model? The linear model is, as it stands, controversial. The second question is how to improve a selected model. Researchers constantly search for a better model.

Some structural and behavioral analogies can be drawn between causal and neural networks. On this basis, modeling causal knowledge as a neural network is a possible direction. Several advantages can be immediately seen. One is that a multilayer neural network can model nonlinear causal processes. The neural network can learn by itself. Perhaps, more importantly, this approach integrates modeling, simulation, and learning in a single entity.

However, the neural network alone is not the whole idea. Conventional knowledge concerning causal modeling and learning such as causal ordering and control of confounding variables is important. Only when all this knowledge is built into the neural network can it be robust and reliable.

Four different causal neural networks have been described. The key idea is that if we can integrate the causal model as a graphic or functional or rule-based structure into the network, then it can behave in an understandable manner while learning on its own to model some unknown factors and noise.

12.7 References

1. Anderson, J.R. 1987. Causal analysis and inductive learning. In *Proceedings of the Fourth International Workshop on Machine Learning*. Morgan Kaufmann, Los Altos, CA.

2. Asher, H.B. 1983. *Causal Modeling* (2d ed.). Sage, Beverly Hills, CA.

3. Blalock, Jr., H.M. 1962. Four variable causal models and partial correlation. *American Journal of Sociology*, 68, pp. 182–194.

4. Blalock, Jr., H.M. 1964. *Causal Inferences in Nonexperimental Research*. The Norton Library, New York.

5. Blum, R.L. 1982. Discovery and Representation of Causal Relationships from a Large Time-Oriented Clinical Database: The RX Project. Ph.D. thesis, Stanford University.

6. Bobrow, D.G. (ed.). 1985. *Qualitative Reasoning about Physical Systems*. MIT Press, Cambridge, MA.

7. Cooper, G. 1984. NESTOR: A Computer-Based Medical Diagnostic Aid That Integrates Causal and Probabilistic Knowledge. Ph.D. thesis, Stanford University.

8. Fishwick, P.A. 1988. The role of process abstraction in simulation. *IEEE Transactions on Systems, Man, and Cybernetics*, 18(1), pp. 18–38.

9. Forbus, K.D. 1984. Qualitative process theory. *Artificial Intelligence*, 24, pp. 85–168.

10. Fu, L.M. 1991. CAUSIM: A rule-based causal simulation system. *Simulation*, 56(4), pp. 251–257.

11. Garson, G.D. 1991. Interpreting neural-network connection weights. *AI Expert*, April, pp. 47–51.

12. Glymour, C., Scheines, R., Spirtes, P., and Kelly, K. 1987. *Discovering Causal Structure*. Academic Press, Orlando, FL.

13. Hertz, J., Krogh, A., and Palmer, R.G. 1991. *Introduction to the Theory of Neural Computation*. Addison-Wesley, Reading, MA.

14. Iwasaki, Y., and Simon, H.A. 1986. Causality in device behavior. *Artificial Intelligence*, 29, pp. 3–32.

15. Kuipers, B. 1986. Qualitative simulation. *Artificial Intelligence*, 29, pp. 289–338.

16. Kulikowski, C., and Weiss, S. 1982. Representation of expert knowledge for consultation: The CASNET and EXPERT projects. In *Artificial Intelligence in Medicine*. Westview Press, Boulder, CO.

17. Patil, R.S., Szolovits, P., and Schwartz, W.B. 1981. Causal understanding of patient illness in medical diagnosis. In *Proceedings of 7th IJCAI*, pp. 893–899.

18. Pazzani, M., Dyer, M., and Flowers, M. 1986. The role of prior causal theories in generalization. In *Proceedings of AAAI-86*, pp. 545–550.

19. Pearl, J. 1986. Fusion, propagation, and structuring in belief networks. *Artificial Intelligence*, 29, pp. 241–288.

20. Pearl, J. 1987. Evidential reasoning using stochastic simulation of causal models. *Artificial Intelligence*, 32(2), pp. 245–257.

21. Peng, Y., and Reggia, J.A. 1987. A probabilistic causal model for diagnostic problem solving, Part I: Integrating symbolic causal inference with numeric probabilistic inference. *IEEE Transactions on Systems, Man, and Cybernetics*, SMC-17(2), pp. 146–162.

22. Simon, H.A. 1954. Spurious correlations: A causal interpretation. *J. Am. Stat. Assoc.*, 49, pp. 469–492.

23. Szolovits, P. (ed.). 1982. *Artificial Intelligence in Medicine.* Westview Press, Boulder, CO.

24. Weiser-Friedman, L., and Pressman, I. 1989. The metamodel in simulation analysis: Can it be trusted? *Operations Research*, pp. 231–243.

25. Zeigler, B.P. 1976. *Theory of Modeling and Simulation.* John Wiley, New York.

26. Zeigler, B.P. 1984. *Multifaceted Modeling and Discrete Event Simulation.* Academic Press, New York.

12.8 Problems

1. Given a set of causal equations

$$X = Z + 5$$
$$2Y = 5Z$$
$$3Z = X$$
$$4W = 2X + Z$$

determine the causal order among the variables X, Y, Z, and W.

2. A set of causal relationships are given as follows:

A causes X.
B causes C.
B causes Y.
A causes Y.
C causes X.
D causes Y.
E causes D.
E causes B.
D causes B.
E causes F.
F causes X.
G causes X.
H causes Y.
I causes H.

Assume that we are investigating whether X causes Y. Identify the smallest subset of confounding variables through which all known causal influences on both X and Y flow.

3. Implement a neural network based upon a set of causal equations given below:

$$X = Y + Z + 5$$
$$2Y = 5Z + W + 1$$
$$3Z = X + Y$$
$$4W = 2X + Y + Z$$

(a) Specify the network structure.

(b) Specify the connection weights.

(c) Show how a constant term is handled.

4. The structure of a set of causal equations is assumed as follows:

$$X = aY + bZ + c$$
$$Y = dZ + eW + f$$
$$Z = gX + hY + i$$
$$W = jX + kY + l$$

where a, b, c, d, e, f, g, h, i, j, k, and l are coefficients to be determined. A set of training instances are given. In each instance, the values of the variables X, Y, Z, and W are specified. Design a neural network based on this equation set.

(a) What variables do the input and the output units correspond to?

(b) Show how to train this neural network.

Chapter 13

Validation and Verification

13.1   Introduction

Before being used, a computer-based system should be evaluated in many aspects. Among these, performance validation could be the most significant. There is often confusion between validation and verification. Validation refers to determining whether the system can perform at an acceptable level of performance in terms of accuracy and efficiency. Verification refers to determining whether the system was correctly implemented. A system needs to be verified first, and then it can be validated.

A number of techniques have been established for validating expert system performance, as described by O'Keefe, Balci, and Smith (1987) and Gupta (1991). All these techniques apply to validating a *performance* system. This chapter treats the validation of both the performance and the learning systems. Validation of a learning system differs from that of a performance system. For example, we evaluate the capability of generalization in a learning system but not in a performance system. An artificial neural network can be both a learning system and a performance system. In the training phase, it is a learning system, while after training, it becomes a performance system.

In the remaining sections, we address the concepts fundamental to performance validation and describe general validation techniques. We examine this issue in the context of learning systems and then in performance systems. We also explore approaches to verification.

13.2   Performance Validation

The definition of "performance" varies with the nature of tasks. For classification tasks, performance can be defined in terms of the correct rate of classification over test cases. For discovery tasks, there is no sense of correctness on discovered concepts, and we might define performance in terms of their

331

interestingness, as in AM.

The *grain size* of performance measures should be addressed as well. In some problem domains, the system's response should be described at multiple levels and/or using multiple variables rather than as a simple yes-no type of answer. A performance measure may be too coarse-grained if it only judges the system's response as good or bad. A finer measure is one which can analyze the quantitative differences between the system's response and the standard one. As more detail is explored, the grain size of performance measurement is reduced.

Another relevant issue is how to choose or define the performance standard against which a computer-based system can be compared. At first, we should discuss what is the gold standard, a generally accepted answer with which the results given by the system can be compared.

There are two conventional views on the standard. One is based on what a human expert (or a group of them) says is the correct answer. The other is based on what actually turns out to be the correct answer. For many kinds of problems, the second view is simply irrelevant since we do not know their eventual outcomes.

As to the performance standard, there are also two views. One is based on human expert performance. A computer-based system is valid if it is comparable to or outperforms human experts. Another view is based on the best existing system (whether it is a human or not). We may call it an *evolutionary* view. A system is valid if it can beat the best existing system in the world. The problem with this view is that it is idealistic. A system can still be acceptable even if its performance is not the best while offering other advantages.

O'Keefe, Balci, and Smith (1987) separate validation methodology into qualitative and quantitative methods. Qualitative methods adopt subjective comparisons of performance, whereas quantitative ones employ statistical techniques to compare performance. Defined in another way, *qualitative validation* refers to validating qualitative results such as categorical responses, while *quantitative validation* refers to validating quantitative results involving numerical values.

In quantitative validation, the *paired t-test* is often applied to compare the system performance against a selected standard. This technique assumes a single-variable response. That is, the system's response is described by a single variable. In some experimental designs, we evaluate performance in terms of error rates across different samples. Since the error rate is a single variable, the t-test can be applied to these cases.

In the t-test, one should note the difference between the two-sided test and the one-sided test. In the two-sided test, the question asked is whether the system's response is equal to the standard response or not. In the one-sided test, the question asked is whether the system's response is equal to or better than the standard response. In practice, a valid system should be at least comparable to the standard.

To apply the t-test, first, we need to formulate a null hypothesis H_o to be tested as "the system's response is the same as the standard response," and we set the level of significance α properly (e.g., $\alpha = 0.05$). Next, we measure the difference between the system's response and the standard response by $d_i = X_i - Y_i$ where X_i and Y_i are the system's response and the standard response, respectively, for the ith case. Suppose there are n test cases. There will be n observed differences. Then, we calculate the t value for d_i's under the null hypothesis. Finally, we determine whether to reject the null hypothesis by the t value, the α value, and degrees of freedom (i.e., $n - 1$). The detailed procedure is summarized as follows.

The Paired t-Test

1. Formulate a null hypothesis:

$$H_o : X = Y$$

   where X stands for the system's response and Y for the standard response. Set the level of significance α properly (e.g., $\alpha = 0.05$).

2. For all i, calculate $d_i = X_i - Y_i$ where X_i and Y_i are the system's response and the standard response, respectively, for the ith case.

3. Calculate the t value by

$$t = \frac{\sqrt{n}(\bar{d} - 0)}{S_d}$$

   where $\bar{d}$ is the mean difference, S_d the standard deviation, and n the number of cases.

4. Look up the t distribution table (one-sided or two-sided, depending on the null hypothesis). Reject the null hypothesis if

$$t > t_{\alpha;n-1}$$

   where $t_{\alpha;n-1}$ is the tabled value for the significance level α and degrees of freedom $n - 1$. Note that in the t table, only positive values of t are recorded.

It is important to recognize two types of errors. Type I error refers to rejecting the null hypothesis when it is true. Type II error refers to accepting the null hypothesis when it is false. Conventionally, we use α to denote the probability that a type I error will occur and β the probability of committing a type II error.

In the event that the system's response involves multiple variables, the single-variable t-test will be insufficient. To validate the system's response on a single-variable basis will neglect the interactions among the variables and is thus misleading. These variables should be considered jointly or simultaneously. In such cases, the Hotelling's one-sample T^2 test (a multivariate t-test) should be used (O'Keefe et al. 1987).

Hotelling's T^2 Test

1. Formulate a null hypothesis:

$$H_o : \mathbf{X} = \mathbf{Y}$$

   where $\mathbf{X}$ stands for the system's response vector and $\mathbf{Y}$ for the standard response vector. Set the level of significance α properly (e.g., $\alpha = 0.05$).

2. For all i, calculate $\mathbf{d}_i = \mathbf{X}_i - \mathbf{Y}_i$ where $\mathbf{X}_i$ and $\mathbf{Y}_i$ are the system's response and the standard response vectors, respectively, for the ith case.

3. Calculate the T^2 value by

$$T^2 = n(n - 1)\bar{\mathbf{d}}^t \mathbf{S}^{-1} \bar{\mathbf{d}}$$

   where $\mathbf{S}^{-1}$ is the inverse of the sample variance-covariance matrix, $\bar{\mathbf{d}}$ the mean difference vector, and n the number of cases.

4. The null hypothesis H_o is rejected at the level of significance α if

$$\frac{(n - p)T^2}{p(n - 1)} > F_{\alpha;(p,n-p)}$$

   where $F_{\alpha;(p,n-p)}$ denotes the upper α percentage points of the F distribution with p and $n - p$ degrees of freedom.

Suppose a multivariate response involves p variables and hence can be described by a p-dimensional vector. The difference between the system's response and the standard response is also encoded by a p-dimensional vector. For n test cases, there will be n observed difference vectors. In the univariate case, we compute the t value, but in the multivariate case, we compute the T^2 value by

$$T^2 = n(n - 1)\bar{\mathbf{d}}^t \mathbf{S}^{-1} \bar{\mathbf{d}}$$

where $\mathbf{S}^{-1}$ is the inverse of the sample variance-covariance matrix, $\bar{\mathbf{d}}$ is the mean difference vector, and $\bar{\mathbf{d}}^t$ is the transpose of $\bar{\mathbf{d}}$. The relationship holds that

$$\frac{(n - p)T^2}{p(n - 1)} \sim F_{(p,n-p)}$$

where $F_{(p, n-p)}$ is the F distribution with p and $n - p$ degrees of freedom.

When the system response is qualitative such as the yes-no type of response, quantitative techniques such as the t-test or T^2 test are inappropriate. We can arrange paired system and standard responses into four groups: (yes yes), (yes no), (no yes), and (no no); and count how many cases fall into these four different groups. Concordance analysis (Agresti 1990) can indicate whether the system's response and the standard response are positively associated and how strongly they are related.

The *chi-square* test has been used in testing hypotheses in a wide variety of situations that involve enumeration data. The chi-square test can also be applied to test the association between the system's and the standard responses. A significant association indicates the agreement between the system and the standard. However, "association" is a weaker indication for such agreement than "concordance." Lack of agreement does not rule out the validity of the system, for it may outperform the standard.

We should also measure the error rates across different samples for further comparison. The concordance or association test concludes whether there is agreement between the system and the performance standard or not, while the error rate test concludes whether the system is equal to, better, or worse than the performance standard.

The error rate of a performance system can be estimated by either assuming a parametric model or testing the system empirically. Consider a classification system which divides the space into two regions R_1 and R_2 corresponding to class C_1 and C_2. Under an assumed parametric model (e.g., multivariate normal distributions), the probability of error is the probability of the case when an observation falls in R_1 (R_2) and the true class is C_2 (C_1). The main question with this approach is whether the assumed model is valid.

In the empirical approach, the system is run on a set of test instances. The fraction of the instances that are misclassified is used as the estimate of the error rate. It can be shown that this estimate is the maximum likelihood estimate for the true but unknown error rate of the system based on the test sample. Unless the sample is fairly large, this estimate must be interpreted with caution. Techniques such as "leave one out" for estimating the error rate are discussed later.

13.3 Validation of a Learning System

What to validate is intrinsically linked to what the learning system is meant for. Suppose the learning system is to improve an existing performance system. Then, the learning system is valid if it can improve the performance significantly. Now, suppose the learning system is to build an expert system from scratch. Then, the learning system is valid if the expert system it built can perform adequately. These facts lead to the performance view of a learning system.

A learning system often improves or learns its knowledge from training data. If we just test the knowledge on the training data, the performance level reflects how well the knowledge fit the data but is not necessarily a reliable estimate for unseen data. For this reason, training data and test data should be drawn independently from the domain. And a learning system cannot build high-performance systems unless it has a good generalization ability. As a result, the performance view of a learning system is actually grounded on its underlying generalization capability.

When a learning system involves an adjustable or random element, its performance may vary. For example, we often randomize the initial weights in a neural network. Different initial weight settings often lead to different learning results. In an unsupervised learning network, different parameter tunings may also yield different cluster structures. We can try a set of different parameter values and evaluate the performance. But we are confronted with the question whether we should take the average case or the best case performance to define the system performance. If we know what is the best, then, of course, we should take the best performance. For example, in the traveling salesman problem, the objective is to find the shortest tour that visits each city only once and returns to the starting point. And we do know how to compare solutions found. On the other hand, we may not know what is the best. For example, a learning system is designed to learn a set of rules based on a very limited amount of training data. In this case, we may keep several versions of rules learned, and taking the average performance over these versions is justified.

13.3.1   Aspects of Validation

The validity of a learning system can be evaluated in the following aspects:

- *Performance:* When a learning system is used to build a performance (problem-solving) system, the first concern is whether the system can provide satisfactory solutions. We measure the performance of the performance system to indirectly indicate how good the learning system is. Assume that learning is based on empirical data. The learning system extracts knowledge from training data by induction or generalization. The learned knowledge should be general enough to deal with unknown data. The generalization capability of a learning system can be tested in normal conditions, in noisy conditions, with missing data, and with irrelevant data. In noisy conditions, the learner should discern right from wrong data. With missing data, the learner should perhaps hypothesize what the missing pieces might look like. With irrelevant data, the learner should not be distracted. All these conditions seem to be part of the real world and must thus be considered when evaluating a learning system.

- *Generality:* If a learning algorithm can be applied to many distinct problem domains, it would be more interesting and more useful. Researchers often use "generality" as a criterion to evaluate the soundness of a learning algorithm. The more domains it can apply to, the more true its fundamental principles.

- *Stability:* "Stability" refers to the ability to retain previously learned knowledge. A learning system may forget old knowledge when its capacity limit has been reached or when new knowledge interferes with old knowledge. Desirably, the knowledge and performance of a learning system should increase monotonically over time.

- *Efficiency:* On this issue, we are concerned about the computational complexity of the learning algorithm and learning speed. An exponential algorithm cannot be scaled up and is hence uninteresting in general. Learning speed is critically dependent on the hardware environment. By offering higher accuracy, a slow learning system is still acceptable. Thus, learning speed alone is a weak criterion for validity.

- *Quality:* When two systems perform equally well, we begin to ask which provides better quality, for example, the size of decision trees or rules or neural networks. In unsupervised learning systems, it may be hard to define "accuracy" for a new concept or cluster discovered. Instead, we measure how interesting or how useful it is.

- *Consistency:* Here, we are concerned whether a learning system can generate systems with consistent performance based on similar data. This criterion is especially important for unsupervised learning systems when we cannot measure accuracy.

- *Incremental learning:* An incremental learning system can continue to assimilate new data. It neither stores old data nor forgets previously learned knowledge. This feature is essential for a learning system which continues to receive inputs from a real-time environment.

- *Sensitivity:* The performance of a learning system may be sensitive to perturbation of system parameters or training data. Hypersensitivity to minor changes in the learning system itself or in the environment may suggest intolerance to noise or faults.

13.3.2 Approaches to Validation

The statistical techniques such as the *t*-test for performance validation introduced earlier can be applied to a learning system. This section contains several approaches which are specifically related to validating a learning system. These approaches include cross-validation, consistency analysis, sensitivity analysis, and goodness-of-fit criteria.

Cross-Validation and Related Techniques

Several techniques for estimating error rates have been developed in the fields of statistics and pattern recognition, which include *holdout, leave one out, cross-validation*, and *bootstrapping* (Weiss and Kapouleas 1989).

The holdout method is a single train-and-test experiment where a data set is broken down into two disjoint subsets, one used for training and the other for testing. A sufficient number of independent test cases (say 1000) are needed for reliable estimation.

Leave one out (Fukunaga 1972) repeats n times for n instances (cases), each time leaving one case out for testing and the rest for training. The average test error rate over n trials is the estimated error rate. This technique is time-consuming for large samples.

K-fold cross-validation (Stone 1974) repeats k times for a sample set randomly divided into k disjoint subsets, each time leaving one set out for testing and the others for training. Thus, we may call this technique "leave some out," and "leave one out" is just a special case of this general class.

Bootstrapping (Jain, Dubes and Chen 1987) is a method for random resampling and replacement for a number of times, and the estimated error rate is the average error rate over the number of iterations.

The basic idea behind error estimation or validation is that the test set must be independent of the training set, the partition of a sample into these two subsets should be unbiased, the respective sample size should be adequate, and the estimated error rate refers to the test error rather than the training error rate. Besides, in order to maximize the use of every sample, it would be preferable to take each case for training at one time and for testing at another.

Leave one out and bootstrapping should be considered for small samples, the holdout method for large samples, and k-fold cross-validation is applicable for both cases. The question remaining for k-fold cross-validation is, What is k? The answer again depends on the sample size. Notice that too few training instances can lead to a poor learning result, and too few test instances can give an erroneous estimate of the error rate. It would be true that as k decreases but is no less than 2, the error estimate is more conservative since we use fewer instances for training and more for testing.

Example. A sample consists of instances 1, 2, 3, 4, 5, 6. Under the leave-one-out strategy, we design experiments as follows:

Experiment	Training	Testing
1	1, 2, 3, 4, 5	6
2	1, 2, 3, 4, 6	5
3	1, 2, 3, 5, 6	4
4	1, 2, 4, 5, 6	3
5	1, 3, 4, 5, 6	2
6	2, 3, 4, 5, 6	1

Suppose the test error rates for these experiments are, respectively, 0.00, 0.00, 1.00, 0.00, 1.00, and 0.00. Then the average error rate is 0.33. The three-fold cross-validation design is illustrated by

Experiment	Training	Testing
1	1, 2, 3, 4	5, 6
2	1, 2, 5, 6	3, 4
3	3, 4, 5, 6	1, 2

Validation on Consistency

In an unsupervised learning system, we can evaluate its self-consistency in the following way.

Suppose we have N training sets $T_1, T_2, \ldots, T_N$ drawn from the same population. We apply the clustering procedure on set T_i so that T_i is divided into k_i clusters $C_{i1}, C_{i2}, \ldots, C_{ik_i}$. The size of each cluster is measured by the proportion it occupies in the whole set. They are denoted by $p_{i1}, \ldots, p_{ik_i}$, respectively, with $\Sigma p_{ij} = 1$. The cross-validation set contains randomly chosen M pairs of cells. The null hypothesis is that the clustering procedure is equivalent to a random aggregation scheme.

The following test scheme is used to test this null hypothesis. Let (x_i, x_j) be two randomly picked cells. Intuitively, if they are classified into the same cluster consistently, then we should think that the clustering procedure has picked up some common characteristics of the two cells. On the other hand, if this pair is classified sometimes in the same cluster but sometimes in different clusters, then we should imply that the clustering procedure is inconsistent for this pair. Thus, we use the frequencies of the M pairs (x_i, x_j) being classified in the same cluster in the N training sets as an indicator of the consistency of the clustering procedure.

Let

$$S_i = \begin{cases} 1 & \text{if a pair is classified into the same cluster} \\ 0 & \text{otherwise} \end{cases}$$

and $P_i = Pr\{S_i = 1\}$. It can be easily shown that the probability of any pair being classified as $(S_1, S_2, \ldots, S_N)$ according to the classification procedures produced by $T_1, T_2, \ldots, T_N$ is

$$P(S_1, S_2, ..., S_N) = \prod_{i=1}^{N} P_i^{S_i}(1 - P_i)^{1-S_i}$$

With some assumptions on random clustering, we can figure out the expected probability of P_i. And the expected probability (and hence the frequency) for M pairs in each configuration $(S_1, S_2, \ldots, S_N)$ can be computed by the above equation. A chi-square test can be used to test the lack of fit by the random hypothesis.

The Chi-Square Test

1. Formulate the null hypothesis:

   H_o: The clustering procedure is random or inconsistent.

   Select the significance level α.

2. Compute the χ^2 value by

$$\chi^2 = \sum \frac{(f_o - f_e)^2}{f_e}$$

   where f_o is the observed frequency and f_e the expected frequency.

3. Look up the χ^2 distribution table. Reject the null hypothesis if

$$\chi^2 > \chi^2_{\alpha;df}$$

   where $\chi^2_{\alpha;df}$ is the tabular value for the significance level α and degrees of freedom df. The number of independent frequencies is the degrees of freedom.

As in any other statistical test, the sample size is of the utmost importance. A rule of thumb is that any expected frequency should be at least as large as 5. With proper formulation of the null hypothesis, the chi-square analysis can be applied to test differences between different treatments, associations between variables, and goodness of fit of an observed distribution to a given one.

Sensitivity Analysis

For example, by changing initial weights, a backpropagation network will have a different performance after training; by adjusting the so-called vigilance parameter value, an ART network may give rise to different clusters. Through sensitivity analysis, we can determine the proper operational range of system parameters.

We may also perturb training data to see how performance becomes different. The data are perturbed by random replacement of attribute values and/or class labels for some percentage of instances. In a supervised learning system, we can measure the change in the test error rate. In an unsupervised learning system, we can count the fraction of cells originally in the same clusters which shift to different clusters because of the perturbation.

Goodness-of-Fit Criteria

Consider an unsupervised learning system whose main function is clustering. Its validity is evaluated by that of the clustering structure it generates. The validity of a clustering structure can be interpreted as how well it can provide the true information or reveal the intrinsic characteristics of the data. Jain and Dubes (1988) describe a number of useful indices for measuring cluster validity with comprehensive discussion.

Sometimes, the cluster validity is subjectively determined by the expert in the domain. The problem with this approach is that the expert often makes a judgement by visual inspection. In the case of a data dimensionality higher than three, the visual technique cannot see the whole structure directly and relies on multiple low-dimensional views of the structure. The more the views, the more difficult to integrate them.

Another alternative to validating the unsupervised system is to let it cluster instances with assigned class labels a priori. Then, we measure the correspondence between clusters produced and classes predefined. The ideal condition is that there is a one-to-one correspondence, and the instances in the same class are also put into the same cluster. The validity of the clustering structure is determined by how close it is to this ideal condition. If there is not a one-to-one correspondence, it is hard to measure the discrepancy between the clusters and the classes. We need to tune the system parameters so that the correct number of clusters is produced. A simple algorithm is:

1. Adjust the system parameters so that the clusters and the classes are equal in number.

2. Establish a one-to-one correspondence between clusters and classes. If most instances in class A appear in cluster X, then these two are paired.

3. Calculate the error rate. If an instance does not appear in the cluster corresponding to its class, then it is an error. The error rate so calculated is used to evaluate the validity of the clustering procedure.

In sum, the validity of a clustering structure can be evaluated by:

- The fit between the structure and the data. For example, we can measure the separation between clusters based upon Fisher's linear discriminant criterion function (Duda and Hart 1973).

- The expert's judgment, usually based on visual inspection.

- The match between the structure and a priori information.

13.4   Validation of a Performance System

A performance system is valid if it can meet the performance standard defined by the expert in the domain. For example, an expert system is evaluated by running test cases, scoring its performance, and comparing the performance against expert opinion. Several points can be briefly mentioned:

- The number of test cases and how widely they cover the domain affect our confidence in the validation result. When only a few historic cases are available, perturbation on existing cases can be tried.

- We often use a more strict standard to evaluate a computer-based system and will accept it only if it outperforms the human counterpart.

- The error rate is not the only evaluation criterion. There exist other performance measures which should be adopted as appropriate.

Several useful validation techniques have been described earlier. This section examines the issues involved in validating a performance system and also reviews several important techniques to evaluate it.

13.4.1 Aspects of Validation

The validity of a performance system can be evaluated in the following aspects:

- *Accuracy:* A computer-based system will not be accepted by its intended users unless it has demonstrated its accuracy in problem solving. "Accuracy" means the correctness of the answer.

- *Robustness:* "Robustness" means that the system can perform adequately under all circumstances, including the cases when information is corrupted by noise, is incomplete, and is interfered with by red herrings. All these cases are typical in domains such as military combat and medical diagnosis.

- *Efficiency:* Here, the concern is how fast the system can arrive at a correct answer and how much computer memory is required. It cannot be overemphasized how important speed is in real-time situations.

- *Consistency:* When we test the performance of a system, we attend to not just the average performance but also how consistently it performs. We are reluctant to accept a system which is good in most cases but plunges occasionally—especially in a risky domain.

- *Adaptability and Extensibility:* A system is of limited use if it cannot be modified or extended. A rule-based system is popular partly because it can be modified by revising rules locally. Revising a neural network seems more laborious because all connection weights will be affected. How to adapt a connectionist structure is addressed in Chapter 4 "Knowledge-Based Neural Networks."

- *Reliability and Fault Tolerance:* We are concerned with how performance degrades when part of the system fails. Fault tolerance can be construed as the ability to degrade gracefully under faults. It is clear that graceful degradation is preferable to abrupt degradation. For example, a neural network is fault-tolerant in that its performance can be maintained in case some connections are broken. Besides fault tolerance, such dependability factors as safety and sociopsychological impact are also important from the human user's perspective.

- *Sensitivity:* A system should be sensitive enough to detect subtle change in the input data, offering precision. At the same time, it should not be so sensitive to noise as to reach an incorrect conclusion. Sensitivity is thus a useful index for the system performance.

13.4.2 Approaches to Validation

Statistical approaches have been described earlier. O'Keefe et al. (1987) describe several qualitative approaches for validating an expert system; their applicability can virtually be extended to any other kind of performance system such as neural networks:

- *Turing Tests:*[1] The system performance and human expert performance are compared without knowing the performer's identity. Such blind evaluation can eliminate any bias for or against computers. The system is valid if a human as the third party cannot recognize which results are provided by the system.

- *Field Tests:* The system is deployed in the field, and its performance is watched by the users. This empirical evaluation will indicate how reliable and how useful the system is for the field application.

- *Face Validation:* The face value and the credibility of the system are subjectively assessed by project team members, potential users, and experts. This can serve as a useful preliminary approach to validation.

- *Sensitivity Analysis:* The effect on the system performance is measured by altering input variable values or system parameters. For example, MYCIN researchers have found that the decisions of MYCIN are not sensitive to certainty factor change of less than 0.2 (Buchanan and Shortliffe 1984). When few or no test cases are available, this technique is especially useful because it can generate additional cases by perturbation.

---

[1]The Turing test was proposed by Alan Turing in 1950 for determining whether a machine can think.

13.5   Validation of Individual Patterns

Uncertainty is naturally associated with the inference process in practical domains, with quite a few exceptions (e.g., in pure mathematics). A rule in a knowledge-based system is often inexact in that when its antecedent is matched (true), its consequent is not necessarily true. Even if each individual rule looks right, they may be wrong when combined because of the incorrect independence assumption. This fact complicates the evaluation of individual rules since we have to consider their interactions. Nonetheless, an individual rule should still be correct to some degree.

13.5.1   Performance of a Rule

Evaluation of individual rules can be categorized into *content dependent* and *context independent*. In the former case, we evaluate a rule along with other rules in the system; in the latter case, we evaluate a rule alone. In context-independent evaluation, we test a single rule's *predictive value*, which is defined as the probability of its consequent being true given that its antecedent is matched among test instances. Rules with low predictive values are filtered out.

We can then proceed with context-dependent evaluation. In such evaluation, we identify rules which contribute to incorrect conclusions. Rules can be ranked according to how much they contribute to false-positive and false-negative evidence (Wilkin and Buchanan 1986). The rule set is revised by removing one or more rules at a time incrementally. Alternatively, a connectionist approach which considers rules all together for revision is described in Chapter 4.

The problem of evaluating and selecting a subset of important rules is an NP-complete problem. Meta-DENDRAL (Buchanan and Mitchell 1978) has developed a domain-specific heuristic for selecting a subset of important rules. It calculates a score for each rule according to the following function:

$$\text{Score} = I \cdot (P + U - 2N)$$

where I = the average intensity of positive evidence data points; P = the number of positive evidence instances; U = the number of unique positive evidence instances; and N = the number of negative evidence instances. Rules are selected on the basis of their scores.

13.5.2   Statistical Significance of a Pattern

In pattern analysis, a frequent question is how significant a pattern is. For example, in genetic pattern analysis, we identify patterns causally associated with a particular trait. In univariate analysis, we test the association between a single genetic marker and the trait. In multivariate analysis, we also wish to know the association between a pattern of markers and the trait.

Depending on the type of variable value, we select different statistical techniques. For qualitative values (on nominal or ordinal scales), the chi-square test is chosen. We create a 2×2 table by asking whether the pattern at hand and the concept concerned are matched or satisfied:

	concept $(+)$	concept $(-)$
pattern $(+)$	n_{++}	n_{+-}
pattern $(-)$	n_{-+}	n_{--}

where the pattern can be univariate or multivariate.[2] Then we run the test to see if there is significant association between the pattern and the concept. For quantitative values (on interval or ratio scales), the correlation test (multiple correlation for multivariate analysis) is taken.

One caveat is that when a pattern is generated from one data set by a certain procedure, the significance of the pattern should be evaluated against another independent data set. This is an important concern in multivariate analysis where the number of possible patterns is great.

13.6 Verification

Here, we look at two strategies for verifying a system rather than verifying program code or data structures to which the software engineering practice can immediately lend itself. One strategy is based on the declarative semantics and the other on the procedural semantics of the performance system.

Verification based upon declarative semantics is independent of control strategies and conflict resolution techniques. This analysis strategy is static in the sense that it does not involve procedural execution by the inference engine. On the contrary, verification based on procedural semantics is coupled with the inference procedure.

13.6.1 Verification of Rule Bases

In the *declarative approach*, the checker uses condition and action pattern matching algorithms to determine the inconsistency and the incompleteness in the rule base (Suwa, Scott, and Shortliffe 1984; Nguyen, Perkins, Laffey, and Pecora 1987). The object of verification is to remove these undesired conditions. Several types of rule-based inconsistencies can be recognized:

- Redundant Rules: Two rules share the same antecedent and consequent.

- Conflicting Rules: The antecedents of two rules are equivalent, but one or more of their conclusions are contradictory. For example,

---

[2]In the multivariate case, we can create more cells in the table. Statisticians point out that the merger of multiple cells is legitimate.

Rule 1: If A, then X.
Rule 2: If A, then not X.

- Subsumed Rules: Two rules have the same conclusions, but one contains fewer conditions than the other in the if-part. For example,

  Rule 3: If B and C, then Y.
  Rule 4: If B, then Y.

Rule 3 is subsumed by rule 4; whenever the former succeeds, the latter also does but not vice versa.

- Unnecessary If Conditions: For example,

  Rule 5: If D and E, then Z.
  Rule 6: If D and not E, then Z.

The conditions "E" and "not E" are unnecessary.

- Circular Rule Chain: The chaining of rules forms a cycle. For example,

  Rule 7: If P, then Q.
  Rule 8: If Q, then R.
  Rule 9: If R, then P.

In this case, the system will enter an infinite loop at run time unless it has a special way to handle this situation.

In the approach by Suwa, Scott, and Shortliffe (1984), the rule checker assumes that there should be a rule for each possible combination of attribute values. This approach is unsuitable in domains where most combinations simply are not meaningful, and we should not consider a meaningless rule as missing. Likewise, unreferenced attribute values do not imply that they should appear in some rule. Still, we can identify several circumstances where the rule base is considered incomplete:

- Illegal Attribute Values: An illegal attribute value occurs when a rule references a value that is not defined a priori.

- Unreachable Conclusions: In a goal-oriented system, if a goal hypothesis does not match the consequent of any rule, then the goal cannot be derived unless explicitly told.

- Unreachable If Conditions: In a goal-oriented system, when an if condition of a rule does not match the consequent of any other rule nor is the condition askable, then the rule will never fire.

In the *procedural approach,* rule verification based on procedural semantics will involve the rule-based interpretation/execution. For example, the following set of rules will lead to a conflict:

If I, then J.
If I, then K.
If J, then L.
If K, then not L.

In this case, when "I" is true, both "L" and "not L" are concluded—a conflict. The procedural approach can identify this problem, whereas the declarative approach cannot.

Taking the procedural strategy, one can analyze the effects of conflict resolution, closed-world negation, and the retraction of facts. Evertsz (1991) describes the abstract interpretation of production systems so that the consistency checker acts on the abstract domain of uninstantiated data. A rule base and the inference engine can be viewed as a function, whose domain is the set of possible inputs the rule base can accept and whose range is the set of final data bases the rule base can generate from the input domain. Abstract interpretation generates a set of final data bases for a given abstract description of the input domain. A full analysis demands generating all possible routes through the rule base.

13.6.2 Verification of Neural Networks

In declarative aspects, we verify:

- Network Properties: architecture (single-layer or multilayer), information flow (feedforward or recurrent), and connection patterns (fully or partially connected)

- Unit Properties: input connections, output connections, and nonlinearities (hard limiter or sigmoid or hyperbolic tangent)

- Behavioral Properties: weight initialization, activation calculation, and weight updating

A neural network model is often characterized by a set of mathematical equations. Verifying that these equations are all implemented correctly is essential.

In procedural aspects, important properties to be verified include:

- *Convergence:* Check whether the network will converge to an asymptotic value by iterations.

- *Stability:* Check whether successive iterations produce smaller and smaller output changes until the output becomes (nearly) constant. Check also whether the intermediate and output values steadily decrease or do not explode.

13.7   Summary

Checking whether a system is correctly implemented and testing if it has reached an acceptable level of performance are two issues known as verification and validation, respectively. Both are important in the development of practical systems, yet they should not be confused. Validation of a learning system and that of a performance system are related but different issues and should be distinguished from each other.

Error rate estimation is not the only means of performance validation. Quantifying the system output and then applying quantitative techniques can increase the resolution of validation results. Concepts such as cross-validation and sensitivity analysis are very useful. The former offers an accurate estimate of the error rate by effectively using available samples. The latter can analyze the system behavior under changes and thereby can explore the suitable operational range of system parameters and generate additional test cases.

In the aspect of verification, it is useful to make distinctions between declarative and procedural approaches. The second depends on the procedural semantics associated with the performance system, while the first does not. Different system properties can be examined under these two different perspectives.

13.8   References

1. Agresti, A. 1990. *Categorical Data Analysis*. John Wiley & Sons, New York.

2. Buchanan, B.G., and Mitchell, T.M. 1978. Model-directed learning of production rules. In *Pattern-Directed Inference Systems*. Academic Press, New York.

3. Buchanan, B.G., and Shortliffe, E.H. 1984. *Rule-Based Expert Systems*. Addison-Wesley, Reading, MA.

4. Duda, R.O., and Hart, P.E. 1973. *Pattern Classification and Scene Analysis*. John Wiley & Sons, New York.

5. Evertsz, R. 1991. The automated analysis of rule-based systems, based on their procedural semantics. In *Proceedings of IJCAI-91*, pp. 22–27.

6. Fukunaga, K. 1972. *Introduction to Statistical Pattern Recognition*. Academic Press, New York.

7. Gupta, U.G. (ed.). 1991. *Validating and Verifying Knowledge-Based Systems*. IEEE Computer Society Press. Los Alamitos, CA.

8. Jain, A.K., and Dubes, R.C. 1988. *Algorithms for Clustering Data*. Prentice-Hall, Englewood Cliffs, NJ.

9. Jain, A., Dubes, R., and Chen, C. 1987. Bootstrap techniques for error estimation. *IEEE Transactions on Pattern Analysis and Machine Intelligence*, 9, pp. 628–633.

10. Nguyen, T.A., Perkins, W.A., Laffey, T.J., and Pecora, D. 1987. Knowledge base verification. *AI Magazine*, Summer, pp. 69–75.

11. O'Keefe, R.M., Balci, O., and Smith, E.P. 1987. Validating expert system performance. *IEEE Expert*, Winter, pp. 81–87.

12. Stone, M. 1974. Cross-validatory choice and assessment of statistical predictions. *Journal of the Royal Statistical Society*, 36, pp. 111–147.

13. Suwa, M., Scott, A.C., and Shortliffe, E.H. 1984. Completeness and consistency in a rule-based expert system. In *Rule-Based Expert Systems*. Addison-Wesley, Reading, MA.

14. Weiss, S.M., and Kapouleas, I. 1989. An experimental comparison of pattern recognition, neural nets, and machine learning classification methods. In *Proceedings of IJCAI-89*, pp. 781–787.

15. Wilkins, D.C., and Buchanan, B.G. 1986. On debugging rule sets when reasoning under uncertainty. In *Proceedings of AAAI-86*, pp. 448–454.

13.9 Problems

1. A neural network generates a univariate response. The test results are shown below:

Test	Network response	Correct response
1	15	20
2	9	7
3	27	15
4	35	38
5	11	45
6	19	17
7	55	50
8	46	41
9	25	28
10	23	21

(a) What statistical test is proper for validating the network performance?

(b) Give the statistical validation result. Set the level of significance $\alpha = 0.05$. Is this network valid?

2. A neural network generates a trivariate response. Assume that the three output variables interact. The network is validated by running the following tests:

Test	Network response	Correct response
1	(1, 5, 6)	(2, 0, 4)
2	(9, 11, 15)	(7, 12, 18)
3	(2, 7, 9)	(1, 5, 8)
4	(3, 5, 8)	(3, 8, 10)
5	(11, 15, 25)	(9, 8, 35)
6	(19, 23, 2)	(17, 25, 6)
7	(5, 5, 8)	(5, 1, 9)
8	(14, 26, 18)	(9, 30, 21)
9	(25, 15, 43)	(28, 10, 40)
10	(2, 3, 9)	(2, 5, 12)

(a) What statistical test is proper in this case?

(b) Give the statistical validation result. Set the level of significance $\alpha = 0.05$. Is this network valid?

3. Devise a statistical procedure to test the noise tolerance of a neural network.

4. Explain why validating an unsupervised learning network is more difficult than validating a supervised learning network. What different properties can be evaluated with respect to each other?

Chapter 14

Rule Generation from Neural Networks

14.1 Introduction

A major weakness of the neural network approach to artificial intelligence is that the knowledge learned by a neural network is difficult to interpret. Some neural network–based systems such as Gallant's (1988) connectionist expert system are augmented with a rule-based explanation capability. The rules can be implemented by extracting them from the neural network or by building them from another source. The latter approach does not really address the issue of *interpretability*.

While most researchers investigating the problem of rule extraction from neural networks are interested in the issue of interpretation or the issue of explanation, rules extracted from a neural network can also be used to build an RBCN (described in Chapter 4 "Knowledge-Based Neural Networks") which outperforms the original network.

This chapter addresses the problem of generating rules from neural networks. It formalizes the relationship between a neural network and a rule-based system. The chapter is intended to provide readers with general understanding of the problem.

A basic principle of a (biological) neural network is that if the sum of its weighted inputs exceeds a certain threshold, then the neuron fires. This principle can be extended to an artificial neural network which uses a smooth activation function such as the sigmoid function. Notice that a neuron using a hard-limiting threshold function produces a binary response (0 or 1), while a neuron with a smooth activation function generates a graded response. Thus, the employment of a smooth activation function creates more "states" for a neural network.

The description of rule generation in this chapter focuses on feedforward networks. Its extension to the recurrent architecture is provided in Chapter 15 "Learning Grammars."

14.2   Basic Definitions

Definition 1. A rule generated from a neural network has the form

If the premise, then the action (conclusion)

or specifically,

$$\text{If } A_1^+, \ldots, A_i^+, \ldots, \neg A_1^-, \ldots, \neg A_j^-, \ldots, \text{ then } C \text{ (or } \neg C)$$

where A_i^+ is a positive antecedent (an attribute in the positive form), A_j^- a negated antecedent (an attribute in the negative form), C the concept, and $\neg$ reads "not." We represent an attribute of n values by n attributes, so an *attribute* is actually an attribute value. The rule is called a *confirming* rule if the action is C, or a *disconfirming* rule if the action is $\neg C$. When the premise holds (that is, all positive antecedents mentioned are present and all negated antecedents mentioned are absent), the concept is true in the confirming rule or false in the disconfirming rule. Here is a hypothetical rule for classifying fruits:

If color-red, size-medium, then apple

The rule's premise is limited to a conjunction of attributes. Disjunction is not allowed. However, the presence of multiple rules with the same conclusion represents disjunction.

We do not restrict the use of the rules to a particular kind of inference engine. They can be used for both exact and inexact reasoning. In the latter case, a rule should be attached with a number indicating the degree of belief in the conclusion given the premise, and an attribute can also be associated with a belief value.

Definition 2. In the neural network, each node is designated by a symbol. Suppose we seek rules confirming or disconfirming the concept C. We define a *pos-att* for the concept C to be an attribute designating a node which directly connects to the node corresponding to C with a positive connection weight. We define a *neg-att* for C in the same way except that the connection weight is negative. The idea is illustrated in Figure 14.1. There should be no confusion between a pos-att (neg-att) and a positive (negated) antecedent of a rule. However, in a confirming (disconfirming) rule, a pos-att exists in the positive (negative) form and a neg-att in the negative (positive) form.

Definition 3. The *activation function* refers to the nonlinearity on the hidden or output units of the neural network. We implicitly assume that the activation function is the sigmoid function:

$$F(a) = \frac{1}{1 + e^{-\lambda a}} \tag{14.1}$$

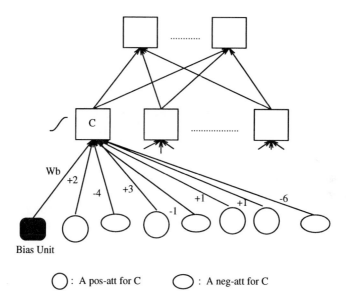

Figure 14.1: The pos-atts and neg-atts relative to a concept. An attribute can be either a pos-att or a neg-att, depending on the concept. $W_b = -\theta$ where θ is the threshold on the node C.

where λ determines the steepness of the function.

Definition 4. We define the function *Act* which returns the activation value, calculated in the neural network, of the node corresponding to the argument object. For example, $\text{Act}(C)$ refers to the activation of the node designated by the symbol C. The activation range of any node in the network is restricted to the interval [0, 1].

The activation (O_j) of unit j (a hidden or output unit) is calculated by

$$O_j = F(\sum_i W_{ji} X_i - \theta_j)$$

where X_i is the input from unit i, W_{ji} the weight on the connection from unit i to unit j, and θ_j the threshold on unit j. The threshold of a node can be made freely adjustable during neural network learning by adding an additional input connection from a node (called a bias unit) whose output is always 1; and the weight on the connection is the negative of the threshold value.

In the case of a hard-limiting activation function, the output of a neuron is given by

$$O_j = \begin{cases} 1, & \sum_i W_{ji} X_i > \theta_j \\ 0, & \text{else} \end{cases}$$

Definition 5. The *validity* condition for a rule is defined as follows. Whenever the rule's premise holds, so does its conclusion in the presence of any combination of the values of attributes not referenced by the rule. In the neural network, the definition is rephrased. Whenever all of the positive antecedents (attributes) contained in the premise take on the value (activation level) 1 and all of the negated antecedents (attributes) in it take on the value 0, the total input to the concept node in the conclusion is greater than its threshold. The validity condition so defined does not preclude a valid rule from being used in an uncertain case when attributes take on a value of neither 0 nor 1. That is, the use of a valid rule is not limited to the binary case. A rule is said to be *valid* if it satisfies the validity condition.

Consider a confirming rule,

$$\text{If } A, \text{ then } C$$

The validity condition for this rule is that the total input to the concept node C is greater than its threshold as long as $A = 1$. In the case of the sigmoid activation function, $\text{Act}(C) > 0.5$ whenever $A = 1$. (See Figure 14.2.) For a disconfirming rule, the total input to the concept node should be less than the associated threshold (or $\text{Act}(C) < 0.5$ in the case of the sigmoid activation function) whenever the premise holds.

Definition 6. The *certainty* condition for a rule is defined as follows. Whenever the rule's premise holds, so does its conclusion in the presence of any combination of the values of attributes not referenced by the rule. In addition, the concept to be concluded or denied must be certain. This means that $\text{Act}(C) = 1$ or 0 where C is the concept concerned. Therefore, the certainty condition is stronger than the validity condition.

Definition 7. A rule *subsumes* another rule if and only if they both share the same conclusion and the premise of the former is a part of that of the latter. In other words, the former rule is more general than the latter. It is easily understood that the rules subsumed by a valid rule should also be valid. Subsumed rules are redundant in making conclusions and can be removed.

Definition 8. The *rule size* is defined to be the total number of attributes mentioned in the rule's premise.

Definition 9. Suppose a neural network has learned n *valid* rules. The rule extraction method is said to be *complete* if it can generate a rule set from the

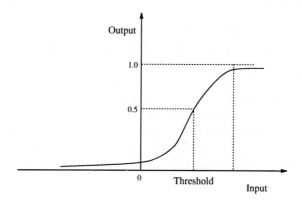

Figure 14.2: A sigmoid activation function. When the input = threshold, the output = 0.5.

neural network such that each of the n rules is either in the set or subsumed by some other rule in the set.

Definition 10. Suppose a neural network has learned m *valid* rules with sizes $\leq k$ where k is a positive integer. The rule extraction method is said to be k*th-order complete* if it can generate a rule set from the neural network such that each of the m rules is either in the set or subsumed by some other rule in the set.

14.3   Search on Adapted Nets

In this section, we present a general rule search algorithm developed by Fu (1991, 1994). The algorithm referred to as *KT* heuristically searches through the rule space expanded in terms of combinations of attributes, which are distinguished into pos-atts and neg-atts according to the concept for which rules are formed. To form confirming rules, the algorithm will first explore combinations of pos-atts and then use negated neg-atts in conjunction to further consolidate the positive combinations. Similarly, to form disconfirming rules, the algorithm will first explore combinations of neg-atts and then use negated pos-atts in conjunction. The distinction between these two kinds of attributes reduces the size of the search space considerably. Furthermore, through layer-by-layer search, the overall search width is exponential with the depth of the network. The algorithm is outlined below.

The KT Algorithm (Overview)

1. For each hidden and output unit, search for a set S_p of a set of pos-atts whose summed weights exceed the threshold on the unit.

2. For each element p of the S_p set:

   (a) Search for a set S_N of a set of neg-atts so that the summed weights of p plus the summed weights of $N - n$ (where N is the set of all neg-atts and n is an element in S_N) exceed the threshold on the unit.

   (b) With each element n of the S_N set, form a rule, "If p and NOT n, then the concept designated by the unit."

The algorithm includes two modules:

- A search module: It searches for valid rules for a given concept and calls two procedures:

  - The Form-Confirm-Rule procedure: It searches for confirming rules and calls two processes:
    * The Explore-Pos process: It explores combinations of pos-atts.
    * The Negate-Neg process: It adds negated neg-atts to the combinations found in the Explore-Pos process.
  - The Form-Disconfirm-Rule procedure: It searches for disconfirming rules and calls two processes:
    * The Explore-Neg process: It explores combinations of neg-atts.
    * The Negate-Pos process: It adds negated pos-atts to the combinations found in the Explore-Neg process.

- A rewriting module: It rewrites rules containing some symbols designating hidden units which do not correspond to predefined attributes or concepts so that these symbols are eliminated from the rules.

The description of Form-Confirm-Rule and that of Form-Disconfirm-Rule are the same except that the roles of pos-atts and neg-atts are exchanged. So, the exposition is mainly focused on Form-Confirm-Rule.

KT generates rules for each concept corresponding to a hidden or output unit (called a concept node). For each concept, KT explores combinations of relevant attributes (pos-atts and neg-atts) systematically by conducting a tree search. Each node in the tree represents a combination of attributes. A node at the ith level generates its child nodes at the $i+1$th level by adding an additional, available attribute in all possible ways. Moreover, KT employs three heuristics to prune the search space:

- $H1_{KT}$: Given a combination of g pos-atts, if the summed weights of these attributes plus other (up to) $k - g$ strongest, nonconflicting[1] pos-atts are not greater than the threshold on the concept node, then prune the combination.

  Example. Seven positive attributes are being considered:

  $$A_1^+(0.20), A_2^+(0.10), A_3^+(0.10), A_4^+(0.15), A_5^+(0.10), A_6^+(0.14), \text{ and } A_7^+(0.05)$$

  (the number in the parentheses denotes the associated weight linked to the concept node). The bound of rule size k is assumed to be 5. The threshold of the concept node is 0.75. Consider the combination

  $$\{A_1^+, A_2^+, A_3^+\}$$

  The summed weights of these attributes and other 2 $(5 - 3 = 2)$ strongest pos-atts (i.e., A_4^+ and A_6^+) are

  $$0.20 + 0.10 + 0.10 + 0.15 + 0.14 = 0.69$$

  which is less than 0.75 (the threshold). So, the combination is pruned.

- $H2_{KT}$: Given a combination of pos-atts, if the summed weights of these attributes plus all nonconflicting neg-atts are greater than the threshold on the concept node, then keep the combination, but stop generating its successors.

  Example. Suppose there are four negative attributes involved:

  $$A_1^-(-0.10), A_2^-(-0.05), A_3^-(-0.01), \text{ and } A_4^-(-0.03)$$

  The threshold of the concept node is 0.40. Consider the combination

  $$\{A_1^+(0.30), A_2^+(0.15), A_3^+(0.20)\}$$

  Assume that A_2^+ and A_2^- are mutually exclusive. The summed weights of the combination plus all nonconflicting neg-atts are

  $$0.30 + 0.15 + 0.20 - 0.10 - 0.01 - 0.03 = 0.51$$

  which is greater than 0.40 (the threshold). Thus, this heuristic rule succeeds.

- $H3_{KT}$: Given a combination of pos-atts and negated neg-atts (possibly none), if the summed weights of the pos-atts plus nonconflicting neg-atts not in the combination are greater than the threshold on the concept node,

---

[1] Nonconflicting attributes are those that can co-exist. A working definition of nonconflicting attributes is that they (i.e., their corresponding activation levels in the neural network) are not negatively correlated. Two variables are said to be negatively correlated if their correlation coefficient is less than −0.7.

then keep the combination, but stop generating its successors.

Example. Suppose there are four negative attributes involved:

$$A_1^-(-0.20), A_2^-(-0.50), A_3^-(-0.10), \text{ and } A_4^-(-0.30)$$

The threshold of the concept node is 0.35. Consider the combination

$$\{A_1^+(0.20), A_2^+(0.60), A_1^-, A_2^-\}$$

The summed weights of the pos-atts in the combination plus all nonconflicting outside neg-atts are

$$0.20 + 0.60 - 0.10 - 0.30 = 0.40$$

which is greater than 0.35 (the threshold). Thus, this heuristic rule succeeds.

$H1_{KT}$ and $H2_{KT}$ are applied during Explore-Pos and $H3_{KT}$ during Negate-Neg. We call the search a *heuristic search* because the use of these heuristics allows us to avoid exhaustive search. The soundness of the three heuristics will be formally shown later.

KT generates rules from a neural network on a layer-by-layer basis. In each layer, it explores rules with sizes up to k where k is predefined. We can view it as a kind of *beam search*. It should be noted that the largest-possible size of rules relating the input attributes (the attributes describing the instances, e.g., color and size) and the output concepts (the concepts describing the instances, e.g., classes) is k^d where d is the number of layers.

The overall objective of the search module is to find all syntactically legal, *valid* rules, each not subsumed by any other rule. It calls Explore-Pos first. The output of Explore-Pos is a set of all combinations of at most k pos-atts, each of which can confirm the concept if *all* neg-atts are absent. Then, Negate-Neg is applied to each such combination in an attempt to find all rules, each of which can confirm the concept in the absence of some or no neg-atts. In brief, Explore-Pos searches for combinations of pos-atts

$$\{\{A_1^+, ..., A_i^+\}\{...\}...\}$$

such that the summed weights of $A_1^+, ..., A_i^+$ are greater than the threshold. Negate-Neg searches for combinations of pos-atts and negated neg-atts

$$\{\{A_1^+, ..., A_i^+, \neg A_1^-, ..., \neg A_j^-\}\{...\}...\}$$

such that the summed weights of $A_1^+, ..., A_i^+, A_{j+1}^-, ..., A_q^-$ exceed the threshold. Note that $\{A_{j+1}^-, ..., A_q^-\}$ is the complement of $\{A_1^-, ..., A_j^-\}$ with respect to the set of all neg-atts.

The search tree in Explore-Pos starts with an empty set as the root node. As depicted in Figure 14.3, a node is expanded by adding a new (not in the node)

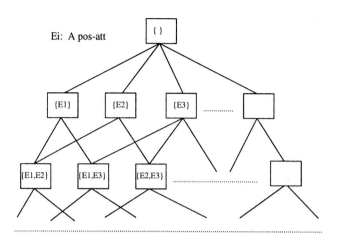

Figure 14.3: The Explore-Pos search.

pos-att in all possible ways. Redundant nodes, nodes with conflicting attributes (such as mutually exclusive attributes), and nodes with more than k attributes are deleted at once. More importantly, the heuristics $H1_{KT}$ and $H2_{KT}$ are applied to prune the search tree. The search ceases when no successor nodes can be generated, and the output of Explore-Pos is all the acceptable nodes in the final tree. The process is summarized below:

1. Pick an unexplored node. If there is no such node, then exit, and the output is all the legitimate nodes in the final tree.

2. Apply the heuristics $H1_{KT}$ and $H2_{KT}$. If they fail, then generate the child nodes.

3. Go to step 1.

If Explore-Pos accepts the combination of the attributes A_1^+ and A_2^+, it may also accept the combination of A_1^+, A_2^+, and A_3^+. Though the latter combination is a superset of the former, they may take different combinations of negated neg-atts in conjunction to form confirming rules, and the subsumption relationship may not exist.

The search tree in Negate-Neg starts with any combination of pos-atts returned by Explore-Pos. Figure 14.4 shows the expansion of a node by adding a new, negated neg-att in all possible acceptable ways. Again, redundant nodes, nodes with conflicting attributes, and nodes with more than k attributes are

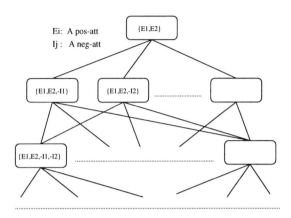

Figure 14.4: The Negate-Neg search.

deleted. The heuristic $H3_{KT}$ is applied constantly. The search terminates when no new nodes can be produced. The output of Negate-Neg is all the nodes to which the heuristic $H3_{KT}$ successfully applies. The process is formulated below:

1. Pick an unexplored node. If there is no such node, then exit.

2. Apply the heuristic $H3_{KT}$. If it fails, then generate the child nodes. Otherwise, put the node in the output set.

3. Go to step 1.

The output of Negate-Neg is a set of premises for confirming the given concept. A confirming rule is formed by putting the conjunction of all members in a premise on the left-hand side and the concept on the right-hand side.

Take a simple example here. Suppose the attributes relevant to a certain concept are A, B, C, D, E, and F. The first three are pos-atts, the rest neg-atts. Their respective associated weights are 0.08, 0.09, 0.03, -0.05, -0.01, and -0.01. Assume that the threshold on the concept node is 0.14. Then, the combination of A and B ($\{A\ B\}$) will be in the output of Explore-Pos since their summed weights are calculated to be 0.17. And the combination of A, B, $\neg D$ ($\{A$, B, $\neg D\}$) will be in the output of Negate-Neg because the summed weights of A, B, E, and F are 0.15.

The procedure Form-Disconfirm-Rule is similar to Form-Confirm-Rule. It searches for combinations of attributes whose summed weights are below, instead of above, the threshold on the concept node. The pruning heuristics are modified accordingly. And the roles of pos-atts and neg-atts are exchanged.

In a multilayer neural network, the distinction between a "concept" and an "attribute" is relative since we can find rules supporting the concept corresponding to a hidden unit (a hidden concept) or use it as an attribute (a hidden attribute) to form rules for a concept at the next higher level.

The purpose of the rewriting module is to eliminate the symbols which refer to some hidden units but are not predefined in the domain. The intended knowledge hierarchy can still be realized. The algorithm is given below:

1. Find a rule (call R_A) whose antecedent contains an undefined (not predefined) symbol. If no such rule exists, then exit.

2. Find all rules (call R_B's) whose consequents reference the symbol.

3. Replace the symbol in R_A by the antecedent of each R_B to generate a new rule. Delete R_A.

4. Go to step 1.

In the process, redundancies, subsumptions, and inconsistencies are removed.

The rewriting procedure is illustrated by the following example. Suppose in layer 1, there is one rule:

- $M_1 \wedge \neg M_2 \longrightarrow C$

"$X \wedge Y \longrightarrow Z$" reads, "If X and Y, then Z." In layer 2, there are three rules:

- $A_1 \wedge \neg B_1 \longrightarrow M_1$

- $A_3 \longrightarrow M_1$

- $B_2 \wedge \neg A_2 \longrightarrow \neg M_2$

Rewriting the rules of layer 1 in terms of the rules of layer 2, we obtain:

- $A_1, \neg B_1, B_2, \wedge \neg A_2 \longrightarrow C$

- $A_3, B_2, \wedge \neg A_2 \longrightarrow C$

The rewriting process is backward in the sense that the antecedent of a rule is rewritten on the basis of rules whose consequents deal with its antecedent. Rewriting starts with the output layer. The rewriting module rewrites rules of one layer every time in terms of rules of the next layer closer to the input of the net.

A sufficient (but not necessary) condition to ensure the validity of rewritten rules is that rules must be rewritten based on rules satisfying the *certainty* condition. The proof is given later. The search module can be programmed to find rules with certainty by tuning up the threshold level. Assume that the activation function is a sigmoid function. When the total input to a neuron is equal to its threshold θ, its activation is 0.5. If the desired activation is 1 (as required by the certainty condition), then the total input should be greater than $\theta + \epsilon$ where ϵ is a small positive real number. The idea is clear from Figure 14.2. When the sigmoid function gets steeper, it approximates the hard-limiting function. In the latter case, the validity condition coincides with the certainty condition.

Experience indicates that rewritten rules are often more specific than necessary. A simple refinement can make the rewritten rule set much more useful. It is done by dropping conditions of each such rule one by one until it begins to cover more negative examples. This refinement often reduces the number of rules.

Since the rewriting procedure may miss some rules, a question is whether we can avoid it. In the case of the neural network with a single hidden layer, the hidden layer can be replaced by a conjunction layer implementing rules extracted for hidden units, and thereby, we convert the neural network to an RBCN where rules are readily identifiable and no rewriting is necessary.

14.3.1   Properties

When KT searches for confirming rules, it does not consider negated pos-atts because a valid rule containing a negated pos-att is subsumed by the rule in which that negated pos-att is deleted and which is still valid. (The proof is simple and hence omitted.) Likewise, KT does not consider negated neg-atts in forming disconfirming rules.

The performance of the rule set generated by KT from a neural network is not necessarily equal to that of the neural network. The network may learn some rules which are invalid according to the validity criterion. The combined effect of these invalid rules may be deleterious to the network performance.

The KT algorithm may miss some exceptional cases for which the rules should be larger than permitted. While it is possible to increase the search width, this may not be cost-effective. Consider a case where KT has extracted rules which cover, say, 95 percent of the training examples. To accommodate the remaining 5 percent of the examples, we may use a simple technique. That is, treat an example as a specific rule, and generalize it by ordering the attributes it possesses and successively removing them one at a time until a certain criterion is met. The attributes may be ordered by some information theoretical measure.

The completeness of the KT algorithm can be considerably improved by using a special procedure to train the neural network. Chapter 4 describes such a training procedure, which involves clustering of hidden units and nullifying of small weights.

A learning program which considers the utility of individual attributes one at a time is referred to as *monothetic*, whereas considering multiple attributes simultaneously is called *polythetic*. In these terms, the decision tree approach is monothetic, whereas the KT algorithm is polythetic. The monothetic approach may miss the case when multiple attributes are weakly predictive separately but become strongly predictive in combination.

The potential number of rules is exponential with the number of attributes involved if no preference criterion is imposed. Assume that there are n attributes under consideration. Without recognizing pos-atts and neg-atts, each attribute may be present in either the positive or the negative form or absent. So, there are 3^n possible combinations of all attributes to form rules. This is the cost of generating rules by exhaustive search. If rule sizes are limited by k, then the cost of rule generation is $O(n^k)$.

Rule evaluation is concerned with the determination of the rule's validity. To evaluate a rule, an exhaustive search will consider all possible combinations of attributes not mentioned by the rule. The cost of evaluating a rule can be as large as $O(2^n)$.

For the search module of the KT algorithm, the rule generation cost in the best case is $O(1)$, and in the worse case $O(p^{k_1} q^{k_2})$ where p is the number of pos-atts, q the number of neg-atts, and k_1 and k_2 nonnegative integers such that $k_1 + k_2 = k$ (k is the predefined upper limit of rule sizes). The rule evaluation cost is $O(1)$. For the rewriting module, the rewriting cost is $O(r_1 r_2^k)$ where r_1 is the number of rules on one layer rewritten based on r_2 rules on another layer.

14.4 Learning in Practical Domains

Rules generated from a neural network can be run by a categorical or noncategorical inference engine (see Chapter 11 "Expert Systems"). In the latter case, we may build an RBCN, as described in Chapter 4. Figure 14.5 shows such an application, in which the rule extraction as performed by KT is used as a kind of regularizing mechanism for the neural network so as to improve its performance. This approach also offers a solution to the problem of overfitting data. As another application, the rules can be refined according to some statistical criterion and used as predictive patterns.

14.4.1 Learning under Noise

Here, we consider three domains as examples. One is the well-known Fisher's iris data set, which is perhaps the best-known data set to be found in the pattern recognition literature. The data set contains 3 classes of 50 instances each, where each class refers to a type of flower, the iris. One class is linearly separable from the other two; the latter are not linearly separable from each other. Each instance in the data set is described by four continuous features. We divided the data set into two equal subsets, A and B, by separating instances at the odd positions from the instances at the even positions in the data set. Then, we ran cross-validation with these two sets. The experiments reported here include three settings. In the first setting, the original data were used and we assumed that it was noise-free. In the second setting, we randomly perturbed 10

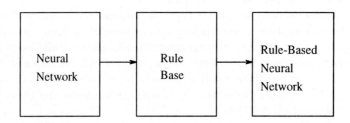

Figure 14.5: Regularization of a neural network. Rule transformation is followed by building a rule-based connectionist network.

percent of the training instances by changing their class labels. For example, an instance originally labeled as iris-setosa was relabeled as iris-viginica. Likewise, in the third setting, we randomly perturbed 20 percent of the training instances. The second and the third experiments were designed to evaluate the ability of noise tolerance. Notice that the principle of cross-validation was applied to all three experimental settings. For example, in the third setting, we perturbed 20 percent of subset A as the training set and used subset B as the test set and then perturbed 20 percent of subset B as the training set and took subset A as the test set.

The second data set divides hepatitis prognosis into two categories: die or live. In this domain, there are 155 instances, each described by 19 features, among which 6 are continuous features and the rest are nominal features. We partitioned the sample into two halves (78 and 77 cases) and ran cross-validation. Like the iris domain, three experimental settings with the noise level at 0 percent (assuming noise free), 10 percent, and 20 percent, respectively, were conducted.

The third data set was obtained from the domain of hypothyroid diagnosis. In this domain, there are 3163 instances available, among which 150 are hypothyroid cases and the rest are negative. Each case is described by 25 features, among which 7 are continuous features and the rest are nominal features. We used all the hypothyroid cases plus the first 150 negative cases in the original data. Again, we created two subsets with 75 hypothyroid and 75 negative cases in each without bias and ran cross-validation. Like the previous two domains, we ran three settings with the noise level at 0 percent, 10 percent, and 20 percent, respectively.

The experimental results are depicted in Figure 14.6. In the iris domain, KT achieved an error rate of 3.3 percent and C4.5 (based on the decision tree algorithm of Quinlan 1983) showed a rate of 6 percent in the absence of noise.

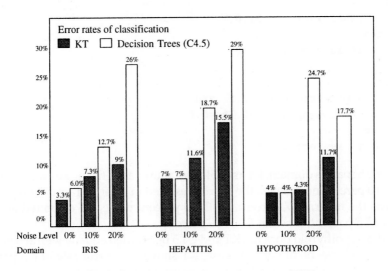

Figure 14.6: Performance evaluation of KT.

KT gained a larger edge over C4.5 as noise was added. At a noise level of 10 percent, KT gave a 7.3 percent error rate, whereas C4.5 yielded a 12.7 percent error rate. In the case of 20 percent noise, the former reached an error rate of 9.0 percent, whereas the latter, 26 percent. The validity constraint appears to bring down the number of rules significantly.

Only five rules were generated by KT at zero noise:

```
R1: If
        petal-length is <=2.7,
    then
        it is setosa.

R2: If
        petal-length is >2.7&<=5.0  and
        petal-width is >0.7&<=1.6,
    then
        it is versicolor.

R3: If
        petal-length is >5.0,
    then
        it is viginica.
```

```
R4: If
        petal-width is >1.6,
    then
        it is viginica.

R5: If

        septal-width is >3.1   and
        petal-length is >2.7&<=5.0,
    then
        it is versicolor.
```

In the hepatitis domain, KT and C4.5 became even in the noise-free condition. At the 10 percent noise level, the former resulted in an error rate of 11.6 percent, whereas the latter, 18.7 percent. With 20 percent noise, KT exhibited an error rate of 15.5 percent, whereas C4.5, 29 percent.

In the hypothyroid domain, KT and C4.5 performed equally well at 0 percent noise. In the case of 10 percent noise, KT showed an error rate of 4.3 percent, whereas C4.5, 24.7 percent. When the noise level increased to 20 percent, the former gave an error rate of 11.7 percent, whereas the latter, 17.7 percent.

In all three domains, KT surpasses C4.5 by a wide margin, consistently for the most part in noisy conditions. The superiority of the neural network in learning rules under uncertainty and the polythetic nature of rule extraction may account for the better results with the KT method.

The results are also consistent with the finding made by Fisher and McKusick (1989) that neural network learning outperforms ID3 on noisy data. Here, we demonstrate that the rules extracted from a trained neural network by KT also outperform those derived from a learned decision tree in noisy conditions.

14.4.2   Learning under Missing Data

Data sets with particular items missing are a common problem. Generally, an item is missing by chance because it has not been recorded or is unavailable for some reason. Sometimes, however, a value is not missing but null. Such cases will be referred to as null values rather than missing values.

Several solutions to missing values have been proposed, such as using a default value, using the most common value, and treating "unknown" as a new value. KT uses a very simple technique to deal with this issue. Whenever an attribute value of a case is missing, all the input units encoding the values of that attribute are clamped at zero when plugging the case into the neural network for training. Note that KT represents an attribute of n values as n attributes, so that making all values 0 does not correspond to any actual value. This solution proves to be effective in domains we have studied. For example, in the domain of hepatitis prognosis, there are 167 missing attribute values, and KT is still able to learn well. However, it would be better to remove cases with many missing values if possible. When abundant cases are available, we can just select those without missing values.

14.4.3 Many-Category Learning

In the iris domain, we learn rules which can classify irises into three categories: iris setosa, iris versicolor, and iris viginica. In the hepatitis domain, we learn rules for predicting "die" or "live." In the hypothyroid domain, we learn rules for diagnosing "hypothyroid" or "negative." When the number of categories (classes) in the domain increases, more interference among different classes rises, and thus more discrimination is needed. A machine learning program which performs well for few-category learning may fall short for many-category learning tasks.

Here, we use soybean (soybean-large) disease classification as an example to show the performance of KT in this respect. In this domain, there are 19 classes, 35 features, and 307 instances. We created two subsets (one with 154 and the other with 153 cases) and ran cross-validation. The error rate for KT was 17.6 percent, whereas C4.5 exhibited an error rate of 60.6 percent.

14.5 Various Rule Extraction Methods

Rules can exist in different formats. The rule extraction algorithm will depend on the kind of rule to be extracted. The if-then rule is a standard format in knowledge-based systems. Rules in this format identified by the rule search program represent the first-level abstraction of the neural network knowledge, although they can be further processed so as to obtain higher levels of abstraction of the network knowledge.

It is a significant advantage if rules can deal with uncertainty. The rule search program only extracts valid rules, but valid rules can also be uncertain. Consider the case of a sigmoid activation function. A (confirming) rule is valid if the target concept is activated in excess of a certain level (viz. 0.5). Since the maximum possible activation is 1, the interval from 0.5 to 1 creates a range of (un)certainty levels that can be associated with rules. Therefore, the rule search program can identify valid rules with or without a degree of certainty. This simple extension greatly increases its applicability.

There is an emerging interest in fuzzy rules, which are rules written under the fuzzy set theory of Zadeh (1965). A fuzzy set is characterized by the membership function which determines the degree of membership of an element in the set. Thus, learning fuzzy rules from a neural network also involves the learning of the membership function. This subject is treated in Chapter 11.

Some networks have special architectures and special training algorithms so that when the networks have been trained, rules are immediately readable from the networks with no or a little search. The KBCNN model (described in

Chapter 4) and the RuleNet (McMillan, Mozer, and Smolensky 1992) are two examples of this approach.

Here, we sample some other rule extraction methods as follows. Gallant's (1988) method is able to find a single rule to explain the conclusion reached by the neural network for a given case. His method involves the ordering of available attributes based upon inference strength (the absolute magnitude of weights). To form a rule, the attribute with the greatest strength among attributes remaining to be considered will be picked. The process continues until the conjunction of picked attributes is sufficiently strong to conclude the concept concerned.

Saito and Nakano's (1988) method can find multiple rules from a trained neural network. Their method searches through the rule space spanned by attributes selected according to given instances. Their method is empirical, observing the input/output behavior of the trained network directly.

Hayashi (1990) describes a simple search technique for extraction of fuzzy rules from a neural network. In his method, the input units are organized as a set of cell groups. In each rule formation cycle, it selects one output cell and one input cell group and does not address the interactions between different cell groups. The weights between the input and the hidden layers are fixed during the learning process. Rule search is conducted directly in the space of primary attributes without involving pattern formation and combination in the hidden layer. The overall search width is limited.

The rule extraction method developed by Towell (1991) is called the NofM method. It explicitly searches for rules of the form

If N of the following M antecedents are true, then . . .

The rules extracted by the NofM method can be viewed as a simplified version of the neural network.

14.6   Summary

Extraction of rules from a neural network is important because it allows us to interpret the network's knowledge and allows the network to explain itself. Furthermore, the rule extracted can be used to build a rule-based connectionist network. This approach can regularize the neural network and prevent it from overfitting the data.

We have addressed almost all the important issues associated with the problem of rule generation from neural networks. We have shown how the network knowledge can be decoded systematically yet heuristically. We have also examined the possible limitation of this process. The soundness of the rule search method has formally been established. The completeness of the method has also been evaluated. It has been shown that the search algorithm is kth-order complete within a single layer. However, through layer-by-layer search, rules with sizes exponential with the network depth can actually be explored. Additionally, the completeness of rule extraction can be considerably improved using a special neural network learning procedure.

Combining neural networks and rule search is an empirically valid method for learning expert rules. Its superiority over the decision tree approach has been demonstrated in noisy conditions. This may be attributed to the better capability of the neural network in handling uncertainty and also the polythetic nature of learning. The rules extracted may outperform the original neural network. A logical explanation for this fact is that we only identify valid rules, whereas the neural network may learn invalid rules.

14.7 Appendix: Formal Bases

In this appendix, we give the formal basis of the KT algorithm. Specifically, the following theorems are proven:

- The rules generated by the search module are sound.

- The search module is kth-order complete where k is the predefined upper bound of rule sizes.

- The rewritten rules generated by the rewriting module are sound.

Theorem 14.1 The rules generated by the search module satisfy the *validity* condition. That is, for any generated rule,

$$R_k: \text{If } A_{j1}^+, \ldots, A_{jn}^+, \neg A_{j1}^-, \ldots, \text{ and } \neg A_{jm}^-, \text{ then } C_j$$

$\text{Act}(C_j) > 0.5$ if the rule's premise holds; that is, if $A_{ji}^+ = 1$, for all $i, 1 \le i \le n$ and $A_{ji}^- = 0$, for all $i, 1 \le i \le m$. Assume that the activation function is a sigmoid function, and A_{ji}^+ and A_{ji}^- denote a pos-att and a neg-att for C_j, respectively.

Let the set $P_k = \{A_{ji}^+ | 1 \le i \le n\} \cup \{A_{ji}^- | 1 \le i \le m\}$ (i.e., the set of all attribute values mentioned in the premise of the rule R_k). Let NET_{rule} be the input to the node C_j from the attribute nodes in P_k. That is,

$$\text{NET}_{\text{rule}} = \sum_{i=1}^{n} W_{ji}^+ A_{ji}^+ + \sum_{i=1}^{m} W_{ji}^- A_{ji}^-$$

where W_{ji}^+ (W_{ji}^-) is the weight associated with A_{ji}^+ (A_{ji}^-), and it is the weight on the connection from the node A_{ji}^+ (A_{ji}^-) to the node C_j. Let NET_{ext} be the input to the node C_j from the nodes X_{ji}'s external to (outside) P_k. We distinguish X_{ji}'s into pos-atts and neg-atts, X_{ji}^+'s and X_{ji}^-'s, with respect to C_j. So,

$$\text{NET}_{\text{ext}} = \sum_{i, X_{ji}^+ \notin P_k} W_{ji}^+ X_{ji}^+ + \sum_{i, X_{ji}^- \notin P_k} W_{ji}^- X_{ji}^-$$

Thus, the activation of C_j is given by

$$\text{Act}(C_j) = F(\text{NET}_{\text{rule}} + \text{NET}_{\text{ext}} - \theta_j) \qquad (14.2)$$

where F is the sigmoid activation function and θ_j is the threshold on the concept C_j. Let $\text{NET}_{\text{ext-ub}}$ and $\text{NET}_{\text{ext-lb}}$ denote the upper bound and the lower bound of NET_{ext}, respectively. Then it is quite obvious that $\text{NET}_{\text{ext-ub}}$ corresponds to the case when all X_{ji}^+'s are 1 and X_{ji}^-'s 0, since the W_{ji}^+ associated with any X_{ji}^+ is positive and the W_{ji}^- with any X_{ji}^- is negative. We call this case S_B. Reversely, $\text{NET}_{\text{ext-lb}}$ occurs when all X_{ji}^+'s are 0 and X_{ji}^-'s 1. This case is called S_W. So,

$$\text{NET}_{\text{ext-lb}} \leq \text{NET}_{\text{ext}} \leq \text{NET}_{\text{ext-ub}}$$

and

$$\text{NET}_{\text{ext-ub}} \geq 0, \ \ \text{NET}_{\text{ext-lb}} \leq 0$$

Given that the rule's premise holds, NET_{rule} is fixed. Because the function F is a monotonically increasing function, the maximum of $\text{Act}(C_j)$ occurs in the situation S_B, and its minimum occurs in the situation S_W. The values of $\text{Act}(C_j)$ in these two extreme cases are denoted by $\text{Act}(C_j)_{\text{ub}}$ and $\text{Act}(C_j)_{\text{lb}}$, respectively. That is,

$$\text{Act}(C_j)_{\text{lb}} \leq \text{Act}(C_j) \leq \text{Act}(C_j)_{\text{ub}}$$

The heuristic $H3_{KT}$ guarantees that

$$\text{NET}_{\text{rule}} + \text{NET}_{\text{ext-lb}} > \theta_j$$

This translates into

$$\text{Act}(C_j)_{\text{lb}} > 0.5$$

since $F(0) = 0.5$. Thus,

$$\text{Act}(C_j) > 0.5$$

The proof is similar for disconfirming rules.

Corollary 14.1 If a rule for the concept C_j is valid, then the NET_{rule} of the rule $> \theta_j$. The reverse is not true. This defines a necessary but not a sufficient condition for the rule's validity.

Lemma 14.1 In the process Explore-Pos, the node (rule) pruned under the heuristic $H1_{KT}$ is not valid, nor are its successor nodes (rules).

Suppose rules are sought for the concept C_j. Consider the node $P = \{A_{j1}^+, ..., A_{jg}^+\}$ which is pruned by $H1_{KT}$. Suppose, the node P forms a premise for the concept C_j, and call the rule R_P. Assume P holds. By $H1_{KT}$,

$$\text{NET}_{\text{rule}} + K \leq \theta_j$$

where K is the sum of the weights of $k - g$ (where k is the maximum rule size allowed) strongest pos-atts external to the rule. Because $\text{NET}_{\text{ext}-\text{lb}} \leq 0$, we obtain

$$\text{NET}_{\text{rule}} + \text{NET}_{\text{ext}-\text{lb}} \leq \text{NET}_{\text{rule}} \leq \text{NET}_{\text{rule}} + K \leq \theta_j \qquad (14.3)$$

In the process Negate-Neg, we may add any number of negated neg-atts to the rule. In the best case, we can make $\text{NET}_{\text{ext}-\text{lb}} = 0$, but still the rule cannot satisfy the validity condition because $\text{NET}_{\text{rule}} < \theta_j$ (from Corollary 14.1). Next, consider a successor node S of P such that $S = \{A_{j1}^+, ..., A_{jg}^+, ..., A_{jh}^+\}$. Let S form another premise of C_j, and call the rule R_S. Again, assume S holds. Let L be the sum of the weights of $k - h$ strongest pos-atts external to the rule. Because attributes like A_{jh}^+ are not necessarily among the $k - g$ strongest, external attributes for the rule R_P, it is clear that

$$\text{NET}_{\text{rule}} \text{ (of } R_S) + L \leq \text{NET}_{\text{rule}} \text{ (of } R_P) + K$$

This fact in conjunction with Eq. 14.3 leads to

$$\text{NET}_{\text{rule}} \leq \text{NET}_{\text{rule}} + L \leq \theta_j$$

with respect to the rule R_S. It means that R_S is not valid either. So, we can simply prune the node P during Explore-Pos.

Lemma 14.2 In the process Explore-Pos, both a (parent) node and its successor nodes which are pruned due to the heuristic $H2_{KT}$ can form valid rules (satisfying the validity condition), and the parent rule subsumes its successor rules.

Suppose the rules are formed for the concept C_j. Let the parent node $P = \{A_{j1}^+, ..., A_{jn}^+\}$. By the heuristic $H2_{KT}$,

$$\sum_{i=1}^{n} W_{ji}^+ A_{ji}^+ + \sum_{i, X_{ji}^- \in N_j} W_{ji}^- > \theta_j \qquad (14.4)$$

where N_j is the set of all neg-atts for C_j. Let the parent node P form a premise for C_j (called the rule R_P), and assume P holds. In this case,

$$\text{NET}_{\text{rule}} = \sum_{i=1}^{n} W_{ji}^+ A_{ji}^+$$

and

$$\text{NET}_{\text{ext}-\text{lb}} = \sum_{i, X_{ji}^- \in N_j} W_{ji}^-$$

From Eq. 14.4,

$$\text{Act}(C_j) \geq \text{Act}(C_j)_{\text{lb}} = F(\text{NET}_{\text{rule}} + \text{NET}_{\text{ext}-\text{lb}} - \theta_j) > 0.5$$

(Note that F(0) = 0.5.) Therefore, the parent node forms a valid rule. Since a successor node is the parent node plus any number (excluding 0) of pos-atts, a successor node S can be represented by $S = \{A_{j1}^+, ..., A_{jn}^+, ..., A_{jp}^+\}$. Let S form another premise for C_j (called the rule R_S), and assume S holds. Then, for R_S,

$$\text{NET}_{\text{rule}} = \sum_{i=1}^{p} W_{ji}^+ A_{ji}^+$$

So, the NET_{rule} of R_S is greater than that of R_P since more positive weights are added. Both rules (R_S and R_P) share the same $\text{NET}_{\text{ext-lb}}$. Thus, the $\text{Act}(C_j)_{\text{lb}}$ due to R_S is greater than that due to R_P. It follows that the $\text{Act}(C_j)$ due to $R_S > 0.5$, and hence the rule R_S is valid. Since $S \supset P$, R_P subsumes R_S.

Lemma 14.3 In the process Negate-Neg, both the (parent) node and its successor nodes pruned by the heuristic $H3_{KT}$ can form valid rules (satisfying the validity condition), and the parent rule subsumes its successor rules.

In the proof of Theorem 14.1, we have shown that the rules generated under $H3_{KT}$ are valid. Here, we only need to show that the successor nodes pruned by $H3_{KT}$ can form valid rules as well and they are subsumed by their parent rule. For the concept C_j, consider the node $P = \{A_{j1}^+, ..., A_{jn}^+\}$ whose successor nodes are pruned by $H3_{KT}$. Each successor node is formed by adding any number (except 0) of negated neg-atts to the parent node. Let R_P and R_S denote the parent rule and any successor rule. Since in calculating $\text{NET}_{\text{ext-lb}}$, we assume every neg-att external to the rule holds, and since the external, neg-atts of R_S are a subset of those of R_P, it follows that the $\text{NET}_{\text{ext-lb}}$ of R_S is less negative than that of R_P. However, R_S and R_P share the same NET_{rule}. As a result, the $\text{Act}(C_j)_{\text{lb}}$ due to R_S is greater than that due to R_P. As R_P is valid, so is R_S. Furthermore, R_S is subsumed by R_P since the premise of the former is a superset of that of the latter.

Theorem 14.2 The search module is kth-order-complete. That is, all valid rules with rule sizes $\le k$ are either in the generated rule set or subsumed by some other rule in the set.

The KT algorithm systematically generates all possible (syntactically legal) rules with sizes limited by k. However, it uses three heuristics to prune the search space: $H1_{KT}$, $H2_{KT}$, and $H3_{KT}$. The first heuristic rule prunes invalid rules (Lemma 14.1), whereas the latter two prune valid but subsumed rules (Lemmas 14.2 and 14.3). Suppose there exists a valid rule with a size $\le k$. This rule must be either found by the KT algorithm or pruned by $H2_{KT}$ or $H3_{KT}$. In the latter case, it must be subsumed by the node whose successor nodes are pruned. The result follows.

Theorem 14.3 The rewritten rules generated by the rewriting module satisfy the *validity* condition. Given rules

R_1: If A_{1i}'s, then M_1,

.

.

.

R_n: If A_{ni}'s, then M_n,
R_o: If $M_1, \ldots,$ and M_n, then C_j.
Rewriting the rule R_o using the first n rules yields
R_r: If A_{1i}'s, $\ldots,$ and A_{ni}'s, then C_j.
If the rules $R_1, \ldots, R_n$ satisfy the *certainty* condition and the rule R_o satisfies the *validity* condition, then the rule R_r satisfies the *validity* condition.

Assume that the premise of the rule R_r holds. We wish to prove that $\text{Act}(C_j) > 0.5$. Since the premise of R_r is the conjunction of those of $R_1, \ldots, R_n$, it follows that each of their premises should hold as well. These rules ($R_1, \ldots, R_n$) satisfy the certainty condition, so

$$M_i = 1 \quad \text{for all } i, 1 \leq i \leq n.$$

Thus, the premise of the rule R_o, which is the conjunction of all M_i's, holds. R_o satisfies the validity condition, and therefore, $\text{Act}(C_j) > 0.5$. Note that the proof is similar when negated attributes are involved.

Theorem 14.4 For the search module of the KT algorithm, the rule generation cost in the best case is $O(1)$, and in the worse case $O(p^{k_1} q^{k_2})$, where p is the number of pos-atts, q the number of neg-atts, and k_1 and k_2 nonnegative integers such that $k_1 + k_2 = k$ (k is the predefined upper limit of rule sizes). The rule evaluation cost is $O(1)$. For the rewriting module, the rewriting cost is $O(r_1 r_2^k)$, where r_1 is the number of rules on one layer rewritten based on r_2 rules on another layer.

A rule generated by the search module involves some pos-atts and some neg-atts with a total number $\leq k$. The cost of generating all possible such rules is $O(p^{k_1} q^{k_2})$, where k_1 and k_2 are nonnegative integers such that $k_1 + k_2 = k$. Note $p^{k_1} q^{k_2} \leq n^k$ where n is the total number of relevant attributes. Thus, the worst cost is polynomial. The practical cost depends on how efficient the pruning heuristics employed by Explore-Pos and Negate-Neg are. In the best case, Explore-Pos and Negate-Neg just generate one or a few nodes, and the cost is $O(1)$.

As to the cost of evaluating a possible rule, KT only evaluates a single case. For example, to evaluate a confirming rule, KT considers only the case when all neg-atts not mentioned by the rule are present (this case corresponding to the situation S_W in the proof of Theorem 14.1). Thus, the cost of evaluation for each possible rule is $O(1)$.

The cost of rewriting depends on the number of combinations of how many ways to rewrite each antecedent in the rule's premise. Suppose the rules on layer 1 are rewritten based on the rules on layer 2, and the numbers of rules are

r_1 and r_2, respectively. For each antecedent in each rule on layer 1, the maximal possible number of ways to rewrite is r_2 (namely, one rewriting based on one rule). So, the cost of rewriting rules is $O(r_1 r_2^k)$.

14.8   References

1. Fisher, D.H., and McKusick, K.B. 1989. An empirical comparison of ID3 and back-propagation. In *Proceedings of IJCAI-89* (Detroit), pp. 788–793.

2. Fu, L.M. 1991. Rule learning by searching on adapted nets. In *Proceedings of AAAI-91* (Anaheim, CA), pp. 590–595.

3. Fu, L.M. 1994. Rule generation from neural networks. *IEEE Transactions on Systems, Man, and Cybernetics*, 24(8).

4. Gallant, S.I. 1988. Connectionist expert systems. *Communications of the ACM*, 31(2), pp. 152–169.

5. Hayashi, Y. 1990. A neural expert system with automated extraction of fuzzy if-then rules and its application to medical diagnosis. In *Advances in Neural Information Processing Systems*. Morgan Kaufmann, San Mateo, CA.

6. McMillan, C., Mozer, M.C., and Smolensky, P. 1992. Rule induction through integrated symbolic and subsymbolic processing. In *Advances in Neural Information Processing Systems*, pp. 969–976. Morgan Kaufmann, San Mateo, CA.

7. Saito, K., and Nakano, R. 1988. Medical diagnostic expert system based on PDP model. In *Proceedings of ICNN*, pp. 255–262.

8. Quinlan, J.R. 1983. Learning efficient classification procedures and their application to chess end games. In *Machine Learning*. Tioga, Palo Alto, CA.

9. Towell, G.G. 1991. Symbolic Knowledge and Neural Networks: Insertion, Refinement, and Extraction. Ph.D. thesis, University of Wisconsin, Madison.

10. Zadeh, L.A. 1965. Fuzzy sets. *Information and Control*, 8, pp. 338–353.

14.9   Problems

1. The trained weights associated with the concept X are given below:

$$W_{XA} = 1, W_{XB} = 2, W_{XC} = 3$$
$$W_{XD} = -1, W_{XE} = -2, W_{XF} = -3$$

where A, B, C, D, E, and F are attributes relevant to X. Each attribute takes on a binary value (0 or 1). Assume that the trained threshold on X is 2. Find all valid rules confirming X.

2. In the previous problem, suppose we are given additional constraints: Attributes A and C are incompatible, and attributes B and E are incompatible. Again, find all valid rules confirming X.

3. Suppose we delete a neg-att from the premise of a valid, confirming rule. Show that the remaining rule is still valid.

4. What network training strategies can be applied to improve the efficiency of the rule search on the neural network?

Chapter 15

Learning Grammars

15.1   Introduction

A number of artificial intelligence and pattern recognition systems employ formal grammars to represent concepts. *Grammatical inference* (Fu 1982) is defined as the problem of learning a grammar from a set of training instances. The origin of grammar learning can be traced to the middle 1950s with the development of formal grammars for modeling the structure of natural language (Chomsky 1957, 1965). Interest in this problem area has encouraged the development of computer programs which assist researchers in constructing grammars for understanding unfamiliar languages. In addition, researchers in the field of pattern recognition use grammars to describe handwritten characters and visual scenes. These researchers' interest has created a need for grammatical-inference techniques.

A grammar is a system of rules describing a language and determining which sentences are allowed in the language. Grammars can describe natural languages (e.g., English) and formal languages (e.g., the computer language C). In natural languages, grammar rules are the generally accepted conventions of constructing sentences. In formal languages, grammars are often more restricted. A formal grammar for a language determines whether a given sentence is grammatical (i.e., in the language) or ungrammatical (not in the language). Thus, the grammar is a description of a potentially infinite set of all valid sentences in the language.

The task of learning a grammar can be viewed as learning the concept "grammatical sentence." Most languages are too complex to be described by a single rule. Instead, a grammar is usually written as a set of rules that describe the structure of the language. For example, a natural-language sentence (S) is a noun phrase (NP) followed by a verb phrase (VP), represented by

<S> → <NP><VP>

This rule describes the overall structure of a sentence. A noun phrase and a verb phrase can be further described by other rules. A grammar can thus be built out of a set of phrase-structure rules (also known as productions). In this way, the concept "grammatical sentence" is broken down into subconcepts like the noun phrase and the verb phrase. Such subconcepts are combined according to the grammar rules. Thus, determining whether a sentence is grammatical involves the sequential application of these rules.

Aside from natural-language understanding, another important application for grammatical inference is in the area of *syntactic pattern recognition*, which is based on concepts from formal-language theory. The syntactic approach to pattern recognition offers the structure-handling capability lacked by the decision-theoretic approach. In the syntactic approach, we create a grammar for each class of objects. The grammar describes the structural relationships involved in decomposing a pattern into subpatterns or primitives. For example, a quadrilateral can be defined syntactically as the concatenation of four lines in a closed loop. An object is classified as a specific class if the object is in the language generated by the class-corresponding grammar.

In the subsequent sections, we describe formal grammars, examine the limitations of grammatical inference, and review symbolic methods for learning grammars. Then, we explore the neural network approach to the same problem. In particular, we describe how to learn symbolic rules under this approach.

15.2   Formal Grammars

A basic system studied in formal-language theory includes a finite set of rules for generating a set of strings in a specific language. The syntax of these rules is described by a *grammar*, which is formally defined by a four-tuple (N, Σ, P, S), where

- N is a finite set of *nonterminals*, or variables.

- Σ is a finite set of *terminals*, or constants.

- P is a finite set of *productions*, or rewriting rules, in the form of $\alpha \rightarrow \beta$.

- S is an element of the nonterminal alphabet and is called the *start* symbol.

It is required that N and Σ be disjoint sets. Let alphabet V be the set N $\cup$ Σ. In a production $\alpha \rightarrow \beta$, α is in V^*NV^* and β is in V^*, where $*$ is the Kleene-star operator denoting any number (including zero) of occurrences of the symbol it follows. This production is interpreted as follows: String α may be rewritten as β, and α must contain at least one nonterminal.

One useful way of defining grammars (and hence languages) is called the Chomsky hierarchy, which is shown in Table 15.1. In the table, V^+ denotes the set $V^* - \{\lambda\}$ where λ is the *empty string*. The context-sensitive grammar describes the fact that a nonterminal can be rewritten only in the context of the surrounding substrings. An equivalent definition for this type of grammar is

Table 15.1: The Chomsky hierarchy.

Type	Grammar	Productions
0	Recursively enumerable	Unrestricted
1	Context-sensitive	$\theta A \delta \rightarrow \theta \rho \delta$ (θ and δ in V^*, ρ in V^+, and A in N)
2	Context-free	$A \rightarrow \alpha$ (A in N and α in V^+)
3	Regular	$A \rightarrow aB$ or $A \rightarrow a$ (A and B in N and a in Σ)

that for any production $\alpha \rightarrow \beta$, the length (i.e., the number of symbols) of β should not be less than that of α. That is, no length-reducing rule is allowed. It is important to note that all regular grammars are context-free, all context-free grammars are context-sensitive, and all context-sensitive grammars are unrestricted. By convention, a language is classified as the type of the most restricted grammar that generates it.

Recursively enumerable and context-sensitive grammars give important results in computation theory. Context-free and regular grammars are important in language theory and syntactic pattern analysis. A large body of work on context-free parsing (i.e., assigning a structure to each grammatical string) has been developed in compilers for programming languages.

To rewrite strings in an orderly manner, we either rewrite only the single leftmost nonterminal in the existing string (called the *leftmost derivation*) or only the rightmost nonterminal (called the *rightmost derivation*) in each step. Either derivation strategy does not restrict the language generated by a grammar. We generally take the leftmost derivation. A grammar is used not only for generating a language but also for recognizing valid sentences (strings or patterns) in a language.

For every grammar, there exists a single language (the set of all strings of terminal symbols derivable from the start symbol by the application of a finite number of productions) and an automation (the machine that recognizes the valid sentences in the language). For example, regular languages can be recognized by a *finite state machine*, where computation is modeled as the transition from one of a finite number of states to another (see Figure 15.1). One state is marked as the start state. One or more states may be marked as final states. The transition from one state to another is determined by the current input symbol. Suppose the machine implements grammar A for class X. If the machine is in a final state and there is no more input, then the input string is classified as X; else it is not. Note that for a given language, there may exist many grammars, which may not all be equivalent in efficiency and usefulness.

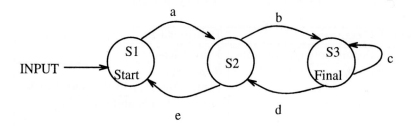

Recognize: ab, abc, abcc, ...

abdb, abdeab, abcdb, abccdeab, ...

...

Figure 15.1: A finite state machine.

In the natural language, both regular and context-free grammars are inadequate, though a finite state machine can be used for lexical analysis and a context-free parser for syntactic analysis. It appears that a machine of the power of a Turing machine is necessary for recognizing natural sentences. *Augmented transition networks* (ATNs) (Woods 1970) provide a way of doing this. An ATN can be viewed as a finite state machine in which the transition arcs between states are associated with words as well as various procedures.

Traditional grammars generate one-dimensional strings and can be used to recognize sequential patterns such as in natural-language sentences or genetic code sequences. To deal with two- or three-dimensional structural patterns, context-free *graph grammars* have been developed that construct a graph of terminal nodes instead of a string of terminal symbols. There are other extensions of context-free grammars.

In so-called stochastic grammars, each production is assigned a probability. During the derivation process, productions are selected according to their assigned probabilities. The probability for the occurrence of a sentence in the language is computed as the product of the probabilities of productions in its derivation. Stochastic grammars have been used for pattern recognition in noisy and uncertain conditions.

Sometimes, the structure generated by a grammar is not so meaningful or useful. Chomsky (1965) developed the theory of *transformational grammar* in which the structure derived from a context-free grammar (called a deep structure) is further altered by transformation rules (into so-called surface form). This process is connected to how a child learns a language.

15.3 Theoretical Limitations

It is useful to view grammatical inference as a search through a rule space of all possible context-free grammars for a grammar that is consistent with training instances. The training instances have been classified by a teacher to indicate whether or not they are grammatical. Under what conditions is it possible to learn the correct context-free language from a set of training instances? This question has been investigated, and several results have been obtained. The most important result is that it is impossible to learn the correct language (or grammar) from positive examples alone. Gold (1967) proved that if a program is given an infinite sequence of positive examples (sentences known to be in the language), the program cannot determine a grammar for the correct context-free language in any finite time. This is because there are too many possible languages to be considered between two extremes. One extreme is the most general (universal) language, which contains all possible sentences. The other is the most specific language, which contains all the sentences seen so far.

In most situations, however, the above limitation can be coped with by exploiting additional information so that a reasonable language, and its grammar, can be learned. Possible sources of this additional information include:

- Knowledge concerning the grammatical structure, the type of grammar, and the prior distribution of possible grammars

- Semantical constraints

- Negative examples

According to studies in cognitive psychology, people are able to learn natural language almost entirely from positive examples. One important source of information may be the meaning of sentences. Some grammars are ruled out consciously or subconsciously simply because they are meaningless. Likewise, a computer program can incorporate semantic constraints for detecting impossible grammars. On the other hand, negative examples can help the program eliminate grammars that are overly general. The use of near-miss negative examples allows the rule space to rapidly converge.

15.4 Symbolic Methods

Learning a grammar from a set of variable-length strings or variable-sized structures could be more difficult than learning a concept from a set of instances described by a fixed number of attributes. In the former case, the learner must be able to extract similar features on relative rather than absolute positions in structures. Despite this fact, learning methods are similar.

Two basic learning strategies are top-down and bottom-up. The first strategy generates hypotheses from a model and then tests them against data. The second strategy generates hypotheses and refines them according to data. Also, we can identify two major learning mechanisms: generalization and specialization. Take an example here. Any one of the following grammars can explain the string ab:

- G1: $S \rightarrow ab$

- G2: $S \rightarrow AB, A \rightarrow a, B \rightarrow b$

- G3: $S \rightarrow Ab, A \rightarrow a$

- G4: $S \rightarrow aB, B \rightarrow b$

These possible grammars are refined by applying generalization or specialization operators as more strings are seen.

Barr, Feigenbaum, and Cohen (1981) describe four symbolic methods for learning context-free grammars from training instances:

- *Enumerative* or *generate-and-test* methods (e.g., Horning 1969) propose possible grammars and then test them against the data. Heuristics include:

  - Find the grammar that maximizes the posterior probability after observing the training sample.

  - Generate only *deductively acceptable* grammars. A grammar is deductively acceptable if it generates every instance in the training sample and if every production in the grammar is used to derive at least one of the training instances.

  - Search through the set of all possible grammars ordered from most specific to most general. Remove grammars inconsistent with training instances until one grammar remains, which is the target grammar.

- *Constructive methods* (e.g., Fu 1975) usually learn from positive examples only. They collect information regarding the distribution and repetition of substrings in the language and use it to build a grammar. Heuristics include:

  - Create a nonterminal symbol for a class of strings that appear in the same context in different sentences—an analysis called the *distribution analysis*.

  - Seek repetition and model it as a recursive production. Consider, for example, the training set $\{a, aa, aaa, aaaa\}$. We can create productions: $A \rightarrow a$ and $A \rightarrow Aa$. As another example, suppose in the string uv^*xy^*z, v and y are always repeated an equal number of times in the language. Such strings can be represented by a self-embedding production of the form $X \rightarrow VXY$.

- *Refinement methods* (e.g., Knobe and Knobe 1977) start with a hypothesis grammar and gradually improve it using various heuristics in order to accommodate new training instances. Heuristics include:

  - Generalization by merging: Replace two nonterminals by another common nonterminal in the grammar.
  - Generalization by disjunction: For two strings s_1 and s_2, create two rules $A \rightarrow s_1$ and $A \rightarrow s_2$.
  - Specialization by splitting: Replace some occurrences of a nonterminal N by N_1 and others by N_2 in the grammar.
  - Replace $A \rightarrow a$ and $A \rightarrow aa$ by $A \rightarrow Aa$.
  - When string s occurs many times on the right-hand side of productions, create a new nonterminal A, replace all occurrences of s by A, and add the production $A \rightarrow s$ to the grammar.

- *Semantics-based methods* (e.g., Anderson 1977) employ semantic constraints to guide the search for correct grammars. Most of these methods have been developed to model language acquisition by children. Heuristics include:

  - Incorporate semantic information in the syntactic structure of the language.
  - Learn transformation rules which convert meaning-bearing deep structures into given sentences.

15.5   The Neural Network Approach

The success of symbolic methods depends on the heuristics they employ. Implementation of these heuristics is often tedious. The neural network approach has recently emerged as a promising alternative. After being presented with a sufficient number of instances, the neural network can automatically learn grammars of certain types by self-adaptation or self-organization. A lot of programming effort can be saved in this way. Most neural networks devoted to this application are at the experimental stage, and the grammars they can learn are of limited complexity. In this section, we examine the neural network architecture and the network training algorithm developed for this purpose. A particular emphasis is placed on how to extract symbolic grammar rules from the trained neural network.

In the first place, the neural network approach must be able to represent training instances (strings of symbols for one-dimensional structures). Learning grammars from sequences of fixed length is easier than from those of variable length. In the former case, one can use a fixed number of input units to encode each sequence during training so that the first unit (or the first group) encodes the first symbol, the second unit the second symbol, and so forth. In the latter case, one may set the number of input units according to the maximum possible length. This length-based approach to determine the size of the input layer is inefficient when sequences are long and especially so in the second case when at least one sequence is long.

Two options exist for selecting the neural network architecture: feedforward and recurrent. The main difficulty with the feedforward network lies in the fact that it is weak in learning the implicit *precedence* relationship in sequences, and this relationship is a critical component of grammars. In contrast, the recurrent network exhibits the capability of learning and encoding such a relationship in the hidden layer where recurrent loops are permitted. For example, we wish the network to learn "a comes before c and c comes before g" regardless of their positions in sequences. Another benefit the recurrent network can offer is the *real-time* handling of the input. Such a network can consider one symbol of a string rather than a whole string at a time, remember some aspects of the past, and then integrate the information collected along the time axis. This ability eliminates the need to distinguish between fixed-length and variable-length inputs. Furthermore, a network with a small input buffer can handle even infinitely long sequences. Cleeremans, Servan-Schreiber, and McClelland (1989), Giles et al. (1992), Pollack (1991), Sun et al. (1990), and Williams and Zipser (1989) have addressed the use of recurrent neural networks in learning grammars. Both regular and context-free grammars can be learned by such networks.

In recurrent neural networks, recurrency involves the hidden or the output layer or both. Figure 15.2 shows a neural network architecture we suggest for learning grammars, which is based on that proposed by Elman (1990). Chapter 10 "Learning Spatiotemporal Patterns" has more discussion on this topic.

Hertz, Krogh, and Palmer (1991) have collected several learning algorithms for recurrent neural networks. The *real-time recurrent learning* (RTRL) algorithm (Williams and Zipser 1989) has proved to be useful for learning grammars. The algorithm is on-line and incremental and can deal with sequences of arbitrary length. It is named RTRL because weight change can occur in real time during the presentation of the input and the output sequences.

Like standard backpropagation in feedforward networks, RTRL minimizes mean squared error by gradient descent. In fact, one can think of RTRL as backpropagation learning adapted to the recursive nature of computation. This is the basis of how the learning rule is derived.

The Real-Time Recurrent Learning Algorithm (Adapted)

- **Weight Initialization**

  Set all weights and node thresholds to small random numbers.

- **Calculation of Activation**

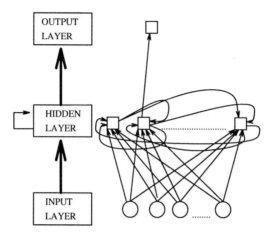

Figure 15.2: A recurrent neural network architecture for learning grammars with recurrency in the hidden layer.

1. The activation level of an input unit is determined by the symbol presented to the network. Each training instance consists of a string of symbols, and at each time step, only one symbol is presented to the network. The activation levels of input units are reset for each symbol presentation.

2. The activation level $O_j(t)$ of a hidden and output unit at time t is determined by

$$O_j(t) = F(H_j(t-1)) = F(\sum_i W_{ji} O_i(t-1) + I_j(t-1))$$

where W_{ji} is the weight from unit i in the hidden layer, I_j is the input from the input layer, and F is a sigmoid function:

$$F(a) = \frac{1}{1+e^{-a}}$$

The activation levels of hidden and output units are initialized to zeros at and only at the beginning of each string.

- **Weight Training**[1]

---

[1]The complexity of a single learning trial is $O(N^4)$ for N fully recurrent units since there are $O(N^3)$ derivatives to maintain and each derivative takes $O(N)$ time to update.

1. Adjust weights by

$$W_{ji}(t+1) = W_{ji}(t) + \Delta W_{ji}(t)$$

where $W_{ji}(t)$ is the weight from unit i to unit j at time t and ΔW_{ji} is the weight adjustment.

2. The weight change is computed by

$$\Delta W_{ji}(t) = -\eta \frac{\partial E(t)}{\partial W_{ji}} = \eta \sum_k E_k(t) \frac{\partial O_k(t)}{\partial W_{ji}}$$

where η is a trial-independent learning rate,

$$E(t) = \frac{1}{2} \sum_k (E_k(t))^2$$

and

$$E_k(t) = \begin{cases} T_k(t) - O_k(t) & \text{if } T_k \text{ is defined at time } t \\ 0 & \text{else} \end{cases}$$

where $T_k(t)$ is the desired (target) output activation and $O_k(t)$ is the actual output activation at time t for output unit k. In the implementation, one hidden unit is taken as the only output unit. The last derivative can be found by

$$\frac{\partial O_k(t)}{\partial W_{ji}} = F'(H_k(t-1))(\delta_{kj} O_i(t-1) + \sum_l W_{kl} \frac{\partial O_l(t-1)}{\partial W_{ji}})$$

and

$$\frac{\partial O_k(0)}{\partial W_{ji}} = 0$$

3. Repeat iterations until convergence. Note that weight training occurs at the end of each string rather than each symbol.

When applying RTRL to the task of learning grammars, we restrict that weight change be performed at the end of each instance string. The desired (target) activation level of the output unit is either 1 for positive examples or 0 for negative examples. Suppose each input unit encodes a particular symbol. At each discrete time step, one symbol from the instance string activates one input unit (to the level 1), and the other input units are zero. However, the activations of hidden and output units are accumulative over a string. The differences between the feedforward and recurrent learning algorithms are obvious from the detailed adapted algorithm, as given above.

Giles et al. (1992) applied second-order recurrent neural networks to grammar learning and claimed their advantage over first-order (ordinary) networks in the aspect of convergence. In a second-order network,

$$O_j(t) = F(\sum_{i,k} W_{jik}O_i(t-1)I_k(t-1))$$

15.6 Learning Rules from Neural Networks

The grammar learned by a neural network can be used to generate or classify sentences or objects. If the neural network performs very well and the only concern is "performance," then it seems unnecessary to understand the grammar written in the neural network language (namely, connection weights). However, this is often not the case, because the neural network may well be entrapped in a local minimum or because human users wish to understand the grammar so as to interactively participate in the learning process or to simply satisfy their desire of knowing. Giles et al. (1992) showed that the extracted symbolic grammar outperforms the neural network from which it was extracted in classifying unseen sentences in many cases. This result reflects the fact that the neural network is prone to local minima, and the process of rule extraction regularizes what the neural network has learned. In this section, we address the problem of extracting grammar rules from a trained neural network. We divide approaches to this problem into *the state space method* and *the weight space method*.

15.6.1 The State Space Method

Recall that a regular grammar can be automated by a finite state machine. This motivates the view of the neural network as a state-based machine in which state transition occurs in response to an input. The basic assumption is that the neural network can form fairly well separated regions or clusters of states during training, which represent corresponding states in a finite state machine. Giles et al. (1992) have developed this idea into the *dynamic state partition* (DSP) procedure.

A definition of a "state" in the neural network is an activation pattern of the hidden layer. Suppose there are N hidden units, each with two states. Then, there are 2^N possible neural network states. In the recurrent learning algorithm, we assume that the activation range of neural units is continuous from 0 to 1. If we partition this range into q subranges, then there exist q^N possible regions in the neural network state space. In practice, it is much less since many regions are never reached. This clustering heuristic is used by the DSP procedure. Other clustering techniques such as that given by Cleeremans et al. (1989) are also available for this task.

The next step of rule extraction is construction of a state (region) transition diagram. Given an input symbol a, we can find a pair of states S_1 and S_2

such that S_1 is changed to S_2 in response to the symbol a. The state transition diagram is drawn based on all such transition pairs, each of which is associated with a symbol. It is then a simple matter to write a transition as a grammar production. In the above example, we write

$$S_1 \rightarrow aS_2$$

If $S_1 = S_2$, a loop is formed in the state transition graph.

The transition digraph (directed graph) can be further minimized by means of standard minimization algorithms as described by Hopcroft and Ullman (1979). The minimization procedure will remove redundant and unnecessary states in the graph. A grammar can be reduced to another equivalent one if both give rise to the same language. To see this, consider an example. A set of grammar rules

$$S_1 \rightarrow aS_3$$
$$S_2 \rightarrow aS_3$$
$$S_1 \rightarrow bS_2$$
$$S_2 \rightarrow bS_2$$

can be simplified as

$$S_1 \rightarrow aS_3$$
$$S_1 \rightarrow bS_1$$

by deleting state S_2.

In general, the state space method consists of the following steps.

The State Space Method Based on DSP

1. Define neural network states.

2. Form the state transition graph.

3. Minimize the graph.

4. Write the minimized graph as a set of productions.

The major issue with this approach is how to partition the neural network space in order to obtain the best grammar, since different ways of partitioning may end up with different symbolic grammars. A heuristic is to try various conditions to generate different grammars and favor the simplest grammar with the smallest number of states.

In its original form, the DSP method only extracts regular grammars, despite the fact that recurrent neural networks are able to learn both regular and context-free grammars.

15.6.2   The Weight Space Method

The weight space method forms rules by searching the weight space, extended from the *KT* algorithm (see Chapter 14 "Rule Generation from Neural Networks"). A basic idea is that if the sum of a set of input weights for a neural node always exceeds its threshold, then the corresponding combination of inputs always activates the neural node, and so a rule can be formed. Thus, rule extraction does not involve identifying the state of the neural network.

In this method, there is direct correspondence between a grammar and the neural network implementing it. Figure 15.3 shows such correspondence. Each symbol defined in the grammar is mapped into a node in the neural network: A terminal symbol designates an input unit, a nonterminal symbol a hidden unit, and the start symbol the output unit. This mapping strategy suggests that we can build a recurrent rule-based connectionist network (RBCN) for learning new or improving existing grammars.

We view the grammar learning problem as concept learning and accordingly reverse the directionality of the implication relationship in rules when they are mapped into the neural network. For example, the grammar rule

$$S \rightarrow AB$$

which says S can be rewritten as AB, is implemented as

$$S \leftarrow AB$$

which now says AB infers (or predicts) S. This view is especially important in pattern recognition.

In a grammar rule, temporal order is implicitly present among the symbols in its premise. For example, in the grammar rule $S \leftarrow AB$, A must be followed by B and not the reverse in inferring S. This fact distinguishes a grammar rule from an ordinary classification (or decision) rule. In the latter case, it does not matter whether we say

If A and B, then X

or

If B and A, then X

While feedforward neural networks can successfully learn rules in many classification tasks such as medical diagnosis, their failure to recognize the implicit temporal relationship in grammars prohibits their general use in learning grammars. One exception is when training instances are fixed-length sentences. In this case, temporal relationship can be explicitly encoded during training, and there is no need to learn it.

Recurrent neural networks can learn the temporal relationship in sequences. One may be curious about how such networks can learn to distinguish between "A before B" and "B before A." Let us return to the example of Figure 15.3.

Grammar:

S ⟶ AB
A ⟶ a
A ⟶ c
B ⟶ b
B ⟶ d

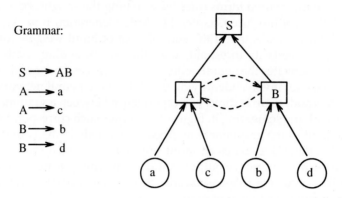

Figure 15.3: A neural network architecture for implementing grammars.

Assume that there is a strong negative inhibition from node B on node A but not the reverse. If A appears first, it will not be inhibited since B is not there, and A will then be scaled up by the nonlinearity in the node. Later, B steps in, but it cannot counteract the full activation of node A. Consider another possible scenario. If B comes first, it will impose an inhibitory wave on A, and when A emerges, its activation is scaled down to zero by the nonlinearity. Consequently, only "A followed by B" will activate the node S, but not in the other way. Although this exposition may help one conceptualize the behavior of the recurrent neural network, its complexity can be far beyond this.

When the recurrent network is employed, the KT algorithm cannot be immediately applied to learn grammar rules because of several considerations:

- In grammar rules, there are no negated attributes such as "not A." Only combinations of positive attributes need to be explored.

- Hidden units corresponding to nonterminal symbols should be preserved.

- Distinctions should be made between rules for recognizing and those for generating valid sentences of a given language. The former may be more general (or discriminative) than the latter. The KT algorithm will extract the first kind of rule, which can be transformed into the second kind by making rules more characteristically descriptive of training instances.

- Some heuristics should be introduced to hypothesize the precedence relationship among symbols in the rule's antecedent:

  - The precedence relationship between nonterminals: One heuristic is to check the weights W_{ij} and W_{ji} for any two hidden units. If

W_{ij} (the weight from node j to node i) is less positive or more negative than W_{ji}, then the symbol of node i precedes that of node j. Conflict resolution is necessary for cases like "$A < B$, $B < C$, and $C < A$" where "$<$" denotes precedence. A resolution strategy is to calculate the sum of weights from all the other symbols and order them according to which one is less positive or more negative.

- The precedence relationship between a terminal and a nonterminal: Since there is no recurrency between a terminal and a nonterminal, we check the precedence relationship between nonterminals excited by the terminal and that nonterminal.

The weight space method includes the following steps.

The Weight Space Method for Learning Grammar Rules

1. Apply the RTRL algorithm.

2. Apply the KT algorithm (adapted for extracting grammar rules).

3. Hypothesize the precedence relationships among the symbols in the rule's antecedent.

4. Test the grammar against training instances. Remove grammar rules which are not used for successful prediction of any training instance.

Inasmuch as rules learned by the weight space method permit any combination of terminal and nonterminals in their premises, both regular and context-free grammar rules can be extracted. This is the advantage of this method over the state space method. On the other hand, the number of nonterminals learned by the weight space method is bounded by that of hidden units in the neural network used.

15.7 Summary

Learning grammars is a special case of learning time sequences. A learning program devoted to this task must be able to learn the temporal relationship implicit in training sequences. Viewing grammatical inference (i.e., the problem of learning grammars from examples) as concept learning, existing techniques for the latter can be extended to the former. However, heuristics characteristic of grammar rules such as distribution and repetition analyses as well as the semantics in the language are very instrumental to the learning process.

Since implementation of these heuristics and semantics could be tedious, the neural network approach shows promise to this problem. Presented with examples, the network can learn grammars by self-adaptation. Thus, much programming effort can be saved. In this approach, recurrent networks offer nonlinear memory in the hidden layer which can aggregate previous information along the time axis, and are hence well-suited for learning grammars. The memory size need not be proportional to the number of training instances, nor need the size of the input buffer, to the length of sequences. These networks can handle both fixed-length and variable-length sentences and learn both regular and context-free grammars. In real-time recurrent learning, the network is run on-line and incrementally updates its knowledge.

Symbolic grammar rules can be extracted from a trained neural network. The state space method identifies particular regions of the neural network state space and constructs a state transition graph, which can be converted to grammar productions. The weight space method, on the other hand, searches for rules in the weight space, obviating the "state" concept of the neural network. In comparison, the weight space method is more general than the state space method, since the former can extract both regular and context-free grammars, whereas the latter (in its original form) only regular grammars. Moreover, the state space method explores states in a number exponential with that of hidden units, while the weight space method learns nonterminal symbols in a number linear with that.

15.8   References

1. Anderson, J.R. 1977. Induction of augmented transition networks. *Cognitive Science*, 1, pp. 125–157.

2. Barr, A., Feigenbaum, E.A., and Cohen, P.R. 1981. *The Handbook of Artificial Intelligence*. Morgan Kaufmann, Los Angeles.

3. Chomsky, N. 1957. *Syntactic Structures*. Mouton, The Hague.

4. Chomsky, N. 1965. *Aspects of the Theory of Syntax*. MIT Press, Cambridge, MA.

5. Cleeremans, A., Servan-Schreiber, D., and McClelland, J. 1989. Finite state automata and simple recurrent neural networks. *Neural Computation*, 1(3), p. 372.

6. Elman, J.L. 1990. Finding structure in time. *Cognitive Science*, 14, pp. 179–211.

7. Fu, K.S. 1975. Grammatical inference: Introduction and survey. *IEEE Transactions on Systems, Man, and Cybernetics*, SMC-5, pp. 95–111.

8. Fu, K.S. 1982. *Syntactic Pattern Recognition and Applications.* Prentice-Hall, Englewood Cliffs, NJ.

9. Giles, C.L., Miller, C.B., Chen, D., Sun, G.Z., Chen, H.H., and Lee, Y.C. 1992. Extracting and learning an unknown grammar with recurrent neural networks. In *Advances in Neural Information Processing Systems 4.* Morgan Kaufmann, San Mateo, CA.

10. Gold, E. 1967. Language identification in the limit. *Information and Control,* 16, pp. 447–474.

11. Hertz, J., Krogh, A., and Palmer, R.G. 1991. *Introduction to the Theory of Neural Computation.* Addison-Wesley, Reading, MA.

12. Hopcroft, J.E., and Ullman, J.D. 1979. *Introduction to Automata Theory, Languages, and Computation.* Addison-Wesley, Reading, MA.

13. Horning, J.J. 1969. A study of grammatical inference. Report No. CS-139, Computer Science Dept., Stanford University.

14. Knobe, B., and Knobe, K. 1977. A method for inferring context-free grammars. *Information and Control,* 31, pp. 129–146.

15. Pollack, J.B. 1991. The induction of dynamical recognizers. *Machine Learning,* 7(2/3), p. 227.

16. Sun, G.Z., Chen, H.H., Giles, C.L., Lee, Y.C., and Chen. D. 1990. Connectionist pushdown automata that learn context-free grammars. In *Proceedings of IJCNN* (Washington, DC), vol. I, p. 577.

17. Williams, R.J., and Zipser, D. 1989. A learning algorithm for continually running fully recurrent neural networks. *Neural Computation,* 1(2), p. 270.

18. Woods, W.A. 1970. Transition network grammars for natural-language analysis. *Communications of the ACM,* 13, pp. 591–606.

15.9   Problems

1. A finite state machine uses the following grammar rules:

$$S_1 \rightarrow 1\, S_2$$
$$S_2 \rightarrow 1\, S_1$$
$$S_2 \rightarrow 0\, S_2$$

Assume that S_1 is the start state and S_2 may be a final state. What kind of strings can be accepted by this machine?

2. A neural network is used to learn a regular grammar. After the network has been trained, we identify the state change in response to an input symbol as follows:

Input symbol	Before state	After state
a	S_1	S_2
b	S_1	S_1
a	S_2	S_2
b	S_2	S_3
a	S_3	S_2
b	S_3	S_3

(a) Write down the grammar rules.

(b) What kind of strings can be recognized by this network?

3. A recurrent neural network has one output unit X, a hidden layer with two hidden units M and N, and two input units A and B. Assume that the activation function is a hard-limiting function which produces a binary output (0 or 1). The thresholds associated with nodes X, M, and N are 5, 3, and 2, respectively. The trained weights are given below:

$$W_{XM} = 3, W_{XN} = 4, W_{MN} = -6, W_{NM} = 2$$
$$W_{MA} = 4, W_{MB} = 2, W_{NA} = 1, W_{NB} = 3$$

where W_{ji} is the weight from unit i to unit j.

(a) Given an instantaneous input (1, 1) at time 0, run the network. Will it reach a stable point? Write down the result.

(b) Given an instantaneous input (0, 1) at time 0 and another instantaneous input (1, 0) at time 1, run the network again. Write down the result.

(c) What is the grammar rule extracted from this network?

4. Physicians use the Electroencephalogram (EEG) to detect epilepsy. The spikes in the EEG often suggest the underlying brain pathology. Suppose we use a neural network for this task domain. The neural network will accept an EEG signal of variable length. To train such a network, which algorithm would be most appropriate?

Part III

Case Studies

Chapter 16

Genetic Pattern Recognition

16.1   Introduction

To understand what genetic patterns are, we need to define the basic terminology first. Roughly speaking, the development, appearance, and behavior of a biological being are determined by its *genes*. Genes are carried by the chromosomes in the cell nucleus. The number of chromosomes varies with the species. The biochemical composition of a chromosome is characterized by a long string (sequence) of DNA nucleotides (a huge biochemical molecule). Genes are biochemical units that are identified from the DNA sequence and carry hereditary characteristics from parent to offspring. The forms of a gene are called *alleles*. Genotype refers to the genetic constitution of an individual or organism, while phenotype denotes the observable characteristics (traits) of the individual as determined by the genotype and the environment. The collection of all the genes of an organism is called a *genome*. A genetic pattern means either a combination of genes of different forms or a DNA nucleotide subsequence.

Sequencing an entire genome is a systematic approach for unraveling the secret of life. However, to know the DNA sequence does not necessarily mean to understand it. Some part of the sequence may control the expression of the genes of another part. Some genes may not be expressive at all. In addition, the same DNA sequence can produce very different proteins, depending on where the process initiates. To understand the human genome, which consists of about 3 billion nucleotides, poses an enormous task. The highly complex nature of this task demands a heuristic approach to information processing. Furthermore, existing background knowledge gathered from such fields as molecular genetics, biochemistry, and physicochemistry should be exploited to facilitate this understanding process since this knowledge can rule out many incorrect interpretations of the DNA sequence and generate plausible

397

hypotheses for experimental verification. Both heuristic and knowledge-based information processing lie at the heart of artificial intelligence.

AI techniques have been applied to the domain of DNA sequence analysis in predicting or identifying certain specialized regions (such as promoters which are related to the control of protein synthesis), in recognizing genes, and in understanding the evolutionary relationships between sequences. These tasks can be formulated as a classification or learning problem. For example, we classify a string of nucleotides as containing a promoter or a gene; we learn the corresponding classification knowledge; we learn the common properties of different sequences. It appears that the fundamental problem is "learning."

Hunter (1991) describes several contemporary AI techniques for this task domain, including the expert system approach, the A* algorithm, model-driven vision, formal mathematical inference, grammar induction, minimal-length encoding, the neural network approach, and case-based reasoning. From the perspective of learning, we classify these techniques into four categories as follows:

- Heuristic search such as the A* algorithm

- Inductive learning, model-driven or data-driven

- Grammatical inference

- The neural network approach

Heuristic search is a topic easily found in standard AI textbooks. It applies a heuristic function to guide the generation of a search space so that the generated space is much smaller than the actual space.

Inductive learning is concerned with the finding of general descriptions of a concept from specific examples. This topic is treated in Chapter 3 "Learning."

Grammatical inference is a problem of learning grammars from examples. It is important in natural-language understanding and syntactic pattern recognition. In DNA sequence analysis, if we treat a sequence as a sentence composed of parts like introns, exons, and promoters, then grammatical inference techniques can be applied to recognize genes in new sequences. For more details about grammatical inference, see Chapter 15 "Learning Grammars."

The application of the neural network approach to genetic data analysis was illustrated in Chapter 4 "Knowledge-Based Neural Networks." There, we apply the KBCNN to predict promoters. Besides, it should be noted that recurrent neural networks are a potentially powerful means for analyzing DNA sequences. See Chapter 10 "Learning Spatiotemporal Patterns."

In this chapter, we focus on a kind of genetic pattern recognition, namely, the problem of identifying the gene combinations (patterns) causally related to a given trait determined by multiple genes (a so-called polygenic trait). Conventional approaches to this problem only recognize individual causal genes without analyzing their interaction patterns. Typically, the presence of a single gene is not strong enough to predict such a trait, only coexistence of multiple genes can.

In the sections that follow, we review background material on polygenic trait analysis, present a computer program called GPDP (genetic pattern discovery program) that was developed for this task domain, show important results, and discuss their significance.

16.2   Polygenic Trait Analysis

The observation that most traits in nature exhibit continuous variation can be explained by quantitative inheritance resulting from multiple genetic factors modified by environmental effects (East 1916). Numerous predictions of this theory have been confirmed by animal breeding studies. Diseases such as hypertension, atherosclerosis, diabetes, and cancer could be investigated in animal strains varying widely for these traits.

Recent advances in molecular genetics have led to the development of methodologies capable of providing data sets that will allow the identification of genes responsible for the expression of polygenic phenotypes (traits) (Paterson et al. 1988; Paterson et al. 1989). In this section, we present important concepts and statistical techniques for polygenic trait analysis.

16.2.1   Genetic Linkage

Since chromosomes come in pairs, a gene *locus* normally consists of two alleles, one from either parent. They are also called a gene pair. Individual alleles can be either dominant or recessive. A recessive characteristic is suppressed when a dominant one is present. Consider a gene with two possible alleles: A and a. Suppose A is dominant and a recessive, and suppose the phenotype associated with the allele A is *red* and that with the allele a is *yellow*. Then there are three possible genotypes as far as this gene is concerned: AA, Aa, and aa. The phenotypes for the first two genotypes are *red*, while that for the last is *yellow*.

In the process of inheritance, a gene pair segregate independently from each other so that the chance of receiving either allele by a child is equal. This principle is recognized as Mendel's first law. Suppose there are two gene pairs. The concept of independent assortment of one gene pair from the other gene pair is known as Mendel's second law. For instance, suppose one gene pair controls the trait *color*, the other gene pair the *height*. The probability of the color *red* in conjunction with the height *high* in a child is simply the product of the individual probabilities of color *red* and height *high* since these two traits are independently transmitted.

Genetic linkage is a phenomenon which cannot be explained by the above Mendelian laws. When two gene pairs coexist in the same chromosome and they are close to each other, it is likely that the traits corresponding to them are coinherited. The coinheritance of alleles at different genetic loci is referred

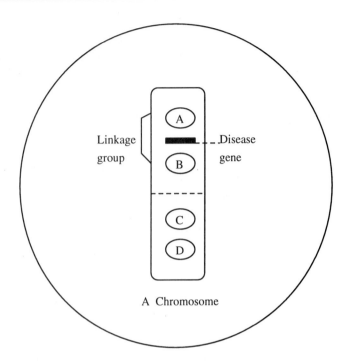

Figure 16.1: Genetic linkage.

to as *genetic linkage*. Notice, however, two linked alleles may segregate due to crossover of chromosomes with a chance proportional to their distance. The concept is illustrated in Figure 16.1. So, when a certain trait (e.g., color *red*) always concurs with another (e.g., height *high*), we should suspect or hypothesize that their genes are linked.

Genetic linkage can serve as an extremely useful basis for discovering or identifying new genes. The idea is as follows. Consider the two traits color and height again. Suppose we know where the gene for the trait color is and we know these two traits are linked. Then, the location of the gene for the trait height must be close to that for color. Furthermore, the technique is available for calculating the distance between the two genes. If known genes are taken as markers and evenly distributed in the entire genome, it is possible to recognize new genes by exploiting the principle of genetic linkage. Through incremental identification of new genes on the basis of known genes, a genetic map can eventually be completed.

16.2.2 Statistical Analysis

A primary objective is to identify the genes which determine the trait under study. It is convenient to view the genes as the cause and the trait as the effect, though some genes do not cause but affect the trait. Under this causal view, the techniques of causal analysis are applicable to genetic analysis.

Two conditions must be considered in establishing a gene-trait relationship:

- Association: The gene is associated with the trait to a high degree.

- Nonspuriousness: There is no known third factor responsible for the association.

However, if the gene is yet to be identified, how can we show its association with the trait? A traditional technique for gene identification is to calculate the association between the trait and each genetic marker. This can be done by chi-square analysis. If a trait-determining gene is linked to a genetic marker, then the marker trait must be associated with the trait concerned. So, once we find a high association between a marker trait and the trait under study, then we hypothesize that the gene of the trait is around the genetic marker. In practice, we define a threshold for the degree of association in order to accept or reject the hypothesis. If it is accepted, we place the gene on the gene map after calculating its distance from nearby markers with some simple algorithm. The location of a gene can be more accurately determined if markers are spaced more densely.

The technique described above maps genes based on a point-to-point analysis since each marker represents a point in the genome. Yet, another approach called *interval mapping* (Lander and Botstein 1989) maps genes on an interval-by-interval basis. More specifically, this approach compares the hypothesis that the trait gene falls in the middle of the interval flanked by an adjacent pair of genetic markers with the hypothesis that it is unlinked to the interval. Since an interval is constituted by numerous points, the interval-based mapping strategy can drastically reduce the complexity of the problem in comparison with the point-based strategy. It is thus not surprising that the former strategy requires a smaller sample than the latter, as demonstrated experimentally.

The issue of nonspuriousness is addressed by controlling confounding factors as described later.

16.3 Genetic Pattern Discovery

The analysis of genetic data sets is extremely complex, in part due to heterogeneity in the manner of inheritance of polygenic traits. In the simplest situation, the inheritance of a phenotype may reflect the additive effects of several independently segregating loci. In this situation, methodologies such as the interval mapping program or univariate statistical analysis are sufficient. However, many complex phenotypes are the result of complicated genetic interactions that may involve dominant/recessive relationships between alleles of a single gene as well as nonlinear interactions between alleles at separate loci. In such complicated situations, more than one genotype may be capable of producing the observed phenotype. And the currently available methodologies for data analysis may not efficiently identify all the genotypes involved in the expression of a complex trait.

An important object is to identify combinations of genes that correlate with the expression of a phenotype. Since some polygenic phenotypes may result from more than one genotype, then all affected individuals may not have identical genotypes at the relevant loci. Consequently, the analysis must be capable of detecting more than one pattern of genes in the affected class. In addition, statistical analysis must be incorporated into the computation to allow an assessment of the significance of the obtained results.

A major difficulty in the identification of combinations of genes responsible for polygenic phenotypes lies in the number of combinations that must be considered during the analysis. For example, a data set containing 40 independently segregating (i.e., unlinked) loci would yield 2^{40} possible loci combinations. The huge combinatorial space prohibits the use of exhaustive search techniques.

The goal of the genetic pattern discovery program (GPDP) is twofold:

- Discovery of disease-causing genes

- Identification of genetic patterns (combinations of genes) for prediction of the disease, and understanding the relationships between genes and the role each gene plays

GPDP basically implements the procedure of learning causal patterns described in Chapter 12 "Causal Learning and Modeling." In the first step, the program generates patterns predictive of a given concept. The patterns are learned by a neural network (see Figure 16.2) and then decoded symbolically by the KT algorithm (see Chapter 14 "Rule Generation from Neural Networks"). Each pattern is then refined to maximize its statistical P value.[1]

The next step deals with the control of confounding patterns since patterns may coexist. The approach which eliminates instances matched by more than one pattern is not feasible since this is the case for most of the instances in our experience. An alternative approach relies on a statistical model. We use the rule-based connectionist network (RBCN) (illustrated in Figure 16.3) for such statistical control. This approach maps the patterns into a three-layer RBCN in which each hidden unit corresponds to one pattern (called a pattern node). The degree of the match between a pattern and an instance is reflected by the activation level of the corresponding hidden unit. And the connection weight between a pattern node and the concept node (called a *pattern strength*) is analogous to a multiple regression coefficient. In the RX project (Blum 1982),

---

[1] The P value is the smallest significance level at which the statistical hypothesis would be rejected. The level of significance is the least upper bound to the probability of incorrectly rejecting the null hypothesis when it is true.

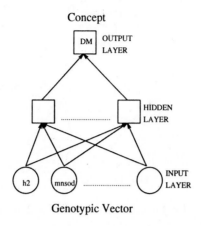

Figure 16.2: A neural network for genetic pattern recognition.

multiple regression coefficients are an indicator of the validity of single causal variables. Here, we extend this heuristic to the case of causal patterns and assign a higher validity to a pattern with a higher strength. Thus, the two bases for determining the significance of patterns are the statistical P value and the pattern strength.

Further analysis of identified genetic patterns requires specific genetic knowledge. For example, the placement of identified genes on the gene map is based upon the knowledge concerning genetic linkage.

The GPDP Procedure

1. Use a neural network to model a set of genetic data. The neural network performs generalization (recognition of common characteristics), abstraction (leaving out unimportant details), and extraction of statistical properties from the data.

2. Rerepresent the network knowledge as a set of symbolic patterns.

3. Delete patterns with insignificant statistical P values.

4. Map the remaining patterns into an RBCN, and train it on the data.

5. Select patterns based on their pattern strengths obtained from the RBCN.

6. Analyze the selected patterns based on genetic knowledge.

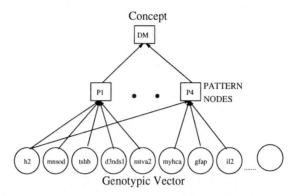

Figure 16.3: A rule-based connectionist network for genetic pattern recognition.

The genetic patterns identified by GPDP have many important applications:

- Prevention, diagnosis, and treatment of the disease: We may diagnose the disease based on genetic patterns, and prevent and treat the disease by blocking causal genes.

- Qualitative understanding of genes: From the genetic patterns, we may learn which genes are mandatory for the disease, and we only need to target those genes for disease prevention or treatment.

- Development of new theory: For example, if we know a certain gene is mandatory for the disease and if the gene is linked to an immunity-related gene, then we may hypothesize an immune theory for the disease.

- Design of a new genetic experiment: The genetic patterns obtained from the last experiment suggest the focus of the next experiment. Thus, a more controlled and focused experiment can be designed.

- Study of partial patterns: There might be microscopic changes for individuals exhibiting a partial pattern.

- Understanding of the evolutionary relationships among genes: The genes of the same pattern may descend from a common root.

- Understanding of the evolutionary relationships among different species: Similarity in genetic patterns between species may imply a close evolutionary relationship between them. Thus, it is possible to transfer research results on one species to another species.

16.4   Experiments

There are two objectives of this study:

- To identify genes which are causally related to insulin-dependent diabetes mellitus (IDDM)

- To identify genetic (genotypic) patterns which accurately predict the IDDM trait with few false positives and false negatives

With some special breeding technique,[2] two groups of mice resulted: One is diabetic and the other nondiabetic. Each gene locus involves two alleles: N and B. The allele N was originally inherited from a pure diabetic strain (NOD), and the allele B from a pure nondiabetic strain. Since the allele B is dominant over N, the genotype NB of a diabetic gene locus will not lead to diabetes and only NN possibly will. It does not matter whether the genotype is NN or NB for the gene locus which does not contain or is not linked to diabetic genes.

In the experiment, we used 80 genetic markers (loci), each with a genotype of either NN or NB. If a genetic marker is linked to a diabetic gene, then their genotypes should match with a high probability. So, if the genotype at a diabetic gene locus is NN, then the genotype at a linked marker locus is most likely to be NN as well. As a consequence, a genetic marker of NN linked to a diabetic gene has some predictive value for the diabetic trait. GPDP will learn the patterns of markers which allow accurate prediction of diabetes mellitus. We assume that each marker in such patterns must be linked to some diabetic gene; otherwise, contradiction arises, for if a marker is not linked to any diabetic gene, then the marker has no predictive value and should not be present in those patterns. Thus, this approach identifies not only diabetic genes but also their interaction patterns, achieving both objectives of this study.

In the program, the genotype of each individual mouse is represented as a feature vector, as shown schematically in Figure 16.4. The data were provided by the Genetic Center at the University of Florida.

16.5   Results

In this study, the GPDP program identified four patterns with statistical P values less than 0.001, which are displayed in Table 16.1. Each pattern is described by a conjunction of genetic markers. For example, the pattern P1 consists of the markers "mnsod at chromosome 17," "tshb at chromosome 3," etc. The information attached to each pattern includes how many IDDM cases and which cases it matches, the accuracy of prediction, and the P value. The information concerning matched cases is important if we want to know which patterns combined together can cover (or explain) all IDDM cases. However, this information may be redundant, because confounding pattern analysis can

---

[2] The technical details are omitted.

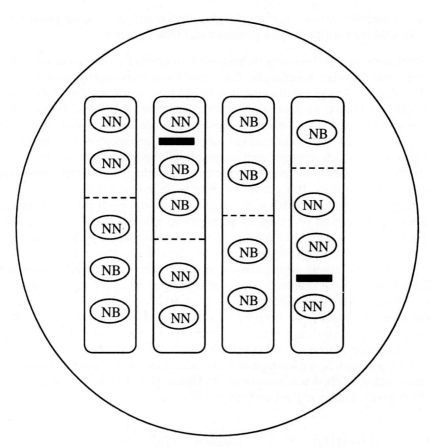

Genotypic Vector: [1 1 1 0 0 1 0 0 1 1 0 0 0 0 0 1 1 1]

1: NN ; 0: NB

Figure 16.4: Representation of genetic data.

Table 16.1: Genetic patterns identified by the GPDP program for predicting IDDM in mice.

Pattern	Description
P1	mnsod at chromosome 17, tshb at chromosome 3, d3nds1 at chromosome 3, mtva2 at chromosome 11, h2 at chromosome 17
P2	myhca at chromosome 14, rp154c at chromosome 9, ncam at chromosome 9, gfap at chromosome 11, il2 at chromosome 3, h2 at chromosome 17
P3	rp154c at chromosome 9, ncam at chromosome 9, il2 at chromosome 3, h2 at chromosome 17
P4	myhca at chromosome 14, gfap at chromosome 11, il2 at chromosome 3, h2 at chromosome 17

provide similar information. It should be noted that the patterns identified may not cover all IDDM cases because these patterns are defined in terms of genetic markers and there is a chance that a diabetic gene and its linked markers have different genotypes. By the same token, a pattern may give a false prediction because a diabetic gene may be dissociated from its linked markers.

The validity of the patterns was further evaluated by controlling confounding patterns and calculating the pattern strength. Table 16.2 shows the statistical P value and the pattern strength for each identified pattern. In order of decreasing validity, the patterns are, P1, P4, P3, and P2. They cover 54 percent, 71 percent, 63 percent, and 54 percent of IDDM cases, respectively. P1 and P4 together cover 96 percent; P1, P4, and P3 together cover 100 percent of cases. As discussed above, the patterns need not cover all cases since there is genetic noise due to crossover or recombination of genes even if they are linked. From this analysis, we prefer to select P1 and P4 as the final patterns, though we have some reservations about P3. An additional observation is that prediction accuracy is not necessarily parallel with validity.

We compare these results with those reported in the literature. A diabetic gene, idd-1, has been located on murine chromosome 17 (Hattori et al. 1986); a possible diabetic gene designated $idd-2$ on chromosome 9 has been reported by Prochazka et al. (1987); and Todd et al. (1991) reported two additional diabetic genes idd-3 and idd-4 on chromosomes 3 and 11, respectively. Assume that a chromosome has at most one diabetic gene. GPDP identified five diabetic genes on chromosomes 3, 9, 11, 14, and 17 (collected from the patterns P1, P2, P3, and P4). We call them $idd-kt-3$, $idd-kt-9$, $idd-kt-11$, $idd-kt-14$, and $idd-kt-17$, respectively. The correspondence of these genes to those reported in the literature is shown in Table 16.3. Only the gene $idd-kt-14$ finds no counterpart in the literature. However, this is not quite true. Todd et al. (1991)

Table 16.2: The validity of the patterns.

Pattern	P value	Pattern strength
P1	< 0.000001	0.34
P2	< 0.000001	0.07
P3	< 0.000001	0.09
P4	< 0.000001	0.17

Table 16.3: The correspondence between the IDDM genes identified by GPDP and those reported in the literature.

Gene (GPDP)	Gene (literature)	Reference
$idd-kt-17$	$idd-1$	Hattori et al. 1986
$idd-kt-9$	$idd-2$	Prochazka et al. 1987
$idd-kt-3$	$idd-3$	Todd et al. 1991
$idd-kt-11$	$idd-4$	Todd et al. 1991
$idd-kt-14$	?	Todd et al. 1991

indicate that genes on chromosome 14 (as well as on some others) could be involved in diabetic susceptibility. The consistency between our results and the findings in the literature is evidence of the validity of GPDP.

The genetic patterns identified by GPDP suggest that at least three genes are required for developing IDDM and two of them should be $idd-1$ and $idd-3$. Such findings have not been made with conventional, univariate techniques. While it seems easy to obtain this result, it is not. The program had heuristically explored a space of 2^{80} possible patterns before this conclusion could be drawn.

16.6 Discussions

A polygenic trait is determined by multiple genes. Conventional approaches focus on the identification of genes or genomic intervals which contribute to the expression of the trait. After identification of these genes, the question ensues of how they interact. It is often the case that each single gene alone is not strong enough to produce the trait. So, one wonders what gene combinations will lead to the trait. The GPDP approach which formulates the problem of gene discovery as the problem of pattern learning has significant advantages since it identifies not only genes but also the patterns of their interactions.

There exist different theories to explain polygenic traits. In one theory, there exists a threshold for the trait (called a threshold trait). A causal gene contributes to the trait to a certain extent. Only when the combined effect of multiple genes exceeds the threshold will the trait appear. Thus, the expression of the trait is all or none. In another theory, there is no threshold for the trait, and the expression of the trait is continuous, depending on the combined effect of genes.

In both theories, a quantitative model can be built to simulate the genetic mechanism. A linear system which assumes that gene effects are linearly additive is simple but may be of little avail. A nonlinear solution is often mandatory.

A probabilistic approach is another alternative. In the case of threshold traits, this approach may be misleading since it may fail to recognize the fact that the probability of a trait is zero when the genetic effect is under the threshold.

By combining the neural network and symbolic techniques, the GPDP approach is able to learn genetic patterns for polygenic traits explained by either theory. Since some genes are important only in conjunction with other genes, GPDP directly attacks the space of possible patterns, rather than selecting genes which are important in some sense, and then tries their combinations. In this way, the completeness of search is ensured.

16.7 References

1. Blum, R.L. 1982. Discovery and Representation of Causal Relationships from a Large Time-Oriented Clinical Database: The RX Project. Ph.D. thesis, Stanford University.

2. East, E.M. 1916. Studies on size inheritance in Nicotiana. *Genetics*, 1, pp. 164–176.

3. Hattori, M., Buse, J.B., Jackson, R.A., Glimcher, L., Dorf, M.E., Minami, M., Makino, S., et al. 1986. The NOD mouse: Recessive diabetogenic gene in the major histocompatibility complex. *Science*, 231, pp. 733–735.

4. Hunter, L. 1991. Artificial intelligence and molecular biology. *AI Magazine*, special issue, pp. 27–36.

5. Lander, E.S., and Botstein, D. 1989. Mapping Mendelian factors underlying quantitative traits using RFLP linkage maps. *Genetics*, 121, pp. 185–199.

6. Paterson, A.H., Lander, E.S., Hewitt, J.D., Peterson, S., Lincoln, S.E., and Tanksley, S.D. 1988. Resolution of quantitative traits into Mendelian factors, using a complete linkage map of restriction fragment length polymorphisms. *Nature*, 335, pp. 721–726.

7. Paterson, A.H., DeVerna, J.W., Lanini, B., and Tanksley, S.D. 1989. Fine mapping of quantitative trait loci using selected overlapping recombinant chromosomes in an interspecies cross of tomato. *Genetics*, 124, pp. 735–742.

8. Prochazka, M., Leiter, E.H., Serreze, D.V., and Coleman, D.L. 1987. Three recessive loci required for insulin-dependent diabetes in nonobese diabetic mice. *Science*, 237, pp. 286–289.

9. Todd, J.A., Aitman, T.J., Cornall, R.J., Ghosh, S., Hall, J.R.S., Hearne, C.M., Knight, A.M., et al. 1991. Genetic analysis of autoimmune type 1 diabetes mellitus in mice. *Nature*, 351, pp. 542–547.

Chapter 17

Drug Discovery

17.1 Introduction

Drug design is concerned with the design of a chemical compound that exhibits a desired pharmacological activity. In our endless battle with diseases, this is always an inevitable problem. Ancient medicine is more or less an empirical science. With the advent of computer technology, it appears all of a sudden that we can shorten the life cycle of drug design tremendously. Novel drug molecules can be invented by computer-based search and their properties evaluated by computer-based analysis and simulation. As more analysis is added and principles developed, drug design becomes more and more a science than an art.

An important part of drug design is to understand the structure-activity relationship of chemical molecules. Without this understanding, drug design becomes an intractable, blind-search problem. Recent advances in molecular modeling have much to offer in this regard since both structures and properties of drug molecules can be modeled before more rigorous analysis can apply.

The procedure of drug design normally consists of the following steps:

1. Select a lead compound with a desired pharmacological property as the kernel for the drug to be designed.

2. Derive new drugs from the kernel under structure-activity principles and evaluate their properties.

3. Update the structure-activity principles from experimental observations on those drugs.

4. Go to step 1 or 2 and iterate unless some drugs have achieved satisfactory effects.

Drug discovery refers to the finding of a new drug which could be a completely new compound or a new derivative of existing compounds. So, drug discovery is the ultimate goal of drug design.

411

In the analytical approach to drug design, discovery of drugs will depend on the clever choice of the lead compound, the generation of promising molecules for evaluation, and the extraction of structure-activity principles from examples. Traditionally, all these tasks are dealt with by medicinal chemists. As chemical knowledge grows and data accumulate rapidly, this brute-force approach is no longer feasible. The alternative is treating those tasks as computational problems, since computers are definitely more advantageous than humans. However, the nature of the problem is not all computational; its solution also relies on the ingenuity of human scientists. For this reason, artificial intelligence techniques will eventually be required to automate drug discovery.

In the subsequent sections, we examine some important issues which arise when machine learning techniques are applied to drug design, describe the drug discovery program (DDP), present results with this program, and conclude with some discussions.

17.2   Machine Learning and Drug Design

The history of applying machine learning techniques to chemistry can be examined from two related approaches: pattern recognition and expert systems.

Pattern recognition was first applied to extract molecular structure from spectral data. Since then, the range of methods and the number of chemical applications have increased rapidly. Kowalski and Kirschner (1979) present many interesting pattern recognition applications to drug design.

In the expert system approach, DENDRAL and Meta-DENDRAL programs (Buchanan and Feigenbaum 1978) were developed for chemical structure elucidation. DENDRAL infers the molecular structure of unknown compounds from mass spectral and nuclear magnetic resonance data. Meta-DENDRAL was developed to learn relevant knowledge that DENDRAL used. It learns fragmentation rules for given classes of molecules by heuristic search, generalization, and specialization.

The learning object in the pharmacological application is the dependency of activity on structural features, which relationship can be used to guide drug design. To achieve this objective, the first step is to obtain a set of molecules which has been tested for a desired pharmacological activity. The next step is to select features to describe or represent the molecules. Then machine learning algorithms are applied to these data. There are three elements involved in this process:

- Data collection

- Feature extraction and selection

- Learning algorithms

"Garbage in, garbage out" is always the rule. It can never be overemphasized how critical the data are. The biological data should especially be well scrutinized since it is often noisy and error-prone. The domain expert must ensure that the data at hand contain, either direct or indirect, useful information as far as the design goal is concerned.

As in other domains, learning strategies can be divided into *supervised* and *unsupervised learning*. Supervised learning methods involve the use of training instances which are classified in the sense that their biological activity is known. These methods attempt to find patterns in the structural features of the training instances that can be related to the biological activity under study. Unsupervised learning methods, on the other hand, do not rely on the known biological activity of the instances. They recognize clusters or other meaningful structures in the feature space, which may contribute to our understanding of the problem.

Traditionally, three types of supervised learning are available for drug design:

- The probabilistic or Bayesian approach

- The linear discriminant approach

- The nearest-neighbor or *k*-nearest-neighbor approach

The first two approaches involve the learning of functions which participate in the classification of objects. The probabilistic approach calculates the probability of classifying an object to each class, and the decision is the class with the maximum probability. The linear discriminant approach bases its decision on the value of the discriminant function calculated with respect to the object. The third approach is implemented by a distance classifier which assigns an object to the class of its nearest neighbor or a majority of k nearest neighbors in the feature space.

Although these techniques continue to be used today, new techniques that have been added to the armamentarium of machine learning can expand the horizon of research in this area. In particular, AI techniques can greatly improve the ability to represent structural data and symbolic knowledge in computer programs. Chapter 3 "Learning" provides a good survey of currently available learning methods ranging from statistical to AI-oriented and to biologically inspired methods.

A structure-activity relationship identified from training instances can be evaluated on a different set of instances called test instances. It is misleading to use the training instances as test instances since the rules learned will tend to fit the training instances. Given a set of instances, there are many ways to partition them into the training and the test sets. Among these, the *leave-one-out* technique removes one instance, uses the remaining instances for training, and then uses the left-out instance for testing. The process is repeated for each of the instances. This is a well-known technique for evaluating a learning method on a limited number of instances. Chapter 13 "Validation and Verification" has a more detailed description of this issue.

Both the structural features and the activity of chemical compounds can be described in terms of continuous numerical or discrete values. If the activity is categorized, pattern recognition and symbolic learning techniques often suffice. Otherwise, such methods as statistical multiple regression and mapping neural networks will take over. Quantitative modeling is a topic treated in Chapter 6 "Mathematical Modeling."

17.3   Feature-Based Learning

This section addresses some general issues of learning, which include feature extraction and selection, dimensionality reduction, and feature transformation. The applicability of the techniques contained in this section is not confined to the domain of drug design. However, examples will be provided for this domain where appropriate.

17.3.1   Feature Extraction and Selection

The task of determining what features need to be measured for learning or pattern recognition is called *feature extraction*. *Feature selection* bears the same meaning, but it may also refer to the selection of features from a set of available features, given certain criteria. In general, feature extraction is based on the following considerations:

- Features are discriminant and characteristic.

- Features are easy to process or to obtain.

- Features are invariant to translation, rotation, and scaling of the pattern.

However, to select features which meet all three requirements at the same time may be impossible. Features are usually extracted based on the laws of the nature as well as specific domain knowledge. The number of possible features can be very large, and therefore, they must be properly evaluated and chosen.

In the pharmacological application, structural features used for describing chemical molecules can be categorized as follows:

- Molecular weight

- Number of particular kinds of atoms, such as oxygens, phosphorus, sulfurs, carbons, and halogens

- Number of particular kinds of bonds, such as double bonds and triple bonds

- Number of particular kinds of bonds over number of particular kinds of atoms

- Number of particular kinds of groups

- Number of particular kinds of derivatives

- Longest chain of nonaromatic carbons

- Combinations of the above features

The physical properties of molecules are also important because they are structure-dependent. Special molecular technology like infrared, mass spectrum, nuclear magnetic resonance, and x-ray diffraction have created very useful features for structural analysis other than those mentioned above.

Given n features available, two questions become relevant:

- How should one select k out of n features which are most effective for learning or pattern recognition?

- How should one select the minimal set of features from these n features while maintaining the same level of effectiveness?

Although it is possible to exhaustively try every combination of features and seek the most effective combination, this approach is feasible only when n is small. In practice, some ordering of the features based on univariate or multivariate analysis is imposed. And features can be added or removed according to this ordering. Thus, the linear ordering converts an exponential to a linear time requirement.

In the univariate approach, we can evaluate the importance of individual features using an information-theoretical measure (entropy), as done in the ID3 algorithm (see Chapter 3). In the multivariate approach, we can perform multiple or stepwise regression on all features and use the regression coefficients so obtained to estimate the effectiveness of individual features relative to each other.

Three strategies of selecting features based on those for statistical stepwise regression (Devore 1987) can be formulated as follows:

- *Backward feature elimination*

- *Forward feature selection*

- *Forward-backward feature selection*

Backward Feature Elimination

Given the initial list containing all features:

1. If the stopping condition is met, then exit.

2. Calculate or recalculate the (relative) effectiveness score for each feature.

3. Remove the least effective feature from the list.

4. Go to step 1.

Forward Feature Selection

Given the initial list which is empty:

1. If the stopping condition is met, then exit.

2. Calculate or recalculate the (relative) effectiveness score for each feature.

3. Add the most effective feature to the list.

4. Go to step 1.

Forward-Backward Feature Selection

Given the initial list which is empty:

1. If the stopping condition is met, then exit.

2. Calculate or recalculate the (relative) effectiveness score for each feature.

3. Add the most effective feature to the list.

4. Apply backward feature elimination.

5. Go to step 1.

Let us return to the previous two questions. If the goal is to select k out of n features, then the stopping condition is when the number of features on the list reaches k. If the goal is to select the minimal, equally effective set of features, then the stopping condition is when the overall performance of features on the list begins to drop in the case of backward feature elimination or reaches a plateau in the other two cases.

17.3.2   Dimensionality Reduction

The demand for a large number of instances grows exponentially with the dimensionality of the feature space. In addition, greater computational complexity is implied by higher dimensionality. Machine learning and pattern recognition systems often suffer from the curse of dimensionality. A variety of methods for dimensionality reduction have been proposed, such as the following:

- *Principal component analysis*

- *Factor analysis*

- *Feature clustering*

The first two approaches reduce dimensionality by forming linear combinations of features. More specifically, principal component analysis seeks a lower-dimensional representation that accounts for as much of the total variation of the features as possible. Factor analysis is also a data reduction technique, but it seeks a lower-dimensional representation that accounts for the correlations among the features. The third approach merges features which are highly correlated since they provide redundant information (Duda and Hart 1973).

A principal component P is a linear combination of the observed features

$$P = \sum_{i=i}^{d} W_i X_i$$

where X_i is the ith feature and the weights W_i's are chosen to maximize the ratio of the variance of P to the total variation, subject to the constraint $\sum_{i=1}^{d} W_i^2 = 1$. The principal components are obtained by computing the eigenvectors of the variance-covariance matrix of the features.[1] The importance of each eigenvector is reflected by the associated eigenvalue. Each instance feature vector can be represented in terms of a linear combination of principal components. A frequent question is how many principal components are deemed adequate for a particular situation. Different criteria have been proposed. Some criteria set a threshold for eigenvalues so that principal components with associated eigenvalues less than this threshold are deleted. Some criteria set a threshold for the variation accounted for and select the principal components with larger eigenvalues first until the threshold is reached. Sometimes we are forced to select a fixed number of principal components with the largest eigenvalues, for example, in the case of visualizing the data in two- or three-dimensional plots. More descriptions about this technique can be found in the book by Dillon and Goldstein (1984).

17.3.3   Feature Transformation

Data are often preprocessed or normalized before being analyzed. Preprocessing hopefully enhances the information contained in the data. Elimination of useless or redundant features is one form of preprocessing. Transformation of the feature space is another. For some types of data, a change in representation can result in a marked improvement in their classification. For example, one study demonstrates that the autocorrelation spectrum of a mass spectrum is a more useful representation for classification of molecular structures than the mass spectrum itself (Kowalski and Kirschner 1979). The functional-link approach (described in Chapter 6) enhances data representation through various functional transformations. The technique of frequency encoding (described

---

[1] Refer to standard textbooks on linear algebra.

in Chapter 10 "Learning Spatiotemporal Patterns") can apply to any types of spatiotemporal data, which certainly include molecular structural data.

Soltzberg and Wilkins (1977) has developed a *molecular transform* which represents a molecule by means of the identity of the atoms in the molecule and the three-dimensional atomic coordinates as follows:

$$I(s) = \sum \sum z_i z_j \frac{\sin(sr_{ij})}{sr_{ij}} \qquad (17.1)$$

where $I(s)$ is the transform intensity at s, z_i and z_j are the atomic number of the ith and the jth atom, respectively, and r_{ij} is the distance between the atoms. The idea behind this transform is the representation of the molecular structure in a numerical manner.

The nonlinear combination of existing features has been suggested to create new, useful features. However, which nonlinearities are useful is always a question. The neural network approach offers an immediate answer since it recognizes important features, implicit or explicit, linear or nonlinear, in the data by self-learning.

17.4   The Drug Discovery Program

The drug discovery program (DDP) implements the design and discovery procedure described in Chapter 8 "Discovery." Like other pattern recognition systems for drug design, DDP learns the structure-activity relationship from chemical molecules. However, unlike most or all of them, DDP represents such relationships as symbolic patterns. The advantage is obvious because the medicinal chemist can directly visualize the patterns and reason about the molecule. The learned patterns can be combined or mutated and tested in the next design cycle.

The first learning task addressed by DDP is the following: Given a collection of molecules, each described by structural features and the strength of the activity under study, find patterns in terms of the structural features that correspond to the desired level of the activity. It is clear that this is just a kind of *learning from examples* in the category of supervised learning.

The concept to be learned is which molecular structure will exhibit the desired level of activity. Often the level of activity is measured across a continuous range. In the initial phase of learning, it is probably true that all molecules are not desirable. Then the question becomes how to improve our knowledge under this circumstance. The decision on the percentage of the molecules that should be labeled "desirable" is based upon whether we can arrive at a statistically significant result. New molecules are designed using previously learned patterns as guidance. Therefore, the patterns obtained continue to improve since better molecules are produced from cycle to cycle.

Another task is to combine patterns in an attempt to derive a better molecule—an idea from *genetic search* (see Chapter 3). At this point, the question is whether we can make significant discoveries by pattern analysis and combination. A pitfall here is that the boundary of possible patterns has been set by the initial molecules, and the final result may well be a local optimum far below the global optimum in nature. A remedy for this problem is to introduce some random elements into the process, say by mutating the patterns. In fact, it has been indicated that genetic search without the random component does not guarantee a global optimum result.

The genetic algorithm has been used in conjunction with the neural network approach for problem solving. In some approaches, genetic operators are applied to modify the weights learned by the neural network. In DDP, genetic operators are used to modify the patterns learned by the neural network. These approaches are similar in that they all take the genetic algorithm as a means to escape the local minimum.

The DDP Procedure

1. Train the DDP network on prepared molecules.

2. Extract patterns from the network.

3. Combine and mutate patterns in order to design new molecules.

4. Go to step 1 unless a (near) optimum drug is designed.

The neural network employed by DDP for learning patterns is designed to handle both symbolic and numerical features adequately. Many descriptions about molecular structures are symbolic in nature, while physical properties like the melting point are numerical. The DDP network deals with symbolic features in three layers but numerical features in four layers. Adding an extra layer for numerical features is under the consideration of improving mapping accuracy.

17.5 Results

In this study, we used the data collected by Kowalski and Kirschner (1979). The data were originally used by Martin and coworkers to determine the structure-activity relationship in a series of aminoindans and aminotetralines to monoamine oxidase (MAO) inhibition. Each compound is described by four structural descriptors (symbolic features), four physical properties (numerical features), and the biological activity of MAO inhibition both in vitro and in vivo. Notice that the physical properties also reflect structural characteristics. The goal of DDP in this study was to learn structural patterns associated with MAO inhibition. The compounds were arranged into two classes: low activity (inactive or slightly active) and high activity (moderately active and most active). The DDP network built for this task is shown in Figure 17.1 and the patterns obtained in Figure 17.2. The design of new compounds based on these patterns was not conducted because of practical constraints.

New drugs are often tested in the laboratory before being evaluated in the clinical setting. Thus, it would be interesting to predict the in vivo activity of a new drug based on its in vitro activity. With this in mind, we divided the compounds into two equal groups, one group for training and the other for testing. First, DDP learned rules which could predict the in vitro activity of the training compounds. Then, the rules were tested by letting them predict the in vivo activity of the test compounds. DDP achieved the least error rate (2/10), compared with ID3 (a symbolic, decision tree–based learning program), and a numerical distance classifier (both with an error rate of 3/10). Using the symbolic features alone did not change the result. However, when physical properties (numerical features) were used as the only predicting basis, DDP and the numerical classifier were equally better than ID3.

17.6   Discussions

Drug design is a very complicated problem. Successes often rely on a great deal of ingenuity and expertise in the domain. As knowledge and experience have accrued and computers have become available, a more analytic and systematic approach is now possible.

The identification of the structure-activity relationship is the central part of drug design. Only when this relationship is clearly understood can better drugs be designed. However, it is difficult to acquire such knowledge since it requires the synthesis and testing of a sufficient number of chemical compounds in the first place. Thus, analytical reasoning is essential, and background knowledge must be exploited as much as possible.

Pattern recognition techniques have been applied to drug design. Most of them represent molecules numerically and attempt to quantify structure-activity relationships. The main problem with this kind of approach is that some structural information can only be represented symbolically, and the notion of distance simply fails to apply.

DDP is designed to deal with both symbolic and numerical information simultaneously. It can learn symbolic patterns which chemists can understand and predict drug behavior more accurately than either a pure symbolic or numerical approach. This capability is largely due to the neural network which can automatically integrate features of different types in the most effective way.

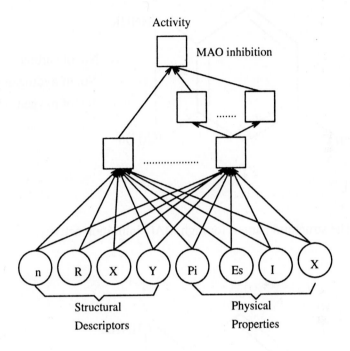

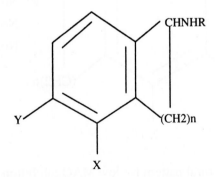

Figure 17.1: The neural network for learning the structure-activity relationship of molecules.

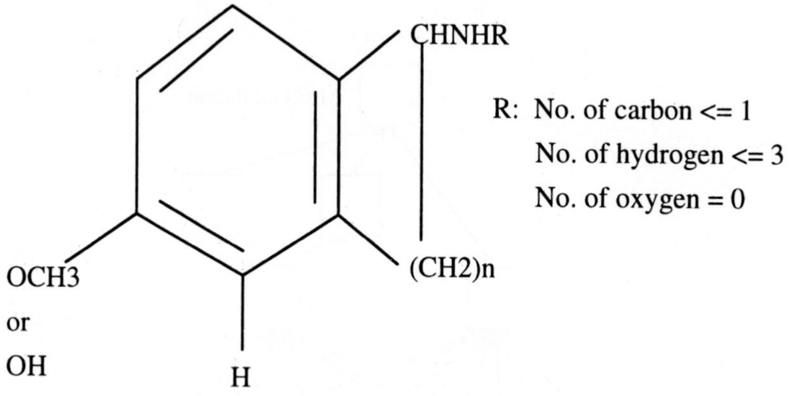

(a) The structural pattern for high MAO inhibition activity.

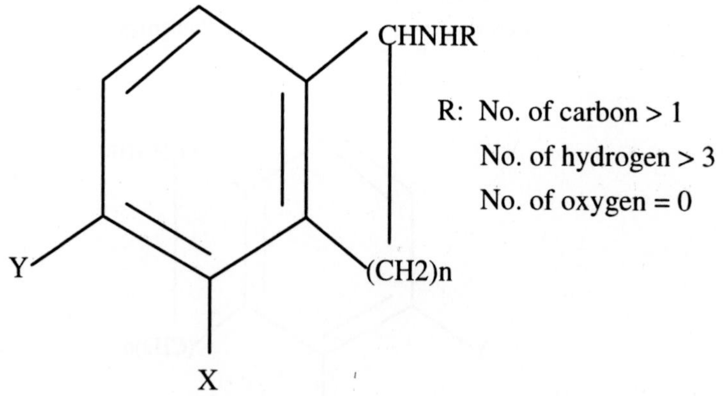

(b) The structural pattern for low MAO inhibition activity.

Figure 17.2: The chemical structural patterns associated with monoamine oxidase inhibition.

17.7   References

1. Buchanan, B.G., and Feigenbaum, E.A. 1978. DENDRAL and Meta-DENDRAL: Their applications dimension. *Artificial Intelligence*, 11, pp. 5–24.

2. Devore, J.L. 1987. *Probability and Statistics for Engineering and the Sciences*. Brooks/Cole, Monterey, CA.

3. Dillon, W.R., and Goldstein, M. 1984. *Multivariate Analysis*. John Wiley & Sons, New York.

4. Duda, R.O., and Hart, P.E. 1973. *Pattern Classification and Scene Analysis*. John Wiley & Sons, New York.

5. Kowalski, B.R., and Kirschner, G.L. 1979. The application of pattern recognition to drug design. In *Drug Design*, vol. VIII. Academic Press, New York.

6. Soltzberg, L.J., and Wilkins, C.L. 1977. *J. Am. Chem. Soc.*, 99, p. 439.

Chapter 18

Flow Cytometric Analysis of Leukemia

18.1   Introduction

The expression of lineage and differentiation-associated antigens in leukemic cells can be analyzed using flow cytometry. This new technology complements traditional morphologic and cytochemical methods currently used in the diagnosis and classification of leukemia and is likely to become indispensable in the future, due to the advantages offered by the specificity of immunological reagents and the quantitative nature of the analysis.

The flow cytometer measures the binding of fluorochrome-labeled antibodies on individual cells. In the simplest analysis, the instrument provides histograms where fluorescence intensity is plotted as a function of cells analyzed. However, the instrument is capable of simultaneously measuring at least two fluorescence spectra and other light signals such as forward and side light scatter emissions. This capability is particularly useful when one measures binding of multiple antibodies to leukemic cells present in heterogeneous samples, such as blood and bone marrow. In these samples, cell subpopulations can be recognized by their particular size (measured by forward light scattering) or granularity (measured by side light scattering). Generally, two light scatter and two fluorescence signals are recorded from each cell for each antibody used. Since a minimum of 10,000 cells per antibody is usually analyzed, the procedure results in a large amount of data which are complex to interpret by current methods.

The potential usefulness of cluster analysis for flow cytometric data has been recognized for a number of years. Cluster analysis is the study of algorithms and methods for grouping or classifying objects. The objective of cluster analysis is to find a useful and valid organization of the data. This analytical method has been used for separating subpopulations in flow cytometric data (Conrad

1987; Crowell et al. 1978; Genter and Salzman 1979; Murphy 1985; Salzman et al. 1975; Salzman et al. 1976). Application of neural networks to flow cytometry data analysis has barely begun (Frankel, Olson, Frankel, and Chisholm 1989).

In subsequent sections, we describe a real-time clustering method based on the neural network model for analyzing flow cytometric data and present the results of its application to leukemic diagnosis.

18.2   Methods

The real-time adaptive clustering (RTAC) algorithm employs a two-layer network: one input layer in which each node encodes a domain feature and one output layer in which each node is designated by a cluster. The network is feedforward (i.e., no recurrent connections) and fully connected (i.e., every input node connecting to every output node). After its connection weights are properly set, we expect that an instance presented to the network (the values of the input nodes set according to the instance) will activate a certain cluster node. The winner-take-all strategy (a competitive learning strategy) is implemented so that the cluster node with strongest activation will shut down all the other cluster nodes. That node which solely remains active denotes the class assigned to the input instance. Since instances in the same cluster should bear similarities, the weights should be set in such a way that similar instances will activate the same cluster. Thus, the neural network is trained to classify a set of instances according to a predefined similarity measure. This task is a kind of unsupervised learning since training instances are not labeled by classes. A commonly raised question is, how many clusters are deemed optimal? Some clustering systems assume that the number of clusters is given, an assumption which may lead to unnatural clustering. The RTAC algorithm rejects such an assumption: When an instance is not similar to any of the existing clusters, a new class will be formed by allocating a new cluster node.

18.2.1   The Theoretical Basis

The basic equation of RTAC is given by

$$\frac{dW_{ji}}{dt} = rO_j(-W_{ji} + O_i) \tag{18.1}$$

where W_{ji} is the weight of the connection from input unit i to output unit j, r is the learning rate, and O_i and O_j are the activations of unit i and unit j, respectively. The weight W_{ji} learns by reducing the error (the squared error criterion) between itself and O_i in the direction of steepest descent. The activation O_j is either 1 or 0 under the winner-take-all strategy. It is obvious that if $O_j = 0$, then $dW_{ji}/dt = 0$ (which means no weight change). This ensures that only the input weights of the winner node can be modified.

In discrete time implementation, we use the following formula for weight updating ($\Delta t = 1$):

$$\Delta W_{ji} = \frac{1}{n_{jk}} O_{jk}(-W_{ji} + O_{ik}) \tag{18.2}$$

where n_{jk} is the size of cluster j incremented by 1, and O_{ik} and O_{jk} are the activations of unit i and j, respectively, when instance k is presented. The learning rate r of Eq. 18.1 corresponds to $1/n_{jk}$ in Eq. 18.2. The choice of this learning rate will be justified in a later analysis.

The activation of an input node is simply the value of the feature encoded by the node. In contrast, the activation of an output node is determined by

$$O_{jk} = \begin{cases} 1 & \text{if } s(\mathbf{W_j}, \mathbf{O_k}) > s(\mathbf{W_l}, \mathbf{O_k}) \text{ for all } l \neq j \text{ and } s(\mathbf{W_j}, \mathbf{O_k}) > \theta \\ 0 & \text{otherwise} \end{cases}$$

$$\tag{18.3}$$

where $\mathbf{W_j}$ ($\mathbf{W_j} = [W_{j1}, W_{j2}, ..., W_{ji}, ...]$) is the weight vector associated with output unit j, $\mathbf{O_k}$ ($\mathbf{O_k} = [O_{1k}, O_{2k}, ..., O_{ik}, ...]$) is the feature vector (the input vector presented to the network) of instance k, θ is the threshold for activation (explained later), and s is a novel function which we have developed to measure the similarity between two vectors:

$$s(\mathbf{x}, \mathbf{y}) = 1 - \frac{||\mathbf{x} - \mathbf{y}||}{||\mathbf{x}|| + ||\mathbf{y}||} \tag{18.4}$$

where

$$||\mathbf{x} - \mathbf{y}|| = \sqrt{\sum (x_i - y_i)^2}$$

and

$$||\mathbf{x}|| = \sqrt{\sum x_i^2}$$

The range of the function s is from 0 to 1 since the difference vector is always smaller than the sum of the two vectors (a property of a metric). This function measures both quantitative and qualitative differences between two vectors and will be justified by statistical validation. The term $||\mathbf{x} - \mathbf{y}||$ is the Euclidean distance between vector $\mathbf{x}$ and vector $\mathbf{y}$, and $||\mathbf{x}||$ and $||\mathbf{y}||$ are lengths for vectors $\mathbf{x}$ and $\mathbf{y}$, respectively. There exist other choices of similarity functions. For example, the *cosine* of the angle between two vectors is often taken as a similarity measure for qualitative clustering. In this measure, two vectors are similar if they point to similar directions regardless of their lengths.

The parameter θ is the threshold for exciting a cluster node, up to the winner-take-all strategy. This parameter is related to the *vigilance* parameter in the ART network (Carpenter and Grossberg 1988). A winner node will be suppressed if its activation is below the θ value. When this happens, no existing cluster node gets activated and a new cluster node j will be allocated, whose weights are initialized by $W_{ji} = O_i$. RTAC is an incremental algorithm. When an instance is assigned to an existing cluster, its statistical properties will be updated. A new cluster is created if needed. This is how RTAC is adapted to the new situation without flushing away old memory, in much the same way as ART does.

The behavior of the RTAC algorithm can be understood further by *equilibrium state* analysis, which has been taken for the competitive learning model (Rumelhart and McClelland 1986). Let p_k be the probability that pattern k is presented on any trial. Let q_{jk} be the probability that unit j wins when pattern k is presented. The system reaches equilibrium (convergence) when no new cluster forms and

$$\sum_k \Delta W_{ji} q_{jk} p_k = 0 \qquad (18.5)$$

Applying the learning rule (Eq. 18.2) to this equilibrium equation, we obtain

$$\sum_k \frac{1}{n_{jk}} (-W_{ji} + O_{ik}) q_{jk} p_k = 0$$

Note that O_{jk} in Eq. 18.2 is replaced by the probability factor. Upon equilibrium, n_{jk} is treated as a constant (i.e., the cluster size has been stabilized given a set of training instances). Thus,

$$W_{ji} \sum_k q_{jk} p_k = \sum_k O_{ik} q_{jk} p_k$$

then,

$$W_{ji} = \frac{\sum_k O_{ik} q_{jk} p_k}{\sum_k q_{jk} p_k}$$

Thus, since $\sum_k q_{jk} p_k$ is the probability that unit j wins over all supplied patterns, W_{ji} upon equilibrium is simply the conditional expected value of O_i, conditioned on the winning of unit j.

Furthermore, we can show that W_{ji} is always the conditional expected value of O_i over all patterns observed so far at each iteration regardless of equilibrium. Let $W_{ji}(n)$ be the W_{ji} when the size of cluster j is n. From Eq. 18.2,

$$W_{ji}(n + 1) = W_{ji}(n) + \frac{1}{n + 1} (-W_{ji}(n) + O_{ik})$$

and thus,

$$W_{ji}(n + 1) = \frac{n W_{ji}(n) + O_{ik}}{n + 1}$$

By mathematical induction, we can further derive that W_{ji} is the average of O_{ik} over all the patterns assigned to cluster j. That is,

$$W_{ji}(n) = \frac{\sum O_{ik}}{n}$$

Recall that when $n = 1$ (pattern k is assigned to a new cluster j), we set $W_{ji} = O_{ik}$.

The stability of the clustering algorithm relies on the fact that clusters formed are well separated from each other. One measure of stability is given by the average amount by which the input to the winning cluster units is greater than that of all the other cluster units over all patterns. In a similar approach, we measure the average intercluster distance and the average intracluster distance and then take the ratio. The larger this ratio, the more stable the system.

The RTAC Network

- **Weight Initialization**

  Weights are initialized according to the first relevant instance.

- **Calculation of Activation**

  1. The activation level of an input unit is determined by the instance presenting to the network.

  2. The activation level O_{jk} of output unit j when instance k is presented is determined by

  $$O_{jk} = \begin{cases} 1 & \text{if } s(\mathbf{W_j}, \mathbf{O_k}) > s(\mathbf{W_l}, \mathbf{O_k}) \text{ for all } l \neq j \\ & \text{and } s(\mathbf{W_j}, \mathbf{O_k}) > \theta \\ 0 & \text{otherwise} \end{cases}$$

  where $\mathbf{W_j}$ is the weight vector associated with output unit j, $\mathbf{O_k}$ is the feature vector (the input vector presented to the network) of instance k, θ is the threshold for activation, and

  $$s(\mathbf{x}, \mathbf{y}) = 1 - \frac{||\mathbf{x} - \mathbf{y}||}{||\mathbf{x}|| + ||\mathbf{y}||}$$

- **Weight Training**

  1. If there is an excited cluster node, then adjust weights by

  $$W_{ji}(t + 1) = W_{ji}(t) + \Delta W_{ji}$$

  where $W_{ji}(t)$ is the weight from unit i to unit j at time t and ΔW_{ji} is the weight adjustment. The weight change is computed by

  $$\Delta W_{ji} = \frac{1}{n_{jk}} O_{jk}(-W_{ji} + O_{ik})$$

  where n_{jk} is the size of cluster j incremented by 1, and O_{ik} and O_{jk} are the activations of unit i and j, respectively, when instance k is presented.

2. In case no cluster node gets excited, then create a new cluster node and initialize its weights.

3. Repeat until no more instances are available.

18.2.2   The Description of the Algorithm

Like any other neural network learning algorithm, RTAC proceeds by presenting training examples to the neural network. The adjustments of connection weights obey Eq. 18.2. At the end of training, weights connecting to a cluster node form the mean vector of the cluster. We also update covariance matrices associated with formed clusters, as iterations go.

The result of the RTAC clustering is affected by the choice of the activation threshold θ (see Eq. 18.3). If $\theta = 0$, then only one big cluster results; if θ is near 1, then each individual tends to form an independent cluster. A proper θ value is found by tuning it across a range (say 0.5 to 0.9).

The algorithm repeats the following two steps until no more instances are available:

- Step 1: Instantiate the input nodes with the current instance. The activation of input unit i is set to the corresponding feature value of the instance.

- Step 2: Compute the activations of existing cluster units by Eq. 18.3. If the activations of all the existing cluster units are 0, then establish a new cluster unit whose incoming weight vector is set to the input vector. Update the weights and the covariance matrix associated with the winning cluster or the newly formed cluster.

Although RTAC is an incremental algorithm, a simple refinement procedure can be added to it for improving the quality of the clustering result. However, refinement requires reviewing old instances a few more times and hence is nonincremental. In the refinement, two operations are performed in sequence:

- Merge: Further merge similar clusters.

- Reassign: Rerun the algorithm using the mean vector obtained in the first round to initialize the weight vector for each cluster unit.

The *merge* operation addresses the case when two seeding instances are far from each other and lead to two distinct clusters, while the gravity center of the two resulting clusters are close enough for merger. The merger of clusters is based on the similarity between their mean vectors measured by the function s of Eq. 18.4. The *reassign* operation deals with the case when an instance is first assigned to an unstabilized cluster. As a cluster grows, its ensemble statistics become more reliable. Thus, the *reassign* operation reduces the randomness from the first-round operation.

While neural network–based, the RTAC algorithm can learn fast, achieving real-time performance. The time complexity of RTAC is $O(nm)$, where n is the number of instances presented to the network and m is the number of clusters formed. When only a few clusters form, the complexity is about linear with the number of the instances. Since $m \leq n$, the complexity is bounded from above by $O(n^2)$.

18.2.3   The Relations to Other Clustering Methods

Conventional clustering methods include partitional clustering such as k-means, hierarchical clustering, the graph-theoretical method (linkage analysis), and histogram analysis. Here we raise some problems with the conventional clustering methods for analyzing flow cytometric data. The k-means technique requires that the number of clusters be given; hierarchical clustering may or may not specify this number; and the last two approaches usually do not use it as a parameter. In the task domain, we may not have this information at hand. Both hierarchical clustering and graph-theoretical methods are too slow to handle the massive amount of flow cytometric data. Histogram analysis does not deal with the case when a cluster exhibits a multimodal distribution.

Such disadvantages of conventional techniques motivate the exploration of new techniques. The neural network approach shows promise in this field, because of its parallel-distributed processing capability and because of its self-adaptability to changing situations. Once the neural network is trained, similar data sets can be analyzed rapidly and objectively. On the other hand, learning may be time-consuming, depending on the algorithm design. One should note, however, the performance of a neural network algorithm can be greatly improved by using a neural network computer instead of simulation on a digital computer.

In terms of clustering, RTAC is related to two other neural network–based algorithms: the Kohonen network (Kohonen 1988) and the ART network. All of these three neural network–based algorithms share the advantage of obviating the assumption of a certain form for within-cluster distributions.

To analyze the flow cytometric data, there are some concerns with the Kohonen network. First, the number of clusters is fixed, and thus the network cannot adaptively allocate a new cluster node. Second, the result is sensitive to how weights are initialized. In contrast, RTAC is able to handle these issues quite well due to a different learning heuristic.

The RTAC algorithm is close to the ART network. They both assume no fixed number of clusters and are adaptive to dynamically changing conditions. They both can be applied to the domains of discrete or continuous feature values. However, the fundamental difference is the choice of the similarity function. See Chapter 3 "Learning" for the description of the ART network. With the same level of vigilance, ART produced fewer clusters than RTAC in

Table 18.1: Cluster sizes in the training set.

Training set i	Proportions (p_{ij}'s)						
1	0.51	0.26	0.09	0.06	0.03	0.03	0.02
2	0.64	0.23	0.09	0.04			
3	0.56	0.16	0.14	0.10	0.04		

our experimental settings. In addition, the implementation of RTAC is simpler than ART, and weight initialization and training are different.

18.2.4 Statistical Evaluation

The clustering program was validated using the technique described in Chapter 13 "Validation and Verification."

Suppose we have N training sets $T_1, T_2, ..., T_N$. We apply the clustering procedure on set T_i so that T_i is divided into k_i clusters $C_{i1}, C_{i2}, ..., C_{ik_i}$. The cluster sizes are measured by the proportions they occupy in the whole set. They are denoted by $p_{i1}, ..., p_{ik_i}$, respectively, with $\Sigma p_{ij} = 1$. The cross-validation set contains randomly chosen M pairs of cells. We use the frequencies of the M pairs being classified in the same cluster in the N training sets as an indicator of the consistency of the clustering procedure.

Let

$$S_i = \begin{cases} 1 & \text{if a pair is classified into the same cluster} \\ 0 & \text{otherwise} \end{cases}$$

and $P_i = Pr\{S_i = 1\}$.

The null hypothesis is that the clustering procedure is equivalent to a random aggregation scheme. We reason "random clustering" in two ways. One is that a fixed number of clusters is required to be produced from a training set. Somehow the clustering procedure produces that many clusters, but they are inconsistent in the sense that future cells are randomly classified. Then the future cells have an equal chance to be classified into any of the clusters. In this case, it can be shown that $P_i = 1/k_i$. Another consideration is that the clustering procedure has a tendency to form clusters of different sizes. Hence it is unrealistic to assume that a new cell has an equal chance to be classified into each cluster. We assume that the new cell will be classified into cluster C_{ij} with the probability p_{ij}. Then it can be shown that $P_i = \sum_{j=1}^{k_i} p_{ij}^2$.

Under either random assumption, the expected frequency for M pairs in each configuration $(S_1, S_2, ..., S_N)$ can be computed. A chi-square test can be used to test the lack of fit by the random hypothesis.

One thousand ($M = 1000$) pairs are classified into three ($N = 3$) training sets. The cluster sizes are given in Table 18.1.

Table 18.2: The observed and the expected frequencies, and the χ^2 scores, under the two different assumptions about random clustering.

Category	Obs. freq.	Exp. freq.(1)	Exp. freq.(2)
0 0 0	380	514.3	219.2
0 0 1	115	128.6	127.3
1 0 0	27	85.7	112.8
0 1 0	36	171.4	198.4
0 1 1	61	42.8	115.2
1 0 1	22	21.4	65.5
1 1 0	130	28.6	102.1
1 1 1	229	7.2	59.31
Total	1000	1000	1000
χ^2		7378.5	864.8

The observed frequencies in each category (S_1, S_2, S_3) are given in the second column of Table 18.2. The expected frequencies based on $P_i = 1/k_i$ and on $P_i = \sum_{j=1}^{k_i} p_{ij}^2$ are given in columns 3 and 4.

It can seen that the random assumption should be rejected without any doubt. Note that a chi-square (χ^2) value of 22.0 is enough to reject the random hypothesis at the 0.005 level.

Since the neural network is nonlinear and self-aggregating, it is very difficult to figure out what the real clustering procedure is. However, since the training sets are random samples, they should have similar characteristics.

If the hypothesis $P_i = 1/k_i$ were true, then we would expect the training clusters to be similar sizes. However, since those clusters are different sizes (as seen in Table 18.1), we feel that the second assignment $P_i = \sum_{j=1}^{k_i} p_{ij}^2$ is more reasonable for the random assumption.

18.3 Results

This cluster algorithm has been tested on some real data collected from the flow cytometry laboratory at the University of Florida. A set of data files were used; each contained the data of 10,000 cells treated with different types of monoclonal antibodies, including anti-CD2, anti-CD8, anti-CD45R, and anti-CD4. Each type of antibody is labeled with certain fluorescein so that anti-CD2, anti-CD8, and anti-CD45R emit green fluorescence, and anti-CD4 red fluorescence. In the data file, each cell is described by four features: cell size, cell granularity, green fluorescence, and red fluorescence.

Table 18.3: Clusters produced by the clustering program on a normal blood sample. Clusters are described by cluster sizes (percents), means, and standard deviations. Features used in the measurement are placed in the following order: cell size, cell granularity, green fluorescence, and red fluorescence. The symbol m_i denotes the mean and s_i the standard deviation of ith feature, respectively.

Cluster	%	m_1	m_2	m_3	m_4	s_1	s_2	s_3	s_4
A	0.53	137.5	163.3	42.9	38.6	28.5	33.7	12.2	11.8
B	0.29	113.7	31.0	134.0	24.7	14.8	11.7	14.0	16.1
C	0.08	223.1	235.3	90.9	63.3	34.8	28.2	42.6	21.0
D	0.06	92.9	30.0	22.0	14.3	12.6	7.5	11.5	10.6
E	0.02	188.9	92.2	114.0	47.2	26.7	28.5	37.5	19.3
F	0.02	67.0	17.2	3.5	6.7	9.0	9.3	5.6	7.8

18.3.1   A Normal Blood Sample

Clusters were produced by the clustering program for anti-CD2 antibodies labeled cells on the basis of similarities in fluorescence and light scatter signals. Clusters are designated by arbitrary symbols, each recorded with several statistical parameters including the percentage, feature means, standard deviations (see Table 18.3), and covariances.

Cell clusters can be visualized as scatter plots. Figures 18.1 through 18.4 are bivariate plots of anti-CD2 antibodies labeled cells. The original data set is plotted in Figures 18.1 and 18.2 using different sets of parameters, and the data after clustering by the clustering program are plotted in Figures 18.3 and 18.4, respectively. Note that the clusters produced by the computer are consistent with what we see on the original plots. The cluster named "B" is well separated from the cluster named "A." Furthermore, one may identify each computer-generated cluster as a known cell type. For example, cluster B may consist of lymphocytes and cluster A of granulocytes (PMNs). On closer examination, cluster B corresponds to T-lymphocytes and cluster D to B-lymphocytes. These two clusters are mingled in Figure 18.3 but clearly separable in Figure 18.4 due to the green fluorescence of the anti-CD2 antibody which specifically targets T-lymphocytes. Thus, through this technique, we actually rediscovered several known cell types.

In this example, some clusters are separable on a two-dimensional plot. It will be harder or impossible to visualize clusters which are separable only beyond three dimensions, and the computer-based algorithm lends itself well to clustering in a high-dimensional space.

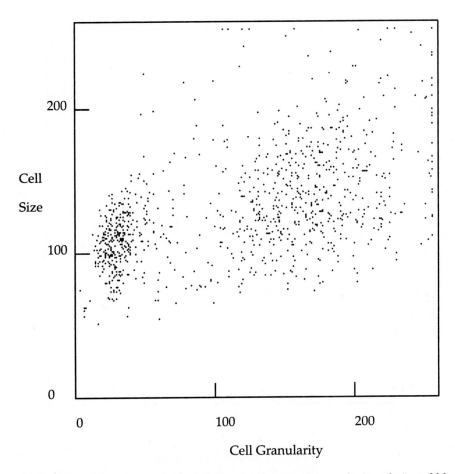

Figure 18.1: Flow cytometric analysis of cell size and granularity of normal blood leukocytes. These are original flow cytometric bivariate data displayed as scatter plots of dots, each representing a cell. Cells with similar physical properties form clusters representing different types of cells (lymphocytes, granulocytes, etc.). Presently, evaluation of these bivariate data is performed by visual recognition and manual definition of clusters that are further characterized by an operator using interactive computer analysis. However, visualization is limited to 2D or 3D plots. In this experiment, four parameters are measured for the analysis, which result in six such 2D plots. It becomes more difficult to integrate these 2D views as the number of parameters increases.

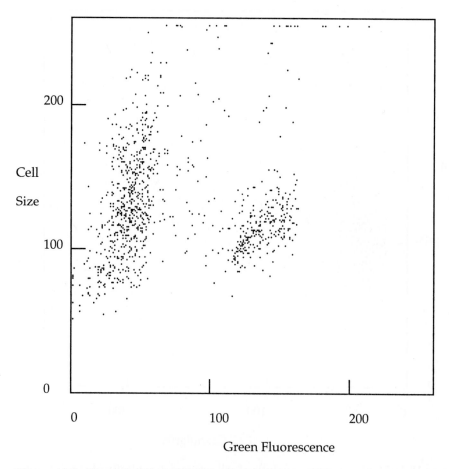

Figure 18.2: Plotted parameters are cell size and green fluorescence from (green) FITC-labeled anti-CD2 antibodies. Cells having similar size and immunofluorescence properties form clusters. The most common analysis currently performed on this type of data is an oversimplified calculation of "percentage positive cells" derived from the comparison of these results to those obtained with a control reagent (irrelevant immunoglobulin). The control reagent is applied to measure the background noise. The information obtained from "percentage positive cells" reveals little concerning the cluster structure, while the structural information is important for identifying abnormalities and classifying diseases.

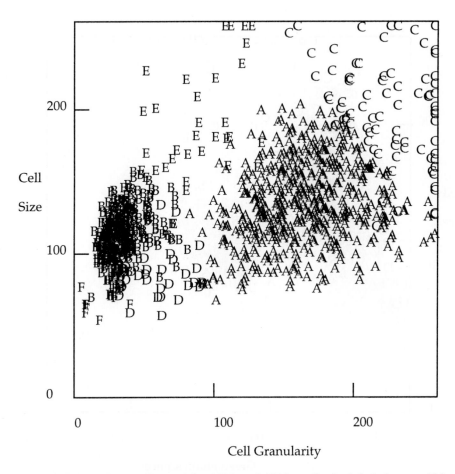

Figure 18.3: A cluster diagram for 1000 anti-CD2 antibody–labeled normal blood leukocytes with respect to cell size and cell granularity. Each cluster is indicated by a distinct letter such as A, B, or C. There are six clusters recognized by the computer program. Some clusters like A and B are quite compact, while others spread around. The clustering program does not use "shape" as a parameter for clustering. This 2D plot may be misleading since the program uses four instead of two parameters for clustering. It is for this reason that some clusters overlap in this 2D plot but are separable in 4D space (not visible).

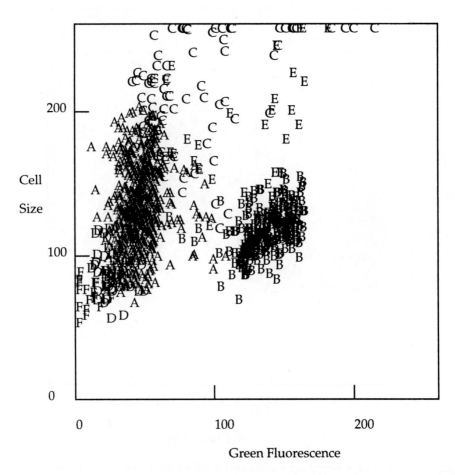

Figure 18.4: A cluster diagram for the same 1000 anti-CD2 antibody–labeled normal blood leukocytes as before, with cell size and green fluorescence as plotted parameters. The same set of labels is used. It is noted that clusters B and D are now separable. The cluster shape changes as plotted parameters vary. The cluster structure is stored as a set of statistical properties such as means, standard deviations, and covariances.

Table 18.4: The clusters of a leukemic blood sample. The symbol m_i denotes the mean and s_i the standard deviation of the ith feature, respectively.

Cluster	%	m_1	m_2	m_3	m_4	s_1	s_2	s_3	s_4
B	0.37	78.5	15.9	127.2	16.5	10.8	4.7	12.9	15.4
D	0.31	67.6	12.8	20.9	17.9	8.4	3.3	12.0	13.0
E	0.25	156.4	53.4	106.6	43.1	35.3	15.8	29.1	16.6
G	0.07	101.9	24.8	39.1	33.6	14.5	8.6	11.0	12.8

18.3.2 A Leukemic Blood Sample

Here, we demonstrate how a leukemic disease can be diagnosed on the basis of flow cytometric patterns. The clustering program was applied to analyze a leukemic blood sample as for the normal sample. To test the sensitivity of this analysis, the sample used was 10 percent leukemic blood mixed with 90 percent healthy blood and stained for CD2. We take the normal sample as a control to recognize abnormalities. In practice, we take the average cluster characteristics of 20 control samples. Table 18.4 shows clusters recognized by the computer program on the leukemic sample. Only four clusters were found. In normal blood, six or seven clusters can be recognized. Without human intervention, the change in the total number of clusters suggests some abnormality.

If a cluster's mean and standard deviation fall in the normal range of a cluster over control samples (20 in our experiment), then the cluster is regarded as normal qualitatively. Such a cluster is also normal quantitatively if its size falls in the normal range too. A cluster which is not normal both qualitatively and quantitatively is an abnormal cluster. From these definitions, some abnormalities can be found in this case. Cluster G identified in this leukemic case is not present as a significant cluster in normal samples. Cluster D is considerably out of proportion in this case as compared with the control. Some clusters like cluster A in normal blood were removed artificially during preparing the sample, and so they were not seen.

Furthermore, we plotted all the clusters recognized. Figure 18.5 is the plot of raw data without clustering by the computer. But we can do clustering with our naked eyes. In the figure, two major clusters can be visualized. The clustering program recognizes them as clusters B and D in healthy blood, respectively, as shown in Figure 18.6. Cluster G is not conspicuous in the first plot but is recognized as a cluster in the second plot.

With our domain knowledge, the four clusters B, D, E, and G may correspond to small T-lymphocytes, small B-lymphocytes, large T-lymphocytes, and large B-lymphocytes, respectively. The increases in sizes for clusters D and G are possibly due to abnormal proliferation of lymphocytes. Presence of large B-lymphocytes as a detectable cluster and the increase of small B-lymphocytes

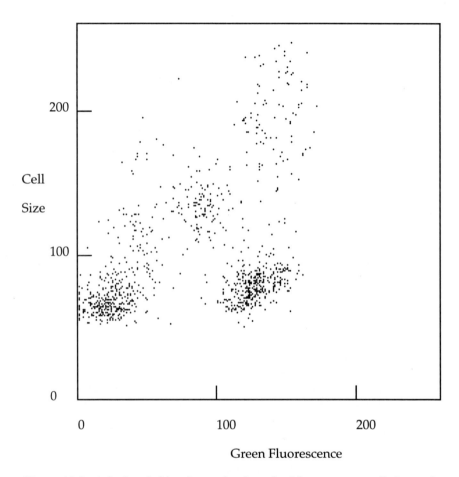

Figure 18.5: A leukemic blood sample plotted with respect to cell size and green fluorescence. This is the original plot without the involvement of clustering. Several clusters can be roughly recognized by the naked eye. Deviations from the previous normal blood sample are due to the leukemic disorder. The "percentage positive cells" criterion only indicates the quantitative change of cells exhibiting high green fluorescence level but fails to tell qualitative abnormality, which information can be obtained by cluster analysis.

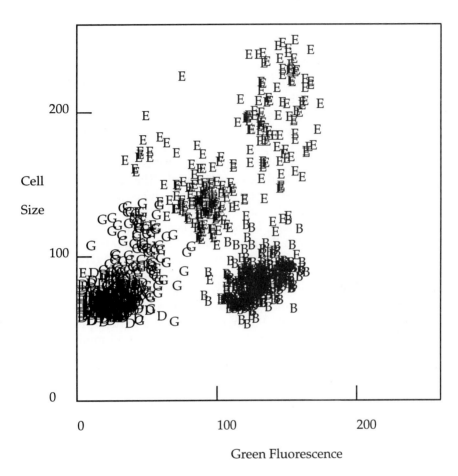

Green Fluorescence

Figure 18.6: The cluster diagram of 1000 anti-CD2 antibody–labeled leukemic blood cells. The plotted parameters are cell size and green fluorescence. The labeling of clusters here is consistent with the previous normal blood sample as much as possible. However, there are only four clusters recognized: B, D, E, and G. Some abnormalities are suspected. In comparison with the previous normal blood sample, cluster G is new, cluster E is more widespread, and cluster D is denser. The central cluster seems to be a stand-alone cluster on this 2D plot, while it is similar to cluster E in 4D space and thus labeled accordingly.

conform to the fact that this case is chronic B-cell lymphocytic leukemia.

The clustering method has been validated formally, as described in the previous section. Now it has also been validated informally by visual verification and confirmation with our domain knowledge.

18.4   Discussions

The RTAC algorithm has several advantages: (1) It is fast, (2) it does not assume a known number of clusters, and (3) it is robust with good tolerance to noise and individual variations. The first advantage is due to its almost linear time complexity. The speed can be further enhanced by using a neural network (parallel-distributed) computer. The second advantage is because of its adaptive nature. The information about a cluster is encoded in weights associated with a cluster node in the neural network. The cluster node issues a top-down signal to test if a new event should be assigned to it. The winner-take-all strategy determines which cluster node should incorporate a new event and update its information pattern. In case there is no winner because none of the top-down signals can match the new event, a new cluster initialized with that event will form. The third advantage can be ascribed to its generalization capability derived from the neural network model. The ensemble statistics are incrementally encoded in the neural network. If there are individual variations, it does not matter much because clusters are formed based on the event characteristics of individuals. So, for example, the computer program can recognize the clusters of neutrophils for blood sample A and sample B, while these two clusters may differ somewhat in size and statistical properties. Despite its success in biological domains, we doubt its capability in recognizing bizarre clusters such as ring clusters. Its relations to other clustering alternatives were discussed. Finally, the developed technique has been validated statistically with respect to self-consistency.

18.5   References

1. Carpenter, G.A., and Grossberg, S. 1988. The ART of adaptive pattern recognition by a self-organizing neural network. *Computer*, March, pp. 77–88.

2. Conrad, M.P. 1987. A rapid non-parametric clustering scheme for flow cytometric data. *Pattern Recognition*, 20, pp. 229–235.

3. Crowell, J.M., Hiebert, R.D., Salzman, G.C., Price, B.J., Cram, L.S., and Mullaney, P.F. 1978. A light-scattering system for high-speed cell analysis. *IEEE Transactions on Biomedical Engineering*, 25, pp. 519–526.

4. Frankel, D.S., Olson, R.J., Frankel, S.L., and Chisholm, S.W. 1989. Use of a neural net computer system for analysis of flow cytometry data of phytoplankton populations. *Cytometry*, 10, pp. 540–550.

5. Genter, F.C., and Salzman, G.C. 1979. A statistical approach to the classification of biological cells from their diffraction patterns. *Journal of Histochemistry and Cytochemistry*, 27, pp. 268–272.

6. Kohonen, T. 1988. *Self-Organization and Associative Memory*. Springer-Verlag, New York.

7. Murphy, R.F. 1985. Automated identification of subpopulations in flow cytometric list mode data using cluster analysis. *Cytometry*, 6, pp. 302–309.

8. Rumelhart, D.E., and McClelland, J.L. 1986. *Parallel Distributed Processing*, vols. I and II. MIT Press, Cambridge, MA.

9. Salzman, G.C., Crowell, J.M., Goad, C.A., Hansen, K.A., Hiebert, R.D., LaBauve, P.M., Martin, J.C., Ingram, M.L., and Mullaney, P.F. 1975. A flow-system multistage light-scattering instrument for cell characterization. *Clinical Chemistry*, 21, pp. 1297–1304.

10. Salzman, G.C., Crowell, J.M., Hansen, K.A., Ingram, M.L., and Mullaney, P.F. 1976. Gynecologic specimen analysis by multistage light scattering in a flow system. *Journal of Histochemistry and Cytochemistry*, 24, pp. 308–314.

Index